Smugglers, Pirates, and Patriots

EARLY AMERICAN STUDIES

Series Editors
Daniel K. Richter, Kathleen M. Brown, Max Cavitch, and David Waldstreicher

Exploring neglected aspects of our colonial, revolutionary, and early national history and culture, Early American Studies reinterprets familiar themes and events in fresh ways. Interdisciplinary in character, and with a special emphasis on the period from about 1600 to 1850, the series is published in partnership with the McNeil Center for Early American Studies.

A complete list of books in the series is available from the publisher.

Smugglers, Pirates, and Patriots

Free Trade in the Age of Revolution

Tyson Reeder

PENN

UNIVERSITY OF PENNSYLVANIA PRESS

PHILADELPHIA

Published by
University of Pennsylvania Press
Philadelphia, Pennsylvania 19104-4112
www.upenn.edu/pennpress

Printed in the United States of America
on acid-free paper

10 9 8 7 6 5 4 3 2 1

A Cataloging-in-Publication record is available from the Library of Congress

ISBN 978-0-8122-5138-8

For Karen

Contents

Abbreviations

ANRJ	Arquivo Nacional (Rio de Janeiro)
ANTT	Arquivo Nacional—Torre do Tombo (Lisbon)
AP	The Adams Papers, Digital Edition, C. James Taylor, ed., University of Virginia Press, Rotunda, 2008–2015 (Charlottesville)
APS	American Philosophical Society (Philadelphia)
ASP:Cl	*American State Papers: Claims*
ASP:CN	*American State Papers: Commerce and Navigation*
BL	British Library (London)
BNL	Biblioteca Nacional (Lisbon)
BNRJ	Biblioteca Nacional (Rio de Janeiro)
CD	Record Group 59, Consular Despatches
CU	Conselho Utramarino (Arquivo Histórico Ultramarino, Lisbon)
GWP	The Papers of George Washington, Digital Edition, Theodore J. Crackel, ed., University of Virginia Press, 2008 (Charlottesville)
HL	Hagley Library (Wilmington, DE)
HSP	Historical Society of Pennsylvania (Philadelphia)
ISM	Independence Seaport Museum (Philadelphia)
JMP	The Papers of James Madison, Digital Edition, J. C. A. Stagg, ed. University of Virginia Press, 2010 (Charlottesville)
LCP	Library Company of Philadelphia (Philadelphia)
LOC	Library of Congress (Washington, DC)
MA–YUL	Manuscripts and Archives, Yale University Library (New Haven, CT)
MAHS	Massachusetts Historical Society (Boston)
MHS	Maryland Historical Society (Baltimore)

MNE	Ministério dos Negócios Estrangeiros (Arquivo Nacional—Torre do Tombo, Lisbon)
NARA–CP	National Archives and Records Administration (College Park, MD)
NARA–DC	National Archives and Records Administration (Washington, DC)
NARA–GA	National Archives and Records Administration (Atlanta, GA)
NARA–MA	National Archives and Records Administration—Mid-Atlantic (Philadelphia)
NAUK	National Archives—United Kingdom (London)
NYHS	New York Historical Society (New York)
PSA	Pennsylvania State Archives (Harrisburg)
TJDC	Thomas J. Dodd Center (Storrs, CT)
TJP	The Papers of Thomas Jefferson, Digital Edition, Barbara B. Oberg and J. Jefferson Looney, eds., University of Virginia Press, Rotunda, 2008–2015 (Charlottesville)
TRL	Thomas Riche Letterbooks

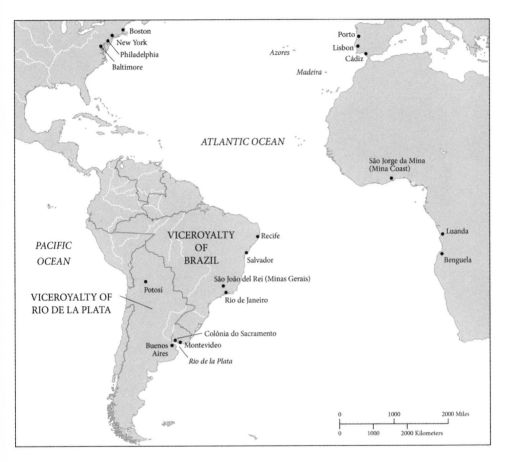

Map 1. North American–Luso-Atlantic trade region.

Contraband, Plunder, and Revolution

On July 15, 1818, Captain Jacob Leandro da Silva and his crew left Rio de Janeiro, Brazil aboard the *União da América* and sailed north toward the Brazilian province of Bahia. The following day, nine leagues southeast of Cabo Frio, a distant ship with a Portuguese flag fired an eighteen-pound cannon ball into the open waters, signaling Leandro da Silva to halt. As the unidentified vessel approached, the crew lowered the Portuguese flag and hoisted the flag of the "insurgents of Spanish America." Leandro da Silva realized too late the intentions of the advancing privateer brigantine called *Irresistible.*[1]

Captain John Danels of Baltimore had weighed anchor at Buenos Aires on June 12 and sailed the *Irresistible* up the southern coast of Brazil with his crew of about a hundred and eighty North Americans. He wielded a letter of marque (also called a commission) from José Gervasio Artigas, the revolutionary leader of the Banda Oriental, or present-day Uruguay. The Portuguese military had invaded the region just south of the Brazilian border in 1816. As an eminent caudillo, Artigas led an army to stave off Portuguese encroachments and to protect the province's autonomy. He offered privateer commissions to North Americans to assist him. The commissions ostensibly allowed captains such as Danels to plunder Portuguese and Spanish vessels according to international legal custom. But Artigas's government lacked recognition from the community of nations. Commissioned by a government of such precarious international status, Danels inhabited a shadowy legal space between pirate and privateer.[2]

Upon capturing the *União*, Danels and his crew brought Leandro da Silva and other officers aboard the *Irresistible* while they pillaged the Portuguese ship until "only a pipe remained for drinking." Aboard the *Irresistible*,

Danels boasted to Leandro da Silva that in twenty days he had captured fifteen Portuguese vessels, and he showed the captain his plunder of one hundred and fifty thousand hard pesos. He taunted the Portuguese royal court, inviting Leandro da Silva to inform the king that the *Irresistible* and other privateer vessels sailed in the region and that he could send against them however many warships he pleased. After Danels's men robbed the *União* of money, cables, pipes, tools, canvas, food, and a few crewmembers, they sailed off and left the crew of the *União* to their luck in the despoiled ship.[3]

In his audacious defiance of Portuguese sovereignty, Danels revealed a willingness to profit from political turmoil in South America. During the Age of Revolution (the tumultuous era between the 1760s and mid-1820s in which Atlantic empires fractured), many traders displayed ingenuity as they sought to enhance their commerce to the detriment of imperial states. Most U.S. traders did not meddle so wantonly in Iberian affairs, but privateers such as Danels marked the culmination of a hope long held among many North Americans that they could profit from revolution in Brazil. As the Age of Revolution progressed, numerous Atlantic theorists and traders extolled the virtues of free trade and decried government restrictions on commerce. Smugglers, pirates, and free trade advocates helped mold commercial policy in the British-American and Luso-Brazilian Atlantics by challenging states for control over commerce. By the early nineteenth century, U.S. republicans viewed free trade as a tool to combat monarchy and empire, whereas Portuguese monarchists assumed it could reinforce them. Their divergent interpretations provoked international conflict that by the 1820s led many North Americans to abandon hope that the Americas would become a hemisphere of free trade republics.

States and Traders

During the eighteenth and early nineteenth centuries, Atlantic commerce developed as a composite of legal strictures and illicit trade practices. States and traders controlled what they could and ceded what they must to maximize their influence in the Atlantic commercial matrix.[4] State authorities contended with free trade advocates, smugglers, rogue officials, slave traders, and pirates—all of whom sought to shape commerce to meet their own ends. But dissidents who challenged state authority did not always enjoy clear victories, for they frequently found their options constrained by state power. Smugglers risked imprisonment and seizure of their cargoes, while revolutionaries faced the ire of imperial militaries. Navies and customs officials suppressed piracy and privateering of dubious legality. Even when they successfully contravened imperial laws, smugglers expended time and money to take precautions they would not have taken if allowed to act without state restrictions. Governments and traders worked out a delicate balance of control over commerce. During the Age of Revolution, they intensified the competition over that balance.[5]

During the eighteenth century, imperial states depended on diffuse bureaucracies, local magistrates, and private trade networks to fill government coffers, thereby weakening their control over commerce. Colonial traders found that their interests meshed well at times with state objectives, and they did not feel interminably at odds with imperial powers. In the mid-seventeenth century, for example, the English government secured commercial treaties with Portugal that gave rise to interimperial commercial networks. The treaties simultaneously benefited private profit and government revenue. When colonial traders believed that state policies impeded their interests, however, they could conspire with those same networks to defy government mandates, usually by smuggling. Paradoxically, they frequently undermined imperial authority by cooperating with the very networks that Atlantic states had fostered.[6]

The British and Portuguese Empires diverged in their approach to such disputes over imperial political economy in the second half of the eighteenth century. In the British Empire, the American Revolution marked the breakdown of the balance between state and private control over commerce. Colonists rebelled against what they saw as heavy-handed policies that limited their economic freedom. Mainland colonists appealed to Enlightenment principles to argue that free trade constituted an inherent right in addition to sound economic policy. The empire fractured as revolutionaries came to associate commercial freedom with independence and republicanism.[7]

By contrast, Lisbon officials liberalized imperial trade policies when revolutionary conspiracies threatened the cohesion of the Portuguese Empire in the 1780s and 1790s. They relaxed prohibitions against commerce among Portuguese dominions and opened trade to a limited extent with Spanish America. They centered their efforts on the slave trade due to its importance to Portuguese-Atlantic commerce and the influence of elite Brazilian slave traders. In some circumstances, they merely legalized practices that

Brazilians had conducted illegally for most of the century. In 1808, the court fled Lisbon in advance of Napoleon's invasion of Portugal, relocated to Rio de Janeiro, and opened Brazilian ports to foreign commerce. Brazilians viewed their opened ports as a welcome culmination of the monarchy's commercial progressiveness. By the early nineteenth century, therefore, Brazilians tended to associate freer trade with the consolidation of monarchical power and imperial strength, not republicanism and imperial fragmentation.[8]

Observers in the United States confronted with bewilderment Brazil's competing national narrative about political systems and free trade. During the Age of Revolution, they hoped to reconcile their own vision of the Americas as a haven for republics with the reality of a monarchy residing in the hemisphere. Most North Americans hoped to see in South American revolutions a reflection of their own ideologies. Many U.S. smugglers, pirates, free traders, and revolutionaries assumed that their efforts to influence Brazilian politics and commerce would result in an independent Brazilian republic. In that sense, Brazil disappointed as Brazilians retained a monarchy even after their independence in 1822.[9]

North Americans desired a republican Brazil not simply because they craved validation for their own ideologies but because they believed it would result in more open trade and greater prosperity. They knew that policies of the Portuguese court had a tangible influence on their fortunes. Since the mid-seventeenth century, North American commerce shared an intricate history with the Portuguese Empire—a relationship supported by the Brazilian gold and slave trades and formalized in treaties with Portugal. As Brazil gained greater influence in the Atlantic economy, many U.S. traders hoped that Brazilian republicans would marshal their productive energy to benefit the United States. As they sought republican trade partners in South America, many North Americans smuggled, plundered, and revolutionized to attain their objectives. Divergent imperial trajectories generated turbulent interimperial exchanges—commercial and ideological—during the Age of Revolution.[10]

Hemisphere of Republics

Fervent North American republicans feared that "an antirepublican neighbour," to use the Philadelphian Tench Coxe's phrase, could cripple U.S. democracy. They believed that the Americas must cultivate republics for their own to survive. North Americans with revolutionary sympathies viewed rebellions in North and South America as an opportunity to free the hemisphere from commercial and political dependence on Europe. In their quest to liberate American commerce, they expected free trade to characterize their new relationships with nascent South American republics.[11]

Traders around the Atlantic had several imprecise definitions of free trade. Some understood the term to mean open intra-imperial trade—a commercial policy that allowed the colonies of a single empire to trade with one another without first routing their goods through the metropolis. Others referred to it as foreign traders paying duties at the same rate as citizens of the nation or empire to which they exported their goods. During wartime, many spoke of free trade as the right of neutral nations to trade without interference from belligerents. In the most fundamental sense, Atlantic traders used the term to mean access to foreign markets without prohibitive duties and regulations. They juxtaposed free trade with mercantilism and imagined the latter as a zero-sum game in the accumulation of imperial wealth based on land and its finite resources. By contrast, they assumed free trade could produce infinite wealth based on capital and labor.[12]

United States free traders drew a tidy syllogism that equated independence from Europe with republicanism, republicanism with free trade, and free trade with prosperity. During the 1790s, the civic virtue inherent in classical republicanism evolved into a private virtue in which the accumulation of individual wealth aided the prosperity of the community and nation. During the years of the early republic, U.S. free traders believed that the perpetuation of their political system depended on the spread of free trade throughout the Atlantic. If the United States secured free markets abroad, U.S. yeomen could exchange their agricultural surpluses for imported manufactures and remain free from the corruption of a manufacturing-based economy.[13]

When empires refused to grant open commerce, many U.S. free traders believed natural rights theory justified smuggling. The American Revolution had impelled free trade advocates to crystallize a philosophy that deemed smuggling an appropriate form of political resistance. Such advocates combined elements of British Whig tradition and Enlightenment-era political economy to cast smuggling, republicanism, and free trade as complementary components of the same liberal ideology. Faced with foreign trade prohibitions imposed by Iberian empires on South American colonies, many U.S. free traders assumed that smuggling could facilitate open commerce until revolution replaced monarchies with republics.[14]

Convinced that monarchies posed a threat to free trade and prosperity, many North Americans hoped to secure republican commercial partners in South America. North American traders did not share uniform business interests or ideologies, and they evinced a willingness to trade wherever they could make a profit. As the Age of Revolution advanced, however, most traders arrived at the consensus that the spread of republican ideologies and institutions throughout the Americas would result in free trade from which prosperity would flow. Imagining such a correlation, they hoped to take advantage of fracturing Atlantic empires to enhance their commerce. They envisioned a future of free trade among the Americas that would serve as a counterpoint to the old, corrupt regimes of Europe. Indeed, some saw the Americas as the region where they would challenge European commercial primacy.[15]

London traders assumed preeminent influence in Atlantic commercial networks. Wealthier, more established traders reaped more business, commanded more credit, and gained more capital than their less affluent peers. With the onset of the Age of Revolution, many American traders took advantage of the opportunity to reorganize their networks. They established new commercial contacts in South America as they sought trade advantages in a relatively untapped market. Some U.S. traders hoped that if they could penetrate Latin American markets they could establish a system of free trade that would liberate the Americas from British commercial dominance.[16]

British traders enjoyed the benefits of imperial power as they conducted commerce—legal or otherwise—in South America throughout the eighteenth century. In 1713, as a reward for victory in the War of Spanish Succession, Great Britain received rights to the *asiento*, or exclusive control over the slave trade to Spanish America. In turn, the British government granted the South Sea Company a monopoly on the Spanish-American slave trade. British traders also conducted a prolific contraband trade with Iberian America. During the Napoleonic Wars, British statesmen and traders sought to permeate new markets to bolster their economic empire against French forces. More than any other non-Iberian nation in Europe, Great Britain stood poised to exploit the chaos that erupted in South America during the Age of Revolution.[17]

Optimistic U.S. traders hoped that a hemisphere of republics would unite their economic and ideological interests to rid the hemisphere of European intrusion and stifle Great Britain's presence in South American markets. In the most optimistic of assessments, they expected that the prosperity of the Americas under a free trade system would provide an example for European nations to follow. The Americas could usher in a new age of commercial freedom throughout the world under the aegis of the United States.

Limits of Free Trade

Many U.S. observers wrapped Brazil into their orderly vision of American republics shaking off the chains of mercantilism and monarchy to trade freely with one another. Between the 1780s and 1820s, several revolutionary movements threatened the monarchical order in Brazil. North Americans observed such movements with interest and assumed Brazilians would soon follow the United States toward independence and republicanism. Many traders hoped that the economic contingency that accompanied civil strife might create favorable opportunities. Business ventures in tumultuous regions faced risks, but intrepid traders gambled on the promise of the new markets.

In that context, the Age of Revolution led to a massive alteration of North American commercial networks away from Portugal and toward Brazil. Although the heady years of 1816 to 1824 resulted in the greatest changes in those networks, the process unfolded during the entire span of the Age of Revolution. Between the 1760s and 1825, most North American traders shifted the center of their Luso-Atlantic trade to Brazil as it came to outshine Portugal as the most promising economic entity of the Portuguese Empire. By 1825, the year the U.S. government recognized Brazilian independence, Portugal seemed to have little to offer the United States compared to Brazil. Many North Americans hoped that if Brazilians would embrace republicanism, Brazil could come to represent American promise contrasted with European decadence.[18]

Instead, Brazil underscored the difficulties U.S. free traders encountered in translating national ideals into state policy. The U.S. government refused to sacrifice the country's international reputation on the altar of free trade and republicanism in the Americas. To assert the government's sovereignty on the high seas in the face of British and French encroachment, Congress passed the Embargo Act of 1807. The act prohibited U.S. exporters from sending goods to foreign dominions and incurred the displeasure of free traders. The embargo went into effect just weeks before the Portuguese monarchy arrived in Brazil and opened its ports to foreign commerce. A monarchy arrived in the Americas and liberalized trade at the same moment the U.S. republic constrained commerce. The juxtaposition exposed the flaws in the U.S. paradigm that contrasted American republics committed to free trade with European monarchies favoring restrictions. Nearly a decade later, when U.S. nationals such as John Danels headed south to sail for Artigas, Portugal mobilized enough pressure from other European monarchies to compel the U.S. government to curtail the extralegal activity. Early U.S.-Brazilian relations revealed the United States at a crossroads between a commitment to liberal ideologies and a concern for respect on the world stage.[19]

Even had U.S. authorities lent stronger support to revolution in South America, the Portuguese government refused to corroborate early U.S. discourse that correlated republicanism with free trade and monarchy with commercial restrictions. Throughout the eighteenth century, the Portuguese Empire never operated as a completely closed system of trade. As in British America, smuggling ran rampant in Brazil, frequently directed by Brazilian governors and other magistrates to the point that they blurred the lines between legal and illegal. Brazilian traders acquired prohibited European and Asian goods and marketed them in the Brazilian interior or traded them for African slaves, many of whom they sold to Buenos Aires for contraband Spanish silver. By the end of the century, to revitalize Portugal's economy, Lisbon officials gradually legalized such activity and punctuated the process by opening Brazilian ports in 1808. After settling in Rio de Janeiro, the Portuguese government repressed republican revolts that many in the United States had hoped would spread throughout Brazil. Portuguese rulers refused to equate free trade and republicanism.[20]

As twilight fell on the Age of Revolution, North Americans revealed the limits of their own commitment to republicanism in South America. In 1817, the U.S. Congress strengthened its neutrality laws to reassure European powers who worried about the U.S. government's commitment to order in the Americas. During the debates over the neutrality bill, congressmen manifested a concern, frequently expressed in racialized terms, that South Americans' inferiority would inhibit the establishment of stable republics in the Americas. North American privateers exposed the government to embarrassment by purportedly associating too freely with mixed race peoples around the Atlantic, cooperating with them in plunder and adopting them into their crews. By 1820, the U.S. government took bold measures to repress the privateers and enhance its reputation among European nations. The State Department also subdued rogue consuls in Brazil who engaged too freely in revolution. Brazil forced North Americans to weigh the promotion of republican ideologies against respect among the community of nations.[21]

In 1822, Brazilian independence resulted from sovereignty disputes with Portugal rather than from a disagreement over political systems. Brazilians retained a monarchy and continued to allow special advantages to British commerce. Like the Portuguese government before it, the Brazilian monarchy repressed republican movements and dampened U.S. hopes that an independent Brazil would gravitate toward republicanism. By the 1830s, U.S. traders had failed to secure republican commercial partners in Brazil. Compared to non-British European nations, they fared well in Brazilian markets. They suspended their hopes, however, that revolution in Brazil would result in prolific business between fellow republics characterized by free trade.[22]

Brazil revealed the fragility of the connections North American free traders drew between republicanism and free trade. Brazilians forged their own trajectory of independence rather than follow the U.S. model. They forced U.S. observers to reconsider long-held assumptions that the United States would guide the Americas toward a new political and commercial order. Brazil also exposed North Americans' struggle to align liberal ideologies with geopolitical realities. Faced with isolation and disrespect from European nations, the U.S. government revealed its tepid commitment to republican solidarity in the Americas. Many white observers began to correlate republicanism with racial homogeneity rather than with the Americas. They viewed their own republic as white and successful and South Americans as racially mixed and incapable of perpetuating stable republics.

Since the eighteenth century, North Americans had depended on slavery in Brazil to sustain their Luso-Atlantic trade, and that dependence persisted throughout the Age of Revolution. Slaves had mined the gold that made Portugal an attractive trade partner to British colonists. They produced the goods for which U.S. smugglers traded. The slave trade generated the wealth that allowed Brazil to eclipse Portugal as the most important commercial region of the Portuguese Empire. Artigan privateers found slave smuggling a profitable component of their business as they captured Portuguese slave ships and kidnapped slave sailors. North Americans had forged their commerce with Brazil through smuggling, piracy, and revolution, convinced that they could secure republican trade partners there. As the era closed, most abandoned such hopes as Brazil and the United States became fellow American slave powers rather than fellow republics.

PART I

Negotiating Empire

BRITISH AMERICANS DEVELOPED THEIR TRADE with the Portuguese Atlantic out of a negotiation between trade networks and state powers. During the mid-seventeenth and early eighteenth centuries, England and Portugal concluded a series of treaties that bound together the commerce of the two nations. In 1640, the Portuguese asserted their independence from a union with Spain that had existed since 1580. The government negotiated with England from a position of geopolitical vulnerability and ceded economic advantages to its northern ally in return for military support. English and Anglo-American traders derived strong advantages from the treaties, such as low duties on goods entering Portuguese dominions. As commerce between the British and Portuguese Empires increased, traders constructed loose commercial networks to facilitate their business. They cooperated in complex webs of suppliers, purchasers, factors, brokers, and consumers.[1]

The trade networks depended on the mutually reinforcing slave and gold trades in the Portuguese Atlantic. Portuguese trade depended on the strength of the Brazilian economy, and the Brazilian economy depended on slaves to mine gold, develop internal markets, and produce agricultural exports. British-American traders sent large quantities of provisions to the Portuguese Empire, and their exports peaked in the late 1760s. Between 1768 and 1772, the middle colonies sent nearly half the value of their grains and grain products to southern Europe, with Lisbon as a key destination. Traders in Portugal used gold and silver from South America to pay for such provisions, usually by smuggling it to British Americans' English creditors. State policy fostered, therefore, a diffuse network of traders in British America, Portugal, the Portuguese Atlantic islands, Great Britain, Africa, and Brazil.[2]

Despite the diffuse nature of their networks, Atlantic traders evinced an ability to cooperate in defiance of state mandates—a defiance that found its consummate expression in revolution. During the eighteenth century, many Enlightenment theorists extolled the virtues of free trade and disseminated their theories around the Atlantic. Atlantic traders had a multitude of competing interests and did not subscribe uniformly to such theories. For many people who lived in the turmoil of the late eighteenth century, however, free trade ideology provided a basis on which revolutionary rhetoric coalesced with commercial profit. During the late 1760s, just as their

trade with Portugal reached its height, mainland British Americans fretted
that new British and Portuguese regulations would ruin their business, and
they decried limitations on their commercial freedom. By that point, revolutionary traders had constructed commercial networks with the vitality
to facilitate rebellion against imperial trade restrictions, and they shared a
common discourse of free trade ideology upon which to base their actions.[3]

Brazilians experienced greater success than British Americans in their
contest over imperial political economy because the African-Brazilian slave
trade comprised a vital component of Portuguese commerce. Beginning in
the 1750s, Lisbon officials concluded that Brazilian development would
benefit the entire empire and ceded to many Brazilian demands, although
they stopped short of opening colonial trade to unfettered foreign access.
While Brazilians and mainland British Americans each vied for greater
commercial freedom, therefore, they arrived at different conclusions about
the fates of kings and empires in the process of trade liberalization. By
the time war erupted between Britain and the colonies, British-American
revolutionaries assumed that empire and monarchy ran counter to free
trade. In contrast, Brazilians found their trade enhanced as officials in Lisbon sought to create a more cohesive empire centered on the slave trade.
The competing narratives plagued U.S.-Brazilian relations with misunder-
standings throughout the Age of Revolution.[4]

Chapter 1

Empire and Commerce

British Americans based their Luso-Atlantic trade networks on a close alliance between England and Portugal first established in the mid-seventeenth century. By the end of the century, they reinforced those networks on the foundation of Brazilian gold and African slavery. Due to the discovery of gold and diamonds in Brazil during the 1690s and 1720s, respectively, the alliance constituted a central component of the Anglo-Atlantic trade nexus throughout the eighteenth century. While the Portuguese government did not allow the exportation of Brazilian gold to foreign empires, British traders participated indirectly in the Brazilian gold trade. According to the terms of the Anglo-Portuguese treaties, English traders exported manufactures to Portugal on liberal terms. Rather than pay for those manufactures with wine as intended by the Portuguese court, Portuguese buyers frequently purchased them by smuggling Brazilian gold to England. Despite strenuous efforts, Portuguese rulers struggled to curb gold smuggling in Brazil and Portugal as British traders carried on a prolific contraband trade on both sides of the Atlantic.[1]

Brazilians obtained slaves and forbidden European commodities by smuggling gold to Africa. Wealthy traders then distributed slaves and manufactures to the Brazilian interior or smuggled them to Spanish America. Brazilian political elites frequently guided or at least winked at such clandestine trade to the point that some contraband constituted semiofficial policy in Brazil, despite contradicting directives from Lisbon. Indeed, many elites took advantage of their positions of power granted by the imperial court to defy the court's regulations. Elite slave traders acquired vast wealth as they developed the Brazilian internal economy, making Brazil the most attractive trade destination in the Portuguese Empire by mid-century. British traders defied imperial regulations to smuggle goods into Brazil and leave with precious metals and raw materials.[2]

British Americans benefited from Portuguese indebtedness to England by exporting provisions to Portugal and receiving remittance from Portuguese importers in the form of bills of exchange drawn on London. By such means, British-American traders sustained their balance of payments with London on the wealth generated by slaves in Brazilian gold mines. Provisions traders in the middle colonies—especially Pennsylvania—enjoyed lucrative business ties with the Portuguese Empire. Due to the profitable alliance, British officials permitted special exemptions from the Navigation Acts for some Luso-Atlantic commodities. For Portuguese commodities not exempted, lax enforcement held sway. Like Brazilians, British Americans enjoyed smuggling under the half-shut eyes and greased palms of customs officials. Throughout the eighteenth century, therefore, British-American–Luso-Atlantic commerce developed as a negotiation between state policy and diffuse trade networks—a compound of legal limits and illegal customs. The result was a prolific trade between British America and the Portuguese Empire by the late 1760s.[3]

Slaves and Gold

In January 1693, the Portuguese court directed the governor of Rio de Janeiro, Antônio Paes de Sande, to head an expedition to the hinterlands of São Paulo in search of gold and silver mines. The king of Portugal, Dom Pedro II, instructed him to organize the region's population and convince them of the "honors and riches" that awaited them if they diligently aided the search for gold. The king expected a report on his progress. Instead, Paes de Sande reported a series of obstacles that prevented the journey. Sometime between 1693 and 1695, nevertheless, *bandeirantes* (frontier prospectors) discovered gold in mountains north of São Paulo (present-day Minas Gerais). Prior to the 1690s, the Portuguese Empire had successfully cultivated sugar and tobacco in Brazil, but the colony remained an after thought compared to the empire's African and Asian dominions. The Portuguese government had long anticipated the discovery of precious metals in Brazil that would match the silver output of Peru in Spanish America. With the discovery of gold in the outer reaches of São Paulo, the Portuguese crown fulfilled one of its most persistent yet elusive objectives in the Americas.[4]

Despite the rapid development of gold mines in the interior, the court failed to send a governor from Rio de Janeiro to inspect the mines and organize expeditions for the discovery of new gold deposits until 1697. The elapsed time indicated Lisbon officials' frail control over the gold-producing hinterlands of Brazil. For more than a century, they tried to control the Brazilian gold trade through governors who lived in political centers remote from the sites of production and transportation highways. In 1764, the Brazilian viceroy, Antônio Álvares da Cunha, pled with Lisbon to place a governor in São Paulo. He despaired at the prolific smuggling in the region and insisted that "it is not possible that it can be governed from Rio de Janeiro." From the very nascence of the gold trade, Lisbon officials struggled to collect revenue from Brazilian mines.[5]

After the new governor of Rio de Janeiro, Sebastião de Castro e Caldas, confirmed the discovery of gold, the Portuguese court regulated its production with a one-fifth tax, the *quinto*. It also prohibited the exportation of gold to any destination besides the metropolis. The government expected miners to bring their gold to one of four smelting houses in São Paulo to have it cast into bars and to leave one-fifth of it in the hands of the government. The miner received an official certificate to indicate compliance with the royal tax. The cumbersome law required Brazilian miners to route their gold through São Paulo just to pay the quinto—a time-consuming and expensive detour. Miners proved disinclined to pay extra transportation costs to comply with a tax. They smuggled gold to the coast along back channels, counterfeited royal seals stamped onto the gold bars, or hid gold dust from patrols stationed along main roads. As early as 1695, Castro e Caldas complained of the frequent evasion of the quinto.[6]

The Portuguese court combatted smuggling in Brazil by imploring governors and customs officials to vigilance. In 1731, the Overseas Council authorized Brazilian governors to search the homes of Brazilians suspected of smuggling, seize any contraband goods, and turn over the offenders to local prelates. Lisbon officials knew little of the inner workings of the mining districts, so they gave broad latitude to local officials to collect the quinto. "Since you have sufficient knowledge of the mines," the minister of overseas affairs, Diogo de Mendonça, wrote the governor of Rio de Janeiro, Gomes Freire de Andrade, "it is not necessary to delineate the means and cautions that you should take," but only that the governor should "position people capable of executing your orders and incapable of descending to the level of those who attempt such smuggling." Once legitimate gold shipments reached the Brazilian coast for export, officials tried to ensure that they shipped for Portugal rather than a foreign destination.[7]

Anglo-Atlantic traders had taken an interest in Brazilian markets since the early eighteenth century. The Brazilian gold strikes provided new life to Portugal's waning economy. By the 1750s, Brazilians exported fifteen thousand kilograms of gold per year. The Portuguese Empire prohibited foreign trade with Brazil, protecting the shipments of precious metal. A seventeenth-century treaty allowed four British factors to operate in the major trade centers of Bahia, Rio de Janeiro, and Recife. After the discovery of gold, however, Portuguese officials prevaricated in the fulfillment of that obligation, and the English presence in Brazil remained negligible.[8]

During the early eighteenth century, British officials and traders struggled to protect their limited trade privileges in Brazil, such as the ability of British merchants in Portugal to trade with Brazilians on their own accounts. As early as 1701, British subjects viewed the colony with envy and complained of the "exclusive Trade" Portugal carried on with "that rich and fertile Tract of Land in America." Faced with prohibitions in Brazil, foreigners infiltrated the Brazilian gold trade through piracy and smuggling. Near mid-century, George Anson, a British naval commander dispatched to the South Atlantic, estimated that at least £1.5 million sterling worth of gold left Brazil legally each year, while another £500,000 sterling left illegally.[9]

The Portuguese government required merchant ships leaving Brazil to sail in periodic fleets to ensure that they did not reroute to prohibited destinations. Rather than follow a consistent schedule, the fleet sailed at the recommendation of the Junta do Comércio (Board of Commerce) when it judged most convenient for Portuguese merchants and state coffers. British-American merchants could sell provisions to Brazil only by re-export from Lisbon. To maximize profits, they sent provisions to Lisbon just before the departure of the Brazil fleet when demand peaked.[10]

North Americans found it difficult to time the departures, for they depended on accurate information from associates in Portugal. Because the Brazil fleets did not sail at regular intervals, merchants relied on their correspondents to inform them when the ships left or arrived at port. In February 1761, John Ayrey & Co. of Lisbon advised the Philadelphia firm Baynton & Wharton that "the departure of our Bahia fleet still remains unknown." Two months later, they informed them that the fleet may not arrive for another year. In early 1762, Baynton & Wharton received word that the Bahia fleet had arrived and would depart again in June. In early April, they learned it could depart in eight or ten days—or a month. As John Ayrey complained, "The detention of the Brazil fleet on that side and this [side of the Atlantic] is what causes a great stagnation to business and Commerce in General."[11]

Correct timing could prove the difference between profit and loss in the Lisbon market. In November 1761, the Pernambuco fleet carried off a large shipment of flour, generating a new demand for the commodity in Lisbon. In December of that year, just before the Rio de Janeiro fleet sailed from Lisbon, Parr & Bulkeley resold flour at 2,800 réis per quintal. The price rose to 3,000 réis immediately after the fleet left Lisbon with large quantities of flour. By the end of the month, it reached 3,200 réis. In 1762, Baynton & Wharton hoped to send West Indian sugar to fill a high demand in Lisbon and Porto. Their Portuguese correspondents discouraged the venture, believing that the shipment would not beat the Bahia fleet and its cargoes of Brazilian sugar. It proved poor advice. Dutch and Italian merchants purchased the bulk of the produce from the Bahia fleet and left Lisbon still in demand for white sugar. North American merchants loathed the fleet system because it served to prohibit foreign trade with Brazil and because it caused volatility in Portuguese prices.[12]

In addition to employing the fleets, the Portuguese government tried to control the gold trade by prohibiting foreign vessels from docking in Brazilian ports except in cases of distress at sea. Although the government allowed British traders in Portugal to trade with Brazil on their own accounts, it stipulated that all goods sailing to and from Brazil had to pass through Portugal.[13]

British traders exploited loopholes in such regulations to smuggle gold out of Brazil. At times, the Brazil fleets sailed on such short notice that customs officials did not have time to conduct regular searches of vessels. Traders could not always count on such instances, but they could take advantage of them when they occurred to leave with contraband. More commonly, foreign crews feigned distress at sea, which allowed them to dock temporarily in Brazilian ports. While they supposedly repaired vessels, recovered from disease, or resupplied, smugglers surreptitiously loaded gold, sugar, and other prohibited goods onto their vessels. On rare occasions in the Portuguese Atlantic islands, firms received special license to trade with Brazil. Although the Portuguese government prohibited shipping Brazilian gold to the islands, the licenses allowed a more favorable opportunity to smuggle gold onto ships in sugar barrels. British subjects could partner with residents on the islands to send a cargo to Brazil on a joint account and re-export illicit shipments for other parts of the British Empire upon the vessel's return to the islands.[14]

By mid-century, Portuguese officials viewed British traders as egregious offenders of maritime laws. With the asiento, British subjects became the dominant slave traders in South America, and they used their position to smuggle goods into Brazil from the Río de la Plata region. In August 1760, the Portuguese court had urged the powerful governor Freire de Andrade to combat smuggling more rigorously, considering how "the English were accustoming themselves to clandestine trade" in Spanish America. The scrupulous governor assured officials in Lisbon that Brazilian customs officers took due diligence to monitor all foreign vessels that entered the port in distress and allowed them to dock only "after showing urgent necessity." At the same time, the Portuguese government decreed that all smugglers in Brazil would face punishment according to the decisions of Portuguese tribunals rather than local officials. Brazilian authorities confiscated the letters of British captains and passengers and sent them to Lisbon to determine if they contained illicit content.[15]

British merchants in Lisbon controlled large portions of the Brazilian gold trade, and merchants outside Portugal received Brazilian gold in exchange for manufactured goods. Throughout the eighteenth century, Portugal engaged in an unfavorable balance of trade as Portuguese traders dispersed gold throughout Europe to pay for foreign provisions and manufactures. The Portuguese crown forbade gold exports, but British and Portuguese merchants shipped the precious metals on board vessels of the British navy or the Falmouth packet because those vessels enjoyed immunity from Portuguese customs searches. Even when gold left Portugal aboard merchant vessels, Portuguese inspectors frequently received a cut in the contraband as payment for turning a blind eye.[16]

Like English traders, British Americans benefited from Brazilian gold even if they could not import it directly from Brazil. They enjoyed a favorable balance of trade with Portugal by supplying Portuguese traders with provisions from the mid-Atlantic colonies. On some occasions, Portuguese traders remitted payment in specie. More frequently, they sent the specie straight to London on British Americans' accounts to pay for dry goods imported from England. Most often, merchants in British America received remittance from Portugal in the form of a bill of exchange drawn on London. By whatever means Portuguese traders remitted payment, Brazilian gold provided the foundation for such transactions. It undergirded the entire economic system by which North Americans paid for manufactures from England by using the proceeds from provisions shipped to Portugal and the Portuguese Atlantic islands.[17]

Brazilians increased their demand for slaves in the interior due to the growth of gold mining in Brazil. By the middle of the eighteenth century, the slave trade played an integral part in the accumulation of capital in Portugal and Brazil. It spurred the development of the Brazilian internal economy and sustained the commercial networks of the Portuguese Empire. Freire de Andrade despaired at the gold smuggled out of Brazil, sent to Africa, and passed to the hands of Dutch, English, and French traders along the Mina Coast as well as to Angola in return for slaves. After the 1750s, Brazilians demanded even more slaves to support the country's growing agricultural sector. Slaves developed Brazil's internal economy through their labor, and Rio de Janeiro traders garnered additional capital by sending them to Buenos Aires in return for contraband silver from the Peruvian mines of Potosí.[18]

During the eighteenth century, Luanda and Benguela in Angola constituted the principal export centers for slaves headed for Brazil. Portuguese merchants resorted to the Angolan slave trade to compensate for the loss of trade in Brazilian cotton and gold, which British merchants in Lisbon had usurped. But British merchants also benefited from the Angolan slave trade due to the relationship between Brazilian slavery and the gold trade. Portuguese merchants imported copious amounts of gold mined by slaves in Brazil and illegally re-exported much of it to London to pay for British manufactures.[19]

African rulers consolidated power by importing European goods for distribution and remitting payment by trading political dependents as a form of capital. They garnered influence as they acquired control over European commodities, but they also accrued debt with European creditors. To balance accounts, they sold slaves to Europeans for export to the colonies. European traders worked with African brokers on the shores, to whom they advanced goods to procure a buyer in exchange for slaves. In those networks, British traders enjoyed an advantage over the Portuguese due to their greater capital. Some Portuguese traders lacked access to textiles from Portuguese dominions in India and depended on British woolens and other goods from northern Europe to trade in Africa. Portuguese and Brazilian traders sent slaves to Brazil to work in mines, in the sugar and cotton fields, or on *engenhos* (sugar mills). Once they arrived in port, middlemen called *atravessadores* frequently cornered the market and sold slaves at inflated prices to engenhos and *lavradores* (small independent farmers).[20]

Once in Brazil, slaves extracted gold from mines and produced sugar and cotton, all intended for export to Portugal. Most often, such goods ended up in the hands of British traders in Portugal, who exported them to London. English manufacturers used the cotton to produce textiles to export around Europe and to the Americas, and British-American importers paid for English manufactures with the proceeds from grain and flour they sent to Portugal. The Brazilian gold trade integrated, therefore, the Atlantic commercial networks of Angola, Brazil, England, Portugal, and British America. The slave system undergirded the entire network by producing the gold and developing the Brazilian economy.

Brazilian traders reaped massive benefits from the slave trade as they accumulated capital and developed internal Brazilian markets independent of capital from Lisbon. Far from a colonial outpost, Brazil assumed an integral role in Luso-Atlantic–British-American trade networks based on the gold and slave trades. By mid-century, it became the most attractive entity of the Portuguese Empire. Still, faced with imperial prohibitions on direct trade with Brazil, British Americans directed most of their Luso-Atlantic trade to Lisbon and the Portuguese Atlantic islands.

Treaties

Brazilian gold maximized the benefits England derived from political and commercial treaties with Portugal, and the alliance fostered the growth of British trade networks in the Portuguese Atlantic. State policies did much more than provide the context for Atlantic trade patterns. They molded commercial networks as they buttressed some at the expense of others. They deemed some legitimate and others illegitimate. Many traders worked within the parameters of state policy whereas others surreptitiously disregarded it. Regardless, imperial states maintained a strong presence in the constitution of commercial networks.[21]

Due to Spain's power and proximity, Portugal lay vulnerable to Spanish aggression in Europe and the empire's American dominions. In 1642, the Portuguese government granted English traders economic advantages in return for English protection against encroachment on its colonies by other empires. In 1654, another treaty prohibited Portuguese authorities from raising duties on British goods above 23 percent ad valorem, further eroding Portugal's economic sovereignty to favor England. It stipulated that English merchants in Portugal approve any increase in customs duties and granted them special immunities from the Portuguese civil authority. In theory, though not entirely in practice, it allowed four English merchant families to conduct business out of Bahia, Rio de Janeiro, and Recife. By the early eighteenth century, Portugal had traded its economic independence for military protection.[22]

The Methuen Treaty of 1703 culminated Portugal's economic subservience to its northern ally. It allowed woolens from England to enter Lisbon and Porto free of duty and reduced duties on Portuguese wines entering England, to the detriment of competing French wines. Throughout the next half century, Portugal imported more English goods than any other state except Holland and the German principalities. Indeed, English shipping generally composed at least 50 percent of the total in Lisbon's ports. Despite their robust wine trade, Portuguese merchants could not compensate for all the manufactures English merchants shoveled into Portugal. Between 1756 and 1760, the balance of trade averaged over £1 million sterling in favor of Great Britain and forced Portuguese merchants to export coveted Brazilian gold. English merchants could then use the specie to reinvest in their own business or re-export to the Amsterdam market as foreign coins for bills of exchange.[23]

The Portuguese government hoped to encourage trade in Lisbon by granting *franquia* privileges. Foreign merchants could pay a franquia fee, which would allow their ships to remain in the Lisbon harbor and, in some cases, store goods on shore duty-free for a maximum of three months. Franquia presented an opportunity for foreign merchants to assess the Portuguese markets and then sell their goods there or carry on to a different port. The Portuguese government assumed that franquia privileges would attract more ships to their ports, and British merchants in Lisbon used it to expand their trade. The British-Portuguese firm of Parr & Bulkeley tried to convince John Steinmetz of Philadelphia that the Lisbon market "is the surest plan to go upon." They cited franquia as a benefit. During the early

1760s, franquia gave local storekeepers the opportunity to go on board and purchase goods free of duties. The privilege attracted foreign ships to Portuguese ports but underscored Lisbon's commercial feebleness in the shadow of the British Empire.[24]

The Portuguese crown often found the alliance advantageous, or at least worth the cost. During the War of Spanish Succession, Portugal depended on the British navy to convoy the Brazil fleet safely across the Atlantic. During the Spanish-Portuguese War of 1735–1737, the belligerents fought for control over the border regions of the Río de la Plata. England supplied the Portuguese with arms and dispatched a fleet of twenty-five warships to Lisbon. In return, Dom João V reaffirmed Portugal's commitment to extend liberal commercial privileges to British subjects within its dominions. In the long run, the uneven alliance ensured British hegemony over British-Portuguese trade throughout the eighteenth century.[25]

Encouraged by the advantages to British trade, British firms migrated to Portuguese dominions, where they usurped control of the wine market. Even where British subjects did not benefit directly from the wine trade, they benefited indirectly from the financial linkages it created. As Lord Tyrawly remarked in 1732, the British "have either freight, brokerage, commission, or exchange upon all that is done by all nations paid us either in Lisbon or at London." Twenty years later, he observed during a visit to Portugal, "A great body of His Majesty's subjects reside at Lisbon, rich, opulent, and every day increasing their fortunes and enlarging their dealings."[26]

British wine merchants established intricate connections with local communities as they conducted business in the Portuguese Empire. In Lisbon, Porto, and Madeira, they established wine factories, the name given to the collection of merchants who formed a sort of guild that regulated the industry and established prices. Merchants used the factories to act in greater concert and generate close ties to local officials. In 1737, for example, the Lisbon factory agreed to allocate 80 moidores (about £108 sterling) per annum to the widow of a murdered British vice consul in Lisbon. The Madeira firm of Lamar, Hill, Bisset, & Co. befriended the health officers on the island who allowed them to import goods of questionable quality. By the 1770s, English firms such as Parr & Bulkeley, Mayne & Co., Thomas Horne, and a handful of others operated in Lisbon and commanded a strong share of the Portuguese market. Other firms, such as Rose & Cock, acted as agents for Portuguese exporters. Cropley Rose arranged his business so that he could stay in London while his partner worked out of

Madeira. British merchants in Lisbon usurped many of the trade benefits that would have otherwise gone to Portuguese merchants as part of the British-Portuguese commercial treaties.[27]

British Americans derived the same privileges from the treaties as their English peers. Parliament relaxed mercantilist policies that affected colonial commerce with Iberian empires because British Americans purchased English manufactures with the proceeds from trade with southern Europe. The British government allowed direct importation of wine from Portugal's Atlantic islands and salt from Portugal, and it permitted British Americans to send breadstuff to the Portuguese Empire. Encouraged by such exemptions, many British-American traders reaped economic benefits from the Portuguese Atlantic trade.[28]

During the 1760s, of the nearly three hundred merchants in Philadelphia, few made the Luso-Atlantic an exclusive market for their trade. Most mixed Portuguese markets with a larger portfolio that included the West Indies and England. In 1755, for example, Thomas Willing recorded sixteen foreign ventures. Six sailed for Lisbon, four to Bristol, two to London, three to Jamaica, and one to Barbados. In November and December 1762, Mifflin & Massey insured goods on three accounts bound for Lisbon, four for Jamaica, two for Martinico, two for Saint Kitts, two for Saint Eustatius, and one each for Havanna, Curação, Liverpool, Portsmouth, and London. Some merchants wove together the West Indies and Portuguese markets. Baynton & Wharton imported sugar from the West Indies and re-exported it to Parr & Bulkeley in Lisbon. Luso-Atlantic ports constituted just one portion of those wider trade networks, but they remained a key part of the mid-Atlantic provisions trade as Portugal's chronic dependence on foreign wheat kept prices high in Lisbon.[29]

By 1764, West Indian merchants struggled to pay the high prices for flour charged by mainland merchants due to the high demand in Lisbon. When Gurley & Stephens of the West Indies placed an order for flour with Thomas Riche, Riche explained that he could not comply with their desired price. He preferred instead to send his provisions to Lisbon, where they fetched a greater value. During the 1760s, England faced high rates of population growth, which cut wheat surpluses and raised the price on exported English wheat. In 1765, due to the high prices of English grain, Portuguese importers relied more on shipments from Sicily, France, Holland, and the British-American colonies. In August, English wheat sold for roughly 440–460 réis per alqueire whereas British-American wheat sold for just 320–360 réis. When prices on French and Sicilian wheat rose, British-American provision traders benefited as Portuguese buyers turned to them for imports. By the mid-1760s, they had secured strong links to Portuguese markets due to a combination of imperial policies and market forces.[30]

Atlantic Islands

State policies fastened British-American trade to the island of Madeira. In 1649, the Portuguese crown granted a monopoly on the Brazil trade to the Companhia Geral do Comércio do Brasil, or General Trade Company of Brazil. Most of the directors came from Lisbon, and they preferred to trade in Lisbon wines rather than import Madeira wine to Lisbon and re-export it to Brazil. Officials in Rio de Janeiro grumbled about the low quantities of wine the company transported to the province. Lisbon authorities maintained the monopoly despite the protests, so Madeira exporters turned to British-American markets to offload their wine. In the 1663 Navigation Act, moreover, the English Parliament exempted Madeira wine from the stipulation that foreign trade to North America must first pass through England. Encouraged by such policies, British Americans constructed robust trade networks with British factors in Madeira in the eighteenth century.[31]

British traders developed a prosperous community on the island of Madeira. By the seventeenth century, the island had become a major exporter of wine. Although small in size, it boasted fertile soil, a moderate climate, and a well-watered landscape. By 1687, English merchants accounted for half of the two dozen foreign merchants at the Port of Funchal in Madeira. In the eighteenth century, merchants such as Richard Hill, Thomas Newton, and Alexander Gordon traveled to Madeira to engage in the lucrative wine trade. By 1775, nonnative traders exported four-fifths of all Madeira wine.[32]

The small island lacked the land mass to raise sufficient wheat given the acreage devoted to viticulture. In 1757, the captain-general of Madeira, Manuel de Saldanha e Albuquerque, estimated that Madeirans consumed nearly 5,475 moios of wheat per year and imported nearly 4,000 of them. During the seventeenth century, shipments of wheat came from Ireland, Holland, and England, as well as other Atlantic islands including Saint Michaels, Terceira, and Porto Santo. In the early eighteenth century, however, Madeira residents turned to British North America for breadstuff, enticed by low wheat prices in the mid-Atlantic colonies such as Pennsylvania, New York, and Maryland.[33]

During the 1690s, Pennsylvania competed with, and eventually eclipsed, western England for Madeira's wheat market. In 1689, Parliament revived the Corn Laws from earlier decades. The laws required the government to pay English exporters a bounty on wheat and flour for exported grain. The government also prohibited the importation of foreign grain into England, to encourage a favorable balance of trade and lend stability to grain and flour prices. Even with the advantageous bounty given to English merchants, Philadelphia grain prices remained lower than English prices throughout the eighteenth century. Between 1720 and 1774, British-American wheat remained an average of 1.44s. (shillings) per bushel cheaper than English grain.[34]

Some Philadelphia merchants exported fish to Madeira via Newfoundland, but Madeirans reduced their demand for fish after the Portuguese Empire forbade its re-export to Brazil as part of sweeping economic reforms in the 1750s and 1760s. The lower demand made it "impracticable," in the words of one Madeira firm, "to sell large quantities together as we used to do." Another confirmed that flour was "the only thing that brings Cash here." As a result, mid-Atlantic merchants loaded most of their Madeira-bound shipments with breadstuff. In return, Madeira traders shipped wines back to the mid-Atlantic, consigned them to the West Indies on the account of mid-Atlantic merchants, or paid with bills of exchange on London.[35]

Consumer preference strengthened the British-American–Madeiran commercial networks. British Americans sought good wine and looked to Madeira firms to fill the demand, raising the value of Madeira wine in North America. In February 1768, Henry Hill recorded a net proceed of £581 15s. 8d. (pence) from fifty pipes of Tenerife wine. During the same period, he earned nearly half as much from just ten pipes of Madeira wine. In 1764, mid-Atlantic distributors could expect £20 per pipe on the best Tenerife wine compared with £25 per pipe for Madeira. To profit on the higher priced Madeira wine, less scrupulous traders colored and fortified cheaper wines to pass them off as Madeira.[36]

In the early spring of 1764, Philadelphia experienced a glut in wine. Only the best wine would sell in such a glutted market, and non-Madeira wine had trouble competing. Azores wine generally sold as a cheaper, low-priced wine. That summer, Thomas Riche advised William Street in the

Azores "to ship the best body & oldest wine you can purchase or we shall never sell them here." In November, the exception proved the rule. Kearny & Gilbert of Philadelphia informed the Madeira firm Newton & Gordon that they could not sell a single pipe of the six pipes of poor Madeira wine sent to them, despite repeated attempts to sell them to wine retailers. "Indeed," they reported, "some of our Customers have gone so far as to question us whether they were Madeira Wines."[37]

With their taste for Madeira wine, British-American consumers integrated a wide range of Atlantic business interests. In August 1763, Samuel Johnston arrived in Philadelphia on a temporary visit from Jamaica and lodged in the Germantown tavern of Sarah Mackinet. While there, he learned that she wanted four annual pipes of high-quality wine. He assured Mackinet that Newton & Gordon of Madeira could meet her needs. He asked them to send her an initial order of two pipes "of the very best wine Ambor Coulor in Hamborough staves." On the face of it, the request demanded little. It engaged, however, an intricate, transatlantic web of producers, buyers, sellers, and consumers.[38]

Most consumers demanded fashionable, amber-colored wine, so producers or distributors had to soften the deep-colored red of Madeira. The demand enhanced the Atlantic trade in brandy and other products used to color and fortify the wine. At times, distributors sent their customers brandy and other liquid concoctions so they could color it as they pleased. In the wine-producing world, opinion held that the best staves came from Hamburg, or Hambro staves. In 1779, the Madeira factory added a special charge of 30s. per pipe for those made of Hamburg staves. Made of white oak—strong, unsawed, malleable, and expensive—those staves protected against leakage and maintained the integrity of the wine they held. With her request for Hamburg staves, Mackinet connected Newton & Gordon with Johnston on one side of the Atlantic, and Hamburg exporters on the other. Further, Johnston instructed the Madeira firm to draw on his partners, Johnston & Jolly of London, to cover the steep price of the staves. The order also engaged other linkages—producers, coopers, dock workers, and sailors.[39]

Johnston expressed appreciation for Newton & Gordon's "punctual Compliance with this small Order." Johnston's description of the order appears incongruous against the backdrop of such a wide-ranging, transatlantic matrix. Atlantic traders developed networks in response to consumer preference within the broad contours of commerce defined by state policy.

To meet the demands of her customers, Sarah Mackinet integrated far-flung points of trade into a single transaction. The "small order" revealed the breadth and complexity of the Atlantic networks engaged in the British-American–Luso-Atlantic trade.[40]

Capital and Credit

London merchants loomed large in British-American networks. Capital ran short in Portugal and British America, so London firms met the need. Approximately twenty English merchants dominated the credit networks of British America. Besides providing the colonies with English manufactures, those firms acted as financial institutions to lend credit to British-American importers. Such merchants could "unilaterally alter," according to the historian Thomas Doerflinger, "the business climate of Philadelphia by withholding or generously extending credit to the dozens of entrepreneurs" who wanted to distribute English dry goods. Many British-American merchants depended on commerce with southern European countries to balance their negative accounts with English firms.[41]

British Americans relied on the Luso-Atlantic to import English dry goods, and they relied on London merchants to trade with the Luso-Atlantic, generating a cycle of dependency on English capital. In 1765, the Porto firm of Holdsworth, Olive, & Newman instructed the Philadelphia house Baynton, Wharton, & Morgan to draw on Watson & Olive of London for payment for a cargo of grain. That same year, Philadelphia merchants Kearny & Gilbert remitted proceeds for wine and the rest of their balance due to Johnston & Jolly of London on account of the Madeira firm Newton & Gordon. In early 1767, Kearny & Gilbert accepted payment from John Alsop in New York. If Alsop could not comply, they would invoice payment to Johnston & Jolly on Newton & Gordon's account. In March, Alsop remitted a £300 draft on Joseph Wharton, Jr. of Philadelphia as partial payment. Kearny & Gilbert invoiced the rest to the London firm. When Samuel Galloway and Stephen Steward of Annapolis shipped a cargo to Robert and John Pasley in Lisbon, Galloway requested they pay for the ship captain's disbursements in cash and remit the rest as a bill of exchange on London to James Russell. English firms wove their influence intricately into the fabric of British-American–Luso-Atlantic commerce.[42]

Merchants bypassed London only when they made remittance in commodities. In 1761, John Ayrey & Co. of Lisbon directed Baynton & Wharton to ship 914,540 réis worth of goods on their account to Newfoundland or to remit the same amount on their account to William Neate of London. In 1773, the Lisbon firm of Parr, Bulkeley, & Co. shipped Keppelle & Steinmetz of Philadelphia 11,991,554 réis worth of wine, lemons, sweet oil, and corks. They imported the goods on six months' credit payable either in goods or bills of exchange on London. In addition, they directed their agent Joseph Banfield to draw on their London associate on the account of Keppelle & Steinmetz to pay for the freight and port charges. Even when not involved directly in payment, London firms remained integral to the transactions between traders in Portugal and British America.[43]

Without credit and capital from London, British-Americans and British-Madeirans struggled to remit payments. In 1762, the Lisbon house of Mayne & Co. advanced Samuel Galloway's captain, Middleton Belt, 33,600 réis to pay for his crew. To cover the sum, Belt drew on Silvanus Grove of London. When the bill came back protested, the Lisbon firm charged the debt to Galloway. When the funds of Lamar, Hill, Bisset, & Co. ran low, they remitted a bill for £452 3s. 6d. to Meredith & Clymer of Philadelphia on Thomas Lamar, the firm's London partner. Whether directly or indirectly, almost every transaction between British America and the Luso-Atlantic involved London firms. Beginning in the 1750s, the Portuguese government sought to attenuate the hold that British merchants had on the country's economic production.[44]

Empire and Profit

On November 1, 1755, a massive earthquake destroyed nearly a third of Lisbon and the surrounding areas. Secondary effects compounded the damage and suffering. An English eyewitness described one of the several seismic waves "rising, as it were like a mountain . . . foaming and roaring, and rushed towards the shore with such impetuosity that tho' we all immediately ran for our lives, many were swept away." Fires decimated the city as candles toppled to the ground and flames escaped their hearths. Wind picked up and intensified the conflagration. In a sort of Aristotelian nightmare, earth, fire, water, and air combined against the inhabitants. Upward of fifteen thousand people perished—perhaps as many as thirty thousand.[45]

Amid the destruction, the eminent Portuguese minister, Sebastião José Carvalho e Melo (better known as the Marquis of Pombal), seized the opportunity to revitalize the Portuguese economy by taking the reins of government from Dom José I. More interested in leisure than power, the monarch relinquished control with alacrity. Pombal laid out an agenda he hoped would restructure the country's political economy and reassert its economic independence. He aimed to end, in his words, "the infractions and abuses" of British trade against Portugal and to reestablish "reciprocal advantages by legal means." While Pombal diminished English influence on Portugal's economy, he also unwittingly reinforced British-American trade with the Portuguese Empire.[46]

Between 1739 and 1743, Pombal had served as the Portuguese ambassador in London. He concluded that the British controlled Portuguese trade in Iberian ports and had designs on Brazil as well. Although suspicious of British motives, he found their economic growth impressive. During his stay, he investigated the inner workings of their political economy, which he later tried to emulate in Portugal. He took interest in British trade companies and the revenue they generated for the empire. He left London convinced that mercantilist policies would rescue his country from dependence on Britain. During the 1750s, armed with his new-found power as first minister, he began to execute his plans.[47]

Pombal hoped state-granted monopolies would advance Portuguese interests. In 1755, he established the Companhia Geral de Comércio de Grão Pará e Maranhão, or the Company of Grão Pará and Maranhão. He granted the company a monopoly on trade to the northern region of Brazil. In December of the same year, the Portuguese government decreed a general prohibition of *comissários volantes*, itinerant traders of Portuguese nationality who controlled much of the clandestine trade with British smugglers. The legislation also prohibited masters and sailors of merchant ships from engaging in direct trade, whether on their own accounts or as agents. In September 1756, Pombal created the Companhia Geral da Agricultura das Vinhas do Alto Douro, or Upper Douro Company. Due to the 1703 Treaty of Methuen, Portuguese growers and distributors in the northern Alto Douro region produced and sold abundant amounts of Port wine. They sent most of it to England. The government granted the company a *nom d'appellation* for Port wine to quash competition from English distributors who purchased cheaper wines and sold them as Port. The company exported wine, brandy, and vinegar to Brazil exempt from ad valorem taxes. Finally, Pombal established the Companhia Geral de Comércio de Pernambuco e Paraíba, or the Pernambuco Company, to reinvigorate the engenhos in the sugar industry. It infused capital and credit into the sugar-growing region of northeastern Brazil.[48]

Pombal assumed the monopolies would reduce the influence of British commercial networks in the Portuguese economy. The Portuguese still depended on British goods and military protection, so Pombal did not wish to break the alliance between the two nations. He did hope, however, to divest British merchants of their influence on Luso-Atlantic trade. He reasoned that if Portuguese merchants could invest in a monopoly company in Portugal's prize dominion, they could attain the capital needed to compete with British merchants. By issuing bonds to Portuguese investors, the monopoly companies threatened to siphon influence from the English credit networks that had impeded the development of sound financial institutions in Portugal. Further, comissários volantes traditionally had provided a key connection between Brazilian ports and British merchants in Portugal. They imported commodities to Portugal and returned to Brazil with goods which they sold on behalf of British merchants. They often engaged in illegal commerce to balance their books. Pombal hoped their suppression would further erode British dominance in the trade.[49]

By the late 1750s, Pombal's reforms began to reduce English economic domination over Portugal. During the second half of the 1750s, British merchants exported to Portugal an average annual value of over £1 million sterling in textiles compared to £459,000 in 1766–1770. During the same time periods, they saw their total export values to Portugal drop from £1,301,000 to £595,000. The reduction came accompanied by a major recession in Portugal that lasted throughout much of the 1760s—a recession exacerbated by the exhaustion of Brazilian gold mines. British merchants lost the ability to acquire exorbitant amounts of Portuguese gold, hampered by the reduction in exports to Portugal and the contraction in Brazilian bullion. William Braund of London, for example, had engaged in the bullion trade with Lisbon for nearly twenty years, but in 1763 his gold trade ceased. In 1760, he imported £12,704 9s. 7d. worth of bullion. By 1763, his imports dropped in value to £443 1s. 6d. With less gold to export to England as remittance, traders in Portugal lost purchasing power, which led to further erosion of Portuguese imports from England.[50]

English traders compensated by exporting more dry goods to Africa, Asia, Ireland, and British America. They began to increase exports to British America during the 1750s. They enhanced the average yearly value of British exports to the mainland colonies by 25 percent from the first half of the decade to the second. By 1764, it rose another 20 percent, and still another 16 percent by 1771. Because British Americans enjoyed a surplus trade with

Lisbon, they paid for increased English imports by exporting more wheat and flour to the Luso-Atlantic. While stifling England's control over Portuguese trade, Pombal had inadvertently strengthened Portugal's ties to British America.[51]

Sea lanes reopened with the end of the Seven Years' War in the early 1760s, and mid-Atlantic merchants improved their trade with Portugal. To secure breadstuff for the war effort, British colonial governments had embargoed British-American shipments to Lisbon and other southern European ports. The embargoes reduced trade between British America and southern Europe by nearly two-thirds. In 1761–1762, after warfare between Spain and England resumed, Spanish privateers impeded shipments to Lisbon. Their activity triggered a decline in supplies from British America to Portugal. Simultaneously, the Portuguese government prohibited imports from Spain and France, generating greater demand for British-American commodities. Those who ventured shipments could expect good returns in Portugal. As Parr & Bulkeley wrote to Baynton & Wharton, traders could accrue a profit on bread, flour, staves, and white sugar so long as the Spanish war lasted. Between July and August 1762, the price of flour in Lisbon increased 6.3 percent and peaked at 3,400 réis per quintal.[52]

With peace came a resurgence of commerce. British Americans increased their trade with Portugal rapidly enough to occasion a drastic decline in prices. Between the August 1762 peak and July 1763, flour prices dropped 24 percent in Portugal. But Portuguese importers did not glut the market, and demand remained high. Portuguese residents depended on foreign provisions due to the limited acreage dedicated to grain crops in Portugal. Parr & Bulkeley noted that wheat and flour "can scarse ever fail of being beneficial speculations." Even with an abundant wheat harvest in Portugal, Portuguese importers demanded cheaper soft wheat of the North American variety to mix with the harder grains grown in Spain and Portugal—an ideal combination for baking bread.[53]

Brazilians also demanded British-American flour, and the demand contributed to steady prices in Portugal because it had to pass through Lisbon before it continued to South America. As Baynton & Wharton's agents in Lisbon, the firm of Raymond & Dea assured them that their flour "will have a constant consumption for Brazil" in addition to Portuguese demand for its domestic market. The combined factors kept breadstuff prices stable in Portugal despite the influx of wheat and flour entering the nation after the war.[54]

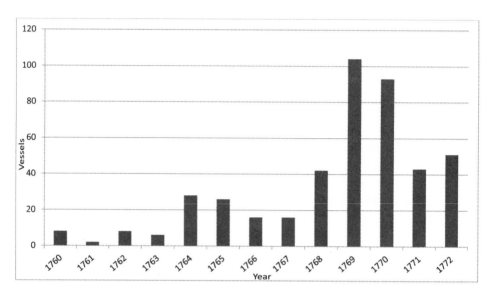

Figure 1. Number of vessels clearing from Philadelphia for Lisbon, 1760–1772.
Source: *Pennsylvania Gazette*, 1760–1772.

In March 1765, Mayne & Co. of Lisbon did not expect any wheat from England as word spread about the possibility of the Parliamentary prohibition on English wheat exports. They anticipated receiving, therefore, much of their wheat from America. If a glut in wheat brought the prices low, they feared that Portuguese natives would simply import wheat and grind it into flour, which would hurt the more lucrative flour trade. By April, however, the price had not dropped sufficiently to justify grinding it in Lisbon. English merchants charged prohibitively high prices on breadstuff, and the Brazil fleet had hauled off a large quantity of flour to the South American colony. Mayne & Co. supposed, therefore, that "Flour from America will . . . stand a good chance." Parr & Bulkeley likewise believed that an embargo on grain exportation from England would drive up prices for American wheat, "for we dont se[e] it can come from any other quarter."[55]

In 1766, Parliament passed the expected prohibition on English grain exports to stabilize high prices in England. Portuguese grain importers turned to British America to satisfy the demand, and mid-Atlantic colonists escalated their trade with Lisbon (Figure 1). By 1767, British-American flour commanded a hefty price of 3,300 réis per quintal. Between 1768 and

1772, New York exporters increased their wheat exports to 53,000 bushels from 38,000 in the early 1760s. By 1769, British-American mainland colonists sent one-fifth of the total value of their exports to southern Europe. They increased their trade with Portugal despite new regulations that required all grains to enter the public warehouse, known as the *terreiro*, before sale. Notwithstanding merchants' complaints that storage in the terreiro exposed wheat to ruin and that the system dampened the price, British-American provisions filled the warehouse. During the 1760s, British colonists enjoyed robust commercial networks with the Luso-Atlantic due to Portugal's and Madeira's strong demand for mid-Atlantic provisions—demand shaped by British and Portuguese imperial policies.[56]

*   *   *

Imperial governments shaped British-American–Luso-Atlantic commercial patterns by establishing duties, privileging certain trade commodities over others, and restricting access to various trade regions. Within the broad apparatus established by states, traders made connections, established contacts, set prices, imported and exported, and remitted payments. They operated in an integrated commercial system that connected traders from North America, Europe, Africa, Asia, and South America in decentralized trade networks. Individual traders constructed networks defined by consumer preference, kinship and social ties, religious affiliations, capital, and credit. By the 1760s, British Americans traded prolifically with the Portuguese Empire. Their commerce expanded as traders sought the best markets for their commodities and state policies generated demand for those commodities in Portuguese dominions.

States may have defined the legal parameters within which traders could maneuver, but traders constructed relationships independent of state authority. They established intricate smuggling webs as they passed Brazilian gold illegally from Brazil to Africa and Europe, from Portugal to England, and in some cases from Portugal to British America. British colonists clandestinely imported Portuguese goods not exempted in the Navigation Acts. If state policies shaped Atlantic trade networks, those networks developed just as much from contravention of state policies.

Many British Americans began to challenge imperial authority to restrict their commerce at the same time their Luso-Atlantic trade expanded in the late 1760s. Over the next decade, they participated in a revolution that eventually released them from the strictures of British mercantilism. As the Age of Revolution advanced, traders altered the entire British-American–Luso-Atlantic trade complex in their quest to do business outside of imperial commercial nexuses. Revolutionaries in North and South America drew on emergent concepts of free trade to expand their commercial parameters and to justify their revolutionary causes. During the prior century, British Americans and Brazilians had participated in Atlantic dialogues that challenged the authority of the state to impose burdensome restrictions on trade.

Chapter 2

The Plague of States

In Europe, Enlightenment thinkers questioned the viability and legitimacy of what Adam Smith eventually called "the mercantile system." Natural law stipulated that commerce, like people, should remain free. Free trade theorists believed that commercial barriers represented unnatural state arbitration and induced suspicion among traders and governments. They disseminated such views throughout the Atlantic, penetrating North and South American populations. On both sides of the ocean, many politicians and traders contested the fundamental premises of mercantilism. They imagined empires as a single entity composed of constituent parts rather than a bifurcation between centers and peripheries. Rather than erode metropolitan finances, they argued, colonial development would spur imperial strength. In their administration of overseas empires, European courts did not possess the economic or political power officials liked to imagine. Mercantilism rarely functioned as an undisputed imperial policy in either the British or Portuguese Empires.[1]

Atlantic traders and intellectuals varied in their definitions of free trade and their views on imperial political economy, and free trade ideology did not remain static from the eighteenth to the nineteenth century. Some envisioned a paradigm of open foreign commerce with minimal or nonexistent duties, whereas others more modestly called for intra-imperial trade. In the Luso-Atlantic, many traders stressed the political and economic expediency of open trade rather than the natural rights language employed by French and British intellectuals. Notwithstanding such philosophical differences, British-American and Brazilian traders operated in an Enlightenment paradigm that assumed that open commerce resulted in greater prosperity. To that end, they smuggled with abandon, underscoring their commitment to trade with foreigners on their own terms. The Brazilian viceroy, Marquis of Lavradio, acknowledged the detrimental impact of contraband on imperial projects when he derided smugglers as "the plague of states."[2]

While smuggling took various forms in the Atlantic, it frequently consisted of interimperial contraband—evading taxes in the process of moving commodities across international boundaries. Traders rarely took the time to intellectualize their trade practices; they did not philosophize about the political or moral implications of their commerce. Smuggling represented, nevertheless, the practical application of a free trade ideology gaining currency in the Atlantic during the eighteenth century. It also exposed a glaring paradox in the Atlantic trade matrix: to participate in illicit trade and defy state control over commerce, traders cooperated with far-flung trade networks that imperial policies had fostered to fill government coffers.[3]

By challenging state policies, colonists pressed imperial officials to consider the welfare of the empire beyond the needs of the metropolis. Beginning in the latter half of the eighteenth century, the British and Portuguese Empires diverged in how colonists and officials chose to negotiate their competing interests. To rebalance what they saw as permissive practices in North America, British authorities sought to rein in smuggling and extend imperial influence more directly over colonial commerce. British Americans responded by severing political ties with the empire to assert autonomy over their trade. Portuguese officials understood that the slave trade underpinned the imperial economy and that Brazil held a central role in that trade, so they compromised with Brazilians' pleas for greater commercial freedom. They restricted most trade with foreign empires and sought to quash contraband, but they hoped that a free, robust slave trade between Brazil and Africa would enhance commerce throughout the empire. By the late eighteenth century, therefore, Brazilians and North Americans began to draw divergent conclusions about the correlation between monarchies and trade liberalization.

A Venture to Brazil

In a failed attempt to trade illicitly with Brazil, the Philadelphia merchant Thomas Riche unveiled a paradox of Atlantic commerce. State policies had stimulated the development of decentralized trade networks—networks that could threaten state authority. Riche benefited from a diffuse arrangement of traders and shippers in his illegal venture. His unfavorable experience revealed that imperial states wielded substantial power over the parameters of commerce. At the same time, it exposed the potential of commercial networks to contravene imperial law.

In September 1763, Riche reached out to William Street, a trader on the Portuguese Atlantic island of Faial, to cooperate in his scheme. Riche had never corresponded with Street, but he learned of him through an intricate network of friends, family, and business associates. A friend from New York put William's brother, Francis, in contact with Riche. Like Riche, Francis resided in Philadelphia. He had tried to settle an account with Zach Nieman and enlisted Riche's help.[4]

After he took notice of a ship ready to depart for Madeira, Riche struck up a conversation with Francis about Portugal's most enviable colony, Brazil. During their talk, Francis informed Riche that William could procure them a cargo to sail to Brazil. William probably obtained a license from the Portuguese government to send one of the few vessels per year allowed to sail from Faial to Brazil. In that case, he could receive a legal return cargo from Brazil to Faial. Riche planned, however, to divert his portion of the cargo or the proceeds in Brazilian gold from Faial back to Philadelphia. His actions would contravene British and Portuguese regulations. Riche "readily agreed" to move forward despite imperial prohibitions. Brought together by a loose network of mutual business connections, Riche and William Street collaborated in a trade that defied the authority of Atlantic empires.[5]

Riche traded aggressively around the Atlantic, doing business with merchants in London, New York, Lisbon, Madeira, Africa, and the Azores. He dealt in a diverse assortment of goods, such as flour, grain, and tobacco, and he occasionally imported slaves. He had begun to develop business relations in the Luso-Atlantic two years prior to his association with William Street. Like other merchants with Luso-Atlantic ties, he used the proceeds on sales of breadstuff to remit payment to his creditors in London. Despite his far-flung financial networks, Riche hoped to reach even farther. Brazil seemed a bright opportunity, especially if he could receive remittances in Brazilian gold.[6]

Riche hoped also to break into the Brazilian sugar and hides trades. British Americans found it hard to import legal sugar at competitive prices. Throughout the eighteenth century, traders in the British West Indies labored with difficulty to compete in the sugar trade with the less expensive sugar from French islands. Sugar exporters in the British Caribbean depended on England's protected sugar market. Mainland importers sought to circumvent the protected market by importing cheaper contraband sugar from the French West Indies. Riche assumed that Brazil could provide an additional supply of suitable, cheap sugar. He hoped that forty or fifty boxes would sell at a good price in Philadelphia.[7]

Toward the end of 1763, he loaded the *Elizabeth & Mary* with over £550 worth of goods, purchased insurance for the voyage from a London firm, and sent it to Faial on a joint account with the Streets. William Street sold the cargo and sent the vessel to Brazil. Captain George Ronnolds sailed with instructions to stow any contraband goods fore and aft to escape detection.[8]

Like other British Americans at the time, Riche suffered from a shortage of specie. As quickly as traders accumulated it, they exported it out of the colonies to pay for imports. Parliament passed the Currency Act of 1764 in the midst of Riche's venture. The act exacerbated British Americans' currency problems, for it prohibited the use of paper bills to pay private debts. Colonists lost their most prevalent form of liquid currency. The legislation hit especially hard in the middle colonies, where Riche lived, and he hoped his venture to Brazil could provide a solution to his cash deficiency. Throughout 1764 and 1765, he complained to his business associates of his "want of money," "poverty," and "disapointments in trade." He called in debts and requested remittances in cash. He asked Street to remit in cash his half in the Brazil venture after the *Elizabeth & Mary* returned to Faial. He erred, however, in hoping that his Brazil scheme would help him regain his financial security.[9]

In the spring of 1765, Riche's contraband trade with Brazil sputtered to a halt due to state restrictions on trade. Because of Portugal's fleet practice, Riche could receive illicit Brazilian goods most securely by routing them through Faial. He could have the goods transferred into wine barrels in the Azores and smuggled into Philadelphia disguised as a legal shipment. The tortuous route exhausted Riche's patience as the *Elizabeth & Mary* sailed to Faial, then to Brazil, probably waited for the departure of the fleet, returned to Faial, and headed back to Philadelphia. By mid-century, Portuguese authorities had increased their vigilance against smuggling, especially by the English, who they correctly assumed carried on a prolific contraband trade in Brazil. In 1762, the Portuguese government had moved the colonial capital to Rio de Janeiro and granted the Tribunal da Relação greater power to confiscate contraband. Just months before Ronnolds arrived in Brazil, officials in Rio de Janeiro had seized the cargoes of several English ships engaged in contraband trade. By the end of the venture, Riche abandoned the hope of curing his financial woes with Brazilian gold or sugar.[10]

Disappointed, Riche practically "gave away" his remaining quarter share of the venture to Francis Street for thirty-five pipes of Faial wine. The amount equaled about £200. When William Street asked him to cooperate in another venture to Brazil, he declined. Riche complained that the *Elizabeth & Mary* took twelve months to complete the previous voyage. "Such Trade I am not fond of," he griped. Without the consent of the state, he found it difficult to sustain lucrative direct trade with Brazil. A year later, he waited for the Rio de Janeiro fleet to take gold to Lisbon so Parr & Bulkeley of that city could pay his creditors in London on his account for breadstuff he had sent the Lisbon firm. Direct trade with Brazil remained closed to him, and he stayed indebted to London and dependent on Lisbon to remit his payments to merchants in the British metropolis.[11]

In his correspondence, Riche communicated in the detached, dispassionate language of a merchant. He cared little about the political or philosophical implications of his illegal commerce. Although he contemplated his venture in terms of sales and profits, it did not occur without serious ideological implications for Atlantic empires. To execute the venture, Riche cooperated with a variety of contacts from around the Atlantic—a network that state policies had fostered. He nonchalantly defied imperial laws in favor of a free trade ideology, albeit an ideology he left unarticulated in his correspondence. His illicit enterprise highlighted the negotiation that occurred between states and private traders as they vied for control over Atlantic commerce. It represented the practical application of Enlightenment discourse that promoted free trade and justified smuggling as an assertion of natural law.[12]

Natural Law

Well before the appearance of Adam Smith's *Wealth of Nations*, many intellectuals, politicians, and traders contested the political economy of Atlantic empires. Historians have tended to overstate the extent to which mercantilism acted as the undisputed economic model of the eighteenth century. As early as the seventeenth century, theorists proposed alternative political economies that they believed would free people and commerce from government strictures. During the Enlightenment, intellectuals grounded free trade ideology in theories of natural law. By the mid-eighteenth century,

free trade advocates applied their ideology to smuggling. They justified illegal ventures on the grounds that such trade represented the natural course
of commerce as opposed to arbitrary government regulations.[13]

The Dutch jurist, Huig de Groot (frequently Latinized as Hugo Grotius), introduced one of the earliest intellectual defenses of free trade in
Europe. In 1609, de Groot published *Mare Liberum* (*The Free Sea*). He
argued in favor of the right of the Dutch to trade in the Portuguese-
controlled East Indies. *Mare Liberum* contested the right of empires to
expand their sovereignty over the seas and believed that attempts to do so
violated the rights of humankind. In de Groot's conception, the Creator
had not formed the oceans to divide, but to connect. Enlightenment writ-
ers such as Victor Riquetti (the Marquis de Mirabeau) and Guillaume-
François Le Trosne expounded on the Dutchman's theory. They
contrasted the natural order of free trade with the manipulated, arbitrary
imposts collected by imperial states. Diderot and Montesquieu discarded
assumptions that foreign diplomacy depended on secrecy, suspicion, and
compulsion. They associated such theories with corrupt monarchies.
David Hume and Adam Smith applied the same conclusions to commerce.
The Scottish thinkers claimed that honesty and transparency would lead
to foreign relations marked by cooperation and mutual interest—
characterized by free trade.[14]

Since the earliest defenses of free interimperial trade, proponents
espoused illicit or unconventional commercial practices to secure their supposedly natural right to access restricted markets. De Groot began his
exploration of free trade at the same time Dutch privateers plundered Portuguese vessels in East Asia. Inspired by the privateers' actions, he wrote *De
Iurae Praedae*, or *On the Law of Prize and Booty*, in which he defended
private warfare as a legitimate method to contest restrictions on the natural
right of free trade.[15]

Liberal political economists such as Le Trosne, Ange Goudar, and Jacques Claude Marie Vincent de Gournay expanded de Groot's defense of
unconventional commerce. They justified defiance of one's own government, defending participation in illicit trade when the state placed onerous
demands on legal commerce. Gournay lambasted the French ban on the
importation of calico. He warned that consumer demand would promote
illicit trade and start a war between smugglers and the government. He
faulted governments, not smugglers, for such warfare if they failed to enact
just trade laws.[16]

Goudar shared Gournay's opinion that ruinous trade laws would spawn violence between smugglers and the government. In his renowned *Testament politique de Louis Mandrin*, he exhorted the government to eliminate the French tax-farming system and avoid imminent chaos. He further suggested that the monarchy grant general amnesty to smugglers. Le Trosne claimed that smugglers acted within "laws of natural order" and that they exercised their right "to buy and sell in a condition of full competition." He placed the impetus on governments to make patriots out of criminals by abolishing the indirect taxes that obliged traders to defy state law.[17]

The Italian philosopher Cesare Beccaria shared Le Trosne's idea that trade prohibitions allowed the government undue power to create a subjective definition of criminality. "To prohibit a host of harmless acts is not to prevent the crimes to which they might lead," he asserted. "It is, rather, to create new crimes; it is to define virtue and vice . . . at one's whim." He denounced the punishment of smugglers beyond confiscation of contraband because the "crime arises from the law itself." He suggested that the smaller the customs duty, the less incentive to smuggle "since men take risks only in proportion to the success that their uncertain enterprise might yield."[18]

Enlightenment-era authors disseminated their ideas throughout the Atlantic and armed colonists with an intellectual basis upon which they began to clamor for freer trade during the latter half of the eighteenth century. If imperial governments refused to yield, such arguments also condoned disobedience to state authority. They did not inherently pit colonies against metropolises, for around the Atlantic many voices contended for a variety of political economies. Facing increased regulations in the 1760s, however, British Americans argued for more open commerce and justified defiance of British law by merging free trade theory with a long tradition of debating imperial political economy.

Contraband and Liberty

Politicians and traders debated imperial commercial systems rather than subscribe to a uniform commitment to mercantilism in the British Empire. Many cited various strains of free trade as counterpoints to mercantilist policies. They politicized the debate in an array of venues from the halls of Parliament to local coffeehouses, and imperial policy pitched and yawed among the discordant interests. As the imperial crisis came to a head in the

1760s and 1770s, mainland colonists saw their economic interests increasingly diverge from those of Britain. In their revolutionary struggle, they drew on an extensive history of English and British polemics to denounce new commercial regulations.[19]

Policymakers and traders promoted variations of free trade in England as early as 1604 with Parliament's so-called free trade debate. Parliamentarians did not call for open commerce between empires, but those who represented provincial ports harangued against the dominance of London merchants, who controlled seven-eighths of overseas trade. The next year, in the House of Commons, provincial members achieved substantive gains in their quest to expand English trade beyond London's control. They fought against the renewal of a royal charter that would have granted the Spanish Company a monopoly on trade in Portugal and Spain. They demanded, instead, that the fish and grain trades to the Iberian Peninsula remain open to all English merchants. The Spanish Company dissolved in 1606, and southern European markets came to symbolize a victory for free trade in England.[20]

Throughout the seventeenth century, Whigs maintained an antimonopoly ideology and demanded the dissolution of the monopolies granted to the East India Company and Royal African Company. Near midcentury, Parliament passed a series of Navigation Acts to regulate colonial trade and compete with Dutch commerce. Some English observers noted, however, that the Dutch owed their commercial success to their "natural liberty." Colonial governors appealed to the example of Dutch trade liberties to argue that freer trade would result in greater prosperity for the entire empire. In New York, middling and poorer merchants felt squeezed by imperial regulations and extolled the example of their Dutch colonial forbears.[21]

Parliamentarians and traders extended the dispute throughout the eighteenth century with intensified implications for the empire's South American policy. In 1711, the Tory Robert Harley, first Earl of Oxford, founded the South Sea Company and aimed to conquer land in Peruvian and Brazilian mining regions. Whigs railed against such territorial aspirations. They claimed that trade rather than land acquisition would enrich the British Empire. William Paterson, the founder of the Bank of England, assumed that treasure-based land grabs impoverished empires. He quipped that the Indies "may be said to have conquered the Spaniards, rather than having been conquered by them." The prominent Whig commentator Arthur

Maynwaring decried Harley's scheme and suggested that "if we cou'd obtain either by *Treaty* or by *Conquest* those *Golden Mines* we dream of, they wou'd not be half so advantageous to us, as the bare Liberty of Trading there, and of exchanging our Goods for Bullion." He insisted that treasure-based empires lay exposed to tyranny whereas those with open trade tended toward liberty.[22]

Radical Whigs maintained that the colonies contributed as much to the wealth of the empire as the metropolis. Because labor rather than land generated wealth, they argued, the colonies comprised the empire's most important entity due to labor's high value in America. According to such arguments, colonists deserved political representation because of their importance to the empire. Early in the century, Daniel Defoe argued that the British Empire should constitute an integrated economic unit rather than a division between colonies and the metropolis. By mid-century, colonists embraced that paradigm to argue for their own economic freedom. Benjamin Franklin maintained that Parliament should consider the colonies as British counties. He wondered in 1754, "What imports it to the general state, whether a merchant, a smith, or a hatter, grow rich in *Old* or *New* England?" He supposed that the empire should afford "some preference" to those "who have most contributed to enlarge Britain's empire and commerce, encrease her strength, her wealth, and the numbers of her people."[23]

Anglo-Atlantic traders staked out rival sides in the debate over political economy. English merchants benefited from mercantilism because it favored their dry-goods businesses and stipulated that the colonies' foreign trade pass through their hands for re-export. In the Americas, traders differed according to a complex variety of elements such as their locations, their specialized markets, and the commodities they traded. Government contractors and factors (agents for European merchants) found mercantilism beneficial, for they enhanced their business in proportion to that of their clients in Europe. As the British West Indies became more dependent on sugarcane monoculture, island merchants supported the protection that the Navigation Acts allowed their sugar-based industries. They despised the unbridled smuggling business between their Franco-Caribbean neighbors and their fellow subjects on the mainland. They badgered Parliament for better regulation of tropical imports in North America.[24]

Mainland traders did not share a single vision for British political economy, but as revolution approached they began to unite in the opinion that the British government had overstepped its bounds. They operated in a political and commercial atmosphere characterized by debate and dialogue rather than an uncontested paradigm of mercantilism. Since England's initial colonization efforts in the Americas, the empire had oscillated between centralized government intervention and a laissez-faire approach to commerce. When it tended toward stricter mercantilist measures in the 1760s, mainland British Americans drew on a century and a half of debate about political economy to protest and resist restrictions on their trade.[25]

Merchants with Luso-Atlantic ties lay especially vulnerable to British trade restrictions because they depended on interimperial trade. They enjoyed the privileges granted to the British Empire in Portugal and the Atlantic islands so long as the government left their Luso-Atlantic trade unfettered. They stood susceptible to financial harm, however, when Parliament intensified regulation of Luso-Atlantic commerce in the 1760s. Smaller merchants also felt threatened by British strictures because they could not absorb the costs of regulation as easily as the merchant princes of Philadelphia, New York, and Boston. Less wealthy merchants tended to specialize to a greater degree than large firms in terms of the commodities they traded and the regions to which they shipped their goods. As small traders with business in southern Europe, Americans such as Solomon Davis and Jeremiah Lee happily promoted revolution and contraband.[26]

British-American smugglers defied legal restraints on their commerce in favor of free trade. Smuggling did not always correlate with an ardent free trade ideology, but it did indicate that traders assumed that their financial interests frequently lay outside of imperial trade parameters. By smuggling, traders manifested their willingness to cooperate with their trade networks in defiance of imperial laws and in favor of their commercial interests.[27]

Colonial smugglers appealed to the intellectual foundation of the Enlightenment to claim the rights of free trade and to rationalize contraband as a means of resistance. As the pseudonymous Tradesman of Philadelphia complained, smugglers argued that "every man has a natural right to exchange his property with whom he pleases, and where he can make the most advantage of it; that there is no injustice in the nature of the thing, being no otherwise unlawful than as the partial restrictions of power have made it so; arguments which may be, and are adopted in extenuation of many other disorderly and pernicious practices." Smuggling had become an ideological statement as well as a financial strategy.[28]

During the eighteenth century, Tories cast illicit trade as unpatriotic—destructive to the common good of British subjects and an affront to the monarchy. In 1765, a writer known as Vindex Patriae accused British Americans of smuggling sugar and tea from foreign markets. Their egregious acts provided "convincing proofs," in the mind of the author, "that they have no tenderness for their mother country." In 1773, John Vardill urged fellow New Yorkers to stanch the inward flow of contraband foreign tea. He suggested that "the *bond* of our *Union* [with England] is *Affection* and *Interest*. Let us strengthen this Affection by mutual Acts of Friendship and increase this *Interest* by preserving . . . a common Advantage." Vardill insisted that those who imported foreign tea aided "the Enemies of their Country." He imagined a mutually reinforcing relationship in which trade would bind the affection of the colonies and metropolis, which affection would compel both entities to desire an exclusive imperial trade.[29]

Tories assumed that colonial smugglers betrayed the good of the empire to pursue their self-interest. Members of Parliament expressed concern that New England contrabandists "carried on a trade pernicious to the interest of this country." One assumed that Parliament could concede "every political point to them" and they still would smuggle because "trading people mind nothing but their present interest, and would trade with the devil for one per cent. extra profit." "As to the Americans," Lord North reportedly told a colleague, "they shall not smuggle the goods of every other country, and be of no service to this country, which has protected them at the expense of so much blood and treasure."[30]

American revolutionaries inverted the Tory paradigm, casting contraband trade as an act of patriotism in the face of unjust laws. After the passage of the Tea Act of 1773, a British editor sympathetic to the colonies inveighed against the duty on tea. The writer assumed the British government could never obstruct illicit foreign tea in a country "where the restraining authority was by all the inhabitants deemed unconstitutional, and smuggling of course considered as patriotism." Rebutting John Vardill's appeal to British patriotism, a commentator who wrote as Tradesman suggested that colonists had no obligation to submit to oppressive laws. He appealed to past English patriots who wrought the Magna Carta and the Glorious Revolution by opposing laws and civil magistrates in favor of just governance.[31]

Smugglers and free trade advocates drew on Whig conceptions of the British Empire as a cohesive unit to argue that colonial trade with foreign powers benefited the entire empire. The *Boston Evening Post* favorably quoted the *London Chronicle*, which asserted that colonial contraband aided the parent country by enabling colonists to purchase English manufactures. Benjamin Franklin reasoned that if British Americans purchased sugars exclusively from the British West Indies, the price of British sugar would increase in England as well as the mainland colonies. The entire empire benefited from illicit trade. By smuggling, therefore, colonists proved their "tenderness for their mother-country." William Cooper, the secretary of the Boston town meeting, argued that "for every penny drawn away from us in the way of Revenue, Britain misses ten in the way of trade." He concluded, "We feel for our Mother Country as well as our selves, but charity begins at home."[32]

Revolutionaries incorporated Enlightenment arguments about natural rights into their calls for freer trade and their justifications of contraband. In his "Summary View of the Rights of British America," Thomas Jefferson claimed "the exercise of a free trade with all parts of the world" as a "natural right." Philip Mazzei, a recent Italian émigré devoted to Enlightenment theories, declared that the colonists would "sacrifice every thing to the enjoyment of liberty and a free trade with all nations."[33]

Colonists translated and distributed *The Sentiments of a Foreigner, on the disputes of Great-Britain with North America*, written by the French radical Guillaume Thomas Raynal, "to whose authority a kind of sanction has been given" according to advertisements. Raynal declared that "contraband was the offspring" of tyrannical revenue laws, and "transgression is the first effect of iniquitous laws." Raynal gave voice to American revolutionaries with his assertion that "FREEDOM of trade undefined, or only restrained within just bounds, would put a stop to these illicit practices." He inverted the traditional British conception of legislation and patriotism by placing the onus on the government to pass proper laws rather than the people to obey.[34]

By the time of the American Revolution, colonial smugglers combined traditional British debates about political economy with Enlightenment rhetoric to defend their right to free trade and to defy the state to obtain it. In April 1776, the Continental Congress invited merchandise from all friendly nations to North American ports—a deliberate challenge to British authority. The literary scholar Ayşe Çelikkol argues that Anglo-Atlantic smugglers "obeyed putatively universal economic laws even as they disobeyed the government." That paradigm made sense especially to British-American revolutionaries, who believed they defended "the Laws of Nature and of Nature's God" in the face of "a long train of abuses and usurpations" by the central government.[35]

Contraband and Empire

Like the British government, the Portuguese court negotiated its political economy with Luso-Atlantic traders and intellectuals who contested the underpinnings of mercantilism. Elite traders garnered vast wealth in Brazil as they smuggled gold to the Mina Coast and Angola to trade for slaves and prohibited European goods. They brought them back to Brazil and traded them illicitly to Spanish America and the Brazilian interior. Once arrived, the captives labored to produce goods for domestic markets and international export. By trading directly with Africa, both legally and illegally, *fluminense* (Rio de Janeiro) traders accrued capital and economic influence independent of the metropolis. The Brazilian hinterlands grew more dependent on merchant capital from Rio de Janeiro than from Lisbon.[36]

Brazilian slave traders augmented their influence over imperial policies due to their control of merchant capital. Faced with Brazil's enhanced economic independence, Portuguese officials considered how best to employ Brazilian resources for the good of the empire. In the mid-eighteenth century, they granted Brazilians greater control over the slave trade. Authorities supposed that the trade would promote economic development in Brazil, and Brazilians could then increase imports from Portugal. They also assumed that as Brazilians increased their presence in Africa the Portuguese Empire would regain its grip on the continent's trade zones. The empire had lost ground in Africa to the British and French since the beginning of the century.[37]

Brazilians demanded slaves because the slave system generated merchant capital and developed the internal economy far beyond the production of agricultural exports. As enslaved laborers developed the Minas Gerais economy, cattle and artisanal industries spread to support the mining community. In Campos dos Goitacazes, most slaves labored for smaller farms, on which they produced coffee, manioc, and dairy products, or they worked on engenhos of less than fifty slaves. On those smaller engenhos, they produced goods destined for the internal market rather than overseas ports. By late century, the agro-export sectors accounted for just half of enslaved labor in the district, and the other half supported industries that sustained local economies. In Bahia and São Paulo, slavery sustained

Figure 2. A Brazilian sugar mill, as shown in Henry Koster, *Travels in Brazil* (London, 1816).

economic production not connected directly to international exports. The slave system supported a wide array of industries and enhanced Brazilians' economic autonomy from Lisbon.[38]

With Brazilians demanding more slaves and Lisbon authorities desiring increased Brazilian production and trade, they fused their interests and supplied the country with an enormous number of captive laborers. The Portuguese government granted an effective monopoly of the African slave trade with the Amazonian captaincies to the Company of Grão Pará and Maranhão. To aid the importation of slaves, it offered Brazilians a subsidized advance of 3 percent interest. Between 1769 and 1778, the number of slaves rose from 3,192 to 4,871 in Campos dos Goitacazes, and sugar output increased 235 percent in the region. Imperial administrators hoped the increased importation of slaves would result in "lucrative engenhos and huge plantations" that would send produce to Portugal in return for manufactures. Between 1750 and 1770, engenhos doubled in Campos dos Goitacazes from 50 to 115. By 1783, the number rose to 278.[39]

The slave trade weakened Lisbon's control over Luso-Atlantic commerce as it infused Brazil with greater merchant capital and a more dynamic economy. Brazilian and Angolan colonists implored the government for direct trade with one another. As governor of Angola, António Álvares da Cunha pled with the court to allow freer trade in the Brazilian-Angolan slave markets. In 1758, Pombal acquiesced. The minister allowed direct trade among Brazil, Angola, and the Mina Coast to strengthen Portuguese territorial claims in Africa and enhance metropolitan capital at the expense of the British. He reasoned that unless Brazil received a sufficient supply of slaves, its economy would suffer and damage Portuguese finances in turn. The change legitimized trade routes that smugglers had carried on for decades, and it served to marginalize the metropolis in one of the most important Luso-Atlantic economic sectors. Pombal had tried to consolidate commercial power in Lisbon through monopolies on Brazilian commerce, but he undermined his own efforts by conceding autonomy to Brazilians over one of the most vital trades in the Luso-Atlantic.[40]

Smugglers thwarted Portuguese imperial designs in the African trade. The Portuguese government had constructed forts to control trade in Luanda, Benguela, and Cabinda to protect imperial commerce, but foreigners continued to permeate Portuguese trade zones in Africa. Brazilians procured prohibited Dutch, English, and French goods in return for tobacco, brandy, and sugar while they traded for slaves on the Mina Coast. Pombal lamented that "our Brazilian colonists have absorbed the commerce and shipping of the African coast to the total exclusion of Portugal."[41]

The Portuguese government unwittingly facilitated illicit trade between Asia and Brazil by allowing direct trade between Angola and the South American colony. Portuguese ships bypassed African ports and made their way from Asia straight to Brazil despite the legal requirement to pass through Angola. In 1772, the government revoked a 1769 policy that allowed direct trade between East Africa and Brazil. Officials found that the trade opened Brazil to contraband Asian goods to the detriment of the Pernambuco Company's monopoly. Authorities hoped, in the words of the overseas minister Martinho de Melo e Castro, to avoid "the pernicious consequences that arise when ships coming from Africa sail directly to Brazilian ports."[42]

Still, traders continued to smuggle with ease due to the close association between Brazilian and African ports. By 1779, Melo e Castro complained that the English, French, and Dutch operated "a free trade by the ports of Africa between those nations and the Portuguese dominions in Brazil without the intervention of the merchants of the metropolis." He stressed that Luanda "has become an entrepôt for a general commerce between Asia, Africa, and America, to the total exclusion of this kingdom." The minister warned that Brazilians would usurp complete control over the important Asian trade if such contraband continued unchecked.[43]

Meanwhile, many Brazilian traders had accrued nearly insurmountable debts to the Pernambuco and Grão Pará and Maranhão companies. By 1777, Rio de Janeiro traders owed the Company of Grão Pará and Maranhão a total of 1.02 billion réis. Few Brazilians had invested with the companies, so many derided the company monopolies in the northern and northeastern parts of Brazil. The Portuguese government had vested the Company of Pernambuco with the power to regulate the supply of metropolitan merchandise, and Brazilians blamed the company for supply shortages and high prices. Colonists complained of the high prices for slaves charged by the Company of Grão Pará and Maranhão. As a result, even sugar-mill owners opposed the monopolies, despite the revitalization of the economy's sugar sector that resulted from the establishment of the Company of Pernambuco.[44]

The Portuguese government made gradual concessions to advocates of more open commerce in Brazil. It abolished the fleet system in 1765 and permitted intercoastal trade the next year. Upon the abolition of the fleet system, the British minister told Pombal exultantly that "freedom was the soul of commerce, and therefore, every liberty which could be allowed must be beneficial to the trade and credit of the nation."[45]

In 1777, Dom José I died, and his daughter, Dona Maria I, ascended to the throne. Deeply antagonistic to Pombal, Maria promptly dismissed the powerful minister and began to roll back some of his most extensive reforms. Enemies of the monopolies saw their chance to raise their complaints and to petition for more open trade. Anti-Pombal forces voiced their approval of extinction, and the Council of State voted six to three to let the companies' charters expire. According to one memorial, anti-monopolists anticipated that the companies' extinction would yield "liberty of commerce and the competition of businessmen" and the end of "a thousand vexations."[46]

In the 1760s, rumors had spread that the British and Portuguese Empires discussed the establishment of a British company allowed to trade directly with Brazil. The British government claimed that Pombal's policies had violated the seventeenth-century treaties. It dispatched a minister to Portugal "demanding immediate redress for all our grievances . . . together with a demand of liberty of trading to the Brazils." Anglo-Atlantic traders maintained high hopes for the mission and spread talk that "beneficial trade to the Brazils is now on the carpet." Brazilians anticipated that direct trade with Great Britain would give them access to cheap English manufactures.[47]

Despite such hopes, Portuguese administrators remained committed to mercantilist policies. In 1761, the Portuguese overseas secretary, Francisco Xavier de Mendonça Furtado, maintained, "All the world knows that the overseas colonies are founded as a precious object of utility of the metropolis . . . from which essential certainty result infallible maxims universally observed in the practice of all nations." Portuguese administrators carried those "infallible maxims" forward over the next two decades. By the 1780s, the Portuguese government received concerned reports from the *Junta das Fábricas*, or Board of Manufactures. The board claimed that manufacture exports from Portugal to Brazil had recently suffered. With the reports in hand, Lisbon officials resisted calls for the establishment of a company to conduct direct trade with Britain. They assumed that in an open market Portuguese manufactures could not compete with those of the British. Authorities still imagined the colonies as a destination for Portuguese products purchased with colonial precious metals. By liberalizing Brazilian commerce, they intended to advance metropolitan objectives, not subordinate them to colonial interests.[48]

During his tenure, Pombal had embedded his adherents into Portugal's government framework. His agents maintained a presence in fiscal and revenue collection agencies well after his dismissal as minister in 1777. Investors in monopoly companies consisted of some of the most socially and financially connected families in the Luso-Atlantic, and they retained the power to recover their debts long after the companies' official expiration. Brazilians continued to purchase goods on the companies' credit for years after the expiration of the charters, and they owed debts to creditors who operated in the companies' names. Moreover, although Brazilian free trade advocates claimed victory at the dissolution of the monopolies, Brazilians still resented onerous taxes.[49]

The Portuguese government remained committed to the collection of the quinto into the late eighteenth century. More than other taxes imposed on Brazilians, the quinto represented the power of the metropolis because the entire tax went to Lisbon rather than remain in local treasuries for colonial administration. At mid-century, the Portuguese government imposed a per capita tax known as the *derrama*, which took effect if gold-mining districts failed to meet a production quota of one hundred arrobas of gold annually. Lisbon officials hoped the derrama would ensure collection of the quinto since it would incentivize traders to report their gold production rather than smuggle the precious metal and risk the imposition of the per capita tax.[50]

Officials in Portugal neglected collection of the derrama in the face of intransigent colonists and lax local enforcement. Between 1763 and 1771, the government collected the tax only four times despite reduced gold production. Local officials blamed overlapping bureaucracies for the inadequate collection of the tax. In 1773, the *Junta da Fazenda* (Treasury Board) of Minas Gerais urged Lisbon officials not to collect the derrama because the mines could no longer support the quota. The government in Portugal did not respond, and the junta accepted the lack of reply as acquiescence. Brazilians could claim another victory against imperial control over their trade, but the Portuguese government maintained a mercantilist orientation throughout Pombal's tenure and the next several decades.[51]

After Pombal fell from royal favor and Martinho de Melo e Castro assumed control of overseas affairs, the governor of Minas Gerais, Rodrigo José de Meneses, informed the minister about the unsustainability of Minas gold production. He implored Melo e Castro to institute a flexible economic relationship between the colony and the metropolis—a relationship that would allow Minas Gerais to diversify its production sectors. Instead, the minister retrenched. He took a mechanical approach to the Brazilian political economy in which each province would produce one or two staples and import necessities from other parts of the empire. Melo e Castro remained convinced that the diminished production of gold resulted from lax oversight rather than exhaustion of the earth. His assumption led him to press for the unabated collection of the quinto into the 1780s. Such assumptions caused friction between the colonists and imperial administrators throughout the rest of the century.[52]

Where Brazilians failed to obtain open commerce through legal or political battles, they illicitly asserted control over their trade. In 1751, the overseas minister, Diogo de Mendonça, instructed Gomes Freire de Andrade to inform the Brazilian authorities of their obligation to satisfy the one hundred arrobas of gold to avoid the institution of the recently decreed derrama. Mendonça assumed correctly that in regions removed from the four main mining districts of Vila Rica, Sabará, Rio das Mortes, and Serro Frio, inhabitants would continue to smuggle gold dust. In their remote locations, they could avoid the smelting houses and the quinto. The minister urged the governor to take all necessary "cautions and rigors" to quash such contraband. In his instructions, Mendonça highlighted the divergence between the government officials' commitment to exploit the colony for the benefit of the metropolis and colonists' endeavors to assert their own control over Brazil's resources.[53]

During the late 1750s and 1760s, Lisbon officials tried to exploit the gold mines to their fullest and quash contraband as gold production decreased. They suspected that Brazilian customs inspectors took a cut of the contraband in exchange for their cooperation. In 1756, customs officers in Lisbon reinspected all vessels from Brazil. The court suggested that the chief inspector in Brazil undermine his subordinates' influence by personally conducting all inspections. In the first half of the 1760s, Furtado implored Álvares da Cunha, now the Brazilian viceroy, to repress the illicit trade. In response, Álvares da Cunha informed the minister that he had placed a patrol along one of the major contraband routes, Rio de São João, between Campos dos Goitacazes and Rio de Janeiro. Such measures failed, however, to quell smuggling. To avoid reinspections in Lisbon, smugglers docked their ships outside of the Rio Tejo estuary. In Brazil, they adeptly evaded contraband patrols.[54]

The Brazilian elite facilitated contraband by the combined influence of colonial officials and privileged merchants. Royal administrators struggled against Brazilian magistrates who invested in contraband and thereby blurred the lines between legal and illegal trade. Local authorities cooperated in and directed contraband ventures. With their support of contraband, they accrued private profit and diversified the colonial economy. Between 1749 and 1760, the governor of Nova Colônia do Sacramento (across the Río de la Plata from Buenos Aires), Luiz Garcia de Bivar, gained notoriety for his abuse of power and involvement in illicit trade. In 1753, the cleric João de Almeida Cardoso claimed that the governor had cooperated in illicit trade, profited personally from confiscated goods, and punished him for denouncing the governor's shadowy transactions.[55]

Colônia do Sacramento merchants were some of the most elite members of society, but they also constituted a class removed from the power structures of the Lisbon nobility. To amplify his power in the Río de la

Plata region, Garcia de Bivar immersed himself in the elite merchant community and enabled traders within his circle to engage more easily in contraband. Hardly the first to abuse his power, Garcia de Bivar carried on a tradition of illicit trade that extended back to his predecessor, Antônio Pedro de Vasconcelos, who had also promoted smuggling networks. Rio de Janeiro smugglers commonly routed their illicit goods through contraband networks in Colônia do Sacramento to trade with the Río de la Plata region. As one writer noted, all the residents of Colônia do Sacramento "live on clandestine commerce."[56]

Colonial officials clashed with residents more over control of the contraband trade than over the prosecution against it. When Luís da Cunha Meneses arrived in Minas Gerais in 1782, he placed his own subordinates in military and civil positions, which allowed them to control the contraband diamond trade. In the process, he cut out local magistrates who had previously benefited from the illegal commerce, causing friction between the governor and lower-level officials.[57]

When they did not directly aid illicit trade, governors turned a blind eye to it for fear of reprisals from the population. In 1770, the Brazilian viceroy, Marquis of Lavradio, complained that although smuggling had "very grave consequences, here it was treated as a thing of no importance." He denounced smugglers as "the plague of States" and worried that measures to repress contraband would "mount against me the spirit of these people that live without knowledge, nor respect for the Laws; as has happened at other times to some of the Governors of the Americas, causing them to slacken in prosecuting the Execution of such Laws." Rather than a clandestine, lawless underground, Brazilian smugglers were some of the most influential members of society who aimed to control local trade at the expense of the metropolis. By 1785, Melo e Castro railed against the "multiplied damages, contraband, and violations across the continent, ports and coasts of Brazil . . . with irreparable harm to the licit and legal trade."[58]

Brazilian smugglers believed that contraband strengthened the colonial economy. Pedro de Vasconcelos maintained that Colônia do Sacramento could not receive the necessary quantity of provisions in the closed imperial system. In 1794, the government detained Caetano Silvestre, a Santa Catarina merchant, for illicit trade in Spanish-American and African ports. Silvestre's business network—including his partners, creditors, and consumers—came to his defense, complaining that the government's attempts to suppress illicit trade would weaken Brazil's economic vitality.

Perceived as an intricate part of the colonial economy and supported by colonial elites, smuggling occupied liminal ground between legal and illegal trade in Brazil.[59]

Like British Americans, Brazilian traders varied in their views on political economy depending on their commercial interests. Many merchants enjoyed imperial protection against foreign competition. Others sought to press the limits of trade even further by requesting trade privileges with Great Britain and Spanish America. In the eighteenth century, with few exceptions, the Lisbon government denied such requests. By integrating imperial trade, the Portuguese court intended to bolster the empire's commerce against foreign influence rather than open it to unfettered free trade. At the turn of the century, Brazilian traders and magistrates frequently contested rather than conformed to imperial trade regulations. As the Age of Revolution unfolded, many Brazilians began to reimagine the Portuguese trade paradigm. They saw Brazil rather than Portugal as the empire's central commercial entity.[60]

*   *   *

In the Anglo- and Luso-Atlantics, traders frequently contested what Francisco Xavier de Mendonça Furtado called the "infallible maxims" of mercantilism. Buttressed by an intellectual environment that extolled free trade and justified violation of imperial commercial restrictions, Atlantic traders tested the limits of imperial power as they expanded their commercial networks. They varied in their definitions of free trade and the extent to which they enjoyed imperial trade paradigms. Although they rarely envisioned a world of unrestricted interimperial trade, they petitioned for the right to trade with partners and markets they deemed most beneficial to their commerce. When governments refused to liberalize imperial policies accordingly, traders often undertook a practical application of free trade by smuggling.[61]

By resorting to contraband, Atlantic traders acquired some control over imperial commerce, but not omnipotence. Thomas Riche defied imperial trade regulations of both the British and Portuguese governments during his illegal venture to Brazil. Despite his efforts to thwart constraints on his business, the lackluster result highlighted the unequal relationship between the state and the individual. His networks remained unchanged after the venture. The Luso-Atlantic wine trade remained the center of his business with the Portuguese Empire. His attempt signaled, however, the potential of decentralized trade networks to challenge state authority.

Colonial subjects vied for greater commercial freedom and assumed increasingly important roles in imperial economies. They forced the British and Portuguese Empires to weigh the needs of the metropolis against their own demands. Beginning in the latter half of the eighteenth century, Britain failed to balance the rival interests of the various components of the empire. The failure resulted in the American Revolution and the independence of most of the mainland colonies. With so much of the Portuguese Empire's economy based on the slave trade, by contrast, Brazilians acquired increased autonomy from Portuguese institutions and capital. As the ties between British America and London unraveled, the Portuguese government moderately liberalized its imperial commerce. As a result, the court stabilized the empire's precarious finances and staved off early threats of republican revolution. It linked trade liberalization with imperial cohesion rather than fragmentation. Although Brazilians and North Americans espoused the virtues of more open commerce by the late eighteenth century, they began to diverge in how they imagined free trade related to empire and monarchy.[62]

PART II

Regulation and Revolution

AS THE BRITISH IMPERIAL CRISIS unfolded, British Americans demanded freer commerce. Faced with economic woes after the Seven Years' War and increased regulation, mainland British-American traders grew more unified in their opposition to commercial restrictions. Although they did not speak with one voice about politics or economics, they arrived at a broad consensus that the central government had exceeded the limits of its power. Merchants with Luso-Atlantic ties agonized as the British government exerted greater control over their trade, which had long enjoyed immunity from regulations by both law and custom. To reassume control over their commerce, they cooperated with business associates around the Atlantic to conduct illicit trade and defy state authority.[1]

Between 1764 and the end of the Revolutionary War, British Americans found their Luso-Atlantic trade disrupted by imperial regulations, colonial boycotts, and warfare. Independence released them from the strictures of British mercantilism, and they welcomed increased trade with Spain and France. With new markets available to them, they diversified their wine trade and marginalized their ties to Lisbon, Porto, and Madeira. At the same time, independence also severed them from the commercial protections of the British Empire. They felt that split keenly in the 1780s, when the Portuguese government restricted importation of U.S. flour into Portugal. The restrictions further eroded U.S.-Portuguese trade. During the 1760s and 1770s, British-American traders had cooperated with their Luso-Atlantic relationships to protest state authority. Paradoxically, they fomented a revolution that eventually attenuated those very relationships.[2]

As their commercial ties to Portugal and the Atlantic islands weakened, by the end of the eighteenth century U.S. traders came to view Brazil as the most important component of the Portuguese Empire. The American Revolution opened a new variety of trade options and introduced a paradigm that pitted independence, republicanism, and free trade against empire, monarchy, and mercantilism. As a result of the revolution and independence, North Americans felt less tethered to Portugal and the Atlantic islands and anticipated free trade with an independent Brazil.

Chapter 3

A Fractured Empire

The British government needed money. By 1763, the Seven Years' War saddled the empire with an enormous national debt, and Parliament looked to America to help improve imperial finances. Officials in London argued that British Americans had benefited from the recent war that cleared their region of dangerous French troops and their Indian allies. Per capita, colonists paid the empire 1s. in taxes for every 26s. paid by subjects in England. The government worked with an annual budget of approximately £3 million besides the amount spent on debt, £360,000 of which went to maintain military support in North America. Central authorities reasoned that colonists must contribute more to their own protection, so they fashioned new laws to raise revenue and restrict contraband.[1]

In the mid-1760s, Parliament threatened British-American–Luso-Atlantic trade with restrictive legislation such as the Sugar Act, Stamp Act, and Townshend Acts. Colonial traders differed from one another in their enthusiasm for patriot causes, but they developed greater harmony in favor of commercial freedom due to the new regulations. They protested Parliament's actions by smuggling dutiable goods and participating in nonimportation movements. In 1774, the Continental Congress adopted the Articles of Association, which prohibited the importation of Madeira wine in response to new taxes levied on it. Rebellious colonists thoroughly politicized Luso-Atlantic trade and cooperated with their commercial networks to resist imperial intrusion.

Luso-Atlantic trade represented the promise and peril of the American Revolution. During the 1760s and 1770s, British-American traders witnessed the erosion of their Portuguese and Madeiran trade networks due to British restrictions, colonial nonimportation movements, and warfare.

By the outbreak of war in 1775, recalcitrant colonists turned from defiance against state restrictions to rebellion against imperial authority. Traders who supported the cause cooperated with their Luso-Atlantic contacts to resist the British government, but the Revolution ultimately attenuated their ties to Portugal and the Atlantic islands. Revolutionary traders engaged their networks to contest imperial power even as they dissolved the mercantilist strictures that bound those networks together. Independence granted North Americans commercial options once prohibited by British policies, but it also stripped them of the commercial privileges they had enjoyed as British subjects. North Americans emerged from the Revolution less fastened to the Portuguese Empire and with a heightened antagonism against trade policies of European monarchies.

Duties

Parliament passed the American Duties Act, better known as the Sugar Act, on April 5, 1764. The government aimed to stop rampant smuggling by reducing the duty on French and Spanish West Indies molasses from 6d. to 3d. per gallon. Parliament had established the 6d. duty under the Molasses Act of 1733. Authorities intended the reduction to placate British Americans. They hoped colonists would choose to pay the lower duty rather than smuggle foreign molasses and risk capture. Anglo-Atlantic merchants had touted such an approach in their appeals for freer trade. As one "eminent Merchant" remarked in 1751, "The only Remedy for Smuggling is reducing the high Duties which encourage it." To compensate for the revenue lost by the reduction on duties for foreign molasses, the Sugar Act imposed new duties on other foreign articles, including wine from Madeira and the Azores. Because "Great Britain does not produce Madeira wine," one American commentator griped, "it will . . . be easily admitted a great grievance to subject the American to the odious alternative of paying this duty."[2]

British-American merchants could have saved a portion of the duty if they routed Madeira wine through England. The act imposed a duty of £7 sterling per ton (double the size of a pipe) on wines imported directly from Madeira and the Azores compared to an overall duty of £4 sterling per ton for wines that passed through the homeland. But colonial merchants would have lost any money they saved on duties to the extra expenses they would incur if they shipped the wine through England. Merchants had little choice but to import the wine directly from the islands and pay the higher rate.

With the Sugar Act, Parliament imperiled a large portion of British-American trade with the Portuguese Empire.[3]

The act complicated traditional smuggling practices in British America. In late 1763, Thomas Riche used his web of Atlantic contacts to avoid duties on Lisbon wine. He proposed that the Lisbon firm Parr & Bulkeley ship two or three hundred quarter casks on their joint account to William Street at Faial. Once the wine arrived at the island, he planned to have it switched into a different bottom and to import it as Faial wine. He could then avoid customs duties when the wine arrived in America. The Navigation Acts exempted Faial wine but not Lisbon. The Sugar Act jeopardized his plan. Parliament scheduled the new duties to take effect on September 29, 1764. If Riche did not receive the wines from Parr & Bulkeley by that date, his scheme would fail. He would pay the duty of £3.5 per pipe—even higher than the duty of 10s. per ton Riche would pay on Lisbon wine. He pled with his correspondents to deliver the wine before September 29.[4]

Like other mid-Atlantic merchants, Riche instructed his suppliers in the Atlantic islands to ship as much wine as possible before the duties took effect. In 1764, British Americans increased their yearly imports of Madeira wine by approximately 400 percent from 1762. Madeira wine glutted the New York and Philadelphia markets. In June 1764, John Searle reported that wine had become scarce in Madeira due to the large quantities exported. Between April 1764 and the first week of January 1765, sixteen vessels entered New York from the Portuguese Atlantic islands. The number increased from the eleven that entered during the same period the previous year. In 1754–1755, only eight vessels had entered the port from the islands. The additional cargoes glutted the market. Searle discouraged more trade until Madeira producers readied the new vintage in November or December. Merchants held overstocked inventories until the end of 1767.[5]

British-American traders warned the government that the Sugar Act would ruin them before it could benefit England. Thomas Hancock of Boston complained that "the heavy taxes laid on the Colonies will be a great Damp to Trade." The Boston Society for Encouraging Trade and Commerce laid out "Proposals to Parliament for the Regulation of the American Trade." The committee warned that the Sugar Act would diminish British Americans' ability to purchase English manufactures. They maintained that only the duty on Madeira could possibly return revenue to the government at the cost of other revenue streams. Due to the glut, however, they calculated that the government could not collect more than £15,000 annually and that the amount would diminish each year due to the high duties. They argued that to generate revenue the government must allow colonists free trade in foreign sugar and molasses, permit direct trade with southern Europe, and reduce the duty on Madeira to the nominal value of 10s. per ton imposed on Spanish and Portuguese wines.[6]

The committee proved prescient in its prediction that British Americans would decrease their demand for Madeira due to the new taxes. The glut coincided with the lower demand, causing prices to plummet. Between February and mid-September 1764, one week before the duties took effect, Madeira wine prices suffered a 28 percent decrease in Philadelphia. Many pipes sold at a loss of between 8.5 to 15.5 percent. The poor market pushed some merchants in Madeira and the mid-Atlantic colonies out of the Madeira trade. Lower demand forced distributors in Madeira to reduce their prices. Madeira suppliers dropped prices from 72,000 réis per pipe in 1764 to between 60,000 and 65,000 réis in 1767. With prices so low, the increased duties constituted an even greater burden on merchants who imported Madeira wine after September 29, 1764.[7]

British-American merchants had little incentive to import legal Madeira. In 1766, Parliament revised the Sugar Act to reduce duties on foreign molasses, but it left intact the duty on Madeira wine. When consumer demand revived in 1768, merchants sought to avoid taxes by smuggling. The New York merchant William Kelly reminded a Parliamentary committee that "wherever there is a great difference of Price, there will be a Daring Spirit to attempt [smuggling] notwithstanding all Preventions." In December 1768, Charles Williams, a British naval officer, reported that six vessels had entered New York from Madeira and Tenerife since November 1767. They declared only twenty-three pipes, twelve hogsheads, and two quarter casks of wine, far below the cumulative capacity of the ships. Williams supposed that New York merchants had smuggled the rest. The Sugar Act propelled merchants with Madeira ties to the center of a colonial commercial culture that endorsed illicit trade as a legitimate means of resistance to tyranny.[8]

Because the Sugar Act targeted southern European products, merchants who traded there became some of the most influential smugglers and proponents of organized resistance. Of the ten Boston merchants who specialized in the southern Europe trade, eight supported colonial resistance. The list included Jonathan Barrett, Melatiah Bourn, Solomon Davis, Jeremiah Lee, Samuel Allyne Otis, Edward Payne, William Powell, and Isaac Smith.

They smuggled and encouraged their fellow colonial merchants to resist British taxation. On October 23, 1768, the advocate general for Massachusetts, Jonathan Sewall, brought a suit against John Hancock and four others in Boston for smuggling one hundred pipes of Madeira wine. Satisfied with the hard-lined approach, Governor Thomas Hutchinson remarked, "It is high time that the Acts of Trade should be more generally observed. We have been so long habituated to illicit Trade that the people in general see no evil in it."[9]

Most often, smugglers declared wines as vinegar, declared only a portion of the wine cargo, or altogether avoided declaring the cargo. The law required shipmasters to present bills of lading to the collector at the port of entry, so the bills had to match the cargo. British-American merchants depended on cooperation from their suppliers in Madeira to load the wine and declare it as vinegar on the bill of lading. They needed shipmasters who would comply with their illicit schemes, for masters oversaw the loading and unloading of cargoes. The suppliers also had to omit a bill of lading in cases where the consignee did not intend to declare any goods. If the consignee planned to declare only part of the cargo, the suppliers had to alter the bill of lading to conform to the goods and amounts declared. Masters then had to ensure that crews unloaded the wine before collectors could inspect the vessel, or they had to hide any wine not included on the bill of lading. Such transactions allowed no legal recourse if the undeclared part of the cargo received damage, if it spoiled or leaked en route, or if the consignee refused payment. Intricate, tight-knit networks cooperated, therefore, to defy new regulations.[10]

Smugglers blurred the lines between profit and politics by resisting the Sugar Act. In 1768, Boston customs officers seized John Hancock's vessel *Liberty* because they suspected the vessel carried contraband Madeira wine. The affair provoked the so-called Liberty Riots. Boston demonstrators injured two customs officers and sparked the movement to impose a non-importation agreement against Britain. In April 1769, the collector at Philadelphia confiscated fifty pipes of undeclared Madeira wine. During the night, locals broke into the storehouse, stole the wine, and abused the customs officers.[11]

Smuggling had a political flavor long before the 1760s, but as the imperial crisis deepened it became a statement about the proper power balance between the colonies and the central government. It relayed the implicit message that the colonists believed they had a right to resist when they felt the government overreached. Colonial traders and consumers resisted the Sugar Act for financial reasons, but new taxes united the colonists beyond a shared economic grievance. The colonists infused political symbolism into commodities whose significance had eroded from a representation of their privileges as subjects of the British Empire to an indication of their colonial subservience.[12]

"A Grievous Burthen"

In February 1765, Prime Minister George Grenville pressed an acquiescent Parliament to pass the Stamp Act. The act imposed a stamp tax on papers that ranged from legal documents to playing cards. The tax moved depression-hit colonists from discontent to indignation with new imperial taxes. Patriot colonists mobilized in protest and violence against stamp commissioners and those who professed sympathy to the hated tax. Mobs warned imperial administrators and legal professionals to ignore the requirements of the Stamp Act. The anger rose to such a pitch that only the most intransigent officials dared impose the rigors of the law by the time it took effect on November 1. Elite colonists coordinated their efforts and formed the Stamp Act Congress to produce a unified appeal against the tax.[13]

Merchants detested the legislation because it required them to place stamps on all official shipping papers. They received warnings from angry colonists and clients not to observe the requirement. British men-of-war patrolled the ports to ensure compliance with the law. To combat the act, merchants made mutually enforced pledges to boycott English imports. They hoped to threaten the business interests of London merchants and compel them to lobby Parliament for repeal of the law. On October 31, 1765, two hundred New York merchants adopted the nonimportation agreements. Just over a week later, Philadelphia merchants followed suit. From there, Maryland merchants joined the fray, followed by two hundred and twenty Boston merchants on December 9.[14]

The 1765 boycotts exempted goods from British merchants in the Portuguese Empire. Because provisions exports played a vital role in the Philadelphia economy, residents refused to boycott markets that imported large amounts of breadstuff. Along with the British West Indies, southern Europe constituted the mid-Atlantic's most important destination for British-American provisions. Merchants could not stomach—and the economy could not sustain—the losses that would have resulted from a boycott on imports from the West Indies and the Portuguese Atlantic.[15]

Rather than boycott goods from the Portuguese Empire, colonial traders cooperated with British firms in Portugal to avoid the onerous stamp tax. The influential Lisbon firm Parr & Bulkeley sympathized with the colonists and countenanced their efforts to avoid stamp regulations. The firm proposed that Baynton & Wharton of Philadelphia send a cargo of wheat and flour on their joint account. Parr & Bulkeley would accept the half shipped on their account as payment for goods sent to the American firm. They hoped Baynton & Wharton would execute the order "with all possible expedition" and in a manner that "may not expose us to any hazard from Captures by British men-of-war which may possibly be the case should your Vessels not be cleared out upon Stamps."[16]

Even before the act took effect in November, mainland colonists made clear that Parliament had undertaken a fool's errand to collect the tax. In March 1766, Parliament repealed the legislation, and merchants on all sides of the British-America–Luso-Atlantic trade breathed a sigh of relief. British Americans received congratulations from correspondents in Portugal, and all hoped to resume normal trade. That same year, Parliament revised the Sugar Act. The revision lowered the duty on foreign molasses to equal the duty on British molasses, but it did not remove the tax on Madeira wine. Imports of Madeira wine remained low due to the glut in the colonies, so merchants did not feel sorely aggrieved at the continuation of the duties until 1768, when demand revived and smuggling increased. For several months in 1766, therefore, Parliament seemed to disarm the tension between London and the colonies.[17]

In 1767, Parliament passed the Townshend Acts, and merchants reinvigorated their resistance through protests, illicit trade, and nonimportation. The acts laid duties on glass, lead, paper, and other items commonly imported into the colonies. To stave off American complaints, the chancellor of the exchequer, Charles Townshend, planned to allow the direct importation of wines and fruits from Spain and Portugal into the colonies. The plan would rescind the requirement in the Navigation Acts that such goods first pass through England. The government could then collect a duty on them in colonial ports.[18]

In the British mainland colonies and in Portugal, most merchants supported direct trade. British-Americans wanted to eliminate the costs of routing shipments through England, and British merchants in Portugal complained that they could not ship fruits through the homeland because the produce spoiled before it reached the colonies. The Lisbon factory favored direct trade with a duty on Portuguese goods equal to that on commodities from England. Such a duty would have amounted to 10s. per ton. Lisbon-based merchants hoped direct trade would dissipate the competitive advantage Madeira traders enjoyed in British America. They supposed that if British Americans could import wine directly from Lisbon, Madeira wine prices would fall from £25 or £30 per pipe to £10 or £11—on par with Lisbon wine. The Lisbon factory claimed that such a reduction would save colonial buyers £200,000 sterling per year.[19]

Townshend's enemies opposed his plan to allow direct trade between Portugal and British America. George Grenville derided it as an attempt to circumvent the Navigation Acts, and he persuaded others to his side. Townshend abandoned the proposal as resistance mounted.[20]

As Pennsylvania's colonial agent in London, Benjamin Franklin claimed to have heard from sound sources that Parliament had dropped the proposal because of opposition from London merchants who stood to gain from shipments routed through their port. Franklin resented what he viewed as the chicanery of London merchants to the detriment of his fellow Pennsylvanians, whose interests he represented in England. He aired his grievances in the *London Chronicle* under the pseudonym of "F. & S." Franklin complained that British-American consumers would potentially pay 3 percent more for Portuguese goods due to the prohibition on direct trade with Portugal. He felt certain that Parliament dismissed the direct-trade legislation so that merchants in London could profit from commissions on the goods that passed through English ports.[21]

Most Portuguese goods passed through the Port of Falmouth rather than London, but Franklin detailed the ways London merchants benefited from the indirect trade route. British-American merchants frequently drew on London creditors to pay the commissions and fees collected by Falmouth merchants. Falmouth and London merchants profited, therefore, from wines that passed through England on their way to the colonies. British Americans chafed at the baleful influence of English merchants in the British-American–Luso-Atlantic trade networks. Franklin directed his ire toward burdensome regulations and the metropolitan merchants who supported them. "When merchants . . . oppose the relieving of their fellow subjects from a grievous Burthen," he wondered, "what can one suppose to be their Motive" other than selfish gain? He sneered that in terms of commerce, London merchants' arms "are as long as those of Kings in Point of Power, for they reach all parts of the trading world." As Franklin's objections attest, colonists aimed to attenuate simultaneously the power of the state and metropolitan merchants. They hoped their struggle would not only ease trade restrictions but also allow them to rework their trade to diminish the power of their English peers.[22]

"Too Narrowly Watch'd"

British-American merchants engaged in direct trade with Portugal on their own terms, enticed by its high demand for American wheat. When colonial ships did not return in ballast, they carried contraband. Charles Wharton insisted to Parr & Bulkeley in Lisbon that if his cargo of corks "have not begune their Rout Via Falmouth, Do send them Directly from your Place by the first vessel that will take them. As I had Rather Run the Risk of them than they should be Burthened with a Falmouth Duty." British-American smugglers preferred to gamble on capture rather than pay additional fees and taxes in England.[23]

Smugglers faced tightened scrutiny by British customs as the imperial conflict worsened. Since the passage of the Sugar Act, Parliament had sent men-of-war to patrol the coast and strengthen oversight of colonial customs. The Rockingham ministry had assumed power in 1765 in opposition to George Grenville's American policy. Even so, it refused to recall the men-of-war from American coasts and left intact heavy-handed vice-admiralty courts to prosecute smuggling.[24]

Men-of-war patrols forced smugglers to take additional, expensive steps to receive goods directly from Portugal. Thomas Riche teamed with Parr & Bulkeley and William Street to import Lisbon wine listed as Faial. Even if they paid duties on the supposed Faial wine due to the Sugar Act, they would not have to pay extra charges to route the shipment through England. Riche betrayed, however, a more anxious tone than in previous contraband ventures as he faced the more effective enforcement of customs regulations.[25]

A man-of-war had recently seized one of his brigs that carried contraband goods to the French port of Cayenne. As a result, he feared for the schooner *Young Nancy*, which carried the illegal wine from Lisbon. He hoped the captain could touch at and leave Faial as quickly as possible, and he asked the Lisbon firm to ensure that the captain packed the wine in an

undetectable manner. He cautioned Parr & Bulkeley not to mention the
wine in their correspondence. Three months later, he felt "a good deal
oneasy" when the *Young Nancy* had not yet arrived. The ship came to
port in the second week of August, but not without causing Riche anxiety
in the meantime. As customs patrols tightened, smugglers found it more
difficult to defy navigation laws. In 1769, according to British officials,
colonial traders continued to import "great Quantitys" of illicit goods
from Europe under the cover of legal shipments from Madeira and the
Azores. Although merchants contravened the law with ingenuity, they did
so with increased expenses and difficulty as men-of-war sailed vigilant for
contraband.[26]

The British government granted Madeira a virtual monopoly on wine
imported into the colonies due to the heightened alertness against direct
imports of illicit goods. Between 1760 and 1765, British-American merchants had increased the variety of wines that they received from Portugal,
Spain, and France. In 1765, they imported nearly six thousand pipes of
wine, of which Madeira constituted just over twenty-five hundred. As customs patrols clamped down on wine from the European continent, non-
Madeira wine imports dropped so precipitously that by 1767 Madeira wine
constituted almost all wine imported into British America. The increase
resulted in part because smugglers relabeled non-Madeira wines as
Madeira, but Parliament also provided a boon to Madeira wine by discour-
aging the importation of other kinds. Due to the "brisk" demand for
Madeira wine by 1769, native Madeiran producers charged the "exorbitant
prices," as one British-Madeiran merchant complained, of 70,000 to 80,000
réis per pipe. In turn, British-Madeiran distributors raised the prices on
British-American importers. Colonists paid dearly for their wine—legal or
smuggled—due to increased imperial regulation.[27]

British Americans began to view the Madeira trade as less of an imperial
privilege and more of a colonial burden. Franklin complained, "Nothing
can set in a stronger Light the Oppression America suffers by the restraint
[on Lisbon and Port wine], and the Advantage foreigners receive by it."
The natives of Madeira "have taken Advantage of the encreas'd Demand,
and rais'd the price thus enormously." The Madeira trade provided a
needed market for British-American provisions, but it unveiled the colonists' subservience to the central government in dictating Atlantic trade
networks. To meet the crisis, colonial merchants devised new ways to contravene imperial laws.[28]

Beginning in 1768, merchants cooperated in nonimportation schemes to coerce the government to drop the Townshend duties. On August 1, Boston merchants agreed not to import British goods until the repeal of the Townshend Acts. By the end of the month, New York merchants had followed Boston's lead. Initially, Philadelphia merchants rejected non-importation, for they feared it would ruin the economy. In March 1769, however, public pressure mounted, and most Philadelphia merchants reluctantly joined the movement. That same month, Baltimore merchants agreed to the boycott. Annapolis merchants followed two months later.[29]

Merchants in the mid-Atlantic abided by the new boycott with greater enthusiasm than they had the earlier nonimportation movement during the Stamp Act crisis. The Townshend boycott melded patriotism with financial interest. Overstocked inventories had reduced the values of a range of goods in the mid-Atlantic, and nonimportation allowed merchants to sell their stores at higher prices. The movement drew a clear political line between the merchants and Parliament as both stuck to their resolves. Thomas Lamar of London wrote his Philadelphia associate Henry Hill, "I do not find [Parliament] to be in the least relaxed in their late determinations respecting America from a firm reliance, no doubt, upon your own resolutions falling to pieces of themselves."[30]

In 1770, Lord North's ministry came to power with a commitment to calm anxiety on both sides of the Atlantic. Townshend's taxes had produced little revenue, and Parliament began to repeal them. British-American importers still murmured about the ban on direct imports from Lisbon and the heightened duties on Madeira wine. As one Virginia resident made clear, colonists expected more than the repeal of the Townshend duties because "Medeira Wine and other things are unconstitutionably taxed. These must be taken off or we shall hardly thank them for the other." If the North ministry believed it had ceded ground to British Americans, the colonists disagreed.[31]

Fewer firms attempted to smuggle as customs officials intensified their scrutiny of cargoes and men-of-war lurked about the ports. In late December 1774, John Smith & Sons of Baltimore sent a large cargo of flour to Lisbon, half on their account and half on the account of Parr, Bulkeley, & Co. They hoped to receive in return three or four hundred casks of wine and fruit, but only if the Lisbon house could dispatch the ship by the end of February. The firm insisted on "immediate dispatch as on that depends the Success of her Voyage, & loading her with such secrecy as is necessary to the risk we run." They worried that by spring men-of-war would patrol their port and seize the cargo if not dispatched on time from Lisbon. If the vessel did not leave by March 10, 1775, they believed the risk too great and directed the Lisbon firm to send a legal cargo of Lisbon salt instead. By April, they refused to order a return cargo of wine, fearing that "we shall be too narrowly watch'd." For the period April 1757–December 1763, 198 illegal cargoes cleared Lisbon for North America compared to just 26 between December 1771 and December 1776. The central government had proven its ability to quash smuggling to the detriment of British-American trade with the Portuguese Empire.[32]

Imperial regulations impeded business in terms of time and money for those who continued to participate in the legal trade with Portugal. In 1773, Keppelle & Steinmetz routed a cargo of Lisbon wine, lemons, oil, olives, and corks, worth a total of £3,959 9s. 4³/₄d. to their Falmouth agent, Joseph Banfield. They estimated that dockage in England would add an additional eight to ten days onto the voyage in addition to the time it took to sail there. By the time the ship left Falmouth for Philadelphia, they had paid £771 9s. in duties, prisage (customs duties on wine), porterage, cooperage, port charges, and a 1.5 percent commission charged by Banfield. In 1774, Parr, Bulkeley, & Co. advanced the captain of Keppelle & Steinmetz's ship *Charming Peggy* money for the duties paid at Falmouth. They debited the amount to the account of Keppelle & Steinmetz. Falmouth charges slashed profits. With the increased costs and decreased opportunities for smuggling, British-American–Luso-Atlantic commerce began to disintegrate under the weight of trade restrictions.[33]

Some merchants dropped out of the trade. Thomas Clifford's firm had conducted extensive business with Portugal, particularly with Parr, Bulkeley, & Co. After 1768, however, the firm ceased correspondence with Portuguese businesses until the 1790s. From April 1757 through December 1763, British Americans received 8.6 percent of clearances from Lisbon in ballast. Between 1771 and 1776, that number increased to 29 percent. The imperial crisis took an enormous toll on trade with Portugal.[34]

After 1772, market forces reinforced men-of-war in their struggle against smuggling between Portugal and North America. In 1772–1773, due to a good wheat harvest in Portugal, merchants in Lisbon relaxed their demand for imported breadstuff. In October 1772, Parr, Bulkeley, & Co. expected moderate markets at best for flour and corn. Four months later, the domestic crop proved strong enough that the firm believed it would run too great a risk for American merchants to venture flour to Lisbon. In spring of 1773, they regretted that North American corn sold poorly even at the season of "briskest Consumption" due to large supplies from Porto and Vienna. In December, the firm reported that Parliament would again allow English grain exports, which would further depress prices in Lisbon. By the middle of 1774, Parr, Bulkeley, & Co. refused to import provisions on a joint account with Keppelle & Steinmetz "till we have some hopes of a fairer prospect."[35]

By the early 1770s, British Americans witnessed their direct trade with Portugal grind to a near halt. While the markets remained high during the 1760s, they had shoveled wheat into Portugal and returned with contraband wines and fruit. If merchants chose not to risk capture for smuggling, they could return in ballast. As Portuguese wheat prices dropped and British customs patrols intensified, traders lost both options. The Portuguese trade fell victim to the imperial crisis. Traders continued to import Madeira wine and smuggled Lisbon wine under cover of Madeira, but colonists began to associate the Luso-Atlantic trade with repression rather than privilege. In September 1774, Parr, Bulkeley, & Co. confirmed an "indifferent" Portuguese harvest for the year, which would raise prices and encourage imports from America. Just as the market regained favor, however, the imperial crisis escalated and created greater fissures in British-American trade with Madeira and Portugal.[36]

Appearance of a Civil War

Colonists fused politics and material culture to protest unpopular imperial policies. Pamphleteers depicted British Americans as oppressed consumers whom the central government burdened with increased taxes on the very items the English had pressed them to purchase. Such items provided a tangible reminder of English duplicity and the importance of the colonies to the wealth of the British Empire. By boycotting the goods that once defined their privileges within the empire, colonists protested what they viewed as their increased subjugation. Madeira wine had possessed political significance since the passage of the Sugar Act. In the 1770s, colonists gave it an even greater political charge by including it in their panoply of boycotted goods. Their actions further sundered the very trade networks they sought to protect.[37]

In October 1774, the First Continental Congress protested Parliament's "ruinous system of colony administration." Earlier that year, Parliament had closed the port of Boston to punish colonists for dumping thousands of pounds of taxed East India Tea into Boston harbor. In an act of solidarity, the Continental Congress approved the Articles of Association, which mandated nonimportation, nonconsumption, and nonexportation of an array of commodities set to begin December 1. As opposed to earlier nonimportation agreements, the Continental Association proscribed the importation of wine from the Portuguese Atlantic islands. The articles prohibited any goods that passed through Great Britain, so they naturally barred wines from Lisbon and Porto. The articles did allow the exportation of goods until September 1775, at which point, if Parliament had not changed course, the colonists would suspend exportation as well.[38]

Colonial merchants created fractures in the Luso-Atlantic trade almost immediately after the articles took effect. As early as December 12, Keppelle & Steinmetz shipped a cargo to Lisbon and instructed Captain Thomas Dowman to return with Portuguese salt—a saleable good not required to pass through England. They wanted him to return, however, with only as much as would set the vessel in ballast. They insisted to Parr, Bulkeley, & Co. that they "are not at liberty" to order any additional wine due to "the resolves of the Congress." Madeira firms smarted from the loss of American markets. In January 1775, Robert Bisset returned to Madeira from a trip to London and found the firm's wines of very poor quality. He decided to sell them and get what little he could rather than "filling our stores with Wines of a precarious quality, especially as we have no prospect of throwing any of them into America for some Months." The following month, a ship arrived in Philadelphia with a few pipes of Madeira wine. The vessel's owner informed the Committee of Correspondence and "declared his intention to send away the vessel and wines, agreeable to the directions of the Congress."[39]

Unable to import Lisbon wines, some British-American firms tried to amortize their debt with English creditors by shipping goods to Lisbon and instructing their associates there to remit payment to London. By early 1775, however, Lisbon firms lost interest in North American produce due to the combination of political turbulence and low demand for mid-Atlantic provisions. In January, rumors spread that Parliament planned to close the ports of Philadelphia and New York as they had Boston, and Lisbon merchants complained that the political chaos made British-American markets unpredictable. In April, the house of Pasley's & Co.

resolved to avoid North American provisions until "the disputes between the Mother Country and her collonys are terminated." They asked their Philadelphia associates to "escuse us for the present, till things are in a more settled situation and our prices and prospects gives proper encouragement." That same month, the Lisbon firm of Parr, Bulkeley, & Co. reported that "America produce in general is at a low Ebb and scarse any demand." For that reason, they preferred "being spectators [rather than] holding a concern" in the cargoes.[40]

With some Lisbon firms rejecting North American business, British Americans strained past relationships as they looked elsewhere for associates who would invest in joint cargoes. Keppelle & Steinmetz turned to another Lisbon firm that would take a larger concern in the cargo than Parr, Bulkeley, & Co. had offered. The Philadelphia firm insisted to their old partners, "We are not bound to consign our Cargoes to your house." Parr, Bulkeley, & Co. found it "distressing" that the American firm did not trust their judgment about the poor state of the Lisbon market.[41]

In the spring of 1775, the Restraining Acts further eroded mid-Atlantic trade with the Luso-Atlantic. In March, Parliament passed the initial act to punish New England for the Articles of Association. It prohibited any trade other than with Great Britain and the British West Indies. The next month, Parliament applied the regulations throughout the rebellious mainland colonies. Although Lisbon firms found their supplies overstocked with breadstuff, Parr, Bulkeley, & Co. believed that within months they would feel the negative effects of halted imports from British America. The firm felt anxious about the state of trade with the British colonies and wished "earnestly . . . for Peace to be restored between G. Britain & the Collonies whereby trade may no longer be interrupted."[42]

The acts heightened uncertainty about the Lisbon market. In April, Parr, Bulkeley, & Co. admitted, "We are puzzled what is best to do for our fr[ien]ds, whether to let the Cargoes upon hand take their saleable chance at loosing [losing] prices, or wait the result of the restraining act." Breadstuff prices would rise in Lisbon due to the prohibition of mainland colonial exports to Portugal. According to Pasley's & Co., however, it remained uncertain how the legislation "may operate on the minds of the Merchants and other trading people in America." On the one hand, if Americans submitted willingly, Lisbon prices would increase. If, on the other hand, colonial merchants defied the legislation, North American produce would continue to flow to Lisbon and prices would change little. John Smith &

Sons requested Parr, Bulkeley, & Co. to sell their ship *Betsey*—which they had used to conduct their Lisbon trade—if they received confirmation that the Restraining Act passed. If the Lisbon firm could not sell it, John Smith & Sons hoped to employ it in a different trade. Otherwise, they would bring it back to America and discontinue its use. Faced with such uncertainty, Parr, Bulkeley, & Co. lamented, "If ever we stood in need of divining, it is at this time."[43]

After mid-April, war erupted and increased the anxiety. In May, John Smith & Sons informed their Lisbon correspondents that they expected the Continental Congress to close the ports of the British-American mainland to avoid the seizure of goods by the Royal Navy. They further reported, "Everything here has the appearance of a Civil War. The people seem more willing to lose their Lives than their Liberties."[44]

As the conflict mounted, commerce grew more precarious. On July 16, 1775, four days before the Restraining Act took effect in Philadelphia, Thomas Dowman left port as captain of Keppelle & Steinmetz's *Charming Peggy*. The vessel carried a cargo to Lisbon. Nine days later, the British man-of-war *Glasgow* apprehended the merchant vessel "as belonging to the Rebels" and brought it to Boston. After the ship's arrival, Thomas Gage, the commander of British forces in America, ordered the ship seized, the cargo appraised, the merchants compensated, and the provisions allocated for the use of British troops. Upon Keppelle & Steinmetz's application for payment, Gage refused their petition. He had sold the provisions to contractors and determined to keep the money as payment for clothing stolen from British troops in Philadelphia.[45]

Keppelle & Steinmetz had approached the breach between Britain and the colonies with moderation. The firm conformed to the British strictures on trade with Portugal and to the Articles of Association. They emphasized that the *Glasgow* had taken the *Charming Peggy* while the merchant vessel proceeded "on a just & legal trade." With the onset of the Restraining Act, Keppelle & Steinmetz initially had not planned to send the ship on voyages to Portugal "untill the present Disputes are settled." They expected either to rent it on a monthly basis or have Parr, Bulkeley, & Co. act as their agents to sell it. Instead, hostilities forced them to terminate prematurely their trade with Portugal. By 1779, their associates in Lisbon lamented the loss of their business due to the "present calamities" and "unhappy contest." Despite efforts to remain on moderate ground, the firm fell victim to the vagaries of warfare.[46]

By the latter half of 1775, demand revived in Portugal for North American produce. Enticed by the improved Lisbon market, some merchants disregarded the Restraining Acts and chanced capture by the Royal Navy. In September, John Smith & Sons of Baltimore assured Parr, Bulkeley, & Co. that "'tis more than probable [colonial merchants] will run Risque & perhaps fill your ports." Just months later, however, the Portuguese government banned vessels from the rebellious colonies. Even if British-American ships slipped past British blockades, they could not enter Portuguese ports.[47]

Portuguese officials kept a wary eye on the rebellion in North America, concerned that it could incite unrest among colonists in Brazil. In 1775, Pombal opined that European powers should "make common cause with England, to help reduce their American subjects to the point of obedience." In early 1776, the Portuguese government prepared a stockpile of ammunition in the Bay of All Saints in Brazil and ordered the Brazilian viceroy and commandants to keep the military ready for possible disturbances among the population. The government believed the measures necessary in case the British colonies tried to contract alliances with Ibero-American colonies that, in the words of one Lisbon observer, "might have bad consequences."[48]

Throughout 1775, the Portuguese and Spanish Empires struggled over dominance in the Río de la Plata region, and Pombal hoped to receive British military support in the dispute. The British withheld assistance, however, and pressured Portugal to come to peaceful terms with Spain. British officials wanted little to do with Portuguese and Spanish quarrels in the Americas. If Portugal incited warfare, it could call upon Britain for assistance according to the terms of their alliance. British authorities hoped to avoid military conflicts that could provoke the Spanish and their French allies to ally with North American rebels against Great Britain. The British government encouraged Pombal to use moderation in the dispute with Spain.[49]

Because the British imperial crisis impeded military aid from London, Pombal weighed in on the matter. In a November 1775 dispatch to George III, he asked what benefits the American colonies would provide the British Empire if France and Spain conquered Portugal. In such a scenario, Pombal claimed, Britain's enemies could obstruct its commerce to the west coast of Europe, the Mediterranean, and Brazil. Furthermore, he doubted the ability of the British military to defeat the American rebels. Brazilian patriots had successfully driven the Dutch out of Brazil in the seventeenth century. Their success exemplified, in Pombal's mind, how well-trained, well-equipped forces like those of the Netherlands could succumb to a war of attrition.[50]

Pombal hoped to see the North American conflict come to a speedy conclusion, so he urged the British crown to allow the colonists their own parliament. He stressed that such a move would not relinquish the crown's sovereignty over the colonies, for the king would retain ultimate authority over the colonial parliament. Pombal concluded that the "small inconvenience" of yielding to colonial demands outweighed the "great risks" of fighting a futile civil war.[51]

The British government refused to entertain Pombal's suggestion, and the Portuguese minister caved. By 1776, he had little leverage to persuade British officials to come to Portugal's aid. His own policies had diminished imports from England, causing Portugal to drop from the third-highest consumer of English goods to sixth. In July, he ordered all ports shut to vessels from the rebellious colonies. Pombal hoped the move would keep Portugal in Britain's good graces. He gave ships from the colonies just over a week to weigh anchor and prohibited any aid for vessels and sailors from British North America, even in cases of distress.[52]

United States authorities decried Pombal's actions. In 1777, the Continental Congress considered helping Spain conquer Portugal if the former provided military support against Great Britain. The plan remained chimerical without a serious commitment from Spain. From their seat in France, U.S. commissioners complained to the Portuguese court that during the "long friendship and commerce" between the two countries, the European power had never sustained "the least injury" from British Americans. The commissioners could "scarcely bring themselves to believe that the said edict is genuine." Despite U.S. objections, the ban continued.[53]

The American Revolution plagued North American trade with Portugal. During the late 1760s, British-American merchants engaged in contraband trade to preserve their Luso-Atlantic networks and to resist imperial coercion. In the 1770s, they instituted nonimportation. The move ironically signaled a willingness to suspend their Luso-Atlantic trade to protest Parliamentary intrusion in their commerce. If they hoped independence would reinvigorate that trade and effect a return to former practices, the Portuguese government disappointed them with its interdiction against U.S. commerce. Many North Americans had felt sure that independence would bolster their business. They followed Thomas Paine's logic that "whenever a war breaks out between England and any foreign power, the trade of America goes to ruin, *because of her connection with Britain*." In Portugal, however, they saw their trade privileges evaporate once they severed their connection to Britain. In response, they again cooperated with their private networks, fusing their commercial and political interests to undermine imperial authority.[54]

Revolution and Profit

By prohibiting trade between North America and Portugal, the Portuguese government inadvertently created new opportunities for resourceful traders willing to take risks in a revolutionary environment. Merchants exploited loopholes in the decrees issued from Lisbon. North American shippers sent goods to Portugal on French and Spanish vessels. Lisbon merchants purchased goods shipped from the former British colonies to other Atlantic ports. Moreover, the Portuguese government still allowed merchants in Europe to export goods to the rebellious colonies, so North American merchants hazarded capture by British warships to receive and distribute Portuguese wine and salt.[55]

Although Portuguese salt had not attracted British-American traders prior to the war, it proved a valuable wartime commodity. The war had cut off the mainland from traditional suppliers in the West Indies, and demand remained high as salted meat composed a staple of continental troops. Several traders hoped to profit from the high demand and risked the dangers of the war-torn Atlantic to import it from Portugal. In 1778, while in Paris, Joseph Wharton planned to send several cargoes of salt from Portugal to North America. He preferred Portuguese salt to French due to its superior quality. Further, British cruisers preyed in Portuguese waters far less than in French. For Wharton, the venture served both a patriotic and financial purpose. It would simultaneously provide the beleaguered colonies much-needed salt "and at the same time . . . benefit myself." Wharton mixed politics with profit as he engaged with the Portuguese trade in defiance of the British Empire.[56]

By the time Wharton proposed his plan, the Portuguese government had begun to soften its stance toward the United States. Dona Maria I ascended the throne in 1777. Still bound by treaties with Britain, the Portuguese government did not open formal commercial relations with the United States, but Maria I relaxed the trade proscriptions. That same year,

Spain and Portugal concluded the Treaty of San Ildefonso, which settled the border dispute in South America. Because Portuguese officials no longer required British assistance in the region, they felt freer to reject British pressure to stifle trade with the United States. The changes did not grant North Americans free commerce with Portugal. They did lend some respite, however, to merchants who defied state decrees and whom the Portuguese government probably would have prosecuted more vigorously under Pombal. On both sides of the Atlantic, merchants felt encouraged by the increased leniency.[57]

The Lisbon merchant Arnold Henry Dohrman took advantage of the less rigorous regulation to cooperate with North American traders and rebels. A Netherlands-born merchant, Dohrman ran a successful firm in Lisbon and carried on limited business with North American firms at the beginning of the Revolutionary War. During the war, he made money by selling clothes and war supplies to the United States. Possessing, in his words, "a strong attachment to the principles of liberty," he offered his services and considerable resources to hundreds of North American seamen captured by British cruisers and left stranded in Lisbon. Although Lisbon officials had warned him not to aid sailors from the rebellious British colonies, he brought the men into his home, nursed them, and provided clothing for them at his own cost.[58]

In January 1779, he procured a vessel to return fifty-three stranded North Americans to their country and loaded it with sixteen cannons and a valuable cargo of wine. When the British consul learned of the departure, the British government pressured Portuguese officials to detain the ship. The following day, the vessel weighed anchor under French colors, but the British privateer *Bellona* gave chase and engaged it in a skirmish that saw one American killed and another's arm shot off. The British overpowered the Americans and imprisoned them aboard the *Bellona*. The British consul accused Dohrman of fitting out a privateer and insisted that the Portuguese punish him. The American crew claimed, however, that they had sailed from France, picked up a cargo in Setúbal, and sailed for Saint Eustatius. Portuguese officials found no arms chest on board, so the Portuguese court saw no reason to detain the Americans or punish Dohrman. Under pressure from London, the court forbade him "on pain of banishment" to provide additional aid to North Americans.[59]

Dohrman exhausted his financial resources due to his generous assistance to North American seamen. At the same time, he created new opportunities. In 1780, Thomas Jefferson thanked Dohrman for the "many

Kindnesses which you have shown to our captive countrymen." He believed that should the United States and Portugal "open an intercourse . . . your actions have pointed out the friend to whose negotiations we may safely confide our interests and necessities." That year, the U.S. government assigned him as a consul in Lisbon. In 1781, George Anderson, a North American familiar with Dohrman's services, recommended him to the Philadelphia trade magnate Levi Hollingsworth, who purchased forty pipes of wine from him and invited future business transactions.[60]

In 1783, Dohrman relocated to New York, believing that his "own interest lies with the United States." He left the daily affairs of U.S. consul in Lisbon to his brother, Jacob. Alexander Nelson, a member of a Richmond merchant firm, introduced Dohrman to John Wilcocks, Jr. of Philadelphia as a proprietor of "one of the most respectable Houses in Lisbon." Nelson lauded Dohrman's "merchantile abilities, knowledge of the world, rectitude of principles, & refined sentiments." Once Dohrman arrived in the United States, Congress reimbursed him for part of the expenses he incurred in relief of North Americans, provided him an annual back salary for his service as agent, and granted him a township in the western United States. He cultivated relationships for his Lisbon firm with businesses from New Hampshire to Richmond and conducted business with Jacob in Lisbon.[61]

At the end of the Revolutionary War, Dohrman's business activities had repaid his gamble to help rebellious Americans. Although he lived in the United States by 1783, he maintained the post of U.S. consul in Lisbon and held interest in Jacob's firm, Dohrman & Co. The Dohrmans could count on the perquisites of the office such as close connections with U.S. merchants, consular emoluments paid by masters of U.S. vessels that entered Lisbon, and a prominent position in the Atlantic trade community. Arnold invested his reimbursements from the U.S. Treasury into a line of ships that sailed throughout Europe. By 1789, he boasted ownership of six recently built vessels between 170 and 450 tons. He held stock in the New York Manufacturing Society and the Bank of the United States, and he purchased an impressive lot in Harlem. He had enhanced his networks and improved his business through the politics of trade. By defying British and Portuguese imperial authority, he gained a high reputation among North American businessmen who invited him into their trade networks.[62]

Like Dohrman, some Madeira houses took advantage of the turbulence of war to increase their goodwill with North American importers. Lamar, Hill, Bisset, & Co. and the Searles had strong American ties, and the two firms smuggled wine to troops and towns under British blockade. They garnered the good graces of North American merchants. John Marsden Pintard maintained that the firm of John Searle & Co. represented the only house in Madeira "whose manifest attachment to our Glorious Cause during the war entitles them to the attention of the Patriotick Merchants."[63]

During the British imperial crisis and Revolutionary War, therefore, many traders cooperated with their networks to defy imperial authority and revive former trade patterns. Even after heightened customs vigilance, colonial boycotts, and a war-torn Atlantic threatened trade between Portugal and North America, merchants such as Wharton, Dohrman, and the Searles increased profits by contesting state power. Ultimately, however, the Revolution severed the mercantilist ties that bound North Americans to the Portuguese Empire. North Americans enhanced their commercial autonomy by dissolving their political association with Great Britain, but they also abandoned the imperial privileges that had undergirded their trade with Portugal and the Atlantic islands.

Severance

The Portuguese government walked a delicate balance of neutrality during the war, torn between treaty obligations to Britain and the military threat posed by Spain and France who had sided with the Americans. The balance generally tipped, however, in favor of Britain. British traders in Lisbon fitted out privateers that preyed on U.S. vessels. The Royal Navy received supplies from Portugal. In 1779, word spread that John Bulkeley held part interest in the privateer, *Bellona*, which had taken Dohrman's ship captive. As a crew member aboard Dohrman's vessel, George Anderson of Virginia complained of Bulkeley's duplicity. He noted that the Lisbon merchant had "made his whole Estate by the Americans." Because the British-Portuguese traders Bulkeley, Thomas Mayne, and John Montgomery had all violated Portuguese neutrality by participating in British privateer ventures, the Portuguese government temporarily expelled them.[64]

Still, many U.S. observers remained skeptical of the empire's declared neutrality. John Adams complained that the "little impotent morsel of a state" had not maintained impartial neutrality. In 1782, rumors spread around Europe that the United States had declared war on Portugal. The rumors proved false, but U.S. vessels engaged in some limited skirmishes with Portuguese ships, and some North American enterprisers applied for letters of marque to sail against Portuguese commerce. At the end of the war in 1783, the tension subsided between the United States and Portugal. On June 19, Dona Maria partially lifted the ban on North American trade, and U.S. and Portuguese officials began to negotiate a possible commercial treaty. But the Revolution had permanently altered former commercial networks and the international politics that had shaped them.[65]

Imperial policies dashed the hopes of North Americans who anticipated resuming strong trade ties with Portugal. In 1779, Charles Wharton assumed that Portugal would soon allow imports of U.S. flour and wheat. The Portuguese court refused to entertain his high hopes. It lifted the blanket ban on U.S. commodities in 1783, but it no longer allowed the importation of rice and flour from any foreign ports. The court aimed, instead, to develop Portuguese domestic production. Rice and flour had constituted two of the most lucrative North American exports during the colonial years. In June 1782, Portugal published a book of rates that listed revised duties on foreign imports. United States merchants learned that they could expect to pay duties "near three times what they used to Amount to." The new restrictions hit mid-Atlantic merchants hard. In 1785, the *Pennsylvania Gazette* maintained that compared to 1773, wheat shipments had fallen nearly 87 percent and corn almost 59 percent. Flour fared somewhat better but still fell more than 24 percent. In the United States and Portugal, traders attempted to rebuild their fractured networks within a new matrix of international relations.[66]

*   *   *

In May 1765, writing of flour imported from British North America, Mayne & Co. of Lisbon remarked that "this article is very subject to great revolutions." The Lisbon firm referred to the commodity's price fluctuations, but the phrase accurately captured the events that agitated the provisions trade with the Portuguese Empire over the next two decades. Until the mid-1760s, British-American traders benefited from the Luso-Atlantic trade due to the privileges accorded the British Empire. By the 1770s, however, imperial restrictions reduced those privileges. Parliament manipulated trade patterns and influenced prices. By increasing scrutiny against direct imports from Portugal, British officials revealed the disproportionate influence of London merchants in the imperial trade matrix. In response,

British-Americans displayed ingenuity as they cooperated with their Luso-Atlantic networks to smuggle and defy state policy. The imperial crisis represented a clash between the power of the imperial state and the power of private networks to define trade parameters.[67]

During the American Revolution, merchants with Luso-Atlantic ties challenged British and Portuguese state power to preserve their commercial networks. Instead, the Revolution accelerated the dissipation of their Luso-Atlantic trade. Following U.S. independence, traders maintained a semblance of the commercial relations they had established during the third quarter of the eighteenth century. The American Revolution exposed, however, the rival interests that would ultimately diminish U.S. commerce with Portugal. The United States escaped the mercantilist ligaments that had bound North American commerce to Portugal. That change attenuated the value of the Luso-Atlantic wine trade as U.S. markets welcomed legal imports of wine from France and Spain. Without the protections of the British government, North Americans faced increased trade regulations in Portugal. Such regulations reinforced the developing notion that European monarchies made poor trade partners, and they made Portugal a less attractive destination for U.S. produce. With disdain for the imperial policies that hampered U.S.-Portuguese commerce, and as Brazil increased in economic influence, many North Americans began to anticipate a future of free trade with independent Brazilians.[68]

Chapter 4

Duties and Discouragements

In 1785, Jefferson predicted that the wines of the Portuguese Empire would always enjoy "an almost exclusive possession" of the U.S. market so long as the court allowed the importation of enough North American produce to purchase them. The Portuguese government rejected his vision for their future commerce. In the mid-1780s, U.S. policymakers tried to negotiate a commercial treaty with Portugal to reopen the flour and rice trades. To protect domestic production, however, Portuguese officials denied their requests and aborted negotiations. Faced with Portuguese restrictions on North American produce, U.S. merchants diminished their trade with Portugal relative to other European markets during the 1780s and 1790s. They found that independence from Britain had dissipated their commercial clout on the world stage.[1]

At the same time, independence allowed mid-Atlantic merchants to send their breadstuff directly to France and Spain and return with French and Spanish wines. By 1807, U.S. merchants sent fewer goods to Portuguese dominions than to any other destination in Europe. Between 1771 and 1775, mainland colonists sent a yearly average of ninety-six vessels to Lisbon. Between 1784 and 1788, only twenty-eight U.S.-registered ships entered the port. North Americans took advantage of their greater freedom of trade to diversify their commerce. As they did, they strained their ties to Portugal and Madeira. By the time the Portuguese court opened Brazilian ports to foreign commerce in 1808, U.S. traders and authorities viewed Brazil as the most significant commercial entity of the Portuguese Empire.[2]

The American Revolution had introduced a paradigm that pitted American independence, republicanism, and free trade against European empires, monarchy, and mercantilism. While he served as U.S. consul in

Lisbon, William Jarvis complained to James Madison, "One would almost suppose that there was Something in an European climate which disposed the mind & heart to intrigue & finesse." Many North Americans imagined that American republicanism countered European corruption. In a letter to the *Pennsylvania Journal and the Weekly Advertiser*, an anonymous author harangued against the commercial regulations of Europe. The writer concluded that "Liberty" had committed to Americans "the guardianship of the darling rights of mankind,—leaving the Eastern world where indolence has bowed the neck to the yoke of tyranny." The author continued the address to Liberty, asserting that "in this Western hemisphere hast thou fixed thy sacred empire; whilst the sons of Europe shackled with the manacles of oppression, sigh for thy safety, and pant for thy blessings."[3]

The U.S. minister in Lisbon, David Humphreys, believed that Portugal represented the worst tendencies of European monarchies, for the court squandered the country's natural economic advantages. He could only imagine Portugal's vast wealth if not hampered by "an unlimited monarchy, a Mad Queen, a foolish Prince-Regent, a weak Administration, an ignorant Laity, a bigotted Clergy & an existing Inquisition." As U.S.-Portuguese trade diminished and North Americans began to associate Portugal with the most atrocious vices of European monarchies, many U.S. traders and politicians coveted trade with an independent, republican Brazil.[4]

Destruction of Merchants

In 1785, while serving as the U.S. minister in Europe, John Adams tried to revive the privileges North Americans had once enjoyed as British subjects in the Luso-Atlantic trade complex. He hoped that U.S. merchants could export flour to Portugal at low duties and return with Portuguese wine. The Portuguese government refused his requests. To diversify Portugal's domestic economy and encourage milling, Lisbon officials wanted to import foreign wheat that Portuguese millers could grind into flour. They allowed, therefore, the introduction of wheat but continued the prohibition on flour except in times of poor harvests. The ban made Portugal a far less lucrative market for mid-Atlantic merchants than prior to the Revolution. The Lisbon merchant, John Bulkeley, feared the prohibition on flour and rice "would confine the American trade for the consumption of Lisbon to a few articles, if not removed by Congress in their treaty of commerce with Portugal."[5]

Bulkeley continued to import wheat from Philadelphia, but the Portuguese government imposed regulations that discouraged U.S. traders from sending the commodity to Lisbon. Since 1765, provisions merchants had preferred to export flour rather than wheat to Portugal due to the restrictions placed on wheat sales at the terreiro. Terreiro proprietors regulated prices and stored the grain in poor conditions. Wheat frequently spoiled in the warehouse before it arrived at market. In 1784, the Philadelphia firm of Willing, Morris, & Swanwick instructed their Baltimore agents to send a cargo of wheat and corn to Antônio José da Cunha Bento of Lisbon. They reminded the Baltimore house that "much money may be lost on for want of care."[6]

To prepare the wheat for storage in the terreiro, merchants incurred extra costs to sack their grain to prevent damage rather than risk the cheaper option of shipping it in bulk. The Baltimore firm of John Smith & Sons explained to Daniel Bowden & Son of Lisbon that "we see no profit offering for our produce equal to the inconvenience arising from the tedious mode of selling wheat . . . at your market." They informed their Lisbon associates that "the only Mode we can with propriety Import your produce is by our own Ships returning from other Ports where Their mode of selling is more agreeable to the Spirit of Commerce."[7]

United States merchants hoped that their government could negotiate an end to the trade restrictions in a treaty. In 1784, Joseph Wharton of Philadelphia mentioned to Charles Thomson "the great disadvantage the middle States lay under from the Court of Portugal refusing admission of our Flour into Lisbon." After Wharton learned of the negotiations underway with Portugal, he hoped U.S. diplomats could convince the Portuguese government to allow U.S. merchants to employ their Portuguese factors to deal directly with purchasers. Since 1775, the Portuguese government required central administrators to retail all flour to Portuguese buyers. Wharton complained that the administrators retailed it in small quantities of approximately thirty-two pounds. Even if the Portuguese government allowed flour imports, therefore, it could take twelve months to dispose of a single cargo. To Wharton, U.S. negotiators needed to convince Portuguese authorities not only to open their ports to foreign flour, but to remove all restrictions that discouraged sales.[8]

Whereas, antecedent to the War, the Port of Lisbon not only consumed at least 150,000 barrels of Flour annually from America, and nea[r]ly all our superfluous Wheat, but the Portugal Trade greatly encreased our Ship building, was a standing nursery for Seamen, furnished us with large and important supplies of Bullion, and facilitated Remittances to other parts of Europe for all our Importations. Hence, it is obvious, unless we have as free Sales as usual, an importation of Flour into Lisbon, instead of being a benefit, will be attended with the greatest disadvantages, through Cargoes laying around for years, to the ultimate destruction of Merchants and the Commerce of the United States.[9]

Prior to the Revolution, North American traders could count on Portugal as a strong market for their provisions. Wharton hoped that if the United States could secure a treaty, U.S. traders could eliminate the obstacles to commerce that accompanied U.S. independence.

Unhappily for Wharton, European powers viewed U.S. independence with suspicion and contempt. They refused to treat the young republic as an equal in treaty negotiations. During the 1780s, Britain rebuffed U.S. officials' attempts to secure favorable trade terms. Spain barred U.S. traders from navigation of the lower Mississippi River. British-Canadians disregarded the terms of the Treaty of Paris, undermining U.S. strength in the Northwest. In addition to such U.S. diplomatic difficulties, U.S. negotiators failed to secure a treaty that allowed the importation of flour into Portugal. Despite Adams's insistence that "nothing would contribute so much to promote the Trade as their receiving our Flour without Duties or Discouragements," the Portuguese ministry refused. Instead, they declared their intention to produce flour from imported wheat. Lisbon officials hoped the prohibition on flour imports would help Portugal avoid the negative balance of trade with North America it had endured prior to the war.[10]

In 1786, Jefferson and Adams proposed a treaty of twenty-eight articles, but the Portuguese diplomat Vincente de Sousa Coutinho lacked authority from Lisbon to approve it. He explained that the Portuguese minister of state and foreign affairs suffered from illness and the queen had traveled to the countryside. Sousa Coutinho claimed that he could not receive his instructions in the near future. Negotiations faded without a treaty.[11]

United States–Portuguese trade languished during the 1780s for lack of an agreement with Portugal. Between 1771 and 1775, mainland colonial merchants sent a yearly average tonnage to Lisbon of 19,508. For the years 1783–1788, U.S.-registered ships brought an average tonnage of just 4,507 per year. Merchants struggled to procure credit from London to pay for Portuguese imports. Even if U.S. merchants received such credit, according to John Smith & Sons, the Portuguese market did not "promise advantage sufficient to Induce them to ask such favor." Without the ability to export wheat, flour, or rice, mid-Atlantic merchants had little reason to send ships to that market. Flour remained in demand and permissible to sell in Madeira, but the island provided a limited market. One merchant lamented that "the prospect of independent Americans" remained "dull" and "dreary."[12]

To make matters worse for U.S. traders, North African corsairs increased their activity during the 1780s. Their presence jeopardized foreign commerce near the Iberian Peninsula. As U.S. vessels sailed to Lisbon, they risked attacks by Algerian crews. With navies strong enough to protect their own commercial vessels, the British, French, and Dutch governments encouraged North Africans to attack competitors from weaker nations. The British government notified Algiers of the United States' independence and made clear that North Americans no longer enjoyed the protection of the Royal Navy. In 1785, Algerians captured two U.S. ships, provoking outrage in the United States. Thomas Jefferson wanted war, but the nation lacked an effective navy. Many U.S. merchants abandoned the markets in or near the Mediterranean to avoid the loss of vessels, captains, and crews.[13]

Due to the North African threat, merchants paid higher insurance premiums for ships that sailed to Portugal. In May 1785, John Smith & Sons complained of British insurers who took advantage of the situation to increase rates beyond due proportion. The firm inveighed that the "jobbing rise of Insurance on American Vessells" had far outpaced the actual danger. Later that year, they refused to import Portuguese wines on their own account if the insurance for the freight surpassed 5 percent of the value. In less perilous times, rates ran closer to 4 percent for shipments from Lisbon to the United States. At the end of the year, they explained to associates in Lisbon that the "risk of the Algerines altho but trifling, effects our Insurance so much that it amounts to a prohibition of the Trade with your port." Although the firm insisted that captures remained rare, the captain of their ship *Unicorn* thought the risk too great to proceed to Lisbon. United States merchants found some relief when the Portuguese government agreed to protect U.S. commerce in the Mediterranean to encourage wheat imports. Still, commerce remained precarious.[14]

With limited access to Portugal, provisions exporters turned their commerce toward British, French, and Spanish ports in Europe and the West Indies. Some U.S. captains took advantage of bureaucratic confusion in Britain to obtain British registers for their ships while others claimed distress at sea to enter foreign ports in the Caribbean. Ships often docked at free ports in the Caribbean to sell their cargoes to foreign vessels. From there, traders forwarded the goods to otherwise prohibited ports. As a result, Delaware Valley provisions recovered faster than most other trade commodities in the U.S. postwar economy. In the West Indies, merchants found high demand and good prices for their provisions, enough to outweigh other deterrents to the trade. In contrast, trade with Portugal remained stagnant. Prohibited from selling flour, unable to sell wheat in great quantities, plagued by North African hostilities, and enticed by trade in the West Indies, mid-Atlantic merchants shrugged at the Luso-Atlantic trade.[15]

Feeding Europe

In 1789, Europeans suffered a poor wheat crop. The scarcity reenergized southern European demand for wheat and flour. Spain, Portugal, and France turned to suppliers in the United States, and mid-Atlantic merchants hastened to the call. In 1790, their firms dispatched multiple cargoes each to southern Europe. By the early 1790s, many traditional tobacco planters had abandoned tobacco and planted wheat due to its greater value.[16]

Europeans purchased U.S. flour to the point that Tench Coxe of Philadelphia declared it "the most valuable article of American commerce," but the Portuguese government remained careful to limit its importation. Due to the dearth in Europe, the court temporarily loosened restrictions on the importation of flour in 1789, opening Portuguese ports on a limited basis to U.S. exporters. Portuguese officials required masters of foreign vessels to apply for a special license to bring flour into the country's ports. That requirement minimized the importation of foreign flour. In 1790–1791, the Portuguese Empire imported 68,648 barrels from the United States. The number fell well below U.S. flour exports to Great Britain, France, Spain, and the Netherlands (Figure 3). In 1791–1792, U.S. traders saw their exports to Portuguese dominions fall by roughly 47 percent. In late 1792, the Portuguese government returned to a more restrictive policy. In 1792–1793, the empire imported only 26,473 barrels. Portuguese Atlantic islands received more than 73 percent of the imports.[17]

Between 1789 and 1792, Portuguese importers increased their demand for foreign wheat as Lisbon authorities encouraged the development of the domestic flour milling industry. United States merchants could sell wheat to Portugal at high prices and offset the additional costs imposed by the terreiro system. The high prices made Portugal a favorable market for the commodity. In 1790, the United States exported 288,518 bushels of wheat to the Portuguese Empire. The Luso-Atlantic trailed only British and Spanish dominions in terms of volume imported from the United States. Only the Spanish Empire imported a higher value of U.S. wheat than the Portuguese Empire. In 1791, U.S. merchants increased wheat exports to Portugal to 331,368 barrels, and Portuguese dominions surpassed those of Spain as the principal importers of U.S. wheat. Over half went to the Azores, Madeira, and other Portuguese Atlantic islands.[18]

Due to the relative values of wheat and flour, North Americans failed to compensate for the deficiency in flour exports to the Portuguese Empire, despite the strong markets for U.S. wheat. In 1790, the Portuguese paid $372,083 for 288,518 bushels of U.S. wheat. In contrast, they paid $459,292 for 68,648 barrels of flour. Given that five bushels of wheat yielded one barrel of flour, U.S. merchants sold wheat to Portugal for approximately 24 cents less per unit than flour. Wheat exports made a poor substitute for flour. In 1790, Portugal lagged far behind Great Britain, Spain, and France in the combined import value of U.S. wheat and flour, even though it trailed only Spain in the value of wheat exports (Table 1).[19]

United States provisions merchants could not compensate for the stymied flour trade even with robust exports of non-wheat grains to Portugal. In 1790, Portuguese dominions imported less than half the total combined value of U.S. grains and flour sent to England. Of the non-wheat grains, corn held the highest demand in Europe. In 1791, U.S. merchants nearly doubled their corn exports to the Portuguese Empire, from 468,537 bushels to 866,905. With the increased exports of corn to Portuguese dominions, North Americans sent a greater value of breadstuff to Portugal than Spain by more than 22 percent. They also increased wheat exports to the Portuguese Empire by 15 percent. That same year, however, flour exports fell by nearly half, from 68,650 barrels to 35,965, and rye exports plummeted from 8,383 bushels in 1790 to 2,912 in 1791.[20]

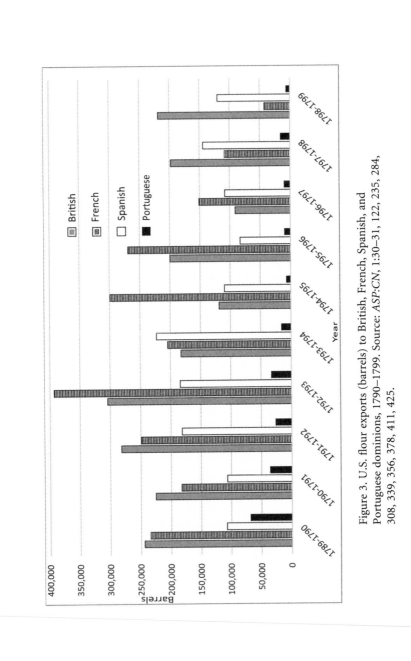

Figure 3. U.S. flour exports (barrels) to British, French, Spanish, and Portuguese dominions, 1790–1799. Source: *ASP:CN*, 1:30–31, 122, 235, 284, 308, 339, 356, 378, 411, 425.

Table 1. Value ($) of U.S. grain and flour exports to major importing empires, 1789–1790

Commodity	Great Britain ($)	France ($)	Spain ($)	Portugal ($)
Buckwheat	10	947	—	—
Corn	325,430	73,023	366,395	256,554
Oats	4,150	14,156	296	30
Rye	120	187	1,971	4,440
Total value of non-wheat grains	329,710	88,313	368,662	261,024
Wheat	355,361	147,654	505,754	372,083
Total value of all grains	685,071	235,967	874,416	633,107
Flour	1,645,738	1,483,195	673,005	459,292
Total combined value of grains and flour	2,330,809	1,719,162	1,547,421	1,092,399

Source: ASP:CN, 1: 26–27, 30–31.

Even with the drastic 1791 increase in corn exports to Portuguese dominions, U.S. merchants still relied less on exports to Portuguese destinations than on those to French or British ports. They sent 16 percent less corn to the Portuguese Empire than to the French Empire that year. Traders in the Luso-Atlantic did not import even half as much U.S. corn as the British Empire. One year later, U.S. merchants saw corn sales to Portuguese dominions plunge to 467,001 bushels. The same year, flour exports dropped again, to 26,473 barrels—a 26 percent decline from the previous year. In 1790, U.S. merchants exported corn to Portugal at just 42 percent of the value of wheat. They enjoyed impressive corn exports to Portugal for just a single year before they declined due to increased competition from Britain, Holland, and the Mediterranean along with an improved harvest in Portugal.[21]

With high European demand for U.S. provisions, prices began to outstrip what Luso-Atlantic traders would pay, further sundering the U.S.-Portuguese trade. Per capita, in 1790, traders in Portuguese dominions spent over 43 percent more than the British on U.S. breadstuff, and they paid more than double the per capita value of the Spanish. In some instances, Luso-Atlantic traders turned to non-U.S. suppliers to avoid the high prices. In 1790, John Bulkeley & Son limited their orders from Thomas

Clifford due to the "extravagant pri[c]es your Farmers require." Several months later, Domingos d'Oliveira's Madeira agent canceled an order for middlings and corn after he learned of the "exorbitant prices those Articles have risen to."[22] Although traders in the Portuguese Atlantic paid U.S. merchants a high per capita value for their goods in the early 1790s, the empire offered less aggregate value to U.S. trade than it had prior to U.S. independence.[23]

United States merchants had shifted their commerce away from southern Europe toward France and Great Britain even before the Anglo-French wars erupted in 1793, when North Americans began to export foodstuff to support the armies of both nations. Southern Europe continued to receive roughly 25 percent of U.S. flour exports between 1790 and 1792, but the percentage had plummeted from 40 percent between 1768 and 1772. In contrast, combined exports to Great Britain, France, Holland, and Ireland increased from 8 percent to 15 percent during the same periods. United States merchants reapportioned their wheat exports as well. They sent 80 percent to southern Europe between 1768 and 1772 and only 60 percent in the early 1790s.[24]

Spain and Portugal constituted the major importers of U.S. foodstuff in southern Europe. By the end of the 1780s, Portugal lost ground to Spain. In 1772 and 1773, Lisbon imported an annual average of 66,300 barrels of flour from British America. Between 1790 and 1792, U.S. traders sent Portugal an annual average of just 24,985 barrels. During the two periods, they increased their wheat exports to Portugal from 228,000 to 272,101. With five bushels of wheat equaling one barrel of flour, however, North Americans would have needed to export 162,475 additional bushels to return to pre-war levels of provisions exports to Portugal. The difference becomes especially pronounced considering that the early 1770s occasioned an ebb in the market from the peak years of 1769 and 1770. In contrast, the early 1790s marked the highest point of Portuguese wheat trade during that decade.[25]

After 1793, the Portuguese government reinstituted blanket prohibitions on U.S. flour. The United States retaliated with high duties on Portuguese wines, increasing their prices and diminishing their demand in the U.S. market. In 1790, John Bulkeley affirmed to Thomas Clifford that they could have procured more freight for the United States "if your Market was encouraging & the duties not so high." To no avail, the U.S. consul in Lisbon pled the U.S. government to lower duties on Lisbon and Port wines.

He hoped that in return the Portuguese government would grant U.S. exporters a monopoly on the fish market in Portugal.[26]

After the European wheat crisis abated in the mid-1790s, western European countries reverted to closer suppliers in eastern Europe. The improved crop caused a precipitous fall in U.S. wheat exports to the continent. In the Caribbean, however, colonists did not enjoy the same milling capacity as European metropolises, so they could not import wheat and grind it into flour. They remained reliant on U.S. flour. As a result, mid-Atlantic merchants hazarded legal danger to smuggle foodstuff to the British, French, and Spanish West Indies rather than to the Portuguese Empire. By 1807, as a destination for all U.S. exports, Portuguese dominions trailed all major western and southern European countries and their imperial dominions. For U.S. provisions exporters, Portugal's importance waned as they pursued new markets.[27]

New Markets

After independence, U.S. merchants enjoyed the freedom to trade legally with nations and empires once prohibited by British policies. In 1778, they had secured a treaty of amity and commerce with France as part of the European country's assistance in the Revolutionary War. By the 1790s, France had become a major importer of U.S. flour. In 1792, Buillon & Co. complained to their French-American associates, Dutilh & Wachsmuth, about poor harvests from their traditional suppliers around the Mediterranean. They hoped that imports from the United States could assuage the crisis due to the "superb" harvest there and the "moderate" prices. They would ship remittances in eaux-de-vie wine and Spanish piastres in return. During the 1790s, Samuel Keith of Philadelphia diversified his wine sales among Portuguese and French varieties. In the mid-1780s, the French native Étienne Dutilh had established his firm in Philadelphia as part of a large influx of immigrant traders. He traded with associates in Bordeaux, Jérémie, and Marseille. By 1790, mid-Atlantic exporters increased their business with French firms to the point that France became the second-most valuable destination of U.S. flour (Table 1).[28]

United States merchants further reduced the value of U.S. trade with the Portuguese Empire as they increased their trade with Spain. No longer tied to Portuguese wines by British mercantilist policies, U.S. consumers

and importers counted on the Spanish market to diversify their wine purchases. The Philadelphia firm Andrew Clow & Co. took advantage of the
heightened demand for mid-Atlantic breadstuff in Spain and the increased
demand for Spanish wines in America. Although they dabbled in Madeira
and Port wine early in the 1790s, they directed most of their Iberian breadstuff exports to Cádiz, Malaga, and Bilbao in return for Spanish wine and
fruit. Their Barcelona correspondents assured them that wheat and flour
were "much esteemed here & constantly wanted for the use of this Place."
They offered high-demand brandies and red wine from Mataró, Villanova,
and Benicarló in return. Valentín Riera & Co. informed Tench Tilghman &
Co. that they had an excellent store of wine that would answer for North
American grains.[29]

In 1805, the New York merchants Jacob and Thomas Walden sent a
cargo of staves and tobacco to Cádiz. They gave the captain the choice to
go either to Malaga or Lisbon in case belligerent powers had blockaded
Cádiz. If the captain chose to proceed to Malaga as they supposed he
would, they directed Grivegnée & Co. of that port to send back two hundred quarter casks of their best wine along with raisins and muscatel. If
he proceeded to Lisbon, they requested Gould Brothers & Co. of that city
to fill the ship with salt ballast and remit Spanish dollars or Portuguese
gold. North Americans reduced their demand for Portuguese wines as
they increased imports of Malaga, sherry, and claret from France and
Spain.[30]

The Portuguese economy remained dependent on viticulture despite
Pombal's mid-eighteenth-century attempts at diversification. By the 1790s,
merchants in Lisbon re-exported limited amounts of tea, nankeens, and
silk from Asia. Portugal had little, however, that U.S. merchants could not
purchase cheaper from Great Britain or the West Indies. In 1790, Theodore
Richter lamented to John Clifford that he probably could not procure a
strong return cargo in Portugal for Clifford's ship *Roebuck*, "as the articles
exported from hence for your Port are few in number, & these divided
among many Ships become a trifle to each."[31]

In 1783, John Adams had predicted the imminent decline of Portuguese
wine consumption in the United States as French wines became available
and popular. He warned Dom João Theolonico de Almeida that although
"port wines, common Lisbon, and Caracavalles had been before the war
frequently used, and that Madeira was esteemed above all other wine . . .
there was no doubt that a variety of French wines would now be more

commonly used than heretofore." Between 1792 and 1794, North Americans still received 64 percent of their imported wines from Portuguese dominions. The percentage marked, however, a distinct drop from the years just prior to the Revolutionary War, when almost all imported wines came from the Portuguese Empire.[32]

Madeira Wine

During the 1790s, North Americans demanded less Madeira and Faial wine than they had during the colonial period. Madeira wine imports plummeted. Prior to U.S. independence, Madeira constituted approximately three-fourths of all wine imported into British America. Between 1792 and 1794, with the increased availability of Spanish and French wines, U.S. merchants halted Madeira imports to the point that they accounted for just 21 percent of all wines imported into the United States.[33]

The Madeira market showed signs of decline almost immediately after the war. Although Madeira firms assured U.S. merchants that the Madeira market remained strong for U.S. produce, North American exporters remained skeptical. In 1784, Scott, Pringle, & Co. of Madeira suggested to Willing, Morris, & Swanwick of Philadelphia that the high demand for breadstuff on the island could command a cargo of four to five thousand bushels of grain, about two hundred barrels of flour, and pipe staves to fill any excess space onboard. They offered to take a concern in half of the cargo if the Philadelphia merchants chose not to venture the entire risk on their own account. The Philadelphia firm took no interest in the offer and passed the information on to their associates, Tench Tilghman & Co. of Baltimore. The Baltimore firm also decided against the venture. Willing, Morris, & Swanwick thought Tench Tilghman & Co.'s decision wise for they believed it would prove difficult to profit on the order.[34]

Willing, Morris, & Swanwick recognized a trend toward cheaper wines in the depressed times of the 1780s. As they informed Tench Tilghman & Co. one year later, "Madeira wine, we find must lie long in Store before t'will sell—the demand for those of inferior quality, such as Teneriffe, Fayal, &c. is much greater & the sale more brisk." Between October 24, 1788, and the beginning of April 1789, the Madeira firm of Lamar, Hill, Bisset, & Co. sent to the United States just ten of their eighty-four wine cargoes. In 1789, Willing, Morris, & Swanwick purchased an "immense" order of Madeira wine, but they purchased it for re-export to the Asian market rather than to sell it in the United States. Between the autumn of 1789 and April 1790, William Seton & Co. of New York managed to sell only a single pipe of wine from a cargo received from the trader Domingos d'Oliveira of Madeira. With the influx of new wines into the United States, the U.S. market could not support the Madeira trade in the same quantities as before the American Revolution.[35]

Madeira remained a strong but limited market for the sale of U.S. breadstuff. In August 1785, the price of wheat reached 700 réis per alqueire, the equivalent of 9s. sterling per bushel. That same month, by comparison, the article commanded just 7s. 6d. sterling per bushel on the Spanish island of Tenerife. Despite the good market for U.S. commodities on the Portuguese island, Madeira's merchants had little to remit as payment besides their wine. With the decline in U.S. demand for Madeira wine, U.S. merchants chose to send their produce elsewhere in return for other varieties.[36]

Some Madeira merchants traded contraband to the United States in exchange for U.S. breadstuff. In 1785, Domingos d'Oliveira paid John Clifford in specie, a prohibited transaction under Portuguese law. The following year, he shipped the Philadelphia house 388.25 Spanish milled dollars, or pieces of eight, for which he expected to receive contraband snuff and soap. He requested that Clifford package the commodities in flour barrels and send them with some legal articles, such as bread, biscuit, and flour. Despite such clandestine trade, Madeira merchants continued to depend on wine exports as a principal mode of remittance, even while demand for the commodity slipped in the United States.[37]

Some Madeira merchants found it difficult to keep business afloat after the attenuation of the once-lucrative North American markets. Before the Revolution, the Madeira firm of Lamar, Hill, Bisset, & Co. built its business around the North American market. In 1762, 72 percent of their known customers came from mainland British America. The American Revolution cut into their business by disrupting the Madeira trade during the 1770s and early 1780s. In 1785, Henry Hill complained to his sister, Mary Lamar, "It is more the want, than the weight of either money or Madeira business that oppresses me." That same year, the firm struggled to pay Charles Wharton and his associates for pipe staves shipped to them. Wharton warned that if they failed to remit payment he would "drop all commercial intercourse" with them regardless of their "long established credit & reputation."[38]

Conditions worsened for the firm as the 1780s progressed. In 1789, Robert Bisset chided Thomas Lamar for incurring increased business expenses despite the decreased profits. He lamented that the partners had reached "the height of the winter of life with almost a certainty of gratifying our . . . oponents in business and of giving them an opportunity to scoff at us and maliciously to say, how are the mighty fallen." By 1796–1797, U.S. customers constituted 61 percent of the firm's buyers, a 15 percent contraction from 1762. Although the percentage of North American importers remained high, it represented a substantial loss from the firm's most prosperous days of the 1760s.[39]

During the fifteen years after the war, the Madeira firm of Leacock & Sons also witnessed the erosion of their North American customer base. In 1797–1798, the firm recorded fifty-nine fewer importers than they had for the years 1763–1765. North American customers accounted for twenty-two of those lost. The firm had only two customers in the United States by the end of the 1790s. Newton & Gordon's customer base increased 81 percent from 1770–1772 to 1797–1798, but the firm saw the North American percentage of their business increase from 2 percent to just 8 percent for the same time periods. United States customers composed just 16 percent of the total increase of the firm's 305 additional customers. Most growth occurred in the West Indies, though the firm saw increases in Africa and Asia as well. After 1789, Madeira firms increased total wine exports from about five thousand pipes per year to peak at over twenty thousand per year in 1805. Despite the substantial increase in exports, they reduced their shipments to the United States in favor of increased exports to Asia and the British West Indies.[40]

Because U.S. traders favored Spanish and French wines, colonists in the French and Spanish Caribbean imported more U.S. grain and flour than did the Portuguese Atlantic islands. Between 1790 and 1792, North Americans sent the Portuguese islands just 8 percent of the combined amount of exports to the Spanish and French West Indies and the Luso-Atlantic islands. Throughout the decade, the percentage dropped to an average of just 5 percent. United States traders preferred French, Spanish, or Dutch neutral ports in the West Indies.[41]

In the mid-1790s, the Pintard firm found that a weak Madeira market in the United States threatened their credit networks after they engaged with customers unfamiliar to the firm. In 1795, Lewis Pintard of New York worried about the poor business acumen of his son, John Marsden Pintard, who resided in Madeira and served as U.S. consul there. John owed the Norfolk merchant Moses Meyers a balance of $12,447. Meyers informed Lewis that a shipment of wine from John could not cover the balance since he could not sell it. Lewis censured his son for continuing to send wines to Virginia, "where you know you must lose so much by them." As the Madeira business lagged, Lewis called in his debts. He requested that Campbell Wilson expedite remittances. But Wilson's firm struggled to pay due to the slow pace of their Madeira wine sales. The Pintards' fortunes worsened when a cargo they had shipped to Salem sold at $10,000 below their cost and another ten pipes sold cheaply at auction. John's personal reputation collapsed when his wife, Betsey, left him and returned to the United States as rumors swirled that he led a drunken and "dissolute life." By the end of 1798, the firm had irreversibly "met with misfortunes & disappointments." The following year, he shuttered the business in Madeira and returned to the United States.[42]

Pintard's business follies and personal difficulties contributed to his financial ruin, but his firm followed the same trajectory as other businesses that operated in Madeira with close ties to North America. By the first decade of the 1800s, U.S. firms on the island had entered a steady decline. Some merged with British firms while others ended their Madeira business in the fashion of Lamar, Hill, Bisset, & Co. and the Pintards. One year before Pintard's business demise, his American cousin John Searle III fled the island from creditors. United States independence had ruptured the North America–Madeira networks.[43]

During the decade after U.S. independence, Portuguese officials hoped to increase the U.S. market for Port wine. Inácio Palyart, the agent of the Douro Wine Company, facilitated business between mainland Portugal and the United States. The Portuguese diplomat Cipriano Ribeiro Freire hoped to establish an agency for the company in the United States to increase imports. Ribeiro Freire assumed that the increase in Port sales would reduce U.S. imports of Tenerife and sherry wines without edging out Madeira imports.[44]

Instead, neither Madeira nor Port commanded strong enough demand in the United States to maintain the Portuguese Empire's position as the principal wine exporter to the new nation. Some distributors such as Henry Sheaff and Charles Smith of Philadelphia sold Port wine among an assortment of Madeira, sherry, brandy, spirits, and peach brandy, but Port never thrived. Between 1782 and 1788, out of forty-five vessels that entered Baltimore from ports in Portuguese dominions, not a single cargo came from

Porto. In Philadelphia, between November 1797 and March 1802, ship entrances from Porto comprised only 4 percent of all arrivals from ports in the Portuguese Empire. Port wine failed to substitute for the decline of Madeira in U.S. markets. As North Americans increased their consumption of Spanish and French wines, Portuguese officials failed to encourage more U.S. purchases of Portuguese wine.[45]

War, Neutrality, and Trade

During the early 1790s, European monarchies observed the French Revolution with concern. Fearful that disorder and revolution would spread beyond French borders and envelop their own countries, Austria and Prussia prepared to invade France. Hostilities erupted in 1792 when French troops repelled an invasion of Austro-Prussian forces. The violence escalated after the French National Convention executed Louis XVI and Great Britain entered the war against France in 1793. Hostilities between them persisted until 1815.[46]

Across the Atlantic, George Washington oversaw tense cabinet meetings in which his secretaries debated the ramifications of the 1778 treaty of amity between the United States and France. On April 22, 1793, Washington declared U.S. neutrality in the conflict. North Americans were divided in their opinions about U.S. neutrality. Jeffersonian Republicans clamored to aid French revolutionaries as repayment for their help during America's war with Britain. Whatever the political debates about the proclamation, provisions exporters hoped to profit from U.S. neutrality by feeding European armies on both sides of the conflict.[47]

The Anglo-French wars further reduced U.S.-Portuguese trade as U.S. merchants focused their exports on the belligerent empires. During the late 1780s, U.S. traders sent between 30 and 40 ships to Bordeaux each year. In 1795, they sent 350. Although they augmented their exports to Portugal slightly after 1796, the increase resulted from a general rise in exports to war-torn Europe. Between 1796 and 1799, U.S. traders sent Portugal an annual average of approximately 1 percent of total U.S. exports.[48]

The percentage enjoyed only a small temporary boost near the turn of the century. United States traders witnessed a short improvement in their trade with Portugal when commerce with France soured during the Quasi-War of 1798–1800. The French government subsequently threatened to seize U.S. vessels that sailed to or from England. At the same time, the

Portuguese increased their demand for North American provisions as they engaged in limited hostilities with Spain in 1801. Napoleon had insisted that his western neighbors punish Portugal for its alliance with Britain. Between 1802 and 1803, the British and French governments agreed to an uneasy truce. During the so-called peace of Amiens, the British and French Empires normalized commerce with their American possessions and ceased reliance on the U.S. carrying trade. The peace led to an improvement in the Portuguese Empire's percentage of aggregate U.S. exports. After hostilities erupted again between France and Britain in 1804, U.S. merchants resumed their prolific trade to the belligerents. United States–Portuguese trade plunged again. By 1807, Portuguese dominions accounted for less than 2 percent of all U.S. exports.[49]

Even as North Americans enjoyed a slight improvement in their commerce with Portugal, the trade was almost negligible compared to that with other regions of Europe. By the late 1790s, U.S. merchants nearly halted sales of flour and wheat to Portugal. In 1799, they exported 1,587 barrels of flour to Portugal compared to 15,146 in 1793. In 1798 and 1799, they did not export any wheat to Portugal. Between November 1797 and March 1802, of all vessels that cleared from Philadelphia, just 1.8 percent sailed to Portuguese dominions.[50]

The Portuguese court maintained its commitment to shed the country's reliance on U.S. breadstuff. In 1798, Francisco Lopez Rodrigues, treasurer of the Portuguese royal gold register, argued for the expansion of Portuguese wheat production. He insisted that Portugal possessed ample lands to grow wheat and sustain its population, and he encouraged the employment of "all land capable of producing wheat." In 1801, vessels from Portuguese ports comprised 0.32 percent of all entrances into Philadelphia. Between 1796 and 1807, U.S. traders exported so little to Portugal that the balance of trade that had long favored North Americans shifted to the Portuguese in 1796, 1799, 1800, 1805, and 1806. Between the 1780s and 1807, North Americans contemplated handsome prospects in France and Britain, a growing domestic wheat sector in Portugal, and Portuguese prohibitions on the most lucrative U.S. provisions. They saw little incentive to target the Portuguese Empire with their goods.[51]

In Portugal, even merchants steeped in the North American trade struggled to maintain their U.S. networks. In 1793, Edward Church, the U.S. consul in Lisbon, claimed that an "immensely rich" English firm in Lisbon "for more than twenty years has enjoyed almost the monopoly of the American trade." Doubtless he referred to the powerful firm of John Bulkeley. Between 1757 and 1776, the Bulkeley family imported 185 cargoes from North America as part of the firm Parr & Bulkeley. The three closest firms imported no more than 84 cargoes each into Lisbon during the same period. After the Revolutionary War, the Bulkeleys tried to capitalize on former networks to maintain their trade with North America. They reminded John Clifford that "we are old friends of your worthy Parents," and they promised to invigorate his trade with Lisbon.[52]

By the late 1790s, family ties constituted the Bulkeley's only significant business networks in Philadelphia—the most important North American port in the Lisbon trade during the colonial period. The Whartons and Walns of Philadelphia had close family ties to one another and to the Bulkeleys of Lisbon. William and Charles Wharton were first cousins once removed. William, whom records often refer to as Moore Wharton, married Mary Waln, the daughter of Jesse Waln. Mary's sister, Sarah, married Thomas Bulkeley, John Bulkeley's son. In 1797, Thomas and Sarah moved to Lisbon, where Thomas served as U.S. consul, and the Bulkeleys acted as the Walns' principal contacts in Portugal. Between November 1797 and March 1802, William Moore Wharton, Robert and Jesse Waln, and Charles Wharton received one-third of all cargoes that arrived at Philadelphia from Lisbon.[53]

Most Philadelphia traders lacked such kin connections and received sporadic shipments of Portuguese goods every few years as pre-Revolution networks unraveled. Between November 1797 and March 1802, Philadelphia received 41 vessels from Lisbon contrasted with 282 between 1769 and 1774. During the 1797–1802 period, fourteen different importers received 34 percent of all vessels that arrived in Philadelphia from Lisbon. They received just 1 each. Of the remaining consignees outside the Wharton-Waln-Bulkeley circle, only David Callaghan received more than three vessels (he received 5), for he specialized in the wine trade. During that same period, four merchants controlled 51 percent of all ships bound from Lisbon to Philadelphia, with most of those (10) consigned to William Moore Wharton. Between 1769 and 1774, by contrast, fifteen merchants had owned 51 percent of all ships that cleared from Lisbon for Philadelphia, and they received an average of approximately 9 vessels each during that period. As Portugal became a less attractive destination, only a few Philadelphia merchants with close Lisbon connections conducted steady business there. Portuguese commerce hardly constituted the bustling business it once had in Philadelphia.[54]

*   *   *

The American Revolution reduced Portugal's importance to North American trade by removing the protections as well as the constrictions of the British imperial system. During the 1780s, U.S. traders confronted the Atlantic commercial world without the support of British treaties and trade privileges that had once sustained their networks. With North America severed from British commercial might, the Portuguese government had little incentive to accord U.S. traders liberal commercial privileges. At the same time, U.S. traders took advantage of independence to engage new markets. They diversified their wine imports, attenuating Portugal's and Madeira's former prominence in their commercial networks.

As revolution and independence caused U.S. trade with Portugal and Madeira to plummet, North Americans viewed Brazil as the future of their Luso-Atlantic trade. In May 1806, the U.S. consul in Lisbon, William Jarvis, suggested that if stripped of Brazil, Portugal would suffer "utter ruin." By heaping "discouragements," in John Adams's words, on U.S. trade, the Portuguese government fortified North Americans' conviction that monarchies inhibited commercial freedom. United States diplomats pressed for trade privileges in Brazil as they tried to secure more open commerce with the Portuguese Empire in the 1780s. The Portuguese government rebuffed their requests, reinforcing the notion among North Americans that independence, revolution, and republicanism remained the surest guarantee of free trade. In the meantime, they asserted their right to trade freely in the Atlantic by cooperating with Brazilians in illicit commerce.[55]

PART III

A Liberty of Trade

DURING THE EARLY YEARS OF the Revolution, many North Americans imagined civic virtue—the sacrifice of private endeavors for the public good—as the keystone that would maintain the integrity of their republic. By the 1790s, they yielded to a more nuanced philosophy that lauded self-interest as a form of public good. Prosperous citizens made a prosperous republic. If the government allowed citizens the liberty to flourish in their private commerce, the electorate would have the economic independence to eschew vice and corruption. North Americans made free trade ideology a centerpiece of their new republican paradigm. They subscribed to eighteenth-century theories that open commerce bred prosperity. Free trade would protect the republic, and republican government would allow traders the liberty to pursue their interests without arbitrary hindrance.[1]

Traders interested in Brazil began to apply such logic to South America. They anticipated a day when Brazilian independence and republicanism would liberate commerce and allow foreign access to Brazilian markets. Meanwhile, North Americans engaged with Brazilian markets on their own terms, conducting rampant contraband trade into the first decade of the nineteenth century. Although other nations smuggled goods in and out of Brazil, Portuguese officials expressed concern that republican ideologies would accompany U.S. contraband.

In a move that confounded North Americans' logic, the Portuguese government combatted republicanism and fortified the empire by liberalizing imperial trade. During the 1790s and early 1800s, the Portuguese court subscribed to the theory that the private prosperity of Brazilian merchant capitalists would enhance the empire's public finances. The government loosened strictures on Brazilian commerce to strengthen the empire and monarchy. In 1807, the Portuguese court fled Lisbon in advance of Napoleon Bonaparte's invasion and established Rio de Janeiro as the empire's new political center. Upon arrival, the prince regent, Dom João, opened Brazilian ports to foreign commerce. With the change, he aimed to enhance imperial finances and consolidate his position as ruler of a united empire. Brazilians associated the Americas and free trade with the revival of the monarchy and the regeneration of Portuguese imperial strength rather than with republicanism.[2]

United States free traders celebrated the opening of Brazilian ports, but the change exposed serious flaws in their paradigm that equated independence and republicanism with commercial liberty. Some observers lamented that the Brazilian monarchy liberalized its trade at the same time their own republican government restricted all foreign exports with the Embargo Act of 1807. With the transfer of the Portuguese court to Rio de Janeiro, moreover, Brazil became the seat of a European monarchical dynasty. The move called into question North Americans' tidy association of American independence with republicanism. It raised doubts among North Americans about whether the monarchy would align its interests more with the Americas or Europe. United States observers also wondered if they could consider Brazil truly independent so long as Dom João and the house of Bragança governed it. To many in the United States, Brazil seemed an unfinished project.

Chapter 5

Republicans and Smugglers

Prior to the 1780s, republican theorists viewed the growth of commerce as inimical to civic virtue, for it impelled citizens to seek their private gain rather than the public good. During the first decade of U.S. independence, traditional republicans abhorred the commercializing tendency of the new nation and found evidence everywhere that civic virtue had corroded. By the end of the decade, the framers of the U.S. Constitution conceded that the survival of a republic could not depend solely on the virtue of its citizens. They would have to devise a governmental structure in which self-interest harmonized with the public good through constitutional checks, balances, and separation of powers. By the 1790s, many North Americans claimed that a society's commercial spirit enhanced science, technology, industry, and ultimately civilization. Some protectionists called for higher duties on foreign manufactures to spur U.S. industry. They argued that citizens should sacrifice low-priced foreign goods for the national welfare. Although committed to duties on imports, even most protectionists opposed closed imperial systems. Free traders embraced self-interest as a new form of virtue. If citizens achieved economic prosperity, they would increase their autonomy and remain incorruptible by external influences. Virtue would proceed from self-interest and private profit.[1]

By the time of the Revolution, North Americans drew on eighteenth-century Enlightenment dialogue to equate free trade with prosperity and to justify contraband. If the survival of a republic depended on the virtue that emanated from a prosperous citizenry, U.S. free traders assumed that liberal political economies would facilitate and protect republican governments. They adhered to mutually reinforcing ideologies in which republican government protected the natural right of free trade, and in turn free trade would produce the prosperity necessary to maintain republicanism. Some free traders defended contraband as a means of asserting their natural right to open commerce. They viewed smuggling as a protest in favor of free trade and against the evils of monarchy and mercantilism. Early U.S. smugglers operated within a commercial culture sympathetic to illegitimate trade as a legitimate means of resistance to abuse of state authority.[2]

Optimistic North Americans anticipated a day when republican revolutions would open prohibited regions to U.S. commerce either by direct annexation or free trade. In 1802, Spanish authorities in New Orleans rescinded the right of U.S. traders to store cargoes at the port free of duty. As Rufus King surveyed American landscapes that year, he foresaw a time when the United States would acquire New Orleans and the Floridas. United States traders would then possess "free navigation and use of the Mississippi." Not one to think small, King assumed that "it cannot be long before all the continental Colonies of [Spain] will imitate the example we have given them." The United States would have free trade in the Americas, whether by diplomacy, smuggling, or revolution.[3]

By the turn of the century, Portuguese officials worried that contraband trade provided the material means by which North Americans would extend the supposedly twin doctrines of republicanism and free trade into the Atlantic. The Portuguese court confronted the ill effects of U.S. independence in the 1780s when conspirators in Minas Gerais extolled the American Revolution and pursued independence from Portugal. Although their plans remained inchoate, they imbued their movement with calls for freer trade and tinged it with republicanism. The plot amounted more to a desperate attempt of debtors to dispel their obligations to the royal treasury than to nationalistic fervor, but it convinced the court that U.S. republicanism menaced imperial authority.[4]

During the 1790s, Portuguese officials liberalized intra-imperial trade to improve public finances, appease discontented Brazilian traders, reduce foreign contraband, and stave off republicanism. Rather than fracture the empire, trade liberalization would revitalize it by reintegrating its constitutive parts and making the prosperity of each entity dependent on the others. While Lisbon authorities relaxed intra-imperial commerce, they repelled republicanism and sought to quash interimperial contraband. As the Age of Revolution advanced into the nineteenth century, North Americans and Brazilians clashed in their interpretations of open commerce as it related to monarchy and empire.

Brazilian Prospects

By the 1780s, Anglo-Atlantic officials and traders viewed Brazil as the most desirable target for commerce with the Portuguese Empire. Brazilian magnates increased their share of imperial merchant capital through the slave trade and extralegal commerce. As one commentator noted, Portuguese merchants "may be considered in no other light than as the intermediate agents or factors between Great Britain and the Brazils." The overseas minister, Martinho de Melo e Castro, admitted that "Portugal without Brazil is an insignificant power."[5]

By the first half of the 1790s, Portugal exported a greater value of goods to Britain than it imported by a difference of £130,000. Since 1781, British traders had increased imports of Brazilian cotton, which first passed through Lisbon. Propelled by British demand, cotton exports grew to account for 11 percent of the value of all Brazilian exports by 1800. British textile manufacturers depended on Brazilian cotton so much that by 1806 Portugal had a negative balance of trade with its own colony due to re-exportation of the product through Lisbon. That year, the U.S. consul in Lisbon, William Jarvis, believed that France and Britain's tussle for Portuguese support amounted to a struggle over control of Brazilian trade.[6]

United States policymakers and merchants hoped to gain direct access to Brazil as its economic influence expanded. In the summer of 1783, John Adams asked the Portuguese ambassador, Vicente de Sousa Coutinho, for permission to trade directly with Brazil. North Americans especially hoped to access Brazilian sugar. The minister replied that Portugal would not allow the United States or any other nation to trade with the colony. Portuguese officials feared that if foreign nations had direct access to Brazil, they would deprive the court and Lisbon merchants of the benefits of the gold, sugar, and cotton exports that flowed out of South America. United States negotiators followed up with a request to designate the Azores as an entrepôt from whence U.S. merchants could import Brazilian sugar, coffee, cotton, and cacao. On that point, too, the Portuguese government parried negotiations, claiming that Lisbon could furnish North Americans the same articles 15 percent cheaper than they could receive them from the West Indies. Many U.S. traders and authorities concluded that only smuggling or republican revolution would give North Americans access to Brazilian ports. By the late 1780s, both methods seemed feasible.[7]

As North Americans fought for access to Brazil, Brazilians clamored for freer trade. They petitioned Lisbon to permit them to trade on their own accounts, rather than as factors of metropolitan merchants. They recommended the establishment of a company to conduct direct trade between Brazil and Great Britain, suggesting that direct trade would diminish contraband English manufactures in Brazil. Instead, the crown issued a 1785 *alvará* (decree) that prohibited manufacturing in the colony. Officials feared non-Portuguese manufactures "would make the inhabitants totally independent of the metropolis." The court directed customs officials to clamp down on contraband trade. The government reportedly confiscated and suppressed a translated manuscript of *Wealth of Nations* from a Brazilian radical. Wealthy and influential Brazilians chafed against the strictures of Portuguese law, especially in the gold and diamond districts of Minas Gerais.[8]

Underground cabals formed with the intention to declare independence "as had done the English Americans," according to later testimony. In 1786, a small contingent of Brazilians appealed to Thomas Jefferson for U.S. support in their quest for independence. In November, while in Paris, Jefferson received a letter from a Brazilian who wrote under the pseudonym of Vendek. The stranger revealed that he and his countrymen "are resolved to follow the striking example, that you have given us." He requested support from the United States and offered payment in silver.[9]

To Jefferson, Vendek's overtures validated his vision of the Western Hemisphere as an "empire of liberty." They also led him to consider the commercial advantages of Brazilian independence at a time when the Portuguese government barred U.S. trade with the colony. In August 1785, Jefferson had proposed that the U.S. government send a minister to Portugal because "our commerce with that country is very important, perhaps more so than with any other country in Europe." He approached Portuguese commercial relations, however, with an eye toward Brazil.[10]

After he learned that John Adams had opened negotiations with Portugal, Jefferson encouraged him to press the Portuguese government to open Brazilian markets to North Americans. During the eighteenth century, British Americans had garnered a strong appetite for Asian goods, and Brazil produced many of the same commodities as the East Indies. United States merchants hoped that they could procure cheaper coffee, sugar, cacao, ginger, spices, and cotton from Brazil than they could from Asia. Barred from trade with the Spanish and British West Indies and allowed only limited trade with the French West Indies, U.S. traders hoped access to Brazil would allow them freer importation of tropical commodities. Jefferson noted that "the Brazil sugars are esteemed with us more than any other" and suggested that the demand for Brazilian produce would escalate if North Americans could import it directly. He doubted, however, that Portugal would allow the United States entrance to the empire's prize possession in the Americas, so he welcomed a meeting with Vendek.[11]

Jefferson arranged to meet the mysterious correspondent at Nîmes "under the pretext of seeing the antiquities of that place." Once arrived, he met José Joaquim Maia e Barbalho, a young revolutionary in ill-health. Maia e Barbalho hailed from Rio de Janeiro, but he studied medicine at the University of Montpellier in France. He acted in concert with a small cohort of twelve Brazilian students who resided in Coimbra, Portugal, and who desired Brazilian independence. The group studied Montesquieu and Diderot. They had circulated a copy of Raynal's *Historie philosophique et politique des établissements et du commerce des Européens dans les Deux Indes*, part of which heralded the virtues of the American Revolution. In another portion, Raynal criticized Portugal for its oppression of Brazil. The revolutionaries also discussed Régnier's French translation of North American state constitutions. They had read and discussed Locke, Hobbes, and Voltaire. The group composed only a small part of a growing body of young Brazilians and Portuguese disillusioned with the empire.[12]

During his meeting with Jefferson, Maia e Barbalho stated the case for a successful revolution in Brazil. Listless and outnumbered, Portuguese troops in Brazil would do little to counter a revolution. Slaves would throw their lots in with their masters. Revolutionaries would fund the war with the 26 million cruzados produced annually by Brazilian mines. From the United States they needed cannons, ammunition, ships, and military personnel. He assured Jefferson that in case of success, Brazilians would establish a republican government disposed to import U.S. provisions.[13]

Jefferson stressed that he did not have authority from the U.S. government to treat on the subject and could express only his individual opinions. He explained that while the United States did not have the means to meddle in a civil war and hoped to cultivate good relations with Portugal, "a successful revolution in Brasil could not be uninteresting to us." Jefferson refused to jeopardize relations with Portugal over an inchoate plot hatched by a small cohort of revolutionaries. But he left the meeting intrigued by the possibility of a Brazilian revolution.[14]

In May, he related the conversation to Secretary of Foreign Affairs John Jay. He insisted that "however distant we may be both in condition and dispositions, from taking an active part in any commotions in that country, nature has placed it too near us to make its movements altogether indifferent to our interests or to our curiosity." United States officials did not carry their correspondence with the hopeful revolutionaries further, but Jefferson revealed the anticipation that only an independent, republican Brazil could open the country's ports to the United States. For him, the Brazilian conspirators represented the promise that the Americas would follow the United States into a prosperous era of free trade and republicanism.[15]

Four years later, as secretary of state, Jefferson sought intelligence about the possibility of Brazilian independence. In February 1791, the Senate confirmed David Humphreys as the first U.S. minister to Portugal, and Humphreys received his credentials in mid-March. Less than a month later, Jefferson sent him encrypted instructions to "procure us all the information possible as to the strength, riches, resources, lights and dispositions, of Brazil."[16]

In June, the assistant secretary of the treasury, Tench Coxe, sent Jefferson a report on Portuguese trade commodities that must have fueled Jefferson's anticipation of Humphreys's report. Coxe supported the development of a protected manufacturing industry in the United States, but he also advocated more open trade in the Atlantic. He maintained that Brazilian sugar, cacao, and coffee "are . . . objects of desire" to the United States. He lamented, however, that U.S. merchants could obtain the commodities only by re-export through Portugal and that they could not export goods to Brazil. He assumed that trade with the Portuguese Empire would increase if North Americans could obtain sugar and other Brazilian articles directly and if they could furnish Brazil with U.S. provisions.[17]

Brazil remained on Jefferson's mind while he waited for Humphreys's report. During a January 1792 meeting with the Senate Committee on Nominations, he related his desire to improve free trade with European nations, including Portugal. He made sure, however, to discuss with the committee the "interesting situation of Brazil." Meanwhile, Humphreys struggled to obtain information for his report to Jefferson due to Portugal's "jealousy" of its colonies. By March 1792, Jefferson had the report in his hands, and he passed it along to George Washington. Humphreys responded favorably that Brazilian wealth was "daily increasing" and that "the ties of attachment [to Portugal] are weakening." As to Brazil's relationship to the metropolis, he insisted that "the Colonists have . . . many causes of complaint; and the Government at home of apprehension, that a separation must one day inevitably take place." Jefferson did not intend for the U.S. government to aid Brazilian revolutionaries, but the report strengthened his anticipation of free trade with an independent Brazil. With his interest in Brazil, he revealed his hope that independent American nations might secure the free trade that Europe prohibited—a hope that remained on his mind into his own presidency.[18]

Just months after his inauguration, Jefferson received a letter from his son-in-law Thomas Mann Randolph. Randolph wrote optimistically, albeit without foundation, that "the Emancipation of Mexico & Brazil cannot be far off when all the products of land must quickly be every where in America or Atlantic Europe at the minimum price." Mann undoubtedly fed Jefferson's own sanguine hopes that cheap commodities would soon flow out of Brazil into the United States free of duties and trade restrictions.[19]

In his flirtation with Brazilian affairs, Jefferson demonstrated a growing supposition among North Americans that revolution and independence would precede prosperous free trade between the United States and Brazil. He had learned by experience that the Portuguese monarchy cared little about a close commercial relationship with the United States. Although North Americans rued the collapse of their trade with Portugal, by the 1790s the Portuguese trade amounted to little without Brazil. If the colony could secure its independence and open its ports to U.S. commodities, North Americans would hardly agonize over the decline of commerce with Portugal.

The Minas Treachery

While he prepared his report for Jefferson, Humphreys received word from the Portuguese foreign minister that a change in gold tax collection had caused "uneasiness" and "remonstrance" in Brazil several years prior. The minister, Luís Pinto de Sousa Coutinho, probably chose deliberately not to divulge the extent to which U.S. independence had stoked unrest in the Brazilian mining districts. Afraid that Brazil might follow the U.S. trajectory of revolution and independence, the Portuguese court liberalized the imperial political economy to the favor of Brazilians. Pinto de Sousa Coutinho revealed only vague details about the episode, but Humphreys learned that the discord prompted the government to relax its demand for gold and instead encourage agricultural exports from Brazil. By the time of Humphreys's report, Portuguese merchants frequently paid with gold for the increased Brazilian imports, reversing the flow of precious metal across the Atlantic and enriching Brazilians. Humphreys and Jefferson assumed that Brazilians' enhanced wealth would benefit the United States when Brazil finally declared independence. Instead, it reiterated to Brazilians that empire and free trade could advance in harmony.[20]

By the late 1780s, Brazilian revolutionaries began to turn vague ideas of rebellion into concrete plans as a small cohort concocted what became known as the Inconfidência Mineira—the Minas Treachery. Brazilians regularly fell short of the annual quota of a hundred arrobas of gold because their output of precious metals decreased after the 1760s. Bureaucratic inefficiencies impeded collection of the derrama, and local and central authorities ignored the tax for most of the 1770s. In 1788, Luís Antônio Furtado de Mendonça, the Viscount of Barbacena, arrived as governor of Minas Gerais with instructions from the Portuguese government to enforce the per capita tax.[21]

The tax placed a heavy burden on the Minas population that was "impossible for them to pay," they complained. Between 1720 and 1807, Brazilians paid a hundred and fifty thousand tons of gold in tribute to Portugal, two-thirds of which came from Minas Gerais. Mineiros (Minas inhabitants) received few benefits for their tribute. The quinto went straight to the crown, entradas (taxes on trade) and subsídios (excise taxes) funded government administration, and tithes supported the church. Discontented with the imperial "yoke," some of them desired to sever political ties with the metropolis "as had done the English Americans." Brazilian revolutionaries shared the sentiment that revolution and independence would result in freer trade and prosperity.[22]

Mineiros knew Joaquim José da Silva Xavier as Tiradentes (tooth puller), for he made a part-time livelihood in dentistry. Tiradentes came from an unremarkable background as the son of a municipal alderman in São João del Rei, Minas Gerais. He struggled early in his life with debt and unsuccessful business ventures in prospecting and retail. In 1775, he entered the dragoons—the regular Minas Gerais military forces. He assumed the modest rank of alferes, a lieutenant. To his consternation, he had not risen above it by 1788. Forty years old, ambitious, and frustrated, he conversed with associates about the potential of political independence for Minas Gerais. By the end of the year, he held a principal position among a small cadre of ringleaders who plotted to rebel against the homeland and to establish Minas Gerais as an independent republic.[23]

The Portuguese court had done its best to suppress unorthodox political ideologies in Brazil. The colony had no institution of higher education until 1792 and no printing presses until 1808. The Royal Censorship Board regulated printed material and suppressed works the court considered dangerous, such as the writings of Enlightenment intellectuals. Many Brazilians skirted the prohibitions. They kept private libraries with illicit material and exchanged ideas and books in Paris-style salons. Several of the Minas conspirators participated in the underground Enlightenment culture, from which they drew their inspiration. Others had contracted large amounts of debt to the crown and hoped the revolution would release them from their obligations.[24]

The conspirators expected that Barbacena would initiate collection of the derrama the following February. They hoped to take advantage of the anticipated discontent to instigate the rebellion. Tiradentes planned to assassinate and decapitate the governor. Francisco de Paula Freire de Andrade, a lieutenant-colonel in the dragoons, agreed to command his troops to stand down amid the tumult. He would ask the multitude what they desired, at which point Tiradentes would hoist the governor's head and demand the liberty of the people. The cohort hoped the rebellion would spread from Minas Gerais to Rio de Janeiro and São Paulo. They received support from Rio de Janeiro contractors who stood indebted to the Portuguese treasury and who believed that Portuguese commercial prohibitions harmed their business interests.[25]

One of the plotters, Joaquim Silvério dos Reis, denounced the plot and his coconspirators to Barbacena in an attempt to have his own debts forgiven. In March, the governor suspended the derrama to avoid rebellion, removing the catalyst that would allow the conspirators to incite a revolution they hoped would terminate their debt. The Portuguese government arrested the plotters, tried them, and sentenced them to death. During the trial, Tiradentes took full responsibility for the concoction of the scheme. The crown commuted the death sentence of the others to banishment and confiscation of their goods. The government hanged and quartered the alferes—the lone casualty of the Inconfidência Mineira.[26]

At the 1789–1790 trials of the Minas conspirators, imperial officials worried that the U.S. example had a deleterious effect on the loyalty of Brazilian subjects. They learned that the defendants "spoke with much pleasure and satisfaction on the establishment of that Republic." The revolutionaries closely studied North American state constitutions and the Articles of Confederation. Tiradentes assumed that if the mineiros could establish an independent republic, they could surpass the opulence of North Americans due to Brazil's wealth of natural resources. Perhaps as early as September 1788, he had received payments from merchants in Rio de Janeiro who asked him to report on the receptivity of Minas residents to the idea of Brazilian independence. The conspirator José Aires Gomes claimed that the merchants backed the planned revolution in Brazil to obtain "freedom of commerce" and "make an English America" in Brazil.[27]

One defendant related an evening discussion at which several of the plotters rhapsodized about the "english Americas"—a "dominant passion" of the conspirator Luís Vieira da Silva. As they surveyed the Minas landscape from a veranda, they imagined the "richness and happiness that would result in these countries [of Brazil] if they achieved their liberty and independence." The cabal had inquired of an Englishman who resided in Minas about "the cause of the uprising of the English Americas," and they compared the taxes on their gold to the duties imposed on the former British colonists. One conspirator, Francisco Antônio de Oliveira Lopes, felt certain that Brazilians would carry on a robust trade with foreign nations once they gained independence. Some members of the group lacked an ideological commitment to republicanism and would have settled for any political arrangement that might free them from their debt to the Portuguese government. The testimony revealed to Portuguese authorities, nevertheless, a worrisome association of republican revolution with independence and free trade—an association that appeared to emanate from the United States.[28]

Faced with the small but sinister independence conspiracy rife with allusions to the United States and free trade, Lisbon officials began to make greater concessions to discontented Brazilians during the 1790s. Imperial officials had instituted the derrama to collect the quinto. By 1791, they recognized that the per capita tax would not fulfill its intended design. Jorge de Abreu Castelo Branco contended that as a means of collecting the quinto, the derrama "satisfies little or nothing." The court looked for more practical and less incendiary ways to collect revenue from Brazilian production.[29]

The Portuguese authorities adopted a strategy that would appease the Brazilian population but leave intact the basic commercial relationship between the metropolis and the colony. First, they loosened some of the strictures on Brazilian commerce. The court allowed Brazilians greater freedom to trade with other Portuguese dominions by removing requirements to route cargoes through Portugal. The government also permitted limited trade with select foreign regions. Second, officials strove to rein in foreign contraband to boost revenue. The dual approach protected the imperial commercial nexus and responded to some of the demands of Brazilians all while dissociating liberalized trade from republican revolution.[30]

Reform

Portuguese officials liberalized intra-imperial trade on the assumption that prosperity in Brazil would reinvigorate imperial finances and deter rebellion. They aimed their efforts at the slave trade, allowing Brazilians greater autonomy in African commerce. The measures intensified a reimagination of the empire as an integrated unit in which the colonies and metropolis would enjoy the benefits of the imperial economy. As minister of overseas affairs, Rodrigo de Souza Coutinho hoped that if the court fostered the political unity of the empire, it could avoid the fate of other empires whose colonies "separated from the mother country." During the Inconfidência Mineira, discontented Brazilians had displayed a tendency to follow such a course unless the court reformed its political economy.[31]

Portuguese rulers subscribed to the theory that imperialism bred an intricate dependency between private wealth and state interest. According to such logic, merchant capitalists benefited from state enterprises and in turn contributed to public revenue. Officials reasoned that if Brazilian commerce flourished from a more open slave trade, the crown would benefit and the empire prosper. Portuguese officials hoped that "economic ideas," as the historian António Penalves Rocha has described, "would combat revolutionary ideas." Such notions countered U.S. narratives of free trade as the offspring of republicanism and imperial disintegration.[32]

Many Lusophone intellectuals and traders argued that if the Portuguese government relaxed intra-imperial commerce, it could increase colonial rents and generate greater revenue in Lisbon. They drew on free trade theorists from England, France, and Spain as they insisted that freer commerce would strengthen the empire rather than weaken it. José Joaquim da Cunha de Azeredo Coutinho argued in a widely read 1794 treatise that freer trade would generate more wealth in Brazil. With greater wealth, Brazilians would purchase more Portuguese manufactures. He insisted that wealth increased in proportion to labor and trade, not finite land and resources. He argued that if officials committed to a more robust colonial economy, they would benefit the entire empire. The government needed only to maximize the liberty of its subjects. In Lisbon, the Junta do Comércio supported his claims. It informed the court that if Brazilians could export produce to Africa in return for slaves, they could afford more manufactures from Lisbon. The board recommended, therefore, that the government remove restrictions on the Brazil-Africa trade.[33]

By the late 1790s, the Portuguese government gave greater heed to such calls. In 1796, Rodrigo de Souza Coutinho assumed the ministry of overseas affairs as an ardent student of political economy. As he pored over imperial finances, he felt convinced that the Portuguese commercial system must accommodate Brazilian elites because "reduced to itself," Portugal "would soon be a province of Spain." Deeply immersed in the theories of Adam Smith and French physiocrats, he liberalized the imperial economy to incentivize intra-imperial trade. He advocated the reduction or exemption of import duties on Portuguese wines, oil, steel, iron, and manufactures; a decrease in duties on slave importation; the abolition of monopoly contracts on salt and whaling; and a reduction of the tax on gold. Following Smith's lead, he believed that colonial trade would produce colonial wealth, and colonial wealth would benefit the colonies and the metropolis.[34]

Souza Coutinho aimed his reforms at the Africa-Brazil trade, for slavery provided a needed labor force, and the slave trade infused Brazil with merchant capital. In 1799, the minister ordered the Junta do Comércio in Angola to give Brazilian traders more leeway to export slaves so long as they did not reroute them to foreign empires. To the north of Angola, merchants in Gabon petitioned for the right to trade with Brazil free of metropolitan influence like their counterparts in Luanda. In 1801, after he received a petition from the eminent Rio de Janeiro merchant João Rodrigues Pereira de Almeida, Souza Coutinho granted Brazilian merchants unrestricted access to Angola.[35]

The minister also legitimized limited transimperial trade. For over a century, Brazilians had made contraband trade with Africa and the Río de la Plata region a pillar of their commerce as they imported slaves and re-exported them to Spanish America in return for silver. The trade ebbed and flowed during the eighteenth century, but it accelerated in the late 1790s as

Montevideo grew in importance as a Spanish-American port in the Río de la Plata. In 1805, the Portuguese government granted limited privileges for Brazilian and African merchants to trade directly with Spanish America to curtail foreign encroachment in the slave trade. The new policy allowed them to send slaves from Angola to the Río de la Plata and bring Spanish-American commodities back to Brazil.[36]

Lisbon authorities assumed that if Brazilians could compete well in the slave trade they could stave off non-Portuguese competition and generate imperial revenue. The Portuguese government allowed Brazilian traders to supplant metropolitan merchants in Angolan markets by permitting direct commerce between Brazil and Africa. Brazilians had long engaged in such trade with the cooperation of local officials, but they could now do so without the risks associated with smuggling.[37]

Portuguese officials viewed the liberalization of intra-imperial trade as an economic expediency rather than an ideological virtue. Unlike North Americans, they maintained their focus on the economic vitality of the empire, not on the right of individuals to trade with whom they pleased. Souza Coutinho subscribed to Enlightenment principles that cast mercantilism as destructive to empires. In his belief that free trade would strengthen the empire and monarchy, he inverted the U.S. paradigm that empire must give way to free trade. Even as it relaxed commercial restraints, the court rejected U.S. free trade dogma. Appeased by the reforms, Brazilian traders disregarded North American associations of republicanism with free trade. Colonists saw little need to revolutionize and overthrow the monarchy as the Portuguese imperial economy increasingly centered on Brazil.[38]

Brazilian traders and political economists tended to seek increased commercial sovereignty within the Portuguese Empire rather than independence and republicanism. Brazilians had used imperial channels to obtain the dissolution of the monopolies in Pernambuco and Grão Pará and Maranhão. Between the 1770s and 1790s, Brazil had not provided a strong source of revenue to the crown compared to other Portuguese dominions. Colonists circulated most of their income within the colony, so they felt more secure in their imperial trade nexus than North Americans had during the 1760s and 1770s. Brazilians assumed that a monarchy could grant greater commercial freedom as easily as a republic. By relaxing regulations further during the 1790s and early 1800s, the Portuguese government confirmed those suppositions.[39]

The commercial relaxation mollified Brazilian traders, but it did not solve the problem of the government's decreased revenue. Portuguese officials worried that they would cause further unrest among the population if they imposed additional tithes and taxes on colonial consumption. Instead, they tried to diminish interimperial contraband, which exposed the limits of their commitment to free trade.[40]

Brazilian traders maintained their desire to trade outside the Portuguese imperial nexus. Africa remained secondary to Europe for most Brazilian traders, notwithstanding the significance of the slave trade to the Brazilian and Atlantic economies. Brazilians demanded foreign textiles, manufactures, and cheap provisions. Of all the legal transatlantic voyages bound for Rio de Janeiro, ships from Africa comprised between one quarter and one half during the 1790s. Most others came from Portugal with domestic goods and re-exports from Great Britain, France, the Netherlands, and the United States. Indeed, Brazilians used African smuggling channels to acquire prohibited European goods in addition to slaves. Slave traders operated on extended, frail systems of credit. Many traders lacked the means to participate in risky ventures. Most of them lacked the capital to finance more than one to three voyages to Africa, so a handful of elite traders controlled much of human trafficking in Brazil. The court set the empire on a sounder financial base by liberalizing the African-Brazilian slave trade, but it did not quell the desires of many merchants to do business outside the imperial nexus. To that end, Brazilians counted on smuggling as a commercial mainstay into the nineteenth century. North Americans controlled much of the contraband trade, and Portuguese authorities worried that U.S. principles could yet creep into the Brazilian population.[41]

Habit of Smuggling

European monarchies grimaced at the connections among U.S. smuggling, free trade ideology, and republicanism. After the Portuguese court rebuffed U.S. attempts to gain access to Brazil in the 1780s, U.S. traders resorted to contraband trade with Brazilians. Traders around the Atlantic had tried to infiltrate Brazilian markets through smuggling since the early eighteenth century. In the minds of Portuguese officials, however, U.S. contraband posed a distinct threat because it represented ideologies of free trade and resistance to authority peculiar to republican government.[42]

United States free traders articulated a more homogenous definition of free trade than their colonial forebears. They relied on Smith's *Wealth of Nations* as they more frequently described free trade as the right to conduct foreign commerce without government prohibitions. While many assumed that governments would retain duties on imports, they believed that officials should reduce the taxes as much as possible and impose them on as few commodities as feasible. The Revolution had promoted a politico-economic ideology that celebrated contraband as an appropriate protest against unjust imperial policies.[43]

Contraband trade permeated the commercial culture of early U.S. commerce. In 1783, the Shelburne government introduced the American Intercourse bill to Parliament. The liberal Earl of Shelburne sought to allow U.S. produce the same privileges as British, accord the United States most-favored-nation status, and permit the importation of U.S. goods in U.S. vessels to the British West Indies. After conservative opposition scuttled the bill, many U.S. traders smuggled to compensate. By 1786, British officials felt such concern about U.S. smugglers that "nothing," according to one American's report, "can exceed the severity exercised towards every useful vessel suspected to be American, touching, or coming near any British port."[44]

Contraband was an open secret. In a 1788 address, Oliver Ellsworth of Connecticut sighed that North Americans looked upon contraband trade in "too favourable a light." In House debates on import duties, Fisher Ames of Massachusetts observed that North Americans had justified smuggling and resistance against "unjust or unpopular" British regulations and now would defy U.S. laws. He admitted that "the habit of smuggling pervades our country, we were taught it when it was considered rather as meritorious than criminal." An early history of the American Revolution reminded readers that "the universal voice of the people" favored acts of defiance.[45]

Throughout the 1790s, most North Americans maintained free trade and neutral rights as the principal objectives of U.S. foreign policy. For North Americans who favored free trade, contraband allowed traders to circumvent cumbersome trade laws and to contest European political economies. It represented the liberty inherent in republican free trade ideology and generated private wealth considered so essential to republican government. As the literary scholar Ayşe Çelikkol argues, whether friend or foe of open commerce, Anglo-Atlantic observers considered smugglers as little more than "underground practitioners of free trade."[46]

In the United States, free trade enthusiasts placed the onus on governments to prevent smuggling by removing trade restrictions rather than expect patriotic traders to obey state regulations. Fisher Ames argued in his 1789 House speech on imposts that even a small duty would lead to illicit trade which the government could not suppress. Why, he asked, pass a law "that is repugnant to the judgement, feelings, and interests of so large a proportion of the people" when such laws would inevitably result in contraband trade? Widespread contraband spoke greater ill of government laws than smugglers. As North Americans observed Brazil's expanding wealth, many of them traded illicitly in the country until independence and republicanism could open Brazilian ports to foreign commerce.[47]

Principles of Republicanism

Portuguese authorities wrung their hands at the loss of revenue occasioned by smuggling. In 1792, a Rio de Janeiro official complained of "the copious and continuous entrance of foreign ships" that unloaded contraband and left with gold dust. In 1790, Melo e Castro complained that by 1785 the expenses of colonial administration in Rio de Janeiro had outpaced revenue by 111,295,722 réis. Portuguese officials determined to remedy "this great evil" in part by quashing contraband.[48]

The overseas ministry intensified the battle against Atlantic contraband as gold output declined during the last quarter of the eighteenth century. In the middle of the decade, the Brazilian viceroy José Luís de Castro ordered the construction of patrol vessels to suppress illegal exports of gold dust, brazilwood, and slaves. The government also tried to ensure that customs officials followed all proper procedures to distinguish between vessels in distress and those that intended to smuggle. At his wits end by 1798, Luís de Castro informed Souza Coutinho that "even having put into practice all the [means] that have occurred to me" to stop contraband in brazilwood, the practice continued. Officials estimated that between 1798 and 1802 Rio de Janeiro customs lost 31,571,543 réis due to smuggling.[49]

While authorities in Lisbon liberalized the empire's political economy during the 1790s and early 1800s, they made clear they would not tolerate contraband and republicanism. Like other European governments during the Age of Revolution, the Portuguese court warmed to limited interimperial trade even as it battled foreign contraband. Jorge de Abreu Castelo Branco suggested in a 1791 report that the Portuguese government could compensate for the suspension of the derrama by reining in illicit commerce. In the diamond districts, colonial administrators expelled smugglers and burned their mining camps. Lisbon officials ordered "the most severe punishment" for smugglers who loaded goods onto foreign ships. By loosening regulations on Brazilian trade with Africa and parts of Spanish America, the court did not compromise with republicanism and contraband so much as it sought to fortify the monarchy and increase imperial revenue.[50]

Revolution erupted in France at the same time Portuguese rulers scrambled to stamp out the embers of republicanism in Brazil. Combined with the American Revolution and the Minas conspiracy, the French and Haitian revolutions put the Portuguese government on guard against republican principles. In 1791, the government arrested several people in Lisbon, including some Frenchmen, for "speaking," as reported by David Humphreys, "too freely in favour of the French Revolution." The following year, the Portuguese government dispatched six cutters to Brazil to constrain illicit trade which, according to one account, had "lately been very frequent there." About the same time, Brazilian officials arrested French officers who arrived in the northeastern Brazilian province of Pernambuco, "where they intended to disseminate their Republican principles throughout Brazil." In 1794, the Brazilian viceroy Conde de Resende ordered the investigation of a literary society he feared supported the French Revolution and subverted Portuguese authority. The government stood vigilant against republicans and smugglers as complementary forces that threatened the sovereignty of the crown.[51]

Even after the more liberal Souza Coutinho assumed power over Brazilian affairs in 1796, he maintained the government's commitment to thwart contraband and republicanism. The government smothered a 1798 conspiracy in Bahia in response to public manifestos that endorsed the motto of the French Revolution—Liberty, Equality, and Fraternity. In 1801, authorities suppressed an inchoate plot in Pernambuco (known as the Suassuna Conspiracy) to declare independence from Portugal and establish a republic. The leaders of the conspiracy, the Cavalcanti brothers (Francisco and Luís Francisco), had received their inspiration in part from Enlightenment discussions that emanated from academic centers such as the Seminary of Olinda.[52]

Bishop José Joaquim da Cunha de Azeredo Coutinho, a Brazilian-born proponent of freer imperial commerce, had established the seminary in

1800. While he studied at the University of Coimbra in the 1770s, Azeredo Coutinho became steeped in Enlightenment thought due to a more Enlightenment-friendly curriculum at the university during the Pombal era. He assumed the bishopric of Pernambuco in 1794 and traveled back to his native Brazil four years later. Although a proponent of liberal commercial policies, Azeredo Coutinho did not explicitly promote revolution. But he turned the seminary into a principal purveyor of Enlightenment ideology in Brazil. The bishop imbued his school with the pedagogical culture he had experienced during his time at the university. The government acquitted the Cavalcanti brothers and did not implicate the bishop in the Suassuna Conspiracy. But Lisbon officials recalled him to Portugal in February 1802 to serve as bishop of Miranda, after protracted conflicts with more conservative elements in Pernambuco. The government refused to tolerate republicanism or educational reforms that might promote it.[53]

Brazilian traders encouraged contraband in their ports in defiance of the central government's efforts to stifle illicit commerce. Many local officials demanded a role as intermediaries in the lucrative contraband trade in return for their acquiescence in the illicit commerce. In 1785, Melo e Castro had warned the Brazilian viceroy, Luís de Vasconcelos e Sousa, about the potential increase in contraband from the United States. He assumed that Brazilian markets would entice smugglers from the newly independent nation, and he feared that they would soon see U.S. ships "infest" Brazilian ports.[54]

By the end of the 1780s, his fears had materialized. Inácio Palyart, the U.S. agent for the Portuguese Douro Wine Company, suggested to the court that a Portuguese consul in the United States might provide added vigilance against U.S. smuggling. The government named Palyart as consul general and sent Cipriano Ribeiro Freire as Portuguese minister to the United States. Like Palyart, Freire recognized that U.S. contraband trade posed an acute problem to Portuguese mercantilism. The minister and consul tried to use "vigilance and severity" to diminish illegal U.S. trade to Brazil, but their resources remained limited and their efforts ineffectual.[55]

North Americans increased their illicit commerce with Brazil between 1800 and 1807 as warfare between Great Britain and France made trade with those empires more dangerous. Adjudicating an insurance claim on a cargo seized by the Brazilian government, one U.S. court observed that during that period "it was generally known, that by the laws of Portugal, all trade by *Americans* at *Rio de Janeiro* was prohibited, though vessels frequently cleared out for, and went to that port from the *United States*, where an illicit trade was carried on." United States law did not prohibit ships from sailing to ports restricted by foreign nations, so a large number of vessels "regularly cleared," as one account noted, U.S. customs houses.[56]

Most commonly, foreign ships arrived in Brazilian ports with captains claiming distress at sea. Imperial officials allowed them to dock for a short period (usually one to four weeks) to resupply and repair their ships. In the meantime, the crew loaded Brazilian goods surreptitiously onto their vessels. In 1800, the court also began to allow foreigners docked in distress to sell goods to pay for supplies. The policy gave smugglers additional cover. Between 1800 and 1807, officials in Brazil noted ninety-eight U.S. vessels that entered Brazilian ports in distress, an unusually high number compared to the twenty-four U.S. vessels recorded between 1792 and 1799 (Table 2).[57]

The Portuguese court seized only several such vessels for contraband, but presumably many more engaged in false pretexts that went undetected. Thomas Waine entered Brazilian ports in distress three times in five years. One time he claimed distress while he sailed for Buenos Aires to aid the British in their invasion of the Spanish viceroyalty of Río de la Plata. His frequent stops seem beyond coincidence considering his apparent willingness to defy imperial sovereignty to enhance his trade. Even when captains docked their vessels in legitimate distress, they used the opportunity to smuggle goods on board before they embarked. In February 1801, the commander of the Brazilian squadron of the Portuguese navy, Donald Campbell (from Scotland), worried about the "innumerable vessels that appear in these coasts under false pretexts to conduct contraband." He murmured about "the difficulty of discovering which are or are not the contrabandists." In 1801, a deputy of the Royal Treasury Board agonized that contraband trade with North Americans had decreased customs revenue to the "greatest excess."[58]

Portuguese officials worried that North Americans' ideological connection among free trade, republicanism, and independence would permeate the Brazilian population. In April 1801, Campbell described smuggling as "hostile to the harmony, and even to the existence of subordination." Smugglers favored private networks over the law, according to Campbell. They threatened the order and deference by which imperial states governed. North Americans acted as the principal perpetrators, "men that have the principles of republicanism firmly engraved in their hearts." Five months

Table 2. U.S. ports of origin/residence of owners of U.S. ships docking in Brazilian ports, 1792–1807

	1792	1793	1797	1798	1799	1800	1801	1802	1803	1804	1805	1806	1807	1792–1807
Nantucket	2	—	3	—	—	1	—	2	1	1	—	—	—	10
Boston	—	1	3	2	1	8	7	5	2	1	3	1	—	34
New York	—	2	—	1	—	—	1	3	—	—	1	3	—	11
Philadelphia	—	—	1	—	1	1	1	2	1	—	1	1	—	10
New Bedford	—	—	—	—	1	—	—	—	—	—	—	—	—	1
Providence	—	—	—	—	1	1	2	2	—	1	1	1	1	10
Rhode Island	—	—	—	—	1	1	2	2	—	1	1	1	1	10
Portsmouth	—	—	—	—	—	3	—	1	—	—	—	—	—	4
Cape Anne	—	—	—	—	—	—	—	—	1	—	—	—	—	1
Salem	—	—	—	—	—	—	—	—	1	—	—	—	—	1
New London	—	—	—	—	—	—	—	—	1	—	—	—	—	1
Norfolk	—	—	—	—	—	—	—	—	—	—	1	—	—	1
Charleston	—	—	—	—	—	—	—	—	—	—	1	—	—	1
Portland	—	—	—	—	—	—	—	—	—	—	2	1	—	3
Newport	—	—	—	—	—	—	—	—	—	—	—	4	—	4
Total	**2**	**3**	**7**	**3**	**4**	**14**	**12**	**16**	**7**	**5**	**11**	**13**	**1**	**98**

Source: Administração Central, CU.
Note: This table excludes ships of unknown U.S. ports of origin/residence of owners.

later, he warned that ideas of Brazilian independence had gained traction among the colonial population and some segments celebrated U.S. independence. He worried that U.S. smugglers imported "licentious liberty" in addition to contraband.[59]

United States smugglers represented a worrisome correlation between free trade and republicanism in Campbell's eyes. They threatened to upset the delicate balance of liberalizing Portuguese trade while protecting Brazil from contraband and republicanism. Faced with a revolutionary Atlantic and calls for greater colonial autonomy, imperial officials viewed the suppression of contraband and the suppression of republicanism as a joint objective.

In 1806 and 1807, Portuguese authorities escalated their aggression against smuggling. In April 1806 the governor of Bahia permitted the port's fortress to fire on any ship that set sail after sunset without permission granted after a final customs inspection of the vessel. Regardless, of the 120 recorded U.S. vessels that entered Brazil between 1792 and 1807, 20 percent docked in 1806. By February 1807, the crown still complained of the large amount of illicit trade conducted by vessels that docked under the pretext of distress at sea. The prince regent directed Brazilian officials to act more vigilantly and to punish smugglers with "great severity" to diminish the illicit trade "so calamitous to the legal commerce of my subjects and so harmful to my royal treasury."[60]

That same year, Napoleon's troops invaded Portugal and compelled Prince Regent Dom João to flee for Rio de Janeiro along with the entire court. Within months of his arrival, he declared Brazilian ports open to foreign commerce. Rather than introduce a republican paradigm into Brazil as North Americans anticipated, the court signaled its commitment to strengthen the monarchy through liberalized trade.

*   *   *

The Portuguese government viewed trade liberalization as an expedient, not a virtue. Officials refused to equate freer trade with republicanism. They tolerated more open commerce only insofar as it benefited government coffers. They condemned U.S. contraband and political ideologies.

Although Brazilians smuggled and pled for more open commerce, Portuguese reforms convinced many that their interests lay with the monarchy. By moving the court to Rio de Janeiro, the government reinforced that logic. Because Brazilians acquired enhanced privileges in the empire, imperial tensions did not reach the same pitch as in North America during the 1760s and 1770s. Due to the move of the royal family to Rio de Janeiro, the court and colonists imagined the Americas as the place where the monarchy would renew its strength and escape the decadence of the French Revolution.[61]

For North Americans with an interest in Brazilian commerce, the transfer signaled the first step toward an era of open trade among the Americas. Brazil became in effect an independent nation—still part of the Portuguese Empire, but no longer a colonial subordinate. United States traders viewed the transfer as a positive change, but they understood it as the first step of an incomplete process. They remained suspicious of monarchy and questioned the implications of an independent kingdom in the Americas. Drawing on their association between republicanism and the Western Hemisphere, many expected that the move would act as a harbinger for political revolution in Brazil. Instead, it inaugurated a reassessment of the Americas' relationship to republicanism and free trade.

Chapter 6

Opened Ports, Restricted Trade

United States traders viewed the relocation of the Portuguese court to Brazil as a positive development for U.S.–Luso-Atlantic commerce, but they worried that Brazil jeopardized the potentially profitable partnership by retaining a monarchy. In the United States, optimistic republicans believed American revolutions would free nations and commerce from monarchies and mercantilism. Since the 1790s, many North Americans believed with James Madison that "the spirit of republicanism will pervade a great part of Europe." Pierre Samuel du Pont de Nemours, an esteemed French exile who resided in the United States, assumed that Europe would follow the example set by the Americas and "turn to Republics" due to "the mistakes and the Wars of her Emperors and Kings."[1]

The House of Bragança inverted that paradigm by settling in Rio de Janeiro and introducing monarchy to the Americas. Portuguese rulers hoped the move would save the monarchy and revitalize the empire. To Brazilians who received the court, the Americas represented the reconstitution of monarchical power. Some North Americans worried that the relocation of the court would obstruct the march of republicanism and free trade in the Americas. After 1807, however, they quarreled more with their own republican government about free trade than with the Portuguese monarchy.[2]

The U.S. government imposed a general embargo on U.S. exports at the very moment the crown opened Brazilian ports to foreign commerce. President Thomas Jefferson hoped that if North Americans withheld U.S. commodities from Europe, they could compel Great Britain and France to respect U.S. neutrality. To the dismay of U.S. traders, their republican representatives impeded free trade with Brazil more than the Portuguese monarchy did. Due to the embargo, British traders enjoyed access to Brazil free of U.S. competition, and they acquired from Brazil many of the goods denied them by the embargo. Meanwhile, U.S.-Brazilian trade suffered.

North Americans jumped into Brazilian markets once the U.S. government lifted the embargo. By September 1810, Brazil accounted for 21 percent of the value of all U.S. exports to the Portuguese Empire and 14 percent of all U.S. exports to the West Indies and South America—a respectable share for a market legally opened within the previous year. After 1810, however, North American merchants turned their attention to the Iberian Peninsula as war-torn Portugal and Spain commanded high prices for U.S. produce. Portuguese and British forces secured Portugal against the French in 1808, and Lisbon became the most important supply port on the European continent until the end of the Napoleonic Wars. Provisions merchants in the United States profited as they sold breadstuff at high prices to British and Iberian armies that fought in Spain. In 1814, they abandoned Portuguese markets as prices plummeted after the war ended and Lisbon remained overstocked with provisions. Thereafter, they resumed their shift from Portugal to Brazil as the center of their Luso-Atlantic trade.[3]

In the face of the embargo and war, North Americans only postponed rather than abandoned the Brazilian trade. As a result of the rocky start to legal trade with Brazil, however, they confronted early challenges to their hope that independence from Europe would lead to fellow American republics that engaged in prosperous free trade. By relocating to Brazil, the court forced North Americans to question whether the Americas could guide the world to an era of free trade and republicanism. Worse still for republican free traders, U.S. officials seemed to betray liberal ideologies to garner respect from European powers—a betrayal magnified as the Portuguese monarchy liberalized imperial commerce. Rather than advance tidy national narratives, the revolutionary age exposed the difficulty of reconciling liberal ideologies with national expediencies.

Liberator of Commerce

As early as 1796, English merchants felt "much concern . . . respecting Portugal." They feared that their trade ally could make only a "feeble resistance" if Spain and France made an alliance. If the countries joined forces, French troops would possess a base from which to invade Portugal. Rodrigo de Souza Coutinho agreed. In 1803, he warned that the conflagration in

Europe threatened Portugal's neutrality and even its independence, for Napoleon would soon subsume smaller and weaker states on the continent. In case of such calamity, he reminded the crown that Portugal was "no longer the best and most essential part of the monarchy" and suggested that "its Sovereign and its People could still go and create a powerful Empire in Brazil." In his advice, the minister revealed the inverted power structure between Portugal and Brazil since the latter half of the eighteenth century. He also expounded a vision of the Americas as a place of monarchical renewal.[4]

Like North Americans, Portuguese officials had come to view Europe as corrupt. For the Portuguese, however, republicanism rather than monarchies had corrupted the continent. Portuguese rulers viewed the American and Haitian Revolutions with concern, but neither came so close to home as the French Revolution. It had unleashed its chaos in Europe, resulted in the Haitian Revolution that bode so ill for slaveholders in Brazil, inspired Brazilian republicans, and paved the path for Napoleon's conquests. Brazil provided a possible antidote for the monarchy's ills, a country of "public prosperity and tranquility," as Souza Coutinho imagined, where the crown could escape the corrosive influence of the French Revolution.[5]

Spain joined France in the war against Great Britain in December 1804. With the alliance, Portugal's situation grew more precarious. In November 1806, Napoleon instituted the Continental System—a prohibition against British commerce on the European continent. The emperor pressured European governments to cooperate under threat of invasion. Until 1807, the Portuguese government wavered on whether it would comply with Napoleon's demands. Portuguese officials demurred while they considered whether Britain or France posed the greater threat to their sovereignty and security. Meanwhile, Napoleon invaded Spain and placed his brother Joseph on the throne. With political control over Spain, the emperor grew impatient with Portugal's vacillation. He abandoned diplomacy and prepared to invade in late 1807.[6]

The British government encouraged the royal family to flee to Brazil. British diplomats reasoned that Portuguese rulers could direct the affairs of the empire beyond Napoleon's reach and maintain its sovereignty. Napoleon might occupy Lisbon, but he could not conquer the empire. After the peace of Amiens ended in 1803, William Pitt spent two years constructing a coalition to fight against French land forces. The Third Coalition disintegrated after the French drubbed its troops at the Battle of Austerlitz in

December 1805. With few allies on the continent, British officials felt increased pressure to maintain Portugal—with all of Brazil's resources—in its sphere of influence.[7]

As the Portuguese envoy to London, Domingos Antônio de Souza Coutinho finalized a negotiation by which the Royal Navy would escort the crown across the Atlantic on condition that the Portuguese government open Brazilian ports to foreign commerce. British negotiators extracted a promise of special trade advantages in return for British assistance. On November 29, the prince regent, Dom João, hastily embarked for Brazil with the rest of the royal family and between ten thousand and fifteen thousand members of the government—more than 5 percent of Lisbon's population. Before he left, he established a regency in Portugal and promised to return after peace.[8]

Souza Coutinho hailed the departure for Brazil as a return to Portuguese imperial roots rather than an ignominious response to French power. He saw it even as the fulfillment of a long-anticipated goal. As early as the mid-seventeenth century, the Jesuit priest António Vieira had suggested that the crown could better secure the empire against Spanish and Dutch aggression and exploit Brazil's resources if the court relocated to America. In the mid-1730s, the Portuguese diplomat Luís da Cunha "dreamily" hoped that Dom João V would move to Rio de Janeiro and assume the title of Emperor of the West. Da Cunha premised his opinion on the recognition of Portugal's increased dependence on Brazil and on the expectation that Rio de Janeiro "would soon become more opulent than Lisbon." Souza Coutinho harked back to such theorists, supposing that the court had not so much fled in exile as it had relocated to a more strategic imperial seat. The crown abolished distinctions between the metropolis and colonies with its relocation to Rio de Janeiro. It reified notions of Brazil as a constitutive part of a cohesive empire.[9]

The governor of the northeastern Brazilian province of Pernambuco, Caetano Pinto de Miranda Montenegro, described January 2, 1808 as "the most wretched day of my life." On that day, he received confirming reports that French troops had driven the court from Lisbon. Despite his concern for the court's tarnished honor, he felt "pleasure and happiness" to know that His Majesty would reside in Rio de Janeiro. He supposed that South America would provide "the surest asylum" from the "Cartesian Turmoil" and "devouring fire of so many Thrones, and Monarchies" that spread throughout Europe. He also hoped that the move would open "immense channels of incalculable riches."[10]

Figure 4. Departure of His R. H. the Prince Regent of Portugal, to Brazil, on 27 November 1807, by F. Bartolozzi. From Henry L'Evêque, *Campaigns of the British Army in Portugal* (London, 1812).

Other Brazilians anticipated the same positive effects. After Souza Coutinho crossed the Atlantic with the Portuguese court, he produced a manifesto that explained the benefits he believed would flow from the court's transfer. He assumed that the move would elevate Brazil's status above a colonial periphery to a co-kingdom with Portugal. If the monarchy did so, it could reconstitute its empire in a manner more favorable to all the crown's subjects, not just those in the metropolis. It could prove to the world that a monarchy could modernize and liberalize its commerce without sacrificing its power.[11]

Still, administrators in Brazil observed the move with some uncertainty. Miranda Montenegro created a list of questions that needed clarification. How should governors receive their clamorous English allies considering the centuries-old prohibition of foreign trade in Brazil? What goods would the court admit and at what duties? Would the court welcome vessels from other friendly nations, "principally from the United States?" In what light should governors view orders from the Overseas Council and other Lisbon-based bureaucracies?[12]

A few weeks later, the crown clarified some of those points in a *Carta Régia*, a decree that declared Brazilian ports open to "all, and any Goods, Produce, and Commodities transported" in foreign vessels that belonged to friendly nations. Although compelled by dire circumstances, the decision further validated the assumptions of many Brazilian officials and traders that monarchy and free trade did not stand in inherent opposition.[13]

One eminent Brazilian free trader, José da Silva Lisboa, applauded Dom João as the "liberator of commerce." Silva Lisboa had studied at the University of Coimbra before he received a royal appointment as a professor of philosophy in his birth province of Bahia, Brazil. He developed a reputation as a chief advocate of open markets while he served as a deputy and secretary to the Mesa de Inspecção da Agricultura e Comércio, or Board of Agriculture and Commerce. He fiercely defended the monarch's decision to open the ports, for he believed the policy would reinforce the strength of the empire. Counter to North American ideas about free trade, he assumed that open commerce would allow the monarchy to thrive in a new imperial order.[14]

Liberal Footing

United States merchants hoped for new trade advantages in Brazil. They had carried on a prolific illegal trade in that country before the Portuguese court opened its ports, but they could now enjoy the benefits of free trade without the risks that accompanied smuggling. England and the United States sent the first foreign ships to Pernambuco following the Carta Régia, just as Miranda Montenegro had expected.[15]

As U.S. consul in the Brazilian port of Salvador, Henry Hill applauded the Portuguese monarch's residency in Rio de Janeiro. In January 1807, Hill had married Lucy Munson Russel who gave birth to their first child ten months later—just before he departed for Brazil to accept his post. He expected profitable business opportunities in South America for his new family and for the United States. He pondered the potential of Brazil's new political dynamic to "give a strong impulse and a new direction to its commerce." He assumed that the U.S. government would not "remain idle and indifferent spectators of an event so extraordinary" as he eyed the move's possible benefits to the "interest and prosperity" of the United States. Hill viewed the opening of Brazilian ports as potentially momentous, but he believed that a prosperous trade depended on two preconditions.[16]

First, the United States needed to procure "a liberty of trade with the Brazils on a liberal footing." If U.S. traders obtained low duties and open navigation in Brazil, according to Hill, they could "greatly enrich and extend our commerce." With beneficial trade agreements, the United States could secure the second precondition for profitable commerce in Brazil— preventing a British monopoly on Brazilian markets.[17]

Hill conceded that "the precise nature of the policy and government" in Brazil remained uncertain. He doubted that it would diverge much from the "old and corrupt Monarchy" of Europe because Dom João carried across the Atlantic "all the prejudices and shackles of Royalty and the Catholic Religion." Still, he hoped that Dom João would liberalize imperial trade policy, since his subjects in Brazil clamored for freer trade. Further, Brazil's Spanish-American neighbors remained under colonial trade restrictions, and Hill believed the prince regent would recognize that liberal trade policies in Brazil would attract foreign commerce. British commercial strength would then remain the sole hindrance to U.S. interests in Brazil.[18]

Despite his general optimism, Hill feared correctly that the British had secured special trade advantages in return for helping the Portuguese court cross the Atlantic. He hoped, however, that because Dom João now resided "remote from, and not in a situation to be overawed and dictated to, by any European power," that he would assert Portuguese commercial independence from Britain. He assumed the prince regent would not turn

Brazilian commerce over to Britain, "having lost one kingdom by a similar course." He suggested that "instant overtures" from the United States could open a lucrative trade with Brazil and believed that Great Britain "could not compete with the United States" in the provisions trade.[19]

Hill opined that the United States should sign a commercial treaty with Brazil that allowed U.S. flour and wheat imports free of duty. United States commerce would then "pour in upon [Brazilians] those articles in a manner to increase their consumption, and sattisfy their wants," all to the profit of North American traders. Hill believed that the United States could supply higher-quality and cheaper breadstuff to Brazil than Brazilians could produce. Further, he assumed correctly that cotton, sugar, coffee, and indigo would continue to dominate Brazil's agricultural production.[20]

Prospects in Brazil depended on the upheaval and unrest that engulfed Europe, according to Hill. "In time of peace," he reasoned, Great Britain "would have an advantage over us perhaps, in those articles which consist of her own manufactures. . . . But under existing circumstances, on account of the war charges upon her commerce, we could carry her own manufactures to the Brazils and sell them cheaper than her merchants." He concluded confidently, "If we are suffered to enjoy a state of Neutrality and permitted a trade on an equal footing with the Brazils, Great Britain cannot compete with us in that market, in any respect whatever."[21]

Rio de Janeiro residents depended on foreign breadstuff, for they lacked a strong local source of wheat and flour. In 1803, the city imported 1,008,000 réis worth of flour and 299,439,000 réis worth of wheat from other Brazilian ports. Wheat and flour constituted roughly 17 percent of the total value of all goods imported into Rio de Janeiro from Brazilian ports. Wheat constituted the second-greatest commodity imported into Rio de Janeiro, just behind hides. The following year, Rio de Janeiro inhabitants received 21 percent of their wheat and flour from other Brazilian ports. Rio Grande de São Pedro (present-day Rio Grande do Sul) supplied Rio de Janeiro with most of its domestic grain imports. Rio Grande merchants sent 60 percent of their wheat exports to Rio de Janeiro between 1804 and 1807. Hill remarked that while Rio de Janeiro imported "plenty of wheat" from Rio Grande, the "flour is very bad" and expensive. He assumed that the ports of Salvador and Rio de Janeiro could support a combined import total of thirteen thousand barrels per year from the United States. He hoped that cheap, high-quality U.S. flour could supplant Brazilian domestic production and make the country reliant on imports from the United

States. Unfortunately for Hill, Brazilian ports opened at a most inauspicious time for U.S. merchants.[22]

The Embargo

Just one month before Brazil's ports opened to foreign commerce, Congress passed the Embargo Act, prohibiting exports to foreign nations. Since the early 1790s, Anglo-French warfare had imperiled U.S. commercial vessels in the Atlantic. United States authorities hoped that if the United States remained neutral, U.S. merchants could exploit the demand for provisions on both sides of the conflict. United States traders trumpeted the slogan "free ships, free goods" and insisted on their right to conduct a neutral carrying trade. Such commerce allowed them to carry non-contraband goods between the British and French West Indies and their respective empires.[23]

Until 1805, the British and French oscillated between encouragement and toleration of the neutral U.S. carrying trade. In 1805, however, British authorities lost patience with U.S. vessels that facilitated trade between France and its West Indies dominions. Merchants in the British West Indies complained to their government that they struggled to provide Europe with tropical goods because U.S. traders overstocked the continent with supplies from the French islands. The Royal Navy began to seize U.S. vessels that carried goods from the French West Indies if the crew could not prove a U.S. port as their final destination. The next year, Napoleon enforced his Continental System, prohibiting trade with Great Britain from any nation.[24]

Congress responded to such affronts to U.S. sovereignty with the Embargo Act in December 1807. The legislation forbade exports to foreign ports. The embargo's supporters hoped it would demonstrate the importance of U.S. commodities to European economies and compel respect for the republic's right to neutral commerce. The embargo lasted until March 1809. Washington replaced it with the Nonintercourse Act, which reopened trade with all nations except Great Britain and France. British traders exploited the intervening period to penetrate Brazilian markets ahead of U.S. merchants.[25]

Jefferson hoped that U.S. traders would sacrifice private interests for the "greater public object" of imposing the embargo. Instead, U.S. traders defied anew state restrictions on their commerce by smuggling. The president worried about the "sudden & rank growth of fraud & open opposition" to the embargo. The act stipulated that traders post a bond before their vessels left port to ensure that they would travel only to other U.S. destinations. But the act made an exception for "dangers of the sea." Crews sailed to ports in the West Indies, unloaded their goods, and returned to the United States. Upon return, they claimed that winds had blown them off course and that their cargoes would have spoiled if they had not sold the goods while in the Caribbean. Even more frequently, traders sent their goods through the interiors of Vermont and New York to Canada, from whence they could reach British markets. Due to the high rates of contraband trade near Canada, the clerk of Genesee County, New York complained to James Madison of "the facility with which the Embargo Laws are here evaded."[26]

Brazil did not offer such opportunities for contraband, so U.S.-Brazilian trade failed to benefit from U.S. smuggling during the embargo. Before 1808, U.S. authorities cared little if private merchants wanted to risk legal repercussions in Brazil for contraband; vessels that sailed there cleared U.S. customs without problem. But United States–Brazilian trade ceased during the embargo. Traders had found it easier to violate Portuguese trade policies than to contravene the laws of their own government. In the meantime, they lost ground to British commerce.[27]

The U.S. government demonstrated a remarkable ability to quash contraband despite the existence of select smuggling routes and the distress of U.S. officials over the evasion of the law. In 1808 and 1809, U.S. authorities enhanced the power of customs officials to enforce the embargo and suppress contraband. Great Britain provided the most convenient destination for U.S. contraband due to the ease with which smugglers routed goods through British Canada. But the Jefferson administration suppressed contraband destined even to British ports. British customs recorded over a 73 percent drop in imports from the United States during the imposition of the embargo. United States merchants did most of their smuggling to Great Britain during the first quarter of 1808, before U.S. customs authorities had received well-established procedures and parameters for enforcing the embargo. Thereafter, U.S. authorities more effectively stifled contraband. British traders saw their importation of U.S. goods decline steadily, from a value of £482,028 during the first quarter of 1808 to nearly zero by the final quarter.[28]

Jefferson ordered militias to suppress borderland smugglers, charged the navy to apprehend contraband, and gave officers the power of search and seizure without a warrant. Officials in Philadelphia seized sixty-three cargoes in 1808. One Boston court heard 150 cases related to violations against the embargo. For republicans committed to free trade and to smuggling where they could not trade freely, Jefferson's measures smacked of tyranny. Orators compared him to King George III. Mobs sang Revolutionary War songs to recall the spirit of rebellion against monarchy and commercial restrictions. Some discussed secession. Such detestation could hardly be expected from a populace able to smuggle at will. The U.S. government obliterated illusions of a unique republican commitment to free trade, and it more effectively suppressed U.S. traders' traditional means of resistance against commercial restrictions—smuggling.[29]

Republican representatives repressed open commerce with Brazil more than the Portuguese monarchy did—to the distress of U.S. free traders. Many North Americans saw clearly that the embargo would benefit British commerce in Brazil. In November 1808, Hill complained to Secretary of State James Madison that the British had already started to procure the upper hand. By October, sixty-nine English vessels had entered Rio de Janeiro "where the English wished for a monopoly" and brought nearly £4,000,000 sterling worth of goods. That year, at least thirty-three British vessels had arrived in the province of Bahia, but not a single U.S. ship. Indeed, the British statesman George Canning assumed Brazil would become "an emporium for British manufactures." By 1809, British traders had established over one hundred firms in Rio de Janeiro. Only several U.S. ships happened to embark prior to the embargo and land in Brazil immediately after Brazilian ports opened to foreign commerce.[30]

Opponents of the embargo worried that it would stymie the new opportunity to trade legally with Brazil. Edward St. Loe Livermore, a Massachusetts representative, complained that "the trade to Brazil (which it will be our own fault if we do not participate in) will be an immense acquisition." Unfortunately, according to Livermore, the embargo threatened legal commerce to Brazil before it could begin. A commentator who wrote as Multa Manent worried that the embargo would allow Brazil to take advantage of its new commercial freedom and usurp U.S. commerce "until they are upon an equal footing with us." Senators James Lloyd of Massachusetts and Samuel White of Delaware insisted that Britain would simply turn to Brazil and the West Indies to supplant U.S. tobacco and cotton.[31]

Livermore agreed with their assessments and assumed that the embargo would allow Brazil to replace the United States as providers of cotton to Great Britain. Philip B. Key of Maryland concurred. He assumed that "the

Brazils will assist to make up a sufficient quantity [of cotton] for consumption" in England. A Liverpool firm maintained that while the embargo diminished cotton imports generally in England, London increased cotton imports by thirty-seven thousand bags from 1807 to 1808. Most of them came from Brazil. A firm in Manchester informed their U.S. correspondents that in response to the U.S. prohibition they imported cottons from Brazil and would "make the Americans . . . pay for the embargo." Rather than facilitate the expected boon to U.S. trade, Brazil provided additional competition due to the U.S. restrictions.[32]

A Savannah merchant learned that "fortunate adventurers" from Britain sold Brazilian cotton and rice in England at almost 100 percent profit. The merchant's London correspondents wondered, "What is the Embargo for, but to throw the U States back 50 years, and divert all their trade to other channels?" They added gratuitously, "It is folly to talk of the freedom of the seas to a Country, who has nearly destroyed the navies of the world, and got almost all the remainder into her possession." North American free trade had died—slain by British might and a coup de grâce from the embargo.[33]

Henry Hill sent a report to Washington that confirmed the Londoners' claims. He complained that the English carried very little sugar or coffee back to Europe. They instead returned with goods that they could have otherwise received from the United States, such as rice, tallow, and cotton. The embargo operated, in his words, "in favor of the Brazils as respect cotton, tobacco, and rice." The consul confronted the irony that the embargo allowed the British to monopolize the very trade he hoped would liberate the United States from British commercial dominance. He could only hope that "the Embargo . . . will distress the Enemies of our Neutral rights & commerce, as much as it does myself."[34]

Hill bore the awkward responsibility to solicit liberal commercial policies from the Portuguese government at the same time the U.S. government placed a general restriction on foreign exports. He received instructions from the State Department to "give such explanations of the policy of the Embargo as to obviate any erroneous or unfavorable impressions which may be likely to result from that temporary restriction on the ordinary freedom of commerce." In his correspondence with the Portuguese court, he praised "the liberal system of the commercial laws of the United States" and at the same time admitted that "the ordinary free commerce" was "under a temporary suspension."[35]

After he had expressed interest in a South American revolution that would open Brazil's doors to U.S. commerce, Thomas Jefferson implemented the very embargo so detrimental to the Brazilian trade. The embargo marked one of the several instances in which Jefferson sacrificed philosophical idealism for governing expediency. Confronted with the realpolitik of the Atlantic world and the realities of constructing a state able to command respect on the foreign stage, he shed his commitment to principles of free trade and limited government. Those competing impulses created a disconnect between a state that had to deal with foreign nations and citizens who remained committed to supposedly natural, unrestricted foreign trade.[36]

United States trade to Brazil demonstrates the complexity of conforming early U.S. policy to national idealism. Facing the outrage of mobs and the subterfuge of smugglers during the embargo, U.S. officials discovered that revolutionary ideologies could endanger the new republic as easily as they could imperial governments. Conversely, U.S. free traders learned that a republic could repress freedom of commerce with greater ruthlessness than monarchies. United States officials maintained that the general embargo functioned as a temporary necessity to garner respect for the vulnerable republic in the midst of ravenous European monarchies. It betrayed, however, the hope that a republic could avoid the heavy-handed policies of monarchies as it asserted economic power in the Atlantic.

Since the 1790s, the Portuguese court had gradually liberalized its trade policies, countering correlations of free trade and republicanism. In the same moment that the Portuguese monarchy culminated that process by opening Brazilian ports to foreign nations, U.S. free traders witnessed their own republican government abandon the principles they supposed would liberate the Americas from European tyranny. Free traders in the United States suffered the disrespect accorded to republican governments by Atlantic monarchies without the benefits of republican free trade. While the Nonintercourse Act of 1809 reopened U.S. commerce to all regions that respected U.S. neutral rights, including Brazil, North Americans did not easily recover from the head start allowed to the British in South America. In 1810, the Virginia Congressman Thomas Newton lamented, "As to the flattering anticipations of commercial advantages with the new empire of Brazil, . . . they vanished like a dream."[37]

United States merchants made a strong push to enter the Brazilian trade after Congress lifted the embargo on friendly nations. Just one month after the embargo ended, several U.S. vessels reached Brazil. In the fiscal year 1808–1809, U.S. merchants sent Brazil 11 percent of all their exports to Portuguese dominions. The following year, they increased the value of their exports to Brazil by 82 percent, to $1,611,738—21 percent of all U.S. exports to the Portuguese Empire. Despite the initial jump, however, over the next several years U.S. merchants found trade with Brazil difficult and less profitable than trade with Portugal.[38]

War

By the end of August 1808, thirty thousand British troops had poured into Portugal to fight the French. Joined by Portuguese forces, they expelled the French invaders and carried their war of liberation into Spain. The troops required copious amounts of provisions. Over the next several years, mid-Atlantic exporters profited by feeding a large army on the peninsula. They sent most of their provisions through Lisbon after British and Portuguese troops liberated the city from French control. United States traders continued, therefore, to center their Luso-Atlantic commerce on Lisbon and Madeira rather than on Brazil due to British commercial dominance in Brazil and the demand for U.S. provisions in Iberia to feed British troops.[39]

Demand in Lisbon increased slowly at first. In 1808, Robert Waln's associates in Cádiz had informed him that a large army had gathered for Spain's defense against France, and it would greatly increase the demand for mid-Atlantic produce. As late as August 1809, however, Levi Hollingsworth complained, "Our exports are confined to Portugal & Spain & her Islands [and] their consumption is unequal to the supply this Country will give." With the Nonintercourse Act in force, U.S. merchants had to route shipments first through the Iberian Peninsula or Madeira if they hoped to send them to Great Britain. In 1809, Cádiz provided a more favorable exchange rate than Lisbon and became the preferred port of the two. The Spanish government paid premium prices for flour imports, drawing mid-Atlantic merchants' attention to Spanish ports. As warfare on the Iberian Peninsula escalated, however, Lisbon became the most important destination for U.S. produce. During the Napoleonic conflicts, therefore, the Portuguese Empire regained some of its centrality in North American trade networks.[40]

The Portuguese government opened Lisbon to flour imports in 1810 due to wartime exigencies. United States merchants sold provisions to British firms in Portugal, which then sold them to the British military. On both sides of the Atlantic, merchants took advantage of the new state of affairs in Lisbon. In April 1811, the Maryland merchants Robert and John Oliver informed their associates in Madeira, George and Robert Blackburn, & Co., that "almost all the Flour shipt from this Country is for account of the British Government." During that month, the Philadelphia firm sent 5,550 barrels of flour to Lisbon to feed British troops.[41]

In May 1810, John Bulkeley & Son informed Robert Waln that so long as Portugal had to "support such large Armies," prices would remain high and prospects in Lisbon bright. They relied "chiefly" on U.S. exporters for provisions. Portuguese currency gained favor on the London exchange as British commissaries borrowed enormous amounts of money to pay for the war. By November, John Bulkeley & Son informed Waln of "the very inviting state of our Market for the sale of Flour Grain & Provisions of all kinds." They explained, "The supplies required for our armies & the Inhabitants of this Capital are immense." They feared that if produce did not arrive soon, "the consequences must be serious," for residents already faced a scarce supply of bread on the peninsula.[42]

With provisions in high demand, the Portuguese government abandoned a health quarantine recently imposed on vessels from the United States. In 1806, officials had instituted the quarantine after they received word of a yellow fever outbreak in New York and Philadelphia. The government forced all vessels from the United States to lay in quarantine at least ten days, and those from Philadelphia and New York for twenty. By 1807, the Portuguese government had reduced the length to three and five days respectively, but it still interfered with U.S. interests in Portuguese ports. By 1810, Lisbon authorities considered the low supplies of provisions for British troops a greater threat than the spread of yellow fever and ceased the quarantine.[43]

United States traders took advantage of the extraordinary demand to charge high prices for their flour. In October 1810, Robert and John Oliver informed George and Robert Blackburn, & Co. of Madeira that flour ran at $9.50, which, "considering the price at Lisbon, can be no object at Madeira." By March 1811, flour sold for between 13,000 and 13,400 réis (roughly $16 to $18) per barrel in Lisbon. In May, Mark Pringle opined to James Ullman that a "cargo of corn and Flour, for Lisbon, would pay a

Figure 5. The Battle of Bussaco [Buçaco], by N. Schioronotti. This engraving depicts fighting between French and British forces in Portugal. From Henry L'Evêque, *Campaigns of the British Army in Portugal* (London, 1812).

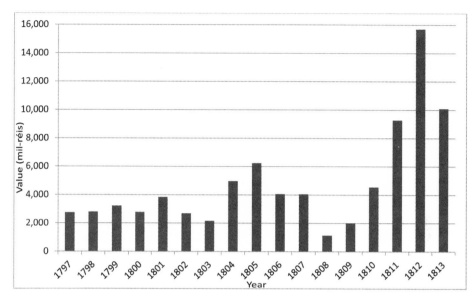

Figure 6. Value (mil-réis) of foreign wheat sold at the public warehouse of Lisbon, 1797–1813. Source: "Mappa dos Trigos Estrangeiros que se venderão no Terreiro Publico de Lisboa desde o anno de 1797 athé 1812," BNRJ.

good freight without risk. I know not a better voyage." Through 1812, foreign wheat poured into Lisbon (Figure 6). By the onset of the War of 1812, Portugal acted as the major Iberian importer of U.S. goods. It eclipsed Spain in 1810–1811 (Figure 7).[44]

By September, flour prices remained strong in Portugal at $15.50 per barrel, even in the face of increased imports. In January 1812, Portuguese demand pushed prices in the United States to nearly $10 per barrel. By the fall, specie left Portugal in droves as Portuguese speculators paid for U.S. provisions in precious metal.[45]

The Royal Navy continued to permit U.S. shipments to Spain and Portugal even after the United States declared war on Great Britain in 1812, in "consideration of the great importance of continuing a regular supply of flour and other dried provisions" to allied armies. The British government granted licenses to protect U.S. vessels that sailed for Spain and Portugal from capture by British warships. Forgers in the United States took advantage of the high demand for such licenses and made quick profits by counterfeiting them. With their trade to the Iberian Peninsula protected, U.S.

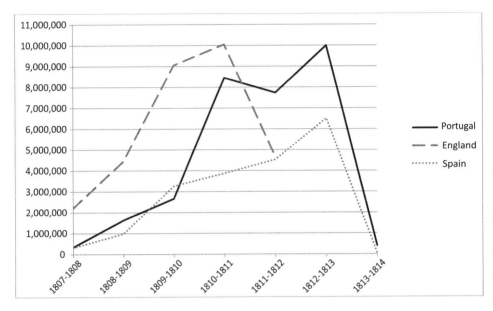

Figure 7. Value ($) of U.S. domestic goods exported to Portugal, England, and Spain, 1807–1814. Source: *ASP:CN*, 1:738, 815, 869, 892, 965, 994, 1023.

merchants exported a higher value of goods to Portugal than to anywhere in Europe after the conflict with Great Britain suspended exports to England (Figure 7).[46]

United States merchants also increased their trade with Madeira after British troops occupied the island in 1807 to protect the important port of call from French invasion. British forces remained there until 1814, and they stretched an already thin supply of breadstuff on the island. In 1806, U.S. merchants had exported $519,213 worth of domestic goods to Madeira. In 1809, they exported $2,336,656.[47]

Between 1809 and 1813, U.S. traders sent nearly double the amount of exports to the Portuguese Empire than in the previous eighteen years combined due to the drastically improved markets in Portugal and Madeira (Figure 8). Between November 1797 and March 1802, only 43 Philadelphia merchants sent goods to ports in Portugal or the Portuguese Atlantic islands. Only 9 sent multiple shipments during that period, and only 2 sent more than three. In 1811, by contrast, 245 merchants shipped goods to the same markets. Sixty-two sent multiple shipments, and 16 made four shipments or more.[48]

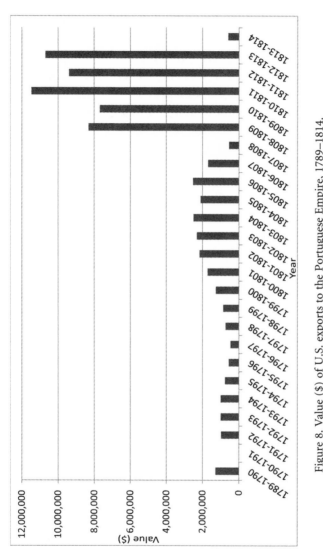

Figure 8. Value ($) of U.S. exports to the Portuguese Empire, 1789–1814.
Source: *ASP:CN*, 1:34, 138, 248, 294, 312, 342, 362, 384, 417, 431, 453, 489, 507, 543, 591, 671, 696, 721, 738, 815, 869, 892, 965, 994, 1023.

North Americans began to import Merino sheep from Portugal in addition to the traditional imports of wine, fruit, and salt. The breed originated in Spain and produced superior wool. Hostilities with Britain had stalled wool imports into the United States. United States merchants took advantage of the resurgent trade with Portugal to acquire high-quality wool and develop a domestic industry. The convulsions in Spain interrupted strict customs enforcement, which facilitated the export of sheep from the Iberian Peninsula. Originally introduced into the United States in 1801, Merino sheep grew in demand as the embargo and nonimportation popularized the manufacture of domestic woolen goods.[49]

The Spanish Junta of Estremadura needed money to support their resistance against the French occupation of Spain, so officials confiscated Merino sheep in the region and began to sell them for foreign export. Merchants in Portugal brought flocks to Lisbon and Porto to ship around the Atlantic, and the Merino trade soared. In 1809, Lisbon merchants exported 29,415 arrobas of Merino wool to foreign ports. The following year, they more than doubled that number to 74,249.5 arrobas. Traders such as José de Cruz da Asenção, William Jarvis, and Nicholas and Daniel Gilman supplied U.S. importers with the impressive breed. In 1811, the pseudonymous Whig observed, "We are indebted to the revolution in Spain, for the Merino Sheep, so fortunately imported into this country."[50]

Writing as R. S. in the *Liverpool Mercury*, one British commentator worried that heightened Merino exports could free the United States from dependence on British woolen textiles. R. S. assumed the United States eventually would catch up to the manufacturing capability of England. The writer fretted that U.S. traders had imported more than six thousand sheep and that clothing manufactured from the wool "was quite equal to our best west country cloths." Indeed, as early as 1809, Merino wool had become such a symbol of U.S. economic independence that James Madison flaunted a U.S.-manufactured suit "made of the wool of Merinos raised in this country" at his inauguration—to the praise of the press.[51]

United States merchants ameliorated their dependence on British finance by importing Merino sheep from Portugal and increasing exports to the Portuguese Empire. Still, London capital remained an intricate part of the commercial networks. London firms such as George and Robert Blackburn, Bainbridge & Brown, and Baring Brothers & Co. financed trade. But U.S. merchants improved their position vis-à-vis their British associates by expanding U.S. exports to Lisbon on British accounts.[52]

In a December 1811 petition to Congress, Philadelphia merchants claimed that due to "the increase of capital in this country, a material change . . . has taken place in the business of importing goods." Formerly, U.S. importers amassed debts by importing commodities on credit, "chiefly on that of Great Britain." By the end of 1811, however, U.S. merchants had liquidated the debt and paid in advance for approximately one-third of British manufactures. In November, Madison had renewed nonintercourse measures against Great Britain. His decision terminated a six-month relaxation of the embargo. The Philadelphia petitioners requested that Congress delay the reimposition of nonintercourse until U.S. merchants received all the manufactures they had paid for in advance.[53]

Several months later, Baltimore merchants petitioned Congress for a repeal of the Nonintercourse Act. They claimed that British firms owed U.S. exporters more than $100 million. *Niles' Weekly Register* maintained, "The mighty aggregate has been chiefly formed by the great shipments to Spain and Portugal; where the British gather up and send home the chief part of the specie, and make payments in paper." British merchants remitted paper currency at discounted rates for U.S. goods shipped on their accounts to Lisbon. Such payments deprived North Americans of remittances equal to the face value of their exports. The Baltimore petitioners hoped they could solve the problem by importing British manufactures in lieu of paper currency.[54]

The petitions indicated U.S. merchants' improved balance of trade with Great Britain. During the Napoleonic Wars, contrary to Henry Hill's expectations, U.S. merchants had improved the balance of trade as a result of commerce with Portugal, not Brazil. The petitioners worried that the trade restrictions imposed by the U.S. government threatened their commerce more than European monarchies. Such realities exposed flaws in the assumptions of many North Americans about free trade among independent republics in the Americas.

Declines

By October 1812, Portuguese markets finally showed signs of a glut. John Bulkeley & Son informed Robert Waln and others that the high number of vessels that arrived from the United States had reduced the price of flour. They predicted it would go lower still if shipments continued to arrive. The following February, Robert and John Oliver assumed that the "immense quantities of Provisions" headed to Lisbon and Cádiz would reduce the price. Beginning in that year, U.S. merchants lost their enthusiasm for Portuguese markets.[55]

After Napoleon's Peninsular War ended in 1814, European merchants ceased demand for U.S. provisions in Portugal and Spain. With the demobilization of armies, U.S. merchants took little interest in Portugal. After the Napoleonic Wars and the War of 1812 concluded in 1815, the Portuguese government raised duties on foreign wheat and flour. The court worried that foreign imports had ruined domestic output and hoped to revitalize grain production in the Portuguese economy. One report noted that higher duties "will be the means of conciliating the interests of the kingdom, in the miserable state in which it stands at this point." At the outset of 1815, the Lisbon firm of Brown, Reid, & Co. offered their services to Baltimore merchants, Robert and John Oliver. The Baltimore firm thanked the Lisbon house for their "good intentions" but responded that the "state of our respective markets will not justify any shipments from this country."[56]

With the end of the war, the British government had no need to offer safe passage to U.S. vessels that sailed to the Iberian Peninsula. North American commerce again lay vulnerable to attack by enemy naval forces. In 1813–1814, U.S. merchants exported the lowest value of goods to the Portuguese Empire since the embargo of 1807 (Figure 7). Between 1809 and 1812, they had enjoyed the benefits of neutrality as they threw provisions into the Iberian Peninsula with abandon. The period represented, nevertheless, a short-lived exception to the trajectory of declining trade with Portugal after U. S. independence.

The Madeira market also declined as U.S. consumers shifted their tastes to Spanish and French wines. In the midst of the War of 1812, Madeira wine fell to less than 1 percent of all wines imported into the United States and rose to just 13 percent after the war. Even while Madeira remained a strong destination for mid-Atlantic exports during the Napoleonic Wars, the island's wine did not sell well in the United States. In 1810, Robert and John Oliver began to phase out their Madeira imports. In October, they complained to the Madeira house of George and Robert Blackburn, & Co., "It is always difficult to sell Madeira Wine in this place." They suggested the firm not send any more on their own account. The Blackburns sent another shipment of twenty-five pipes the next year, but the Olivers informed them that they foresaw "no opportunity of being able to sell it at present." The previous April, they refused to open business engagements with Scott & Co. of Madeira due to their desire to "curtail our mercantile operations."[57]

In 1813, the Olivers failed to procure a license to ship foodstuff to Madeira, further sundering their business connection to the island. They suggested that the Blackburns receive their wheat and flour from the surplus in Lisbon and Cádiz. Thereafter, the War of 1812 severed communication between the associates until April 1815, when they reopened trade with one another. By March of the following year, however, the Baltimore firm believed that the "state of our respective markets will not justify shipments from either side." Between 1809 and 1813, nearly twenty-three vessels sailed from Philadelphia to Madeira each year. Over the next five years, the annual average dropped to eight. After 1813, U.S. merchants gradually abandoned what remained of their Madeira trade networks.[58]

Prospects appeared little better in Brazil. In 1810, the British government secured a treaty with Portugal that gave Great Britain special advantages in Brazilian commerce. The treaty established trade between the two powers and their dominions on a most-favored-nation basis and gave special legal advantages to British subjects who lived within the dominions of the Portuguese Empire. It permitted the election of local judges-conservator in Brazil chosen by British subjects within their jurisdiction. The Portuguese government also allowed British imports into all Portuguese dominions for a lowered duty of 15 percent. The liberal terms expanded Great Britain's favorable position in Luso-Atlantic commerce. The treaty benefited British merchants to the almost total exclusion of Brazilians from non-Portuguese trade with Europe. Because of the advantages derived from the treaty, British exporters sent cheap manufactures to Brazil that Brazilians used to trade for slaves in Africa. The treaty, therefore, led Brazilians to favor British trade because it allowed them to purchase captives in a way U.S. trade could not.[59]

Disadvantaged by warfare and the Anglo-Portuguese treaty, U.S. merchants struggled to compete in Brazil. During the fiscal year 1808–1809, they sent Brazil 10.6 percent of all exports to the Portuguese Empire. The next year, the percentage doubled to nearly 21 but dropped drastically after 1810. In 1810–1811, it fell to just under 15 percent. In 1811–1812 it nearly halved, to under 8 percent, and by 1812–1813 it fell to less than 1.5 percent. United States merchants saw the value of their domestic exports to Brazil plummet from $721,899 in 1809–1810 to $137,821 in 1812–1813.[60]

During the War of 1812, U.S. merchants nearly halted shipments to Brazil, for the British government only permitted ships that sailed to Portugal and Spain to pass through their blockades. In March 1812, Henry Hill sent a cargo from Salvador to Philadelphia, consigned to his agent, Thomas Reilly. Hill recognized the potential for war with Great Britain and instructed Reilly not to send back a return cargo if violence erupted. Instead, he insisted that the agent disburse the proceeds from the original shipment. Without assurances of protected commerce, U.S. traders fared poorly in their business with Brazil during the war. Their failures countered assumptions that Brazil would become the jewel of U.S. trade with the Portuguese Empire. By the end of the War of 1812, they again found their Luso-Atlantic commerce in tatters, Brazil among the rest.[61]

*   *   *

Between 1808 and 1815, U.S. merchants became embroiled in conflicts that revealed the flaws in their expectations that American political independence would lead to a hemispheric order of republicanism, free trade, and economic independence. A European-born monarch resided in the Americas. North Americans failed to secure economic hegemony against Great Britain in Brazil. They increased their economic autonomy from Great Britain due to trade with Portugal rather than Brazil. Most disheartening for them, their own republican government restricted trade by instituting embargoes and nonintercourse measures that weakened traders' ability to compete against British commercial might in the Atlantic. Between 1809 and 1812, U.S. goods flooded into Portugal, but the spike constituted a fleeting exception to the decline that began with the American Revolution. United States traders sustained the trade only by upheaval, political turmoil, and war. With peace, they again abandoned Portuguese and Atlantic island markets. The Brazil trade suffered during the wars, but peace in Europe promised new opportunities in South America.

After the Napoleonic Wars and the War of 1812, North Americans hoped to witness the fruition of their ideal paradigm of American political and economic independence. Although governed by a monarch, Brazil had opened its markets and legitimized U.S.-Brazilian commercial networks. While the Napoleonic Wars diverted trade from Brazil back to Portugal, they also created a new opportunity in South America by driving the Portuguese court to Rio de Janeiro. Britain had flexed its commercial muscle in Brazil, but perhaps Brazil could yet integrate into an American system of republicanism and free trade. Between 1809 and 1815, U.S. observers delayed rather than abandoned that vision. Despite the tentative commencement of U.S.-Brazilian trade, North Americans increased their commerce with Brazil until it became the center of the U.S.–Luso-Atlantic trade nexus by the end of the 1810s. Between 1816 and 1822, U.S. merchants made that shift as revolutionary fervor spread from Spanish America to Brazil. In the midst of such fervor, many North Americans reanimated their hope that Brazil would eventually constitute an independent republic that favored U.S. commerce.

PART IV

"Connexions of Commerce and Liberation"

WITH THE MOVE OF THE Portuguese court to Rio de Janeiro, Brazil became an independent kingdom within the empire. Dom João made the change official with a decree in 1815. Many North Americans felt ambivalent toward the presence of a European monarchy in the Americas. They had hoped that the Portuguese government would give the United States preference over European (particularly British) traders. After 1816, however, many U.S. free traders remained convinced that the Portuguese government would retain high duties and privilege British trade over American. They welcomed unfolding revolutions in the south and northeast of Brazil that they supposed would liberate the country from monarchy.[1]

United States traders anticipated the revolutionary events as an opportunity to secure republican trade partners in the country. They shipped munitions and supplies to revolutionary regions, outfitted privateers to prey on Portuguese vessels, and welcomed Brazilian political refugees into the United States. Their actions frequently defied U.S. neutrality laws and Portuguese sovereignty. They hoped that in return Brazilian republicans would favor American commerce over European. Between 1816 and 1825, the year the U.S. government recognized Brazilian independence, U.S. traders made Brazil their most important commercial partner in the Luso-Atlantic.

Faced with defiance from their citizenries, the U.S. and Portuguese governments sought to secure sovereignty over the commerce and transnational interactions of their people. The U.S. government passed laws that more strictly regulated movement in and out of the nation's borders. Officials also brought the weight of the courts to bear on citizens who violated neutrality laws. In the late 1810s and early 1820s, U.S. administrators consolidated the power of the state to rein in unruly elements. In contrast, the Portuguese monarchy confronted revolutions in Portugal and Brazil that weakened and ultimately fractured the empire when Brazilians declared independence in 1822.

After Brazil's independence, U.S. free traders hoped that Brazilians would follow the pattern of the United States and Spanish-American revolutionaries by establishing a republican government open to inter-American free trade. They retained their hope that if American republics traded freely with one another they could supplant the British in South

American commerce. Such hopes ended ambivalently as Brazil maintained a monarchical system of government and continued to favor British commerce. In 1824, the Brazilian monarchy quashed a new republican insurgency in Pernambuco. North Americans had to settle for trade with an independent Brazilian monarchy in an inferior role to the British. As the Age of Revolution faded, U.S.-Brazilian trade exposed the chimera of the North American syllogism that linked independence, republicanism, free trade, and prosperity. To grapple with their failed assumptions, many North Americans promulgated racialized explanations about Brazilians' failure to establish and maintain a republic.

Chapter 7

Patriots of Pernambuco

In November 1810, Henry Hill sent a report to Mariano Moreno, an official of the Primera Junta in Buenos Aires. Observing the nascent revolutions in Spanish America, he believed that the Americas could remain independent and united against European dominance only if bound together by "an alliance of interest, and connexions of commerce and Liberation." He proposed, therefore, a commercial alliance among the Americas by which they would enjoy most-favored-nation status with one another. Hill believed that republicanism would facilitate such a liberal economic policy and enhance prosperity. In time, he supposed, the Americans could induce European nations to liberalize their trade. He expected that such a course could put the "commerce of the whole world on the same free, uniform, and liberal footing," without disturbance from the "selfish genius of Monopoly and unprincipled commerce."[1]

Envisioning such a sublime world economic order, Hill hoped that the Portuguese government in Rio de Janeiro would not interfere with the spread of republicanism in South America. He supposed that if Americans could compel the monarchy to liberalize its commerce, its system of government would not impede the progression of his proposed cooperative system. He worried, however, that the Portuguese government retained a monarchical inclination toward trade regulations.[2]

The previous year, he had informed Thomas Sumpter, the new U.S. minister in Rio de Janeiro, that the court had already reverted to mercantilist economic policies. In May 1808, for example, the crown established a royal manufactory of gunpowder at Rio de Janeiro to act as the sole purchaser of saltpeter and sole distributor of gunpowder. Hill believed that such actions revealed "how difficult it is wholly to separate Monopoly from Monarchy."[3]

To reinforce his point, he listed additional infractions on free commerce imposed by the court following the Carta Régia of January 1808. He took principal issue with a June 1808 decree that granted Portuguese ships and cargoes favorable duties, whereas the January Carta Régia had made no such distinction. The Portuguese government also retained export restrictions on brazilwood, diamonds, wine, oil, and aguardente. Hill concluded that while the Portuguese government in Rio de Janeiro manifested a more "enlightened & liberal" policy than formerly, "there are many and serious evils, political as well as moral still existing, to militate against the interests of this Country & prevent it from reaping the benefit which might otherwise be expected from its commercial Laws." By Hill's logic, so long as the Portuguese Empire maintained its monarchical system of government, Brazil could never reach its full trade potential. He hoped that a "radical change in the whole political and Judicial system" would cure such evils.[4]

In 1817, republican insurgents promised that very possibility in the northeastern Brazilian province of Pernambuco. In their quest to secure republican trade partners in Brazil, U.S. merchants challenged the authority of both the U.S. and Portuguese states by cooperating with Brazilian revolutionaries. Many hoped Pernambuco would introduce a new political order in Brazil and turn its commerce over to republican governments aligned with the United States. They viewed the revolt as the commencement of Brazil's future as a fellow republic and reliable trade partner. By the middle of the year, they watched their hopes for Brazil thwarted once again as the Portuguese monarchy blockaded Recife—Pernambuco's principal port—and quashed the rebellion. If North Americans saw in Pernambuco the promise of Brazilian commerce and republicanism, they also witnessed the fragility of that promise.

"Live, Pernambuco!"

Prior to 1808, inhabitants in provinces distant from Rio de Janeiro interacted minimally with the colonial capital. In 1815, the crown elevated Brazil to the status of a kingdom, making it equal to Portugal in terms of political sovereignty. The court appointed officers to new administrative positions accountable directly to Rio de Janeiro to join the provinces into a more cohesive kingdom. At the same time, the government sought to transform a large colonial city into an imperial capital. It collected taxes to initiate expensive building and art projects. In the peripheral regions of Brazil, residents saw their earnings siphoned away to pay for projects for which they received no immediate benefit. As one English traveler declared, "A tax is paid at Pernambuco for lighting the streets of the Rio de Janeiro, whilst those of Recife remain in total darkness."[5]

Economic challenges deepened Pernambucans' resentment of the imperial court. In 1816, Pernambucans had suffered through a severe drought that decreased production of cotton and sugar. They also smarted as high export duties on those commodities frustrated economic growth in the region. Locals chafed at the taxes that flowed to Rio de Janeiro to support the opulent court. Native Pernambucans remained deeply indebted to the Pombaline monopoly companies decades after the expiration of their charters. Resentful of the intermediacy of Lisbon merchants in the agricultural trade, they maintained their long-held distrust of monopoly companies and the monarchy that supported them.[6]

On March 6, 1817, Pernambucans rebelled against the provincial government of Caetano Pinto de Miranda Montenegro. A member of the military assassinated his commanding officer, and rebellious troops mutinied. Civilian rebels joined the troops, and together they forced Miranda Montenegro to retreat to a fortress and compelled him to surrender the following day. They allowed him to depart for Rio de Janeiro two days later. The revolutionaries instituted a provisional government and council of state to establish an autonomous republic. The revolt received support from Brazilian military officers, sugar planters, small farmers, artisans, and intellectuals. To the dismay of planter elites, slaves also joined the revolt, hoping to secure their freedom as part of a new order. Following Pernambuco's lead, inhabitants rose up in the nearby provinces of Alagoas, Ceará, Paraíba, and Rio Grande do Norte.[7]

Intellectuals justified their cause with rhetoric that associated republicanism with liberty and the protection of property. Many of the clerics who supported the revolution had received their training in Azeredo Coutinho's Enlightenment-friendly seminary in Olinda. Such revolutionaries departed from past Brazilian assumptions that a monarchy could protect property as well as a republic could. Provisional leaders proclaimed that the revolution would liberate the inhabitants from "the weight of enormous tributes." They promised that the country "will rise to that point of grandeur to which it is entitled, and you will gather the fruit of your work, and of the zeal of your countrymen. . . . A rich nation is always a powerful one." The proclamation revealed an imagined link among liberty, republicanism, and wealth—both national and individual. United States newspapers translated and reprinted the proclamation. Like North American liberals, Pernambucan revolutionaries believed that republicanism, natural rights, and private prosperity advanced in harmony.[8]

Pernambucans imagined ideological connections to North America. Padre João Ribeiro noted that the revolution needed "its Franklin," and observers called José Pereira Caldas, a prominent official in the provisional government, the Franklin of Brazil. Another counselor in the provisional government, José Maria de Vasconcelos Bourbon, took to signing his name as "Wasthon [Washington]." A visitor from New York observed, "Like the revolutions that so often take place in our own country, the *ins* went *out*, and the *outs* went *in*, to the great joy of the majority." He reported with satisfaction that Domingos José Martins led the provisional government and "is (as well as all the natives of the country,) very partial to the Americans." Pernambucan emissaries stoked such sympathy by contracting with U.S. newspapers to print favorable news about the revolt. As one revolutionary saw it, "The two Americas English and Brazilian are hand-in-hand, nothing can stand against us."[9]

Enemies of the revolution agreed with the New Yorker's assessment. Brazilian loyalists spurned revolutionaries as "Imitators of English America." The governor of Bahia complained that the "government of the United States of America has given many proofs of shrewdness before the world all of which may permit suspicion that it shall protect the vilest crimes perpetrated by a half-dozen outlaws." The insurrection resulted from internal grievances of diminished provincial autonomy and unpopular taxes, but revolutionaries framed their moral arguments with Enlightenment rhetoric in the North American style.[10]

By the early nineteenth century, many U.S. observers felt alienated as the lone republic in a world of monarchies. They welcomed the outbreak of republican fervor that they believed they witnessed in South America. Sympathizers of South American republicanism received word of the Pernambucan uprising with delight. They repeated word from Pernambucan informants that the province would take the U.S. government "for their model." One correspondent assured a Baltimore commercial firm that "the Americans are hailed as brothers." The *National Advocate* drew a parallel among the revolutions in "Mexico, Buenos Ayres, Chili and Pernambuco, united by a common interest, and governed by mild and tolerant laws, encouraging education, industry and morality, any attempt to bring them again under the yoke must fail."[11]

North Americans sung hymns to their new fellow republic. The *Aeolian Harp* included a selection of "the most popular songs" of the time, including "The New Republic."

"Live, Pernambuco!" be the voice
That echoes o'er Columbia's plains;
"Live, Pernambuco!" we rejoice
That thou hast burst thy tyrant's chains.

Hail, Pernambuco! ever hail!
Columbia hails thee, sister brave,
She sends thee health upon the gale,
Her greeting on the Western wave.[12]

To North Americans, Pernambucan revolutionaries validated the assumption that republicanism would govern the Americas. Although the Portuguese court elevated Brazil to a kingdom and opened its ports, many U.S. observers assumed the country's progress remained incomplete without the transition to a more liberal political system. In 1820, Moses Ray, a merchant of Philadelphia, reflected on events in Pernambuco and insisted that "we earnestly wish to see all Countries not only perfectly free, but independent of Kings & Monarchs—but governed in that plain, simple manner which must always be congenial to the sentiments and feelings of our Republican character." Pernambucans promised to bring the process to fruition. From there, U.S. traders could finally grasp prosperous commerce in northeastern Brazil.[13]

Liberty and Commerce

For more than a century, Pernambuco had served as one of the most important ports of the Portuguese Empire. By 1816, it exported nearly the same value of goods to Portugal as did the empire's Asian dominions combined. Of the major Brazilian ports, only Bahia surpassed it in terms of the value of goods exported to Portugal at the time of the revolt. During the Pernambucan drought of 1816, streams dried up and left mills inoperable.

Unable to grind wheat and other grains in northeastern Brazil, Pernambu-cans increased their importation of U.S. mid-Atlantic flour. Pernambuco already outpaced Faial and Porto as a destination for Philadelphia pro-visions.[14]

After the War of 1812, Pernambuco was the first Brazilian port to enjoy a revival of commerce with Philadelphia. In 1813 and 1814, Philadelphians did not send any ships to Pernambuco, but in 1815, they sent six, and the next year they sent ten. The number constituted 28.5 percent of all ships bound for Brazil from the port. Between 1814 and 1815, Pernambucans increased the value of their imports from the United States from 18,804,400 réis to 48,448,400. In 1816, the value jumped to 100,696,000 réis. In return for cargoes of breadstuff, Pernambucan hides promised a strong sale to tanners in the mid-Atlantic's emergent boot and shoe industry. On the eve of the Pernambucan revolt, U.S. merchants had rapidly expanded their trade with the province.[15]

Sympathetic North Americans viewed the revolt in Pernambuco as a harbinger for both political and commercial change in Brazil. United States observers described Pernambuco as "the most valuable part of Brazil" and noted that it "is a flourishing and populous province, and its commerce is very considerable." The *Providence Patriot* associated the Pernambucan insurgency with the revolution in Chile, asserting, "Both of these events are highly interesting to the United States, particularly in a commercial point of view." The *Boston Patriot* predicted that "the friendship of the pa-triots of Pernambuco may at no distant day be important in a commercial point of view."[16]

A report in the *Daily National Intelligencer* expounded on the link between the nascent republic and U.S.-Brazilian commerce.

> Brazil is an interesting country to commercial nations. Its climate is mild, and its productions abundant, particularly the province of Pernambuco, which has received from nature so large a proportion of her most precious gifts, and which, on this account, was ever frequented by foreigners, notwithstanding the discouraging policy of the royal government. Now that other laws and other customs are taking the place occupied by tyranny and slavery, and a free constitution secures to strangers all the privileges of liberty and commerce it will be more frequently visited.[17]

The editor of the *Savannah Republican*, Frederick Fell, praised Pernambucans for their refusal to submit their commerce to "old colonial restrictions." United States free traders did not remain satisfied with a monarchical government that opened Brazilian ports to foreign commerce. Republicanism unbound the liberties of the people to pursue trade and wealth. Free trade advocates felt confident that republics would unite their commercial interests to the detriment of monarchies.[18]

A Philadelphia resident, Henry Brackenridge, felt reluctant to provide aid to Pernambucan revolutionaries, but he did not try to refute the assertion that liberal political and economic institutions in South America would benefit the United States. In 1817, he accompanied a government-sponsored tour of South America to evaluate the independence movements there. He spoke highly of South American revolutions but held reservations about the revolt in Pernambuco. He claimed that "whatever we may think of the form, the Brazilians had already obtained the great object for which the Americans are contending, *a government within themselves.*" As conceived by Brackenridge, Pernambuco had no just cause to revolt. He formed his opinion in part due to his respect for the popular Portuguese minister plenipotentiary in Washington, José Corrêa da Serra, whom he considered "too much a republican for Europe."[19]

Still, Brackenridge supposed that North Americans would benefit materially from a republican Brazil. He claimed that independence from Europe "is the first great object to be attained," but he also believed that "governments, founded on the most free and liberal principles" would "tend to our own happiness . . . and the more rapid improvement of America." He maintained further, "The independence and freedom of this continent, are two things we should, as far as is practicable, consider as inseparable." The United States could "obtain a much more solid and permanent footing" in South America than the English if liberal governments ruled the continent. With respect to Pernambuco, he simply worried that "we are too much in the habit of intermeddling with the interior concerns of other nations."[20]

The chief delegate of Pernambuco's provisional government, Antônio Gonçalves da Cruz, rebutted Brackenridge's opinion that Pernambucans should not receive U.S. aid. He reminded Brackenridge that the Portuguese monarchy had shut Portugal's ports to North American commerce during the American Revolution and had accused the colonists "of being rebels, traitors, and criminals." He hinted that Pernambucans had disagreed with the court's actions at the time, and he compared Pernambucan revolutionaries to "the Bostonians of 1774." Gonçalves da Cruz demonstrated a keen grasp of early republican attitudes about commerce and monarchy. In the nationalistic fervor that gripped North Americans after the War of 1812, they could not have failed to understand his allusions to Parliament's 1774 Coercive Acts. The acts had closed Boston ports as punishment for colonists' unruly behavior during the Boston Tea Party. Gonçalves da Cruz made his message clear. Tyrants closed ports; revolutionaries opened them.[21]

Like other South American countries, Brazil seemed a beneficial partner with whom to conduct free trade, for it promised a ready market for U.S. provisions and did not threaten the U.S. manufacturing industry. Despite the imposition of modest duties following the ratification of the U.S. Constitution, protectionists had not formed a united movement to safeguard U.S. industries with tariffs. Manufacturing increased in the United States, however, as warfare stymied trade. A congressional committee on commerce and manufactures claimed that one hundred thousand people worked in U.S. cotton factories after the war. Protectionists called for tariffs to shield the fledgling industry from cheap foreign imports. In June 1816, Congress responded with a 25 percent duty on woolens and cottons along with some additional taxes on low-priced cotton cloth.[22]

Protection advocates called for restrictions against British goods, but they rarely denigrated the ideal of free trade. Hezekiah Niles denounced the United States' commercial dependence on Great Britain despite U.S. political independence. He claimed that North Americans "calmly look on, talk about independence, and quietly bend our necks to the yoke—being tributaries to England, and relieving her wants at the cost of our own distress." Protectionists asserted that a commitment to free trade with European nations could harm the United States if those nations did not share that commitment. Representative Cyrus King of Massachusetts wanted to avoid "an extensive, odious, restrictive system" of trade. Still, he wished to "retaliate upon [Great Britain] some of those embarrassments, which her rigid colonial system is at this moment inflicting upon us." Representative William Lowndes hoped restrictions against European nations would have the good effect of "inviting a change of their system" to a more liberal commercial policy. Free trade remained the goal, even if it took heavy-handed measures to convince European nations to go along.[23]

South American countries had few manufactures with which to threaten the young U.S. industry, and they retained a high demand for U.S. agricultural goods. They made, therefore, less controversial free trade partners than European nations. The restrictions on cotton affected finished pieces that came from British Asia rather than the raw cotton from other quarters such as Brazil. Even the 1816 duties did not amount to a prohibition on British goods, and commodities continued to flow into the United States from British Asia. Niles and other protectionists hoped that protected markets would spur U.S. manufactures that merchants could send to South America. Most North Americans retained in full vigor their wish to trade freely with South American republics.[24]

Portuguese officials noted North Americans' ideological sympathy with the Pernambucans, and they worried that the rebels would seek supplies and munitions from the United States. Indeed, the provisional government allocated approximately £17,000 to purchase weapons and stores in North America. In April, the Englishman Charles Bowen reached the United States with credentials to purchase arms and munitions on behalf of the Pernambucan rebels. Bowen had lived in Pernambuco for years and had the trust of the provisional government. He opened negotiations with the firm of S. & P. Christian of Norfolk and relied on the London firm of Lyne & Co. to underwrite the contract. After S. & P. Christian decided to back out of the talks, he headed to Baltimore to find suppliers. In that city, the firms of Von Kapff & Brune and Thomas Tennant & Co. obliged him with two cargoes of gunpowder and munitions to the province. They filled the order with one thousand quintals of powder from the Dupont factory in Brandywine.[25]

The French and Spanish ministers in Washington suggested to the Portuguese minister plenipotentiary, José Corrêa da Serra, that the British probably lay behind all such plans. But U.S. officials proved keener to encourage the revolutionaries than the British. The English minister in Washington twice rejected meetings with Bowen, whereas the U.S. interim secretary of state Richard Rush received him at least in an informal capacity. Pernambucan revolutionaries implored U.S. president James Monroe for assistance and praised the United States' "brilliant revolution which we seek to imitate."[26]

They promised in return "absolute liberty of commerce, and the most perfect reciprocity." Revolutionaries imbibed copies of U.S. state and federal constitutions. On March 29, the revolutionary assembly had passed a constitution that fashioned the new Pernambucan government, according to a report in England, "like the North American States—liberty of conscience, and unbounded freedom of trade, being the leading principles." In the United States, sympathizers felt gratified that the revolutionaries invited "an intercourse with them upon the most liberal and friendly terms." Monroe allowed U.S. merchants to trade with Pernambucans, moved by a "friendly disposition towards republicks constituted on the same principles as our own." His decision legitimized their belligerency. From politicians to traders, North Americans supported the insurgency with greater enthusiasm than their English counterparts.[27]

On May 5, Gonçalves da Cruz (colloquially called Cabugá) reached Boston and proceeded to Philadelphia, leading the official delegation of the Pernambucan provisional government. The Brazilians arrived to newspaper cheers of "HAIL! PERNAMBUCO! Hail, THE NEW REPUBLIC!" Well-traveled, intelligent, and respected, Gonçalves da Cruz earned the high esteem of many North Americans who compared him to "our own illustrious ADAMS and HANCOCK."[28]

Gonçalves da Cruz had orders to request aid and to offer U.S. merchants twenty years of duty-free trade with Pernambuco. He and his fellow delegates convinced U.S. merchants to send munitions to Recife, and they published praise for the revolt in U.S. newspapers. They contacted Bonapartists who had fled to the United States after the emperor's fall and paid them to sail to Pernambuco to aid the revolutionary cause. Several Bonapartists agreed and traveled to Brazil with munitions and plans to prepare the province as a base to which Napoleon could flee from exile. The delegates worked with locals in Philadelphia to outfit a privateer to sail against Portuguese vessels. Soon after, a ship called *Gertrudis* left port with a small crew and without arms. Corrêa da Serra learned, however, that the vessel made its way to Cape Henlopen in Delaware Bay where it received a full complement of arms and men and changed its name to the *Hornet*. He fumed that despite his efforts to detain Gonçalves da Cruz's ship, "the local authorities favored [Gonçalves da Cruz] shamelessly and against the laws."[29]

The Portuguese crown dispatched twenty-five hundred soldiers from Lisbon and three thousand from Rio de Janeiro to crush the rebellion. Between March and May, royal armed forces besieged Pernambuco and blockaded Recife. By May 20, they had defeated the rebels. Officials arrested nearly two hundred and sent the principal conspirators to Bahia for trial.

The central government executed and dismembered twenty. Vice Admiral Rodrigo José Ferreira Lobo commanded the blockade and instituted an interim government on behalf of the monarchy until a new governor, Luís do Rego Barreto, took control on July 1. Despite the Portuguese government's victory, Corrêa da Serra despaired at the conduct of "the greedy and immoral part of [U.S.] commercial citizens" who supported the revolutionaries. He worried especially about the U.S. consul in Recife, the Philadelphia merchant Joseph Ray.[30]

The Consul

Ray arrived in Recife on July 6, soon after the Portuguese military had suppressed the revolt. As consul, he issued passports, acted as an intermediary between local officials and U.S. sailors, and tracked U.S. trade with the Port of Recife. Consuls did not receive a salary from the U.S. government, so they conducted private business in the regions where they served— usually as merchants. Ray operated, therefore, as an agent of the state and as a private trader. His government post called for neutrality while his financial interests lay with the local, defeated rebels. He negotiated poorly between the two roles and sided with the rebellious population rather too overtly for the comfort of Portuguese and U.S. officials.[31]

Soon after his arrival, unconfirmed rumors spread that he had formed a lodge of Freemasons—a society that had helped instigate the revolt. Worse, Ray lent protection to suspected conspirators. He pled with the Portuguese government for the release of a Bonapartist agent employed in the rebel cause. He contravened Portuguese law as he bribed Portuguese officials, tried to help the agent escape to the United States, and paid him clandestine visits in prison before he finally secured his release. Ray hid dissidents in his home to help them escape punishment. He probably spirited away some rebels to Philadelphia.[32]

Ray harmonized his republican sensibilities and financial interests as he aided the rebels. British merchants acted as Ray's main competition in Pernambuco, and most of them opposed the revolt in fear of their safety and that of their businesses. Pernambucans accused British merchants and the deposed governor of speculating in U.S. flour and other provisions at the expense of the military and local population. The British commodore William Bowles prepared to protect British property and subjects. He warned London of the danger of the "insurrection spreading unfortunately to other regions where strong prejudices are fostered against us."[33]

Brazilians resented British traders who had interloped in their commerce since the securement of the 1810 treaty. They did not complain about the open trade decree, but they protested British abuse of the commercial treaty and British monopolies on foreign commerce. By 1814, some considered the "English usurpation of the seas" as the enemy of "liberty of Commerce and Navigation." Ray seized on the discord with British firms to create sympathy for his firm among the locals and emerged as the dominant U.S. merchant in the region. Portuguese officials feared his support of former rebels and refused to tolerate him as U.S. consul.[34]

Recife policemen had caught wind of "outlawed leaders of the rebellion" who stayed with Ray. They invaded his home, captured the fugitives, and brought them to the local jail. Corrêa da Serra presented to the Monroe administration the court's grievances against Ray. He described the consul's conduct as "criminal to the highest point." The minister accused Ray of conducting illicit correspondence with Pernambucan rebels, paying illegal visits to conspirators, and harboring fugitives in his home. In 1820, the U.S. government replaced Ray with James Hamilton Bennett, signaling the government's commitment to favor international norms over American republicanism.[35]

Ray retained his goodwill with the Pernambucan community long beyond his dismissal as consul. In 1822, Moses Ray, a close relative of Joseph's, traveled to Pernambuco from Philadelphia to do business with the former consul. Moses had fallen on hard times since the War of 1812, and he hoped to revive his fortunes in Brazil. After his arrival, he commented on Joseph's prestige in the province. He reported to his wife, Mary, that "Joseph has a fine house in the most eligible situation in town for business of which he deservedly gets a very respectable share and that unsolicited." He remarked with satisfaction on Joseph's country seat of thirty acres. "Indeed, you would presume him to be the greatest character in the place[.] Amongst the people he passes for the complete Gentleman, Merchant and Philanthropist." Ray fared well in his business as he combined trade and revolution.[36]

Trade and Revolution

Ray's success mirrored that of U.S. commerce with Pernambuco in 1817. The United States outperformed most European nations in terms of the value of exports to Brazil but remained far behind the British. In 1816, U.S. merchants sent Pernambuco 9.7 percent of the value of all foreign imports into the province, compared to the 42.4 percent that came from the British Empire. During the 1817 conflict, however, United States exporters improved their proportion due to a strong market for their produce occasioned by the shortage of breadstuff in the Brazilian North.[37]

By the end of March, Pernambuco's rebel government had declared a moratorium on duties on provisions and munitions imported into the province. It also reduced export duties on provincial produce and abolished taxes on warehouses, shops, and vessels. United States newspapers translated and published a declaration from the provisional government. The statement encouraged liberal commerce with Pernambucan revolutionaries "to support the glorious cause they have undertaken." On March 18, in the adjacent revolutionary province of Paraíba, the provisional government had opened ports to foreign vessels on the same terms as national ships. The act cut the duties on foreign goods by half.[38]

North Americans celebrated the liberal policies by charging exorbitant prices on provisions in the Brazilian province. A New York visitor in Pernambuco claimed that the revolutionaries "calculate on supplies from the United States" as they lacked breadstuff. He supposed North Americans could "afford them plentiful supplies" if the Portuguese government did not blockade the Port of Recife. True to his prediction, the insurgents depended on U.S. produce. They paid as much as 18,000 réis per barrel for flour. In 1811, Lisbon buyers had paid just 13,000 réis at the height of the flour boom in Portugal. By mid-April, North Americans sold flour to Pernambuco for $37.50 per barrel. The figure tripled Lisbon prices.[39]

Enticed by such rates, U.S. merchants tested the blockade that the Portuguese had established by mid-May. Determined to send vessels to Pernambuco, they ignored early claims that the Portuguese had commenced the blockade. Corrêa da Serra felt it urgent to close U.S. trade with Pernambuco to suppress aid for the revolutionaries. In his haste, he breached diplomatic protocol by announcing the blockade in U.S. newspapers before he informed the U.S. State Department. An ardent supporter of South American independence, Richard Rush expressed skepticism about the intelligence that supported Corrêa da Serra's notice. Newspapers questioned the veracity of the declaration. They cited the vague language of the announcement and contradictory reports. Word spread that the provisional government had outfitted a twenty-two-gun brig to protect vessels that entered

Recife, so "it appears," a sympathetic newspaper claimed, "that vessels bound to Pernambuco, will have little difficulty in reaching that port."[40]

United States merchants gambled on trade with Pernambuco in light of the inconsistent information. On May 16, the firms of Rodman & Waln and Keith W. Wells sent a joint cargo of flour to Pernambuco along with codfish, sperm candles, and other commodities. The blockading vessels captured two U.S. ships that carried munitions to the rebels, imprisoned the crews, and sent them to Rio de Janeiro. Portuguese forces attacked a third U.S. vessel, but it slipped away.[41]

In 1817, U.S. commerce improved in Pernambuco despite the temporary blockade. Pernambucans increased the value of their U.S. imports by 8.1 percent, and U.S. imports grew to 21 percent of the value of all foreign goods brought into the province. In contrast, British goods dropped in value to 20.6 percent of the total value of foreign imports in Pernambuco. Portuguese imports fell in value 10.5 percent. French goods increased in value by just 1.4 percent. In 1817, therefore, the United States constituted the only nation to record a significant increase in the value of exports to Pernambuco.[42]

Pernambuco's drought continued until mid-summer of 1817, and U.S. provisions remained in high demand in the province. By August, however, Brazilians welcomed an improved crop of manioc, which they could grind into flour, so they depended less on U.S. breadstuff. Pernambucans had depended most on U.S. flour during the spring convulsions of the revolt and its summer aftermath. The province seemed to promise everything U.S. free traders hoped—a South American republic that would import U.S. provisions free of restrictions and allow U.S. traders to compete with Great Britain.[43]

Calmness returned to Pernambuco by mid-July, but North Americans continued to extend their support to ex-revolutionaries into the later months of the year. In mid-August, Frederick Fell hoped that Pernambucan patriot forces would "hang together until their strength shall have increased sufficient to hurl destruction on the minions and blood-hounds of despotism." Corrêa da Serra supposed that news of the royal government's triumph could not "absolutely defeat the opposition of lies and falsehoods that the revolutionaries have spread" in the United States. But even in Pernambuco, Ray asserted, "The fire which burst out on the 6th of March is not yet quenched it is only smothered and the slightest air will fan it into a flame."[44]

Brazilian refugees clung to the hope that their movement had not died, and they pled for aid from the United States. By August, approximately forty Pernambucan rebels had fled to the United States for refuge. Some expected to regroup and return to Brazil to institute a new rebellion, and they continued to solicit the support of North Americans with promises of open trade. One refugee, either Gonçalves da Cruz or somebody who echoed his arguments to Brackenridge, wrote to "THE PEOPLE OF THE NEW WORLD" in the *National Intelligencer* as Patricio Republicano, or Republican Patrician. The writer asserted that had republicanism reigned in Brazil at the time of the American Revolution, "North Americans . . . would have had our ports open—Portugal would not have closed them against them; nor would its government treat them as rebels." Patricio Republicano knew the minds of his U.S. audience and drew on the equation of republicanism with free trade to arouse support for Pernambuco's moribund rebellion.[45]

Patricio Republicano gained sympathizers in the United States with his passionate pleas. The *Savannah Republican* raged that the court at Rio de Janeiro had even surpassed "the excessive impositions mentioned by 'Patricio Republicano' in his manifesto." The editor fumed at the confiscation of rebels' property following their defeat, a practice "unknown in republican and other liberal governments" but all too common "in Spain and Portugal." Liberal North Americans could not stand for a monarchy in their hemisphere. The Pernambuco revolt allowed them to imagine Brazil in their own image.[46]

A year and a half after the rebellion, Portuguese officials fretted that "the fugitives of Pernambuco . . . continue to be very well received in Philadelphia, where they work to effect a new revolt in this or that place in Brazil." Corrêa da Serra complained that Pernambucan "demons" in Philadelphia received recruits from Brazil and formed "a body of infernal intrigue." The new arrivals included two sons of P. José Ignácio, whom the government had executed in Bahia, and two other "mysterious personages," who he assumed acted as spies in the field. Corrêa da Serra agonized, "Look how the fragments of rebellions in every part of the world come here gathering and increasing ferment in this part." Two months later, he seethed as Gonçalves da Cruz hosted a party with prominent Philadelphia citizens and South American insurrectionists to toast the liberty of South America and "vengeance of the martyrs of liberty in Pernambuco." Nothing came of the alleged plots of renewed insurrection, but Corrêa da Serra lacked patience with North Americans, who he believed fostered and supported such movements.[47]

North Americans witnessed their Pernambuco trade lose ground to Great Britain for several years after the revolt. They increased the value of their exports to the province from 108,860,000 réis in 1817 to 147,782,010 in 1820. In the same years, however, Great Britain increased the value of British exports to Pernambuco from 347,245,500 réis to 638,712,800. The U.S. value increased 35.8 percent, but the British value increased 83.9 percent. The difference contrasted sharply with that in 1817, when North Americans enjoyed a significant increase in trade value with Pernambuco while Great Britain suffered a drastic decrease. The change correlated as much with the demand for North American flour as with political ideology, but it reinforced the notion that North Americans competed with Great Britain best in fellow republics.[48]

As the revolutionary movement evaporated in Pernambuco, so did U.S. trade privileges in the province. After the Portuguese court restored its authority in the Northeast, it compelled several U.S. traders to pay duties on goods that they had evaded paying during the insurrection. The Portuguese government arrested at least seven North Americans as prisoners of the state and held them in the Recife jailhouse in the aftermath of the rebellion. It detained a U.S. vessel for violating a prohibition on foreign vessels conducting coastal trade in Brazil. Thomas Ray of the *Sally Dana* had unloaded a cargo from Philadelphia in Pernambuco while the insurrectionists held the province. He then sailed to Mozambique to secure additional supplies for the rebels only to learn upon his return that the Portuguese government had retaken Pernambuco and prohibited him from entering the port. In 1821, the *National Advocate* repeated word that royalists in Recife were "as poor as rats" and assumed that such poverty "is very natural considering their *kingly* predilections." The newspaper oversimplified Pernambucans' ideological inclinations, but it highlighted the belief that republicanism best fostered prosperity and the regret that republican agitation had failed in Brazil.[49]

*   *   *

Pernambucan revolutionaries held out for just two and a half months, but they captured the imagination of North Americans who contemplated the benefits of a Brazilian province as an independent republic. In 1808, U.S. free traders had cheered the removal of the Portuguese court to Brazil, for they anticipated freer commerce there due to Brazil's elevated status. They feared, however, that the enviable country could never attain its full commercial potential so long as the Portuguese monarchy ruled it. Sympathy translated into support as merchants shipped provisions and munitions to Brazilian revolutionaries. Attracted in the short-term by high prices and low duties, North Americans hoped that in the long-term Pernambuco would throw off the Brazilian monarchy to foster free and prosperous commerce between republics.[50]

Joseph Ray solidified the favor of local revolutionaries and used it to increase his trade. The dismissed consul typified the North American experience in Pernambuco. In 1819, Corrêa da Serra noted about the United States, "There were here infinite Rays." He added that most North Americans wished "to have one in every port of Brazil." Barreto suspected that even after the revolt Ray maintained contact with North American privateers that sailed on behalf of revolutionaries in the Banda Oriental—the region just south of the Brazilian border and north of the Río de la Plata, where Portuguese authorities hoped to secure political control. The Portuguese government had quashed the rebellion in northeastern Brazil by mid-1817, but its problems in the Banda Oriental had just begun.[51]

Chapter 8

Republican Pirates

In 1816, the Portuguese government ignited a four-year conflict with South American revolutionaries after it sent forces to invade the Banda Oriental. The caudillo José Gervasio Artigas led troops against the Portuguese invaders in defense of republicanism and political autonomy in the region. After the revolt in Pernambuco erupted the following year, sympathetic North Americans applauded revolutionaries in both conflicts, whom they imagined as republicans who warred against a corrupt Portuguese monarchy. The *Savannah Republican* lauded Artigas's republican aspirations and the Pernambucan uprising in a single breath, exulting, "Each of them are sufficient to excite souls which have not entirely lost the elasticity of their moral bearings under the degrading weight of the house of Braganza." Many U.S. observers saw the insurgencies as the dawn of republicanism in Brazil. They anticipated that the revolutionaries would eliminate the supposed incongruity of a monarchy in the Americas.[1]

Artigas provided North Americans with letters of marque in 1817, and the letters ostensibly authorized the bearers to prey on Portuguese and Spanish commerce. United States traders responded with alacrity. Investors, captains, and sailors outfitted privateer vessels to sail on behalf of the revolutionaries, contesting the power of the U.S. and Portuguese governments to regulate the transnational interactions of their citizenries. They violated U.S. laws that forbade citizens to fight in wars in which the United States had declared neutrality. The War of 1812 had given the U.S. republic, in the minds of most North Americans, "a separate and dignified station among the powers of the earth." The war ensured that the United States would maintain its independence, but Portuguese officials remained skeptical of the legitimacy of the republican experiment. The republic could hardly take its place among modern state powers if the U.S. government could not exercise sovereignty over its citizens and compel them to maintain its declared neutrality.[2]

During the early nineteenth century, privateering declined in favor of state-operated naval warfare. After the War of 1812, U.S. officials operated in an international context in which European rulers valued the state's ability to repress private maritime violence. Artigan privateers disregarded such state power, damaging the U.S. government's reputation among European nations. With their illicit raids in the Atlantic, they planted a wedge between many North Americans' vision of South American republicanism and the government's desire for respect among the community of nations.[3]

In 1818, U.S. officials hoped to sign a commercial treaty with the Portuguese Empire, and they broached the subject with Corrêa da Serra. Authorities in Rio de Janeiro refused to make an agreement until the U.S. government repressed privateering from its ports. United States administrators labored to prove that the republic could take its rightful place among the community of nations by honoring its international treaties and obligations. They endeavored to reassure the Portuguese government and Europe that they could control their citizens' transnational movement. They did not view the extension of state sovereignty into the Atlantic as an incidental objective—a means to facilitate overseas commerce or export legal frameworks from metropolises to peripheries. Rather, they hoped it would command respect from the community of nations, the very essence of the U.S. nation-building project after the War of 1812.[4]

United States officials began to pursue the privateers more tenaciously in criminal courts—particularly in the privateer hub of Baltimore. Congress passed laws to stymie the movement of privateers into U.S. ports. After 1819, U.S. officials significantly curtailed illicit privateers. They revealed in their efforts the difficulty of harmonizing the North American ideals of hemispheric republicanism with the realpolitik of international negotiations. In their quest for national legitimacy, they could ill afford to alienate European monarchies, including the Portuguese monarchy in Brazil.

North American privateers showed as much interest in profit as politics, but they represented a vision of South American republicanism pitted against the U.S. government's pragmatic approach to international relations. They revealed the United States caught at a crossroads between a commitment to republican solidarity and a determination to command respect on the world stage. By promoting commercial negotiations with the Portuguese government at the expense of revolutionary activity, U.S. authorities upended assumptions that republican revolution would have to precede advantageous trade in South America.

Artigan Privateers

Portugal had relinquished its remaining territorial claims in the Banda Oriental to Spain in 1777 as part of the Treaty of San Ildefonso. The Spanish government incorporated the region into the viceroyalty of Río de la Plata and designated Montevideo as a mandatory port of call. During the Peninsular War, Napoleon had deposed King Ferdinand VII of Spain and sent the Spanish national assembly on the run. In May 1810, leading residents of Buenos Aires established a junta to assume autonomous control over the viceroyalty. The May Revolution led to the establishment of the United Provinces of Río de la Plata and eventually to Argentina's independence movement. In Montevideo, however, imperial officials and many residents opposed the revolution in Buenos Aires.[5]

Many Montevidean commercial elites supported royalism because they associated the monarchy with their commercial advantages over Buenos Aires, such as Montevideo's position as a mandatory port of call. After the May Revolution, Artigas fought in concert with *porteño* (inhabitants of Buenos Aires) revolutionaries to defeat royalists in the United Provinces. In 1811, *orientales* (inhabitants of the Banda Oriental) laid siege to Montevideo to wrest it from royalist control. The besieged party appealed for help to Portuguese authorities, who still harbored designs on the border region. Portuguese troops mounted a short-lived invasion before British officials pressured the government to withdraw them. The Portuguese government left Montevideo in the hands of orientales who secured it for the United Provinces. In September, a triumvirate took control of Buenos Aires and the Argentine littoral, including the Banda Oriental.[6]

Orientales resisted the centralization of power in Buenos Aires. They agitated for a federal form of government to preserve their autonomy and prepared to defend it against encroachments from Spain, Buenos Aires, and the Portuguese Empire. Artigas mustered a multiethnic army composed mainly of creoles and Indians committed to a radical republican platform, such as local control over tax collection and land redistribution. By 1815, he assumed the role Protector of the Free Peoples of the Littoral and enjoyed widespread influence in the region.[7]

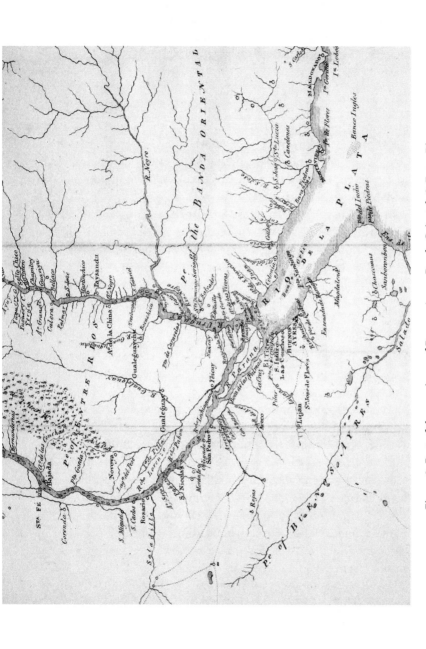

Figure 9. Part of the provinces of Buenos Ayres, Banda Oriental, & Entre Rios. From J. A. B. Beaumont, *Travels in Buenos Ayres, and the Adjacent Provinces of the Rio de la Plata* (London, 1828).

The Portuguese government sought to take advantage of the unstable situation on its southern border and reclaim territory in the Banda Oriental. In September 1816, its military launched another invasion into the province. One Portuguese official, the Count of Palmela, justified the incursion due to "the threat to Brazil of the Jacobin principles espoused in the Spanish Provinces." He worried that Artigas's movement drew "supporters from our territory" and promoted "the uprising of slaves." Buenos Aires officials viewed Artigas's federalist tendencies as a liability to the United Provinces and refused to aid his struggle against the Portuguese. The Portuguese government took control of Montevideo in just over a month and relegated Artigas's influence to the interior of the Banda Oriental. To revive his movement, the caudillo recruited private U.S. citizens to prey on Spanish and Portuguese commerce.[8]

From Mexico to Buenos Aires, Spanish Americans employed U.S. nationals to attack Spanish vessels, to the disgust of the Spanish minister in Washington, Luis de Onís. Roughly three thousand North Americans sailed on behalf of South American independence movements. Between 1816 and 1820, at least fifteen vessels preyed on Portuguese commerce. Letters of marque from Artigas had special appeal because they ostensibly authorized the bearer to attack Spanish and Portuguese vessels. One privateer captain reportedly returned his commissions to Buenos Aires so he could carry "better" commissions from Artigas. By 1819, the U.S. State Department recognized that the Portuguese Empire suffered particularly acute damages at the hands of the privateers.[9]

Baltimore investors leapt into the privateer business, and the city served as a principle port of clearance and entrance for the privateers. During the War of 1812, Baltimoreans served the wartime demands of the U.S. government. Baltimore clippers carried nearly half of the U.S. wartime foreign trade. When the end of the war threatened to disrupt their economic lives, many merchants and investors turned to privateering for South American revolutionaries. In 1816, Thomas Taylor, a U.S. citizen who resided in Buenos Aires, arrived in Baltimore with letters of marque from the United Provinces. During the next several years, U.S. investors purchased over one hundred such commissions from the South American province.[10]

In late 1816, Buenos Aires officials instructed Taylor to allow Captain Fisk of the *Romp* to prey on Portuguese vessels if the empire attacked the United Provinces. Portuguese ministers objected that "it was easy to foresee the abuse" of such instructions. They feared that the privateers would use them to justify unwarranted depredations against Portuguese vessels. Indeed, on November 30, 1816, Captain Rose of the *Independent* captured the Portuguese schooner *Flora*. The privateers had commenced their war on Portuguese commerce even before Artigas issued his own commissions.[11]

Artigas resolved to issue his own letters of marque to U.S. investors in late 1817, and he found an anxious ally in Thomas Lloyd Halsey of Rhode Island. Halsey served as U.S. consul in Buenos Aires and felt a keen economic interest in the success of the independence movements in the region. In 1815, he had warned Secretary of State James Monroe that unless the United States assisted in some way, the revolts would fail and "the ports will be shut against foreign trade, more particularly against the flag of the United States." Halsey viewed South American independence as a vital component of a prosperous U.S. trade in the region.[12]

United States exporters found the Río de la Plata region friendlier to U.S. commerce when not under Spanish control. In June 1806, the British military invaded and occupied Buenos Aires to deprive the empire's Spanish enemies of vital ports and to extend British commerce to the Americas. United States merchants enjoyed freedom to trade in the port city during the occupation. By August, porteños retook their city in favor of the Spanish Empire, and the port closed to U.S. commerce except with special contracts. In the early months of 1807, Montevideo fell into British hands for most of the year. United States merchants could sell their goods in that city, "being the only port in the River," as one trader put it, "in which the cargo would be permitted to be sold being in possession of the British."[13]

After the porteños expelled the British from the Río de la Plata region, Spanish authorities adopted more stringent measures against foreign trade. United States–Río de la Plata trade plummeted. In mid-1811, porteño revolutionary forces laid siege to royalist-held Montevideo. During the siege, the Spanish viceroy ordered U.S. vessels out of the port to keep supplies in the city rather than allow foreign merchants to purchase them. By contrast, the local junta of Buenos Aires facilitated trade with the United States by low duties on foreign goods.[14]

As Halsey's plea to Monroe revealed, privateering for Artigas aligned with the goal to secure independent trade partners in South America. In late 1817, the consul met Artigas at Purificación, where the Protector delivered him a handful of privateer commissions to send to the United States. Halsey then gave them to Thomas Taylor, who distributed the letters to investors in Baltimore.[15]

United States investors constructed a web of transatlantic relationships to take advantage of the commissions. Brokers such as Taylor received commissions from Artigas through intermediaries such as Halsey. They distributed the letters to privateer investors who hired agents to assemble a crew for the vessel. Some privateers filled multiple rolls. Clement Cathell, John Danels, and several others invested in the ships they captained. Thomas Taylor worked as both a broker and a captain. Investors pooled their capital to purchase vessels and hire crews. One Baltimore network included such prominent citizens as Joseph Karrick, a merchant and insurance company director; Joseph Snyder, a chandler and grocer; Joseph W. Patterson, the scion of the eminent William Patterson; Matthew Murray, the former sheriff of Baltimore County; John Sands, a merchant; and John S. Skinner, a postmaster. They purchased and outfitted one of the most aggressive privateer vessels, *La Fortuna*.[16]

Many North Americans cheered Artigas's republican movement and his defiance of the Portuguese monarchy. One writer lauded the "deserving patriots" who fought against the Portuguese Empire. The author supposed that native Brazilians along the southern border "are ripe for independence, many of them having joined Artigas." The *Baltimore Patriot* published a letter that derided Buenos Aires's "scandalous" abandonment of Montevideo to Portuguese forces. The author assumed, however, that "king John . . . will soon find himself checked by Gen. Artigas, who with a brave, formidable, and intrepid army, is already under the walls of Monte Video." William F. Redding, editor of the *Maryland Censor*, decried the Portuguese invasion as "one of the most unprovoked and unblushing measures of royal aggression upon human rights, that ever occurred." He agreed with the *Daily National Intelligencer* that "we care not . . . who rules the Banda Oriental, provided the Republican form of government be perpetuated." In that spirit, he hoped that "before long, a sufficient number of Republican 'pirates' commissioned by General Artigas will repay H[is] M[ajesty] the King for the unjust and unprovoked attack that he has made in Monte Video."[17]

In contrast to such ebullience, Corrêa da Serra assailed Artigas's commissions as illegal. Many privateers carried a letter from Artigas in addition to commissions from other revolutionary governments, but international legal custom proscribed simultaneously holding commissions from different nations. The U.S. government did not formally recognize Artigas as a belligerent in a civil war with the Portuguese Empire. Consequently, according to Corrêa da Serra, he had no right to issue letters of marque to anybody, least of all to citizens of a neutral nation. Finally, the minister pointed out that the Portuguese government controlled the port at Montevideo. Because Artigas "had possession of no sea-port," his commissions were "mere absurdities."[18]

Neutrality

On December 20, 1816, Corrêa da Serra shot off a letter of protest to Monroe. The minister worried that U.S. privateers in Buenos Aires might attack Portuguese commerce. He complained that a "very thin veil . . . has been deemed sufficient to screen the culprits from the effect of the actual insufficient laws." He warned that "nothing but the enactment of new laws, sufficient for the emergency, can justify [the United States] in the eyes of the civilized world." Six days later, President James Madison asked Congress for a stricter neutrality law.[19]

One month later, Congress took up the task with a bill that dealt with the free movement of U.S. citizens. John Forsyth, the chair of the House Committee on Foreign Relations, worried that while the Neutrality Laws of 1794 and 1797 authorized punishment of rogue privateers, they did not allow "the Executive to prevent the commission of the offence." The proposed law would require armed ships owned in whole or in part by U.S. citizens to post a heavy bond that certified they would not engage in foreign privateering. It stipulated that customs collectors could detain any armed vessels they suspected might violate U.S. neutrality. Collectors could even hold unarmed vessels if they believed the crew would receive munitions after they cleared port.[20]

Congressmen sympathetic to South American revolutionaries protested the restrictions on free movement of U.S. citizens. Erastus Root of New York found the provision that allowed customs officers to detain suspect vessels "the most objectionable." He did not believe the situation "sufficiently urgent to subject the citizen to inconvenience, and inflict on him sore injury." Robert Wright of Maryland refused to "bind over the American people on mere suspicion of their intention to violate the law." He could not fathom why the government "should take part against our own citizens to please Spain!" Henry Clay disparaged the bill as an attempt "to discountenance any aid being given to the South American colonies in a state of revolution against the parent country." The bill's proponents, such as John Randolph of Virginia, argued for the necessity of such measures "to restrain any of our citizens who were sufficiently base . . . to engage in such expeditions." The congressmen debated the essence of U.S. foreign policy as they pitted the freedom of North and South Americans against the U.S. government's international reputation.[21]

Supporters of the bill drew on a narrative that cast South Americans as incapable of self-governance. Daniel Sheffey of Virginia lamented that "after the experience of past years" North Americans should have learned not to anticipate civil liberty from an "ignorant and unenlightened" population. He sneered, "The contest in South America . . . is a contest of slaves to become freemen." His remark appealed to Southerners who had received gruesome reports of slave violence during the Haitian Revolution of the 1790s and early 1800s. After Haitian independence in 1804, many white Southerners feared that hemispheric revolutions equated to blood thirsty slaves who indiscriminately killed whites. They viewed independence movements as a disease rather than as a virtue.[22]

Even opponents of the bill shrunk from gainsaying rhetoric that questioned the ability of South Americans to self-govern. Solomon Sharp of Kentucky hoped for the eventual self-governance of South America, but he conceded that South Americans were "not so much enlightened as our people were to the struggle of our Revolution." Henry Clay disputed Sheffey's point by claiming that tyranny rather than innate inferiority kept South Americans in ignorance. Even so, he entertained Sheffey's suggestion, declaring, "Let them have free government, if they be capable of enjoying it; but let them have, at all events, independence." Though supportive of South American revolutionaries, Clay revealed an incipient tendency to assume that the independence of the Americas remained the ultimate goal, whether or not it came accompanied by republicanism. The debate exposed apprehension that South American inferiority may cripple republicanism in the Americas.[23]

Congress passed the bill as the Neutrality Act of 1817 over the objections of its opponents. Patriotic fervor gripped the United States after the War of 1812. Policymakers embarked on a nationalistic foreign policy they hoped would garner international respect for the United States. During the war, North Americans contested the British concept of perpetual allegiance, which rooted an individual's citizenship immutably in their nation of origin. United States jurisprudence applied a more fluid definition to citizenship, allowing for renunciation and naturalization. While the Neutrality Act

of 1817 did not address citizenship questions, it signaled a new commitment by the U.S. government to regulate the international associations of
its citizenry. The act did not outlaw self-expatriation, so privateers could
renounce their U.S. citizenship and sail for wherever they pleased despite
U.S. law. Most sailors, investors, and captains ignored such formalities. The
new law applied, therefore, to a large swath of privateering participants.[24]

Authorities subdued rogue consuls to further ensure U.S. neutrality.
Halsey found, like Joseph Ray in Pernambuco, that his commitment to
republican revolution put him at odds with the State Department. In the
winter of 1817–1818, the government commissioned William G. D. Worthington as a special agent to investigate Halsey and "his meddling in the
Privateering System." Halsey's superiors dismissed him from his consulship
in early 1818, but by the time of his discharge, U.S. investors had purchased
so many Artigan letters of marque that his dismissal failed to halt foreign
privateering.[25]

Defiance

Privateers ramped up their depredations on Portuguese commerce, unde-
terred by the government's actions. In 1817, they captured at least six Portuguese vessels. The number rose to approximately thirty-two in 1818. To
avoid the strictures of the Neutrality Act, crews adopted unconventional
means to arrive at sea fully armed. In 1818, James Hooper worked as a
recruiter for Robert M. Goodwin's vessel, *Republicana*. He outfitted it with
about one hundred men, captained by Clement Cathell. Goodwin and his
partner, Obadiah Chase, had registered the *Republicana* as a foreign war-
ship. As a result, U.S. law allowed it to dock temporarily in Baltimore if it
did not take on or drop off additional crew members or munitions. Goodwin wanted to replace the old ship, however, with the faster vessel *Athenian*.
After the *Republicana* left Baltimore, Hooper sent a schooner to meet it
near Annapolis and surreptitiously supplied it with munitions. Cathell then
met the *Athenian*, transferred the entire complement to the new ship, and
renamed it the *Republicana*. It headed out to sea with its crew and at least
a dozen twenty-four-pound guns. Once outside the United States, the privateers enjoyed the freedom to interact with people of other nations unre-
strained by state regulation, and they established networks around the
Atlantic to facilitate their business.[26]

Once Artigan privateers captured a prize, they sought safe harbors to sell their plunder and to rearm their vessels. Artigas did not control the port of Montevideo, so they sent their prizes illegally to other ports. They preferred places where government officials disregarded regulations on international movement. Swedish, Dutch, and Danish Caribbean islands provided ideal ports as impecunious colonial governments on Saint Barthélemy, Saint Eustatius, and Saint Thomas loosely enforced customs transactions. Constrained by unfavorable topography, such islands could not produce sugar and other agricultural goods in the same quantities as the more affluent Caribbean islands. Since at least the mid-eighteenth century, they adopted illicit trade as a major element of their economies. As one Portuguese official put it, rather than send privateer prizes "to a port where they would certainly be restored to their true owners, they have sent their prizes to a Swedish island called S^m Bartholomeu and from there have the ships brought [to Baltimore] with a Swedish flag."[27]

Privateers sought close ties with the islands' residents so they could bring their vessels into Caribbean ports. On the Danish island of Saint Thomas, they found a ready ally in Benedette, an aide to the island's commandant. In January 1818, Captain Cathell and the *Republicana* captured the *Miguel Pereira Forjaz* and brought the prize into Watermelon Cay on the island of Saint John, about twenty miles from Saint Thomas. The crew unloaded the cargo and brought it piecemeal to Saint Thomas, where Benedette acted as the "principal purchaser." For a share of the plunder, the manager of a local estate cut the cables in Watermelon Cay and took the ship on shore. The Danish colonial government then seized the prize as an abandoned vessel and sold it at public sale.[28]

In November 1818, the *Congresso* captured the Portuguese brig *Paquete de Santos*, took it to Saint Thomas under French colors, and sold its cargo. Benedette gave an official letter of recommendation to the *Paquete de Santos*'s pretended owner, a Frenchman named Marieu. Marieu used the certificate to obtain a "Burgher's brief," which allowed him to own a Danish vessel. He thereby converted the captured brig into a different vessel outfitted with a crew, munitions of war, and new Danish papers—no longer under the flimsy disguise of French colors. Richard Alsop, a U.S. citizen who served as a Portuguese agent in the Caribbean, summed up the problem in Saint Thomas: "There are but few in or out of office who have not been directly or indirectly concerned in or some way benefited by the privateers."[29]

Privateers facilitated their business by securing Caribbean connections in high places. In 1819, rumors circulated around Saint Barthélemy that Governor Johan Norderling had accepted bribes from the privateers. Robert Monroe Harrison, the U.S. consul on the island, claimed that Norderling had "accumulated the enormous sum of 180.000 dollars by the *facilities* afforded to those piratical vessels." Whether or not he accepted bribes, the governor admitted to the Swedish Secretary for Colonial Affairs, "Since I began to close my eyes [to illicit trade] dubloons and sound piastres are everywhere." The colonial government sought revenue and the privateers wanted hospitable ports, so the two parties made natural allies. Once outside the boundaries of the United States, therefore, privateers depended on illicit movement and interaction with people of other nations and empires. They frequently secured such transnational connections on the high seas by taking human plunder in defiance of U.S. government power and Portuguese sovereignty.[30]

Borderwaters

Like other modern states, the U.S. government struggled to align geography and law. Early modern empires contended, in the words of the historian Lauren Benton, with "imperfect geographies"—areas where they attempted to construct legal zones and practices without full control of the territory. More than a highway that connected ports around its peripheries, the Atlantic Ocean acted as a sort of borderland—a borderwater. It constituted the site for a wide array of intricate associations among people of different empires, nations, races, and cultures. North American privateers illicitly incorporated crew members from around the Atlantic, developing polyethnic crews that favored localized relationships in defiance of well-defined national affiliations. Their actions contested the ability of the U.S. government to extend its sovereignty into the Atlantic, violated slave-trade laws, and exposed the government to embarrassment among European powers.[31]

On June 12, 1818, Captain John Danels of Baltimore and his crew left Buenos Aires aboard the *Irresistible*. On July 10, the *Irresistible* approached the *Maria de Lisboa*, captained by José Antônio Moreira and destined for Montevideo from Rio de Janeiro. The *Irresistible* fired on the *Maria* without warning, causing "great destruction" and wounding three men. The privateers boarded the ship and looted money, cables, canvas, and other supplies. They sailed away and left most of the Portuguese crew on the damaged vessel. The North Americans took with them, however, three African slaves who belonged to Moreira along with four French passengers and an Italian.[32]

As the episode reveals, Artigan privateers contested a significant feature of modern nation-states—their monopoly on the legitimate means of movement. The historical sociologist John Torpey argues that states sought a monopoly on the legitimate means of movement, "particularly . . . across international boundaries." They assumed, by extension, an intricate role in regulating the transnational associations of their national citizenry.[33]

Artigan privateers took advantage of the weak U.S. government of the era to develop transnational relationships on their own terms. They augmented their crews by bringing slaves, sailors, and passengers of different nationalities onto their vessels. They cultivated ties with merchants, government officials, sailors, and residents of South America and the Caribbean. By participating in such extensive transnational interactions, Artigan privateers developed integrated, syncretic networks that resisted the imposition of a clear national identity. In the Atlantic borderwater, they defied the authority of the U.S. and Portuguese governments to regulate their illicit movement and commerce.

As a captive aboard John Danels's *Irresistible*, Gabriel Lacayo y Coronado revealed the privateers' interest in diversifying their crews and fostering transnational associations independent of state authority. In June 1818, at the mouth of the Río de la Plata, Danels captured a French galley that carried Lacayo y Coronado, a Hispanic American who traveled with a passport from the Spanish captain general of Guatemala. Danels seized Lacayo y Coronado and others, put part of his crew aboard the French ship, and sent it to the island of Margarita. Lacayo y Coronado continued aboard the *Irresistible* as it sailed north along the coast of Brazil. After the *Irresistible* plundered the Portuguese brigantine *União da América* near Cabo Frio on July 16, Danels allowed Lacayo y Coronado to board the Portuguese vessel and sail for Rio de Janeiro.[34]

During Lacayo y Coronado's sojourn aboard the *Irresistible*, Danels explained to him that he wanted a Spanish American aboard to make his Artigan commission appear more legitimate. The captain had begun his cruise only the week before he captured the French galley, and his vessel remained conspicuously non–Spanish American. Indeed, the captain of the *União da América* observed that only one member of Danels's crew spoke Spanish. Danels made an offer, therefore, to Lacayo y Coronado.[35]

"The captain offered me eight shares of [the] prizes" to join the crew, Lacayo y Coronado later informed Portuguese officials in Rio de Janeiro. Danels proposed "bringing me along with the title of his secretary plus 1000 [pesos] more for me to teach him [Spanish]." Lacayo y Coronado accepted "tacitly" by remaining coy, and he continued to receive good treatment. Meanwhile, he hoped to leave the privateer vessel, and the *União da América* presented the chance. Lacayo y Coronado incensed Danels with his request to board the Portuguese vessel, and the North American threatened to kill him. Lacayo y Coronado never explained why Danels finally released him, but he assured Portuguese officials that he had almost sacrificed his life "so that it is never said that a son of Granada . . . of good parents has made war" against the Portuguese Empire.[36]

In his interactions with Lacayo y Coronado, Danels challenged state authority to regulate transnational movement. The privateers already sailed with unrecognized commissions from Artigas in violation of U.S. neutrality, and they complicated their legal status even more by bringing on individuals from other nations. They had to manipulate crew lists to pull off the scheme. The United States did not adopt a standard passport system until 1856. The government relied, instead, on crew lists to control movement across its borders. Congress had passed an 1803 law that required captains to obtain a certified list of their crews—with physical descriptions of each crew member—before they left port. Captains entered a bond redeemable after they presented an accurate account of their crew upon return to the United States. By bringing crew members aboard in the middle of a voyage, Danels either had to manipulate the lists, as he suggested in Lacayo y Coronado's case, or make the new crew members surreptitiously disembark. Such actions highlight the weakness of state-required paperwork to control movement in and out of the United States, much less in the vast expanse of the Atlantic Ocean.[37]

Danels assembled his crew in a manner to imbue it with a syncretic quality. To augment the crew, he extended handsome offers to a diverse assortment of captives. He urged Miguel Thadeo Montufaz of Guatemala to accompany him to Baltimore, where he would "accommodate him at his home, and . . . indemnify him of all loss and hardship." He invited a French captive named Anglada to join the crew, "treating him magnificently" and offering him an elegant table clock and a valuable epaulet.[38]

Lacayo y Coronado, Montufaz, and Anglada chose not to accompany Danels, but many Artigan privateers successfully incorporated diverse crew

members into their labor force. Just weeks after the *União da América* inci-
dent, Danels captured the *Ceres*. Captain João Luiz Victor noticed that
Danels's crew consisted of North Americans and a mixture of "Portuguese,
Spanish, and French men."[39]

Sailors of African descent stood particularly vulnerable to capture.
Lacayo y Coronado reported the size of Danels's crew at 130, "including
the Negroes from the prizes." The quartermaster of the *União da América*,
whom Danels took aboard the *Irresistible*, saw "a negro who appeared to
him to be Portuguese." Whites in the Atlantic associated blackness with
slavery, so blacks could not choose to leave as easily as Lacayo y Coronado,
Montufaz, or Anglada. Even if allowed to return to a Portuguese vessel,
black captives probably faced a life at least as precarious as the one they
endured aboard a privateer vessel.[40]

Captains obtained a ready source of labor by bringing aboard captives
skilled in seafaring. In June 1820, Richard Moon of the *General Ribeira*
captured the *Fenix* off the coast of Olinda, Brazil. The Portuguese ship had
just sailed from Luanda on the coast of Angola with a cargo of 348 slaves.
Moon abandoned most of the Portuguese crew on shore just north of Goiana, but he kept seven Angolan sailors. They included Paulo, José, Francisco, and Manuel, who belonged to Agostinho Luis Pinto de Carvalho, the
owner of the *Fenix*. The three others, Manuel and two men named José,
belonged to the shipmaster. Pinto de Carvalho testified that the privateers
took, along with the slaves in the cargo hold, "seven Ladino [acculturated]
slaves who entered into the crew." Pinto de Carvalho did not explain
whether he referred to the privateer crew or whether he meant to clarify
that the Ladino slaves had served as crew members aboard the *Fenix*.
Regardless of the owner's meaning, Moon almost certainly used the men as
crew members.[41]

By the time he captured the *Fenix,* Moon had already augmented his
labor force with captives, including at least one Portuguese slave named
Domingos Gomes. The seven slaves from the *Fenix* ranged in age from
about sixteen to twenty years old, ideal for the rigorous work of manning
a vessel. Pinto de Carvalho valued the slaves in the cargo hold at 180,000
réis each, and Moon probably intended to sell them in the Caribbean or
smuggle them into the United States. Pinto de Carvalho claimed an exorbitant 400,000 réis each for the slaves taken from the crew because they were
"well-skilled in seafaring." Fellow seamen aboard the *Fenix* described the
slaves as "good sailors," so much so that the captain refused to sell one man

for 600,000 réis. Moon would have benefited from the slaves' skills if he kept them aboard as his past practice suggests he probably did.[42]

Moon exposed the insecure position of black seamen. Even if he chose not to incorporate the enslaved sailors into his crew, he had the option to sell them along with the other slaves. The men were legal property, so the captain would not have hesitated to bring them aboard as part of his plunder. Whether or not they found more liberty on his vessel than on the *Fenix,* they had little choice in the matter. Such illicit movement presented a challenge to the U.S. government's ban on the importation of slaves.

Captain Henry Ford demonstrated the government's predicament. In October 1818, Ford had outfitted the *General Artigas* and plundered Portuguese vessels. He took "twelve negroes, or persons of colour" among the booty. The following March, he brought the vessel into Severn River, Maryland and paid Captain John Dameron $80 to take him and his crew up to Baltimore in a schooner. The crew boarded Dameron's vessel in the middle of the night. The next morning, Dameron "felt a good deal alarmed" to find that the supposed crew consisted of twelve black men and a young black boy who waited on Ford. He suspected that Ford would try to smuggle them as slaves. When he confronted Ford, the privateer captain insisted that he employed the men as crew members. Ford allayed Dameron's fears with assurances that privateer crews in general "were made of people of all colours." Once they arrived in Baltimore, Ford and Dameron left Ford's crew on the schooner during the night. Dameron returned the next morning to find that the men had vanished.[43]

When the courts tried Ford for slave smuggling, sailors aboard the *General Artigas* corroborated his claim that the black men came aboard his vessel as part of his crew. One officer testified that while Ford sailed through the West Indies, a man offered to buy the black men. The officers urged Ford to make the sale, but he "utterly refused." The officer claimed that all "negroes taken on board were so taken merely as seamen." Not only did Ford take them aboard as sailors but he also employed them in attacks on Portuguese ships. A crew member named John Wilson swore that "they fought the same as the rest of the crew when they engaged a Portuguese schooner, and did duty as the rest of them." He further testified that when Ford distributed supplies, "the black men received the same as the other part of the crew."[44]

Records do not indicate if the courts convicted Ford nor whether the black men came ashore as free men or slaves. Regardless, the U.S. government faced the same negative implications of Ford's actions. Privateers enhanced the diversity of their crews as they transferred African slaves from Portuguese ships to their vessels. That diversity complicated easy identification of slaves whom captains smuggled across U.S. borders. Artigan privateering fostered a fluidity of identity that made easy discernment of legal and national status impossible.[45]

Some slaves, free blacks, and a few free whites voluntarily boarded privateer vessels. On March 5, 1819, just north of Santo Agostinho, Brazil, an unidentified U.S. privateer captured the *Infante Dom Sebastiao*. The privateer crew consisted of ninety men, including seven or eight blacks, nine to eleven white Portuguese, and one Spanish Indian. After the capture of the *Infante Dom Sebastiao*, the privateer crew added at least six to their number who deserted the Portuguese vessel "by their free will." They included José Pinto, José da Fonseca, Joaquim José da Silva, Antônio Maria, Rufino da Costa, and Tomás.[46]

Antônio Maria and Rufino da Costa had boarded the *Infante Dom Sebastiao* as *grumetes*, though records do not make clear exactly what that meant. The word means "cabin boy" in Portuguese, but the term also described Luso-African creoles along the Upper Guinea coast who participated in maritime trade for wages. In the Senegambia and Sierra Leone regions, West Africans had a reputation as established seafarers, and many put their skills to use in the service of Europeans. They possessed a degree of individual autonomy as wage earners, participating in many facets of the Portuguese trade. Grumetes rarely held positions of high rank aboard Portuguese vessels, however, and they often attended to the personal service of the captain and crew. Maria and da Costa likely received meager wages for undesirable labor, whether as Portuguese cabin boys or Luso-African seafarers. In any case, they felt dissatisfied enough to conclude that service aboard a privateer vessel offered greater prospects than labor on a Portuguese courier ship.[47]

Tomás came from Cabinda in west central Africa and served as a slave to the commander of the *Infante Dom Sebastiao*. Black sailors faced discrimination and slavery, but they also saw maritime labor as a chance to assume greater freedom of movement. Records do not reveal Tomás's status aboard the privateer. By boarding voluntarily, however, he indicated that, like Maria and da Costa, he anticipated some degree of liberation.[48]

Artigan privateers broadened the meaning of illegitimate international movement beyond entering and clearing national borders. The Atlantic Ocean constituted a region of fluid, transnational interaction outside government control. Such movement occurred with various degrees of consent among the captured. The experience ranged from those who joined voluntarily, such as Tomás, Maria, da Costa, and white Europeans, to slaves in cargo holds taken by force. They all participated in an intricate transnational exchange on the ocean. Divided into captors and captives, participants did not always associate on equal grounds, but they did associate intimately. According to John Torpey, governments seek to regulate international movement in ways that make their citizens "dependent on states for the possession of an 'identity' from which they can escape only with difficulty." North American privateers challenged such dependency as they moved people across vessels, erasing former national and legal identities.[49]

Some privateer captains officially changed their nationality, further defying state-imposed identities. To give some legal cover to their activities, they needed to become citizens of the South American revolutionary governments for whom they claimed to sail. Several captains jumped through that loophole, including Danels and perhaps José Almeida and James Chaytor. Those official changes mattered only within the legal framework of U.S. courts. National affiliation mattered little in the Atlantic borderwater. Most crew members disregarded the necessity of perfunctory legal changes in citizenship.[50]

Even formal citizenship changes indicated just how diluted national origin had become as a marker of identity among South American privateers. By the time his sailing days ended, Danels claimed citizenship in the United Provinces and Colombia, although he hailed from Baltimore. He maintained a precarious national status while he sailed for Artigas even though he had become a naturalized citizen of the United Provinces, against whom Artigas fought. José Almeida was born in Portugal, became a naturalized citizen of the United States, claimed citizenship in the United Provinces, and acted as a member of the governing council of Saint Barthélemy. In the Atlantic, privateers could don and doff national affiliation as easily as their tunics.[51]

Diplomacy

Privateers threatened the fragile U.S. state-building project due to their exploits in the Atlantic borderwater. They challenged U.S. sovereignty in the Atlantic and made the government vulnerable to disrespect from European nations as they illicitly formed polyethnic crews, smuggled slaves, and trivialized national citizenship. They forced government officials to weigh the reward of republicanism in South America against the cost of contempt from the international community. United States officials exposed the nation to international criticism by appearing to protect privateers who associated too closely with supposedly degraded races. With the young U.S. republic in a vulnerable position, Corrêa da Serra sought to reveal to U.S. officials the dire economic consequences of isolation from the community of nations.

A child of the Age of Reason, Corrêa da Serra initially viewed the United States as the splendid fruition of Enlightenment philosophy. Soon after his appointment as minister to Washington, he assured James Madison that "no foreign minister ever came to the United States with such heartfelt attachment to this nation as myself." Some U.S. admirers referred to him as the Franklin of Portugal.[52]

He soon soured toward republican government as he wrestled with democratic politics that interfered with the punishment of the privateers. He complained that juries had acquitted them for "fear of the people" and that the judges had "disgraced the commission they have from the United States." He loathed Richard Rush, the interim secretary of state, and denounced Rush's sympathy for South American insurgents and dangerous "revolutionary tendencies." He resented the abuse he received in U.S. news-papers and griped, "The [U.S.] government has no power to give any satis-faction, because the same or worse is published about the president and his ministers, and about the members of Congress, and this is what they call freedom of the press." To Secretary of State John Quincy Adams, he politely understated his concern "that the lukewarm acts of some of the United States officers in the sea ports, does not give me the full confidence in them that I wish to have."[53]

In January 1819, he summarized his problems to the Portuguese secre-tary of foreign affairs and war, Tomás Antônio de Vilanova Portugal. The "jacobin and piratical party" held a tight grip in Maryland and spread its subversive ideology throughout the entire nation. President Monroe had no control over his cabinet and the government had no control over the people. "This is very different from monarchies," Corrêa da Serra wrote, "in which the known will of the King is the law which the ministers and vassals follow. Here the government cannot sustain itself without relying on the strongest party, because a republic is a government of parties, and those who think otherwise are deceived. Those that govern do not have any

Figure 10. José Corrêa da Serra, shown here in an undated and unsigned drawing, was the Portuguese minister in Washington, D.C., from 1816 to 1820. From the Biblioteca Nacional (Lisbon).

power and force besides the parties which elect them for a short while, and can get rid of them at the end of it. They are dependent administrators rather than sovereign lords." He hoped to convince North Americans that the privateers posed a threat to their own republic and to shake the executive branch from its apparent apathy.[54]

That year, he posed as a North American pamphleteer and published *An Appeal to the Government and Congress of the United States Against the Depredations Committed by American Privateers on the Commerce of Nations at Peace with Us*. He warned that privateer captains and crews consisted of rogue, nationless individuals who scorned state authority. By accepting foreign commissions, he averred, the privateer "virtually renounces the sovereignty of his own government." The state exposed its weakness by failing to pass and enforce effective laws to regulate the privateers, and it shirked its "duty to make and enforce our own laws against our own citizens." Corrêa da Serra admitted the peculiarity of his antics in a letter to Vilanova Portugal, but he hoped they would throw popular opinion in his favor and force the U.S. government to act. He reminded Vilanova Portugal of his fortune "that you do not have to deal with a democratic republic."[55]

Corrêa da Serra embarked on a parallel plan to compel the U.S. government to cooperate. In December 1818, he met with Rufus King, a member of the Senate Committee on Foreign Relations. King proposed a commercial treaty between the United States and the Portuguese Empire. A few days later, Corrêa da Serra had the same conversation with Thomas Newton, chairman of the House Committee on Commerce and Manufactures. In January 1819, he had a similar discussion with John Graham, whom the government had recently appointed U.S. minister to Rio de Janeiro. That month, Henry Hill wrote to John Quincy Adams of the advantages that North Americans would derive from a commercial treaty with the Portuguese Empire. He hoped the treaty would help the United States extend trade into Asia, a region where the Portuguese "watch closely the flag of other nations," as one Philadelphia merchant described.[56]

Corrêa da Serra gave the same response in each conversation. "My answers were," he explained to Vilanova Portugal, "that certainly the advantage for both appeared great, but that the piracies practiced against us, and so imperfectly repressed [in the United States], must necessarily cool our good will." He felt it a shame that "a few reprobates . . . had excited the obstacles to such good work." He expressed his opinion that the "lack of laws, and that a poor execution of those which existed was the effect of the spirit of faction," which he saw as endemic to republican government.[57]

Corrêa da Serra insisted to John Quincy Adams that the Portuguese court would refuse to engage the United States in a commercial treaty so long as the U.S. government could not fulfill its obligations as a neutral nation. In April 1818, Congress had codified the major provisions of the Neutrality Acts of 1794, 1797, and 1817 into the single Neutrality Act of 1818. Adams tried to assure Corrêa da Serra that the new legislation contained all the provisions of the 1817 law. The act prohibited U.S. citizens from privateering for Artigas, but it did not disallow vessels that flew Artigan colors from docking in U.S. harbors. To that end, Corrêa da Serra proposed an ultimatum. "If the Artigan flag is once declared illegal and the prizes made under it acts of piracy, all occasions of bitterness and mistrust are done away and our two nations are immediately in . . . perpetual amity on both sides and friendly, mutually advantageous intercourse for ever."[58]

Vilanova Portugal reinforced Corrêa da Serra's message. In September 1819, Graham expressed to the minister that the U.S. government "anxiously desired" to remove differences and progress in commercial talks. Vilanova Portugal replied that "it is impossible to deal with commercial advantages so long as this state of piracy exists. Confidence in the banner of the United States is almost lost."[59]

Corrêa da Serra expected that he could compel the U.S. government to act. "Now that I have this hook and bait secure," he wrote to Vilanova Portugal, "I believe that we will be able to fish something, especially if there is shown resentment and alienation." By March 1819, he informed the magistrate that "our objectives come along much better with the expectation of improving even more" due to the bargaining leverage the proposed treaty provided him. In April, he claimed that never since the passage of the Neutrality Act of 1817 had circumstances looked so favorable. Although piracies continued, he averred, "I believe it will not be so for much longer. It seems to me that I perceive in the government a more effective desire than it had shown before to get rid of them."[60]

Corrêa da Serra accurately assessed the U.S. government's newfound commitment. In 1819, the executive branch bore down on privateering and piracy. Privateers in Venezuela had received license from the revolutionary government to seize any goods aboard Spanish vessels—including goods that belonged to neutral nations. United States commerce suffered at the hands of revolutionary privateers. The indiscriminate plunder stoked fears that foreign privateering had degenerated into outright piracy. On March 3, Congress passed the Piracy Act with little debate. It granted the president power to use the U.S. Navy to suppress piracy and made the crime punishable by death. The executive branch assumed that the act would "operate principally" against vessels fitted out in the United States. The act had particular application to Artigan privateers since, in Monroe's words, Artigas's "whole maritime force, ships, officers and men, [partake] so much of adventure and struck out piracy, that it is difficult to class it under any other head."[61]

Later that month, John Quincy Adams received a visit from the French minister in Washington, Hyde de Neuville. The minister told him that the Portuguese envoy to the Congress of Aix-la-Chapelle, the Count of Palmela, had presented a memorial to that body "complaining in the most energetic manner" against Artigan privateers. Palmela portrayed the U.S. government as incapable of controlling its borders. He complained of "crews gathered from every port from every country" who sailed out of U.S. ports and "found means to elude almost all of [the] clauses" of the Neutrality Act of 1817 (codified by that time under the Neutrality Act of 1818). The congress made a formal declaration of "displeasure and indignation" against the privateers and agreed to send "amicable expostulations" to the United States via the European ministers in Washington.[62]

By appealing to the Congress of Aix-la-Chapelle, the Portuguese government assailed the U.S. republic in a vulnerable area—its reputation among European powers. Great Britain forged a more cautious foreign policy that did not upset their commerce with South American revolutionary governments or alienate Spain in their alliance against the French. Corrêa da Serra praised the British and Dutch governments for condemning vessels that flew insurgent flags. He reserved his ire for the United States and the "ridiculous Swedish and Danish colonies" in the West Indies. Foreign privateering presented a unique challenge to the United States, a young republic that faced European governments skeptical of its political institutions.[63]

Hyde de Neuville informed Adams of the congress's concerns and later presented him a copy of Palmela's memorial. Adams assured the minister that "we had [the privateers] in as great abhorrence as the Congress could have." He hoped that the Piracy Act passed earlier in the month "would show the continued solicitude of this government for the suppression of such offences." By spring of 1819, the U.S. government felt the weight of international pressure to curb foreign privateering.[64]

Suppression

After the meeting with de Neuville and under instructions from Monroe, Adams wrote to Elias Glenn, the U.S. attorney for the District of Maryland.

He condemned the privateers' depredations and expressed concern that the attorney general had made only feeble efforts to prosecute those who sailed out of Baltimore. He hoped Glenn would "use every effort in your power to vindicate the character of the nation and the authority of its laws." Days later, Adams sent J. J. Appleton, the secretary of the legation to Rio de Janeiro, to Baltimore to follow up on his instructions to Glenn.[65]

Glenn had ineffectually prosecuted privateers until 1819. Between 1817 and 1818, he had brought criminal charges against nineteen individuals for violation of U.S. neutrality or piracy. Records reveal the outcome of six of those cases. Glenn convicted only the merchant Joseph Karrick for violating U.S. neutrality by acting as an agent to procure new gunpowder for a privateer. Even in that case, the court released Karrick on an arrest of judgment. After Karrick's release, Corrêa da Serra complained that the people arrested on criminal charges "all remain strolling the streets of Baltimore."[66]

One week after Adams censured Glenn's tepid efforts, the attorney responded. "You may assure the President," he seethed, "that I shall as I heretofore have done, use my utmost efforts to vindicate the honor of the nation and the authority of its laws." In 1819, Glenn nearly doubled his prosecution and conviction rates. That year, he brought charges against forty-one alleged privateers for piracy, neutrality violations, or slave smuggling. He secured seven guilty verdicts of the twenty-three known results. Graham hoped that Vilanova Portugal would see in such prosecutions "proofs and pledges" of the government's desire to suppress the privateers.[67]

In the middle of the year, the U.S. government dispatched Oliver H. Perry to Venezuela to protest the ravages of the privateers. The president charged Perry to inform the revolutionary governments in Venezuela and Buenos Aires that the United States would no longer tolerate privateer vessels that fit out in its ports. Further, it would no longer recognize privateers that held more than one commission, as many Artigan privateers did.[68]

Portuguese ministers felt encouraged by the government's new efforts. José Joaquim Vasques, the Portuguese consul general in the United States, visited Baltimore that June. While there, he "had the pleasure to see that this business of Piracy has diminished very considerably by the lack of means which has been taken from it; by the opposition which it has encountered in the system of introducing its prizes here." He hoped that as soon as the Portuguese could impede the privateers' entrance into the West Indies he would "see an end to this horrible system of piracy." To that end, he recruited Richard Alsop, a U.S. merchant, to act as a Portuguese agent to investigate the privateers' Caribbean connections.[69]

By 1814, Alsop had moved from Connecticut to New York, where he probably met Vasques, and by 1815 he had created favorable business ties with Lisbon firms. As an ascendant merchant with prospects in Lisbon and a good relationship with the Portuguese consul general, Alsop stood to gain favor with his business contacts by aiding the struggle against Artigan privateers. He also probably worried about the security of his own trade on the Atlantic. On June 2, 1819, he departed for the Caribbean and stayed there until February 1820. He worked with a Swedish partner, M. C. Von Hausewolff, as he traveled around the Caribbean to reclaim Portuguese prizes and restore them to their owners.[70]

Toward the end of his stay, he sent a report to Corrêa da Serra that used racialized rhetoric to attack the privateers' transatlantic networks and the diversity of their crews. He recounted the labyrinthine process to clear vessels and enter Caribbean ports and painted a derogatory picture of the privateers' associates on the islands. Only a few "miserable beings" inhabited the island of Saint Barthélemy, he wrote. They comprised an assortment of "refugees of all nations . . . native creoles, a miserable race of norman French extraction." Contraband characterized the entire economic history of the island, according to Alsop. The colony enticed mainly "unprincipled adventurers" and "unworthy Americans." Alsop also maligned the diversity of privateer crews, which consisted of "rudy, unconnected, disunited & depraved individuals, the outcasts of all society." Their officers "are composed of most all nations except Spaniards and the crews a motley collection of every colour and tribe."[71]

The privateers' counted their international contacts among their primary assets, but Alsop hoped to turn them into a liability by attacking their racial composition. He portrayed crews as misfit bands bereft of nationality with whom only "unworthy Americans" would interact. His report convinced Corrêa da Serra more than ever that he must compel the U.S. government to pass legislation that would impede privateers from leaving U.S. ports.[72]

In December 1819, Monroe urged Congress to pass a law restricting foreign armed vessels from entering most U.S. ports. Congress acceded the following May. The new law prohibited entrance of such ships into ports that brimmed with privateer activity. To avoid open violations of U.S. neutrality, privateers registered their ships as foreign rather than U.S. vessels, albeit often by fudging ownership records to reflect foreign owners. With their vessels registered under foreign ownership, however, the new law impeded them from returning to U.S. ports after their cruises. It granted the president broad discretion over land and naval forces to enforce its provisions.[73]

The legislation took enforcement of U.S. neutrality out of the hands of local customs officials by charging the U.S. Navy to keep foreign armed ships clear of Baltimore and other ports sympathetic to the privateers. In the Atlantic, local legal interpretations often conflicted with the intentions of central authorities. With the new legislation, the U.S. government sought to repair that divide by removing the influence of local officials—at least those whose views differed from those of the central government.[74]

That same month, Congress renewed the Piracy Act and included additional provisions that targeted the illicit movement of slaves on the high seas. The new legislation deemed persons as pirates who transferred "any negro or mulatto" from one vessel to another with the intent of selling them into slavery. In their attacks on Portuguese commerce, North American privateers commonly captured slave ships and smuggled the slaves into the United States or Caribbean. They also captured Portuguese enslaved sailors and incorporated them into their crews. United States officials feared that such exchanges would allow privateers to smuggle slaves into the country by passing them off as crew members. After 1820, privateers faced the death penalty for such violations as stipulated in the Piracy Act.[75]

Congress passed both laws with little contention. During the summer of 1820, Monroe pressed Baltimore officials for "increased vigilance" against the privateers, and he instructed his cabinet to waste no time in enforcing the new laws. In July, Adams informed Corrêa da Serra of his hope that the acts demonstrated "the determination, both of the Legislature and the Executive to discharge, with the utmost fidelity, all their duties towards friendly nations," particularly the Portuguese Empire. The Portuguese government drew a direct connection between the passage of the acts and its recent efforts to use a commercial treaty as leverage. In a report probably written by the Portuguese chargé d'affaires José Amado Grehon in 1822, Grehon assumed that the laws came about partly because the U.S. government felt "very desirous to contract a Commercial Treaty with Portugal."[76]

In September, Corrêa da Serra extolled the effectiveness of the laws and "the numerous death sentences" of the piratical reprobates. Grehon reported that during the winter of 1818–1819, grand juries indicted three men for piracy and forty more for violation of neutrality laws. "After great oratory harangues, and legal difficulties," he lamented, "the three were acquitted, and of the others only one was convicted." He noted, however, that after the new laws took effect, "the punishment of the Pirates began . . . to be more serious, and there were nearly 40 executed, or condemned to death." Incomplete records make it difficult to determine the exact number of convictions and executions, but U.S. authorities executed at least seven men and commuted twenty-four other death sentences to time in prison. The Portuguese ministers believed, nevertheless, that they witnessed a stronger commitment from the U.S. government to punish Artigan privateers. Indeed, all seven of the executions took place in 1820. Two of them occurred even though four thousand Baltimoreans petitioned Monroe to pardon the perpetrators.[77]

Artigan privateering began to decrease well before Artigas's defeat in late 1820. The decline correlated with the stronger posture of the U.S. government via the Piracy Act of 1819, heightened prosecution rates, and the two 1820 laws (Figure 11). In 1818, Artigan privateers had their most productive year, seizing 58 percent of all Portuguese vessels taken during that period. Between 1818 and 1819, such captures declined by 66 percent. The Panic of 1819 ruined some of the largest investors in South American privateering and contributed to the drop in their activity that year. Regardless of the effect of the financial collapse on foreign privateering, U.S. officials took primary concern with the nation's reputation among world powers. Perception was as important as reality. Portuguese officials felt convinced that the decline resulted from the U.S. government's recent actions.[78]

In January 1820, the Portuguese military pushed Artigas's army out of the Banda Oriental, and the region came firmly under the control of the empire. Worse still for Artigas, he lost the support of the littoral provinces of Entre Ríos and Corrientes—participants in a federal league Artigas had organized for the defense of the interior. In September, he met his final defeat and fled to Paraguay. Artigan privateering ceased except for two prizes taken the following year. The Spanish and Portuguese governments brought libel suits against the privateers in civil courts, which resulted in the restitution of hundreds of thousands of dollars to the original owners. The legal actions occurred in admiralty courts, in which a federal judge rather than a local jury decided the case. Only a few privateers continued in the service of Venezuela and Colombia in the 1820s. Even if it received

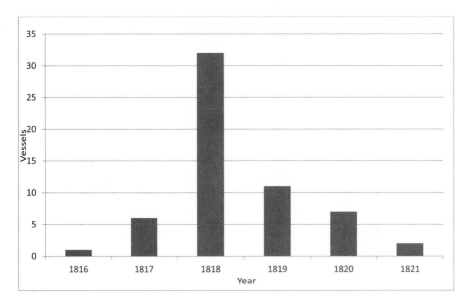

Figure 11. Number of Portuguese vessels captured by foreign privateers. Sources: "General Table of the value claimed by subjects of Portugal, in consequence of captures made by American Privateers, under insurgent Flags, specially Artigas," [n.d.] box 116, Vasques to Pereira, September 30, 1818, box 273, Corrêa da Serra to Adams, March 8, 1818, box 552, "Termo de Juramento e declaração que faz Jacob Leandro da Silva," July 23, 1818, box 116, "Depoimento de Antonio Bernardes," September 7, 1819, box 117, and Corrêa da Serra to Pereira, November 7, 1817, box 552, all in MNE, ANTT; "Declaração que faz João Luiz Victor," August 12, 1818, Série Interior, IJJ9–243, ANRJ; *Daily National Intelligencer*, August 13, 1829.

unacknowledged aid from market forces, the U.S. government could claim the termination of foreign privateering.[79]

*   *   *

The Age of Revolution unfolded as a negotiation between private networks and state power, not as an ineluctable victory for revolutionaries. Many U.S. officials sympathized with the South American revolutionary movements, but the privateers diverged from the government in their willingness to take direct action to effect change. They contested the power of the U.S. and Portuguese states to control their international interactions, national identities, and commerce. Adventurous investors took advantage of the revolutionary atmosphere to the south of Brazil to profit from plunder and liberate a potentially strong trade region from Portuguese control.

William F. Redding believed that the "republican pirates" represented the march of liberty across the Americas; the U.S. government saw them as an obstacle to national projects. Artigan privateers thwarted negotiations for an advantageous commercial treaty with the Portuguese government in Brazil. Ironically, it appeared that republican enthusiasm would endanger rather than promote trade in the South American country.

Even worse for the Monroe administration, the privateers damaged the United States' standing among the community of nations. State Department officials refused to compromise the national reputation with an unpredictable attempt to secure a republican trade partner in the Banda Oriental. Like smugglers during Jefferson's embargo, the privateers fought against their own republican government for control over their international transactions. United States officials suppressed foreign privateering to advance commercial negotiations in Brazil. They signaled a willingness to settle for advantageous trade with monarchies rather than gamble on republican revolutions. Since the 1790s, the Portuguese court had operated on the assumption that republicanism need not accompany liberalized trade. United States authorities seemed convinced.

Chapter 9

Republics, Monarchies, and Commerce

Corrêa da Serra had grown exhausted with the U.S. democratic process during his struggle against foreign privateering, and he concluded that the unruly republic did not merit a commercial treaty with the Portuguese Empire. He threatened that the Portuguese court would agree to a treaty only if the United States participated in a joint commission to investigate damages claimed by Portuguese subjects against the privateers. The U.S. government rejected the ultimatum, considering it a violation of national sovereignty. Corrêa da Serra viewed the rejection as a final affront despite his satisfaction at the repression of privateering. In August 1820, after he learned that the United States refused to cooperate, the minister warned that "commercial restrictions would be certain." In November, he returned to Portugal, and the empire ceased negotiations. By that point, however, U.S. officials shrugged off Corrêa da Serra's actions, as the fortunes of the two governments began to diverge.[1]

In the early 1820s, U.S. diplomats casually dismissed the breakdown of treaty negotiations with the Portuguese Empire. Discontented Portuguese subjects demanded that Dom João return to Lisbon. Their protests exposed the empire to a crisis of sovereignty between Brazil and Portugal. The empire began to fracture in the face of financial disaster. The rupture culminated with a Brazilian declaration of independence in 1822, which curbed U.S. policymakers' enthusiasm for a commercial agreement with the Portuguese Empire. By the early 1820s, U.S. traders sent to Brazil nearly 80 percent of their Luso-Atlantic exports. Rather than pursue negotiations with Portugal, the U.S. government prepared to recognize Brazilian independence and secure a commercial treaty with the new nation. The change brought to fruition a process that had unfolded since the American Revolution by which U.S. commercial ties to Portugal unraveled while trade with Brazil increased. By enhancing the importance of Brazil within the Luso-Atlantic, private commercial networks had undermined the strength of the Portuguese Empire.[2]

By the early 1820s, the United States occupied an ambiguous place in the world. In December 1823, Monroe delivered his annual message to Congress days after U.S. officials received word that the Portuguese ministry would discontinue negotiations. He announced that the Western Hemisphere remained off limits to European recolonization and that the United States would view any attempt to do so as a national threat.[3]

Monroe's message presented a bold statement on foreign policy with no provisions to enforce it. It revealed a nation confident about its future influence but unsure about its present power. By then, however, the United States had garnered greater respect on the world stage. Ironically, in the case of its relations with Portugal, the U.S. government marked its emergence as a rising power not by concluding the treaty but by the nonchalant reaction of U.S. officials to the failure of negotiations. While the eminent strength of Britain had frustrated the process, the U.S. minister in Lisbon, Henry Dearborn, viewed Britain's interference more as a sign of Portugal's subservience to British commercial might than as U.S. weakness.[4]

Free trade remained a potent ideological force in the United States into the 1820s despite increased support for protection that led to the tariff of 1824. Even proponents of tariffs claimed, at least for rhetoric's sake, that protectionist policies complemented free trade, especially in South America. Henry Clay heralded the Monroe Doctrine as a wise and friendly policy toward South America and hoped it would enhance U.S. commerce. Clay viewed South America as an integral part of what he termed "the American System"—his vision of internal improvements, tariffs, and the growth of U.S. industry. United States merchants would secure ready markets for their raw materials and protected manufactures if the government recognized South American nations and safeguarded the independence of the Western Hemisphere. He assumed that the tariff would complement free trade with independent republics in South America. Even as tariff debates intensified, North Americans remained broadly committed to free trade with South American republics.[5]

By the time the U.S. government recognized Brazil, officials realized that rather than transition to a republic, Brazilians would accept Dom

João's son, Dom Pedro, as a monarch. By retaining a monarchy, Brazil exposed the flawed assumptions of U.S. traders that independence from Europe would lead inexorably to republican commercial relationships defined by free trade among the Americas. Some North Americans hoped that renewed commotions in Pernambuco and Montevideo would open new opportunities to trade with independent republicans. But their hope dissipated as the Brazilian government suppressed Pernambucan rebels and chaotic geopolitics stymied economic growth in Montevideo.

Brazil never became the trade bonanza North American free traders had anticipated. United States commerce with Brazil surpassed that of most European nations by the end of the 1820s, but it never supplanted British trade. United States traders had rearranged their Luso-Atlantic commercial networks by the 1820s, but those changes failed to produce the liberal commercial and political systems North Americans once envisioned. Instead, they revealed the complicated legacy of trade and republicanism during the Age of Revolution.

Breaking the Last Link

As Artigan privateering disappeared, the power balance began to shift between the United States and Portugal. In 1818, Gulf Coast Indians became "dependent nations" in the United States due to the First Seminole War. In October of that year, the British made substantial territorial concessions along the Canadian border. In 1819, Spain relinquished Florida. The U.S. government achieved political and cultural homogeneity in regions acquired from the Louisiana Purchase. Beginning in 1820, U.S. officials suppressed the illicit importation of African slaves. Of all slaves smuggled into the United States from Africa between 1808 and 1859, nearly 80 percent arrived in or before 1820. In 1822, the U.S. Navy dispatched a permanent squadron to the West Indies to suppress Spanish pirates that preyed on U.S. commerce near Cuba and Puerto Rico. United States officials confidently rejected British proposals to allow the Royal Navy to board U.S. vessels suspected of carrying contraband slaves. Between late 1818 and 1822, the U.S. government consolidated its power over its domestic territory, extended its reach farther into the Atlantic, and garnered greater influence abroad. Although the United States remained relatively weak among Atlantic powers, North Americans had assumed a consciousness of their rising strength.[6]

Conversely, in 1820, liberal revolutions shook Portugal and destabilized the government as Portuguese subjects resented what they viewed as the court's increased partiality to American interests. In Europe, Palmela hoped to negotiate the return of the Banda Oriental to Spain to avoid alienating the Portuguese Empire from the European community and to avert a possible war with their Iberian neighbor. According to negotiations, the Portuguese court would return the region to Spanish control and receive indemnification for the treasure it expended to secure it from revolutionaries. The court in Brazil demurred, reluctant to relinquish the Banda Oriental. The Spanish government tried but failed to raise a military force to secure the region, so the Portuguese Empire retained control of the province. By risking war with Spain in Europe to secure the Banda Oriental, the government betrayed a preference for the American portion of its empire.[7]

After Napoleon's defeat, European powers met to reshape Europe at the Congress of Vienna. Many Portuguese observers complained that the court failed to ensure that the powers rewarded Portugal for its fight against the French. They had viewed the congress as a chance to renegotiate the Anglo-Portuguese treaty of 1810 with expanded privileges for Portugal. But the British demanded the full abolition of the slave trade in return for trade advantages for Portugal. The court refused to cede that point, again tilting its political economy in favor of Brazil. Palmela observed the dilemma: "We cannot help but consider that the Portuguese Monarchy has two distinct interests, the European and the American, which cannot always advance jointly, but that must not be sacrificed one or the other."[8]

Riots erupted in Porto in 1820, as people became convinced that the court no longer had Portuguese interests at heart. The commotion spread throughout Portugal within months. Revolutionists convened the Cortes—the Portuguese national assembly—for the first time since 1698. They imposed a constitution on the monarchy and demanded the return of Dom João from Brazil. Many Brazilians took up the cause of constitutionalism but differed from Portuguese revolutionaries in their vision of what it meant for the monarchy's future. Portuguese constitutionalists supported the constitution as a means to compel the monarchy to return to the old imperial order with Portugal as the hegemonic entity in the empire. Brazilians saw it as an affirmation of the new imperial order that commenced in 1808. They balked at suggestions that a return of the monarchy to Lisbon should accompany constitutionalism.[9]

Near the end of the year, an anonymous pamphleteer (perhaps the cavalry commander Francisco Cailhé de Geine) argued that the royal family should not leave Brazil. The author warned that if the monarch returned to Portugal he would leave Brazil amid a "revolutionary tempest" that raged in South America. Merchants and landowners pled with Dom João to stay. They wondered how he could leave "the most interesting part of [the] monarchy" and "suffocate the giant in its crib." A body that represented business interests in Rio de Janeiro, the *corpo do comércio*, warned that "Brazil so abandoned" would soon become independent. Nevertheless, in 1821 Dom João sailed for Lisbon with his court and left his son, Dom Pedro, in South America as prince regent. True to the petitioners' predictions, Dom João's return exposed Brazil to agitation for independence.[10]

After the court departed for Lisbon, many Brazilians expressed their dissatisfaction with the new imperial arrangement and demanded autonomy within the empire. The Portuguese government exposed Brazilian traders to new pressures of foreign competition by opening Brazil to foreign commerce—principally British. Brazilian merchants took advantage of freer trade during the 1810s, but they also complained that the crown did too little to fend off outside competitors. In one remonstrance, merchants averred that free trade should foster the wealth of imperial subjects, not saddle them with unfettered foreign competition. Brazilian merchants believed that the imperial courts unfairly protected Portuguese merchants by forgiving their debts to Brazilian creditors without doing the same for Brazilian debtors. Brazilian slave traders decried the empire's 1815 concession to Great Britain to prohibit slave imports from Africa north of the equator.[11]

Brazilians denounced attempts of the Cortes to make Portugal an entrepôt for Brazilian products for re-exportation to foreign nations. One Pernambucan member assailed the stipulation as the price Brazil must pay "to conserve its union with Portugal." The Portuguese envisioned the changes as a union of the constituent parts of the empire, but Brazilians viewed them as a return to colonization. After the return of Dom João to Portugal, they came to imagine the empire as a set of self-governing entities with free trade. Brazilian complaints revealed elemental fissures among the crown, Portugal, and Brazilian traders. They also exposed the disparate visions for free trade in Brazil between Brazilians and North Americans.[12]

In the Northeast, Brazilian patriots sought to depose royal governors and declare autonomous juntas. Inhabitants disputed the nature of their

Figure 12. Departure of the Queen from Rio de Janeiro. By Jean Baptiste Debret, in *Voyage Pittoresque et historique au Brésil* (Paris, 1834–1839). From the New York Public Library.

changed relationship to Portugal and the degree of autonomy Brazilian provinces should enjoy under the new constitution. Chaos erupted in Bahia, Goiana, Recife, and Olinda as officials and residents vied for power in the vacuum left by the Portuguese court. Revolution erupted in Goiana and spread until nearly nine thousand patriot troops threatened to enter Recife and depose by force the royal governor of Pernambuco, Luís do Rego Barreto. Rival forces fought in small skirmishes until the Portuguese Cortes recalled Barreto to Lisbon and allowed the election of a new provisional junta.[13]

Beyond the northeast of Brazil, the entire country looked primed for a political revolution. The Portuguese government had waged a war it could not afford when it invaded the Banda Oriental in 1816. Just before hostilities erupted, the government had embarked on a plan to rehabilitate its precarious public finances by selling shares in the national bank in return for titles of nobility. Once the invasion commenced, the government lost its chances to recoup its debt. In 1818, tax collectors warned that the military interventions in Pernambuco and the Banda Oriental had dried up state funds. The government funded the war with printed money unsupported by specie. The precarious strategy diminished Brazilians' trust in the imperial economy. The empire's finances had improved little by 1820, and Brazilian elites saw their interests diverge from those of the crown. Liberals in Portugal hoped to reestablish the empire's financial stability by compelling Dom João to return to Lisbon and restoring the pre-1808 economic order. With his return to Portugal, Dom João assured that the divergence with Brazilian merchant elites ended in rupture.[14]

By late 1822, Portugal had fallen into political chaos and appeared destined to lose its prize possession in the Americas. Shortly after Dom João arrived in Lisbon, the Cortes refused to recognize Brazil as an independent kingdom within Portugal's empire. Portuguese representatives believed Brazilian free trade had undermined their commerce. They also demanded that Dom Pedro return to Portugal. Brazilians hoped that Dom Pedro would defy the orders of the Cortes, remain in Rio de Janeiro, and maintain Brazil's status as a co-kingdom.[15]

By October 1821, rumors had spread that Dom Pedro supported Brazilian independence and "intended to be proclaimed King or Emperor of the Brazils." On January 9, 1822, from the balcony of his palace, he declared his intention to remain in the country. Over the next several months, he consolidated his support among the Brazilian population. He received word on September 7 that the Cortes had nullified his claim as prince regent of Brazil. Rather than capitulate, he advocated Brazilian independence. The following year, he assumed the role of an independent, constitutional monarch who ruled the Empire of Brazil as Dom Pedro I.[16]

As early as 1820, U.S. officials had recognized their leverage in their relations with Portugal. On several occasions throughout his tenure, Corrêa da Serra proposed "an American system to be concerted between the two great powers of the western hemisphere." He hoped the governments would work in unison to suppress piracy throughout the Americas. In September 1820, Adams privately scoffed. He maintained that "Portugal and the United States are the two great American powers much as a jolly-boat and the *Columbus* [a seventy-four-gun U.S. Navy vessel] are two great line-of-battle ships. . . . As to an American system, we have it, we constitute the whole of it." As the U.S. government increased its power, officials questioned the value of cooperation with Portugal.[17]

United States traders increased their commerce with Brazil concomitantly with the changing power balance between the two countries. Mid-Atlantic merchants benefited from poor Brazilian harvests that resulted from war and famine. They flooded the country with high-quality flour, which impaired Brazilian domestic production. In Rio Grande do Sul, residents witnessed their flour exports to Rio de Janeiro fall from an average of 218,261 alqueires per year between 1812 and 1816 to 83,528 alqueires per year between 1817 and 1822. The wheat crop failed in Rio Grande in 1822, and the dearth raised prices on U.S. flour even higher in Rio de Janeiro.[18]

North Americans produced flour in quantities that Brazilian producers could never hope to match. During the first two decades of the nineteenth century, Philadelphia and Baltimore developed more efficient methods to mill and transport wheat. The improved technology generated a rapid expansion of the mid-Atlantic's milling infrastructure. In 1821, Philadelphia merchants nearly doubled their domestic exports to Brazil from the previous year. By 1822, U.S. merchants exported $835,787 worth of flour to Brazil, surpassed only by the value sent to Cuba. In 1823, they continued to flood Rio de Janeiro with "excessive importations of Flour." As Henry Hill had predicted in 1808, U.S. merchants elided Brazil's domestic production as they inundated the country with provisions.[19]

During the early 1820s, mid-Atlantic merchants abandoned what remained of their trade networks with Portugal and made Brazil the center of their Luso-Atlantic business. Between 1809 and 1816, the Willing family of Philadelphia consigned cargoes to Portugal on twenty-seven occasions, usually under the firm of Willings & Francis. After 1816, the firm did not send any shipments to Portugal. Between 1821 and 1823, the Willings shipped goods to Brazil on at least five occasions. Paul Beck, Jr. and his son, Harvey, each jumped into the Brazil trade after 1820. They shipped goods there on twenty-two occasions between 1820 and 1824. Of the twenty-five cargoes Henry Pratt sent to Brazil or the Río de la Plata region between 1817 and 1824, twelve went in 1823 and 1824.[20]

Other Philadelphia traders made similar transitions to Brazilian markets in those years, including Robert Ralston, John Goddard, J. J. Borie, Jr., Perit & Cabot, George D. Blaikie, J. & J. Keefe, and Snowden & Wagner. In 1815, Richard Alsop of New York began a transition from a poor drifter to a respectable merchant by engaging in the Lisbon trade. By 1820, he viewed Brazil as the more auspicious trade region of the Portuguese Empire. The former Portuguese agent requested consulships in Bahia and Rio de Janeiro. By the time the upheavals of the 1820s occurred in Brazil, the country constituted the undisputed center of trade for U.S. traders who did business in the Luso-Atlantic (Figure 13).[21]

Some North Americans observed with enthusiasm what one called the "rising spirit of liberty" in Brazil, optimistic that a new age of freedom would soon dawn in that country. Captain Richard Fox surveyed the agitation in the Brazilian northeast and predicted that if "the Patriots gain their point in Pernambuco, the revolution will spread all over the country, from Maranham to the river Plate." He sympathized with a handful of subjects transported to Lisbon "to be tried for their lives, on account of their republican sentiments," and he drew comparisons between the persecuted Brazilians and "our own forefathers." The *Daily National Intelligencer* celebrated that "Brazilians seemed universally to desire an emancipation from a yoke which had hitherto held them in the most disgusting ignorance and oppressive bondage."[22]

Some U.S. observers assumed that Brazilian independence would secure new trade benefits for the United States. In an 1822 assessment of Brazil, the *Intelligencer* cited with approbation Dominique-Dufour de Pradt's *Des Colonies, et la Revolution Actuelle de L'Amerique*. Writing in 1817, de Pradt had supposed that Brazilian free trade would result in the "absolute independence of the country; its separation from Portugal, by the impossibility of making it retrograde from the commerce of the whole world to that of

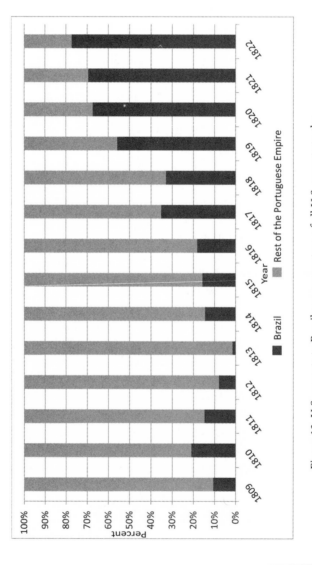

Figure 13. U.S. exports to Brazil as a percentage of all U.S. exports to the Portuguese Empire. Source: *ASP:CN*, 1: 815, 869, 892, 965, 994, 1023, 2: 22, 55, 95, 158, 388, 469, 575, 706.

Portugal alone. So that is very evident, if ever the Sovereign established at Brazil repasses to Portugal, he will leave Independence behind him." The periodical echoed de Pradt's assumption that the United States would align with the new South American countries in a mutual accord of commerce and independence from Europe, especially to the detriment of England. The *Intelligencer* made the connection clear: Brazilian liberty would enhance commerce with the United States and marginalize Great Britain.[23]

Several months before Dom Pedro declared independence in 1822, the acting U.S. consul at Rio de Janeiro, Peter Sartoris, reported that the regent decreed the convocation of a Brazilian congress at Rio de Janeiro. The decree demonstrated that Dom Pedro intended to govern Brazil independently of Portugal. Sartoris gushed, the decree "breaks as it were the almost last link, which bound America to Europe, and may eventually be productive of great benefits to the trade of the U. States." North Americans drew a direct correlation between Brazilian independence and increased trade between the two countries. In such an atmosphere, they hardly felt compelled to reengage Portugal in commercial negotiations.[24]

In 1822, the Portuguese chargé d'affaires in Washington, José Amado Grehon, returned to the subject of a commercial treaty. United States officials first approached Corrêa da Serra about a treaty in 1819, but they now felt little pressure to negotiate with the weakened Portuguese government. As Adams told Dearborn, "We are neither solicitous, nor unwilling to treat with Portugal upon subjects of commerce." If the Portuguese government treated "on the broadest and most liberal principles of reciprocity," the United States would oblige.[25]

United States officials continued to refuse Portugal's demand that the government participate in a joint commission to indemnify Portuguese merchants for losses sustained at the hands of Artigan privateers. By 1822, Portuguese negotiators had lost leverage, and they dropped the condition. In October, Dearborn requested that Portugal include Brazil in the treaty in case the country ultimately remained part of the Portuguese Empire. The government reluctantly acquiesced, further exposing Portugal's weakened power. The Portuguese court had little time to focus on negotiations, however, as it dealt with the imposition of a constitutional monarchy and Brazilian independence.[26]

Complicating negotiations further, Dearborn stipulated that any treaty should allow the United States to enjoy the same privileges in Portugal as did the most favored nation—Great Britain. The British-Portuguese treaty of 1810 obligated Portugal to give Great Britain special advantages in manufacture imports. Portuguese ministers tried without success to renegotiate the 1810 treaty to allow them to trade with other nations on similar terms. A report to the Cortes confirmed that, in Dearborn's words, "England, as might be expected, is very unwilling to relinquish any of the exclusive advantages she now enjoys." In November 1823, the Portuguese foreign affairs secretary, the Marquis of Palmela, informed Dearborn that the Portuguese could not "with propriety" conclude a treaty with the United States on the proposed terms.[27]

With an indifferent response, Dearborn indicated the inverted fortunes of the United States and Portugal. He had received instructions not to "press [Portugal] on the subject of a treaty," and he had no mind to do so. Months earlier, he had informed the Portuguese foreign ministry that he would "readily acquiesce" to suspend negotiations until the Portuguese concluded their talks with Great Britain. When it appeared that Britain's inflexibility would bring the negotiations to an end, he maintained that he had no complaint, nor "a disposition to urge the renewal of the negotiation." Without Brazil, Portugal hardly seemed a nation worth treating with. "Under existing circumstances," Dearborn informed Adams, "I have not deemed it expedient to press the subject any further." By March 1824, Dearborn had heard nothing more on the issue from Palmela. "Of course," he reassured Adams, "I am quite at leisure."[28]

Cisplatine Province

Montevideo played a key role in the growth of commerce between the United States and Brazil. The port city enjoyed a geographical advantage in the southern Brazil–Río de la Plata trade. United States traders had better access to Montevideo than to Buenos Aires because large sand banks impeded easy entrance into the latter port. Montevideo also enjoyed a privileged history as the mandatory port of call in the Spanish Empire. Porteño merchants commonly depended on traders in Montevideo to act as their agents, which reinforced the city's prize position in the estuary. After they unloaded cargoes in Rio de Janeiro, U.S. captains and supercargoes frequently continued to Montevideo to look for a favorable return cargo.[29]

The Portuguese government hesitated to incorporate the Banda Oriental into Brazil, fearful of reprisals in Europe. Since 1817, the Portuguese commander, Carlos Frederico Lecór, managed Montevideo affairs as a military governor, but he cultivated the favor of the city's residents and sought to increase trade. To achieve his goals, he tried to secure stronger commercial connections with North America, believing that the United States and Brazil should unite their interests against European domination.[30]

In April 1821, Lecór received permission from Dom João to call the Congresso Cisplatino, the Cisplatine Congress. The special assembly convened to vote on the fate of the Banda Oriental—whether to become a Brazilian province, return to the United Provinces, or rejoin the Spanish Empire. Lecór recognized the waning power of the Portuguese monarch and anticipated Brazilian independence. He and his close collaborators manipulated events to secure the Banda Oriental for an independent Brazil. Dom João had insisted that popular elections determine the congressional deputies, but Lecór contravened those orders as he handpicked nine of the eighteen participants. He allowed pro-Portuguese *cabildos* (municipal institutions in Spanish America) in the province to choose the other nine. His machinations stacked the congress with representatives who wanted to incorporate the province into Brazil.[31]

In July, the congress voted to unite with Brazil after provincial elites formed a delicate alliance among pro-Spanish, pro-Portuguese, and pro-Artigan forces to promote the project. Dom João hesitated to annex the province under such questionable circumstances. Lecór collaborated, therefore, with Dom Pedro, who welcomed the region as the newly established province of Estado Cisplatino.[32]

With his political maneuvers, Lecór ensured that Montevideo would constitute part of an independent Brazil when the time proved ripe to declare Brazilian independence. The U.S. consul in Montevideo, William Gilchrist Miller, assumed that the region would prosper under the arrangement "from the liberality of its commercial regulation." After it secured the Banda Oriental, the Portuguese government lifted its blockade on Montevideo, and U.S. commerce flowed into the port. In the decade before 1820, Philadelphia merchants consigned a total of $7,996 worth of goods to Montevideo. In 1821 and 1822, they sent $62,485.96 worth of domestic goods alone.[33]

United States merchants increased their trade with Montevideo due to a poor harvest and turbulent politics. Like Rio Grande, the Río de la Plata region suffered a wheat failure in 1822, which raised flour prices in the region. In June, flour sold for $23 per barrel in Buenos Aires versus $16 per barrel in La Guaira, Venezuela. In late 1822, after Dom Pedro declared Brazilian independence, three thousand pro-Portuguese troops invaded Montevideo, repelled pro-Brazilian forces, and demanded that the province remain united to Portugal. The turmoil impeded agricultural production to the benefit of U.S. traders. In 1823, Philadelphia exporters consigned $44,775.62 worth of domestic goods to Montevideo. The figure constituted 21 percent of the value of all U.S. domestic exports to Brazil. Only Pernambuco received a higher share of the value, at 34 percent. Between 1818 and 1822, seventy-seven ships entered Montevideo from U.S. origins, compared to seventy-two that arrived from British origins. North Americans could yet hope for influential trade partners in Brazil committed to independence from Europe.[34]

Despite North Americans' bullish attitude toward the Cisplatine Province, provincial leaders had based their decision to join Brazil on free trade, not republicanism. Over the past century, traders in Montevideo had forged strong transimperial commercial relations with Brazilians. Many elite traders had enjoyed the protections of the Spanish government. After Montevideo fell to revolutionary forces in 1814, some royalists fled to Rio de Janeiro, where they supported the Portuguese invasion of the Banda Oriental. Like many Brazilian merchants, therefore, they did not equate free trade with republicanism. Indeed, after the royalist junta had taken power in 1810, it declared the port open to foreign merchant vessels.[35]

In 1817, a Montevideo delegation had traveled to Rio de Janeiro to request incorporation into Brazil on the condition that the Portuguese Empire guarantee the province free trade. The delegation did not negotiate on behalf of the people of the Banda Oriental. Instead, it represented the province's cabildos—a form of representation based on monarchical political structures of the ancien régime. After Brazil annexed the province in 1821, the government agreed to articles of incorporation that included free trade provisions. By joining Brazil's monarchical system with free trade guarantees, Montevideo elites could preserve political hierarchies and retain their foreign commercial networks.[36]

In their feverish trade with Montevideo, North Americans betrayed a willingness to abandon their association of liberal political economies with republicanism. By incorporating the Cisplatine Province and granting its residents free trade, the Brazilian monarchy shattered assumptions that republicanism and free trade would spread together throughout the hemisphere. United States newspapers printed the seemingly paradoxical news that the province "has been annexed to the Crown of Portugal . . . and a free trade with the whole western coast of that extensive country is antici-pated." The *Independent Chronicle and Boston Patriot* refused to believe that inhabitants of the province would freely choose incorporation into a monarchical political system. The editors assumed Lecór restrained free expression and effected the move by "compulsion, seduction, and terror." Regardless, U.S. traders took advantage of Montevideo's open ports. As Brazilian independence advanced, they recognized that they would have to settle for open trade without accompanying political revolutions in Brazil.[37]

Recognition

Near the end of August 1824, a pamphlet circulated in Rio de Janeiro with the caption, "Congratulations to the Brazilian Nation." The publication celebrated the reception in Washington of José Silvestre Rebello as an accredited chargé d'affaires for the independent Brazilian government. On that occasion, the United States became the first nation to take the critical step toward official recognition of Brazilian independence. On September 11, Condy Raguet, the U.S. commercial agent in Rio de Janeiro and a busi-ness partner in the Philadelphia firm of Clapp, Raguet, & Co., informed John Quincy Adams of the "importance given to that measure, by the [Bra-zilian] ministry." He recognized, however, that both conservative and liberal segments of the Brazilian population observed the event with trepi-dation.[38]

Anti-independence Portuguese natives "were excessively enraged" by the news, "maintaining that it was a disgrace for a Monarchy to solicit the patronage of a Republick, and one so insignificant in the scale of nations." At the other extreme, Brazilian liberals chafed at the monarchical nature of the new government and worried that Rebello's reception "is a sort of approval of the form of the government" on the part of the United States. Indeed, the Brazilian government tried to cast it as such. By recognizing Brazil, the U.S. government raised the question of whether an independent republic and an independent monarchy in the Americas could cooperate in diplomacy and commerce.[39]

North Americans with business in Brazil viewed hemispheric indepen-dence from Europe as their primary goal, even if that included an indepen-dent monarchy in South America. Many began to adopt the racialized assumption, previously manifested during the 1817 congressional debates on neutrality, that the inferior Brazilian population could not sustain a republic. Some U.S. nationals assumed that at best they could hope for an independent Brazilian monarchy. Henry Hill believed that the revolutions in Spanish America would have little effect on Brazilian political institutions. He even suggested that North Americans should not wish for such a change, "considering the nature of the Population of the Country," whom he believed unable to perpetuate a republican government.[40]

Hill continued to complain about "the tendency of the [Brazilian] Government to check industry and oppress individual liberty." He supposed, nevertheless, that Brazil "is gradually approximating to an Independence from Europe, and will naturally find its interest in an amalgamation with the American family, which it will fall into insensibly, by an assimilation of manners, habits, the dissemination of Education, progress of public opinion and political relationship." Independence constituted the primary goal—all the better if republicanism followed.[41]

Like Hill, Raguet doubted the immediate prospects for a republican government in Brazil. As he described to John Vaughan of Philadelphia in 1823, "There is no press—there are no associations—there are no persons who read, or who have much pretension to science or philosophical research, or if there are, it is impossible for a foreigner to find them." He supported recognition of Brazilian independence even if Brazil retained a monarchy, supposing that the move would help absorb the Brazilian government into the American community. If the U.S. government credentialed a chargé d'affaires in Rio de Janeiro, he believed, it could enhance commercial ties with Brazil. Raguet fretted, however, that Brazil aligned more closely with "the principal monarchs of Europe." Equally as bad, the "secret dread of the moral influence of our Republick must have a perpetual tendency to produce a coldness towards us on the part of the government." He hoped that full recognition by the United States could allay such worries.[42]

Raguet assumed that if the United States recognized Brazil quickly it could gain favor there to the detriment of Great Britain and France, "who are desirous to see Brasil as ever heretofore, direct her eyes to Europe, and not to North America." He observed that the British felt envious that the United States had taken the lead in recognition by receiving Rebello. In March 1825, the U.S. government promoted Raguet to chargé d'affaires in Rio de Janeiro. With the appointment, the United States officially recognized Brazilian independence.[43]

Raguet still believed that monarchy stifled trade. As early as 1809, Henry Hill had noted that the Bragança monarchy in Brazil manifested a tendency to regulate trade in a manner more consistent with antiquated European mercantilism than with American liberalism. Little changed after independence, according to Raguet. In July 1824, he met with the consuls general of Britain and France and the Brazilian foreign minister, Luis José de Carvalho e Melo. He hoped to secure "the removal of the obstructions to commerce and navigation which have ever so much abounded here." The meeting proved fruitless, for Raguet had received little cooperation from the British and French consuls. Worse still in Raguet's view, "the obstinate devotion of the minister [Carvalho e Melo] to old habits and rules, were so great that I do not see how this country ever can gain upon the 300 years which she is behind us or Europe."[44]

The new chargé believed that Brazil possessed a two-pronged fate: either the "form of government may gradually assume the character of a Despotism, or ultimately, by the adoption of the American system, be changed into that of a Republick." By December, however, Raguet lamented that "greater is the number of those, who are of opinion, that an absolute government is now more likely to be established in Brasil, than a Republick." Indeed, the Brazilian military had just quashed another spirited but short-lived rebellion in Pernambuco.[45]

Confederation of the Equator

In June 1822, the Cortes had approved the convocation of a Brazilian constituent assembly. Brazilians grew restless as they perceived that the assembly would remain subservient to the Cortes in Lisbon, and deputies to the assembly clamored for greater autonomy in Brazil. The assembly functioned as Brazil's central legislative body after Dom Pedro declared independence in September. It superintended the new constitution that yielded significant power to Dom Pedro as monarch. The emperor had acceded to the demands of Brazilian liberals to convene the assembly to legitimate his rule in Brazil. By November 1823, however, he had consolidated his power as monarch and dissolved the assembly. The following March, Dom Pedro promulgated a new constitution that centralized political power in the monarchy. The move sparked fears of despotism.[46]

Pernambucans decried monarchical centralism. Local elites had sought to recoup autonomy over regional affairs since the return of Dom João to

Portugal. They had anticipated greater power for the provinces after Brazil declared independence. They rested their arguments on the theory that, in the words of the periodical *Typhis Pernambucano*, "Brazil became sovereign, not only in the whole, but in every one of its parts or provinces." In Pernambuco and the surrounding regions of Ceará, Rio Grande do Norte, Paraíba, and Alagoas, provincial leaders revolted against the centralization of power in Rio de Janeiro.[47]

At the end of 1823, electors in the province's Great Council rejected Dom Pedro's appointment of Francisco Pais Barreto as provincial president. Instead, they supported Manuel de Carvalho Pais de Andrade. Carvalho had fled Pernambuco to the United States after the failed 1817 revolt. During his exile, he absorbed U.S. republican ideology. One U.S. newspaper described him as a man "of firm republican principles." Brazilians called him "an American in ideas, in manners and in customs." After his return to Pernambuco and election to the presidency of the province, he advocated a federalist constitution in Brazil to reserve autonomy for provincial governments.[48]

On July 2, 1824, Carvalho issued the "Proclamation of the Confederation of the Equator," in which he denounced political centralization in Rio de Janeiro and outlined his federalist goals. Supported by an unstable coalition of constitutional monarchists, moderate unitarians, and federalists, he set aside his preference for a Pernambucan republic. He limited his proposals to the reconvocation of the constituent assembly and a representative government, whether in the form of a constitutional monarchy or a republic.[49]

Foreigners believed they saw in the Confederation of the Equator the wellspring of a democratic republic. In December 1823, the French consul assumed that Carvalho hid his true radicalism "to appease the court." Maria Graham, an English visitor in the province, observed that North Americans in Pernambuco pressed for republicanism, "showcasing their own government as the most convenient model for the recently emancipated American states." She believed that Pernambuco had turned "decidedly republican, no doubt owing to its constant exchange with the United States." The *National Advocate* assumed, "Every thing seems to indicate a change of system in this country, more congenial with the democratic or republican feelings of the Brazilians than that of an Imperial government."[50]

The Brazilian monarchy prepared a military force to suppress the rebellion, and Carvalho requested aid from the U.S. government. One U.S. ship captain noted that "all the Republicans look to the United States for assistance." Although the Monroe administration declined to help, the rebels once again received succor from U.S. merchants.[51]

The former consul Joseph Ray had remained in the good graces of Pernambucan residents since his dismissal as consul in 1820. In January 1824, eighty-nine people petitioned Carvalho to use his influence to have Ray reinstated as consul. They gave Ray preference to fill the post due to his friendly attitude to Carvalho's government and his antagonism toward Dom Pedro's royal surrogates. The current consul, James Hamilton Bennett, remained unengaged with the Pernambucan rebel cause, and his disinterest cost him diplomatic and commercial influence in the region. Ray outperformed Bennett in business, consigning approximately three times as many outbound ships as the new consul. As the Pernambucan petition in behalf of Ray suggests, he also garnered stronger social ties to the community than Bennett. Locals described him as Carvalho's "intimate friend."[52]

Ray exerted his energy in the case of a young New York idealist named James Rodgers, who aided revolutionaries in Pernambuco. The Confederation of the Equator lasted only a few months, and its viability waned by the end of the summer of 1824. Royal forces established a blockade and defeated the rebellion. They arrested and tried many of the rebels, including Rodgers. The Brazilian government accused the U.S. national of attacking royal troops and killing some "in the most unheard of cruelty." Ray tried to bribe the military court to secure Rodgers's release and with a small group of U.S. traders petitioned Bennett to use his influence to ensure a fair trial for Rodgers. Regardless, the Brazilian military executed the young man on April 12, 1825.[53]

As many as fifty Pernambucan rebels fled to the United States, and the Brazilian government assumed Ray had assisted them. It remains unclear how many people Ray helped, but he recommended at least one fugitive, J. B. S. Rangel, to J. P. B. Storer of Boston, who then introduced him to John Vaughan, an eminent Philadelphia merchant. Storer attested, "During their long residence in this city, the Brazilian exiles have gained the respect and confidence of all good men not more for their sufferings, than their fortitude and dignified deportment." By the early 1820s, U.S. commercial networks intertwined intricately with revolution in Brazil.[54]

As in 1817, U.S. merchants found that ideological sympathy with Pernambucans generated favorable trade opportunities. By the end of the year,

they had flooded the province with approximately fourteen thousand barrels of flour—a year's supply. Between 1816 and 1820, Pernambuco
imported an average of 119,717,002 réis worth of goods from the United
States each year. The figure constituted an annual average of 4.4 percent of
the value of all goods imported into the province. By 1826, the numbers
nearly tripled as Pernambuco imported 423,344,400 réis worth of goods
from the United States. Those goods accounted for 17.4 percent of the
value of all imports.[55]

British trade with Pernambuco grew as well, but it failed to do so at
such a high rate. Pernambucans increased their importations of British
goods from 22.6 percent of the total in 1820 to 32.8 percent in 1826. United
States trade far outpaced the British in terms of its rate of growth. Condy
Raguet's correspondence suggests that such growth came, at least in part,
due to the ideological connection between Pernambucans and the United
States. In January 1825, he informed John Quincy Adams that in Bahia and
Pernambuco "the feeling towards our country, is more fraternal" than in
Rio de Janeiro. For the second time in a decade, North Americans looked
to Pernambuco to bring to fruition the promise of republicanism and
favorable U.S. trade in Brazil. But the province seemed to promise only
false starts. Despite the impressive growth in trade with Pernambuco, U.S.
merchants faced sustained disadvantages in Brazil compared with the
British.[56]

Obstacles

As early as 1823, Raguet felt pessimistic about the trade with Brazil. He
informed Stephen Girard of Philadelphia that U.S. manufactures could not
compete with those of European nations. He reported further that U.S.
produce remained subject to volatile prices. Worse still, Brazil favored trade
with Great Britain, allowing the British a 9 percent advantage in duties over
the United States—an advantage Brazil continued to offer as a holdover
from the Anglo-Portuguese treaty of 1810. Girard chose not to enter the
Brazilian trade.[57]

After the State Department appointed Raguet as chargé d'affaires in
Brazil, he attempted to conclude a treaty that would place the United States
in a stronger trade position against Great Britain. Although the Brazilian
government expressed interest in a trade agreement, the Estado Cisplatino
experienced renewed commotion and ruptured negotiations.[58]

Brazil and the United Provinces inherited Portugal and Spain's dispute of sovereignty over the Banda Oriental. After pro-Portuguese troops abandoned Montevideo, Buenos Aires laid claim to the province. Officials of the United Provinces argued that sovereignty over the region reverted to the United Provinces once Brazil declared independence from Portugal. In December 1825, Brazil declared war on the United Provinces and blockaded their ports.[59]

Raguet questioned the legality of the blockade. He argued that Brazil did not have sufficient naval power to enforce a blockade of all enemy ports. He claimed that in the absence of a fully effective blockade, neutral ships lay exposed to capricious harassment by the Brazilian navy. Tension heightened when the navy captured a U.S. merchant vessel and impressed some of its sailors. Raguet threatened Brazil's foreign affairs minister that "if Brazil was desirous of avoiding a war with the United States, she must respect [North Americans'] liberty."[60]

Ideological overtones colored the diplomatic strain between the Brazilian monarchy and the U.S. republic. "One would suppose," Raguet wrote Clay, "that a monarchy so young as Brasil and surrounded by Republicks," and so financially weak, would try to cultivate good relations with "all the States with which she was in amity." After he quarreled with businessmen and civil officers about some issues with his private affairs, he concluded that the disagreements arose from "their Imperial hostility against the Representative of a Republick." For their part, Brazilian authorities suspected that North Americans favored republican Buenos Aires in the war. José Silvestre Rebello declared that the tilt could "only be attributed to the Republican intolerance." Once again, some U.S. citizens fit out privateers to sail for Buenos Aires against the Brazilian monarchy, although to a much lesser extent than against Portugal during the 1810s.[61]

The renewed conflict gave hope to North Americans who cheered for republicanism in Montevideo. By February 1824, U.S. observers repeated rumors that the Montevideo cabildo planned to rejoin Buenos Aires and, as one U.S. newspaper put it, "avoid being consigned to the yoke of the imperialists of Brazil." Another newspaper called Brazil's 1821 annexation of the Cisplatine Province "the *colonization* of a free people." The editors complained that during the intervening four years the monarchists "abandoned themselves to every excess which generally accompanies the career of usurpers." In such conceptualizations, Montevideo remained in need of republican liberation even if governed by an independent nation in the Americas.[62]

Tumultuous provinces again offered a taste of hope that republicanism would characterize the United States' most important trade regions in Brazil. In 1824, Philadelphia merchants consigned seven vessels to Montevideo and four more to the general region of the Río de la Plata. The eleven vessels constituted nearly 40 percent of all shipments sent to Brazil from Philadelphia that year—a significant increase from the four vessels that had arrived the prior year. Philadelphians sent nearly 18 percent (five vessels) to Pernambuco despite a Brazilian blockade in force during the commotion caused by the Confederation of the Equator. One U.S. newspaper called the blockade "the most interesting [subject] to commercial men, as well as to friends of freedom in South America." In the United States, the blockade symbolized the dissonance between monarchy and commercial freedom. United States free traders saw Pernambuco and Montevideo as regions where they could harmonize trade, republicanism, and independence— commercial and political. Their hopes never materialized.[63]

In 1828, Brazil and Buenos Aires ended the Cisplatine conflict in a stalemate. The two powers agreed to relinquish claims to the Oriental province, granting the region its independence as Uruguay. Great Britain mediated the conflict to stabilize the region, and the British Empire remained an integral part of Montevideo's economy throughout the nineteenth century. Geopolitical turbulence stunted the Uruguayan economy as France and Britain vied for commercial dominance in the new nation and Uruguayans resisted foreign influence. With the end of the war, the United States and Brazil resolved many of their differences. In December, the two nations agreed to a most-favored-nation treaty—twelve years before the United States and Portugal concluded a similar agreement.[64]

Although the treaty facilitated more favorable trade with Brazil, it hardly allowed the United States to keep pace with Great Britain. In 1823, John Devereux of Philadelphia began to trade in Pernambuco, and his brother, B. H. Devereux, joined him in the trade several years later. In 1840, the house drew on the powerful banking firm of Baring Brothers & Co. of London for £5,000 sterling in favor of L. G. Ferreira & Mansfield of Pernambuco. The following year, they drew on the London firm for an additional £7,088 19s. 10d., an indication of the strong presence British houses maintained in the trade, even in traditionally strong markets for U.S. merchants such as Pernambuco.[65]

Condy Raguet complained that "Brasil in imitation of Portugal has completely thrown herself into the arms of England." By 1848, of the seventy-seven recorded merchants in Recife, only three came from the United States. Twenty came from Great Britain, ten from Germany, nine from France, and eight from Portugal. Between the years 1835–1836 and 1839–1840, Pernambucans imported 58.3 percent of foreign goods from Great Britain and only 5.8 percent from the United States. The percentages mirrored trade with the rest of Brazil. In 1842, Brazilians received 48.4 percent of all their foreign goods from Great Britain and just 11.8 percent from the United States.[66]

Such figures only constituted a poor trade if viewed from the lofty expectations that U.S. merchants could supplant British commercial strength in Brazil. By such a metric, most western nations had failed in their commerce. Based on the size of their domestic economy, U.S. merchants enjoyed a healthy share of South American trade, particularly mid-Atlantic merchants. Between 1819 and 1827, Brazil constituted the most valuable non-Caribbean destination in the Americas for domestic goods that left Philadelphia. United States merchants in Recife constituted about 4 percent of the city's total merchant population, but U.S. ships brought nearly 14 percent of all tonnage to Pernambuco between 1842 and 1845. In 1842, Brazilians imported values of U.S. goods nearly on par with those of France. That same year, U.S. exports to Brazil outpaced those of Portugal by £214,928 sterling and nearly doubled those of the German principalities, the two closest national competitors in the country. If North Americans could not compete with Great Britain, they competed very well with the rest of the world.[67]

Slave Trades

Many U.S. traders found success in an increasingly lucrative contraband trade with Brazil—the slave trade. During the mid-1820s, the British government made clear that it would not recognize Brazilian independence unless Brazil abolished the transatlantic slave trade. In 1827, the Brazilian court agreed to terminate the trade, drawing the ire of the elites of the Brazilian slavocracy. Over the next several decades, Brazilian slavers counted on U.S. smugglers to supply them with African labor because the U.S. government refused to allow the British Royal Navy to search U.S. ships for slaves.[68]

As their own government suppressed slave smuggling across U.S. borders, many North Americans supported the illicit trade in Brazil. Between

1831 and 1850, U.S. vessels carried 429,939 of the 738,198 slaves imported into Brazil, with the remainder divided among Brazilian, Portuguese, French, and Spanish vessels. It remains difficult to gauge how many vessels came from the United States given the propensity of traders from other nations to sail under false U.S. colors to avoid British searches. Regardless, U.S. traders certainly accounted for the largest share of slaves brought to Brazil. In the face of a conservative backlash against the abolition of the slave trade, Brazilian officials did little to stem the illegal flow of slaves transported on U.S. vessels. At the close of the Age of Revolution, North American trade with Brazil finished where it started—with a prolific contraband trade underlain by the Brazilian slave regime.[69]

Even if they could not rid Brazil of British influence, North Americans learned that they could take advantage of Brazilian commerce, and they depended on slavery to do so. Southerners and Northerners alike participated in the illicit slave trade to Brazil. Traders exchanged mid-Atlantic produce for Brazilian coffee grown by slaves. With so much of the U.S.-Brazilian trade—legal and otherwise—supported by slavery, slavery's advocates began to contemplate Brazil as a country in which to profit from the transatlantic slave trade. They condemned Britain's attempts to stifle the trade and demanded that the United States, as the Southerner Duff Green declared, "raise the banner of free trade" in opposition to British incursions. By 1844, Green insisted that white Southerners "make common cause with Brazil & Cuba" to resist the Royal Navy. As imagined by Green, free trade with Brazil advanced U.S. interests in South America to the detriment of Great Britain.[70]

By the 1850s, the native Virginian Matthew Fontaine Maury contemplated a doomed attempt to open the restricted Amazon region to U.S. commerce and plantations. He made his plans on the assumption of Brazilians' inherent inability to establish a republic. North Americans would do for Brazil what Brazilians had proven unable to do. He asked, "Shall [Brazil] be peopled with an imbecile and an indolent people or by a go ahead race that has energy and enterprise?" His answer: Brazil could "no more prevent American citizens . . . from going there with their goods and chattels to settle and to revolutionize and republicanize and Anglo Saxonize that valley, than it can prevent the magazine from exploding after the firebrand that has been thrown into it." His visions went beyond free trade in the Amazon, as he added, "That Valley is to [be] the safety valve for our Southern States, when they become over-populated with slaves, the African

Slave Trade will be stopped, and they will send their slaves to the Amazon." The Amazon, he declared, would serve "for all commercial purposes as a sort of an American Colony."[71]

Maury assumed that white Southerners rather than Brazilians would republicanize Brazil. The Virginian conceptualized the country as a place more in need of colonization than liberation. He viewed Brazil as a solution to the slave problem in the United States, and he fused older notions of republicanism and free trade with the more immediate concern of a U.S.-Brazilian slave trade. If North Americans could export slaves to Brazil, the South could reap the benefits of slavery without the costs of anticipated slave uprisings and racial mixture. Native Brazilian republicans had no place in Maury's imagined future. To white Southerners, South American republics had displayed a dangerous tendency toward abolitionism. Only North Americans could develop the sort of republic Maury foresaw—a republic friendly to slavery. Maury viewed Brazil as an extension of the Southern slave empire rather than as an independent republic that invited free trade from North Americans.[72]

Many white Southerners manifested less concern with Brazil's political system than its labor system. As early as 1832, the slavery advocate William Harper mused, "The only portion of the South American continent which seems to be making any favorable progress, in spite of a rich and arbitrary civil government, is Brazil, in which slavery has been retained." Slavery would enrich American nations, as conceived by Harper, whether governed by monarchies or republics.[73]

By 1854, the *Southern Standard* believed that the United States should "look to Brazil as the next great slave power." The editors hoped that the U.S. government could secure a treaty to open the Amazon to U.S. plantation development and to divide control of the Caribbean between the two countries. They foresaw "ruptures" in Europe that would leave the Caribbean vulnerable to annexation or colonization by the United States and Brazil. "The time will come," they predicted, "that all the islands and regions suited to African slavery, between us and Brazil, will fall under the control of these two slave powers." Such expectations discarded an earlier vision of Brazil and the United States as sister republics and replaced it with an image of the two countries as fellow slave societies.[74]

*   *   *

Between 1816 and 1824, Brazil became the most important destination in the Luso-Atlantic for U.S. produce. Many North Americans sought to influence Atlantic politics and diplomacy by supporting Brazilian independence movements. They formed commercial networks that sold munitions and supplies to revolutionaries, helped fugitives escape punishment, and preyed on Portuguese commerce. They capitalized on ideological similarities and food shortages caused by blockades and warfare to increase their trade with revolutionary regions. During the early 1820s, U.S. policymakers and merchants marginalized Portugal. By 1824, U.S. diplomats shrugged off their failed negotiations with Lisbon in light of Brazil's increased commercial influence and its declared independence.

Portuguese trade policies had given shape to the very commercial networks that ultimately undermined the empire. By severing trade with North Americans during the American Revolution, prohibiting flour imports, and opening Brazilian ports to foreign trade, Portuguese authorities facilitated a process by which Brazil eclipsed Portugal as the center of U.S. trade with the empire. With the new balance of power, the U.S. government decided to recognize Brazilian independence—a move they hoped would secure favorable trade privileges.

North Americans founded such hopes on the dual assumption that Brazil would soon align ideologically with other South American republics and that American republics would trade freely with one another. By the end of the 1820s, however, they recognized that such expectations would not come to fruition. North Americans remained unable to contend with British trade in Brazil even if they competed well with non-British European nations. The Age of Revolution failed to validate their equation of independence, republicanism, and free trade. Instead, it caused them to question the paradigm. They had to settle for trade with a Brazilian monarchy in a subordinate position to Great Britain. Republicanism and free trade remained powerful ideologies in the United States until the Civil War. All the same, Brazil obliged North Americans to reconsider old assumptions that the two ideologies would march together throughout the Americas, with the United States as a primary beneficiary.

By the time of the Civil War, North Americans defined their relationship with Brazil by slavery, not republicanism. Anti-slavery advocates denounced the illicit involvement of their compatriots in the Brazilian slave trade, while proponents of bondage insisted that Brazil would support the vitality of U.S. slavery. Maury revealed that pro-slavery rhetoric did not preclude allusions to republicanism and open trade, but he also crystallized the assumption that Brazilians would never attain a republican government. Slaveholders looked with suspicion on republicans in Spanish America who threatened to abolish slavery. Slavery's advocates looked to secure Brazil as an asset in the fight against abolitionism, whether by colonizing Brazil as a slaveholding republic or by allying with the Brazilian monarchy. As the Civil War approached, they worried less about Brazilians' commitment to republicanism than their commitment to slavery.[75]

Epilogue

Two Americas

Just before he departed for Portugal, Corrêa da Serra paid a visit to his old friend Thomas Jefferson in August 1820. The minister vented to the aging former president his disgust with "the piracies of Baltimore." Jefferson hoped that the minister would "distinguish between the iniquities of a few plunderers, and the sound principles of our country at large, and of our government especially." He hoped further that Corrêa da Serra would "promote . . . the advantages of a cordial fraternization among all the American nations, and the importance of their coalescing in an American system of policy, totally independent of, and unconnected with that of Europe."[1]

Jefferson had not altered his opinion much from more than thirty years prior, when he hoped that a revolutionary Brazil would prove beneficial to U.S. commerce. Even then he had expressed an unwillingness to upset European powers and the Portuguese monarchy by promoting revolution in Brazil. With particular forcefulness, however, he now condemned the revolutionary elements that promised to bring his earlier vision of an independent, republican Brazil to its fullest fruition. The man who had envisioned an empire of liberty across the Western Hemisphere revealed a growing supposition among North Americans that they may have to settle for a sovereign kingdom in the Americas. At best, they could hope it identified its interests more with American republics than with European monarchies. Brazil forced North Americans to reconceptualize connections among independence, republicanism, free trade, and prosperity.

Between the 1760s and 1820s, North American traders had hoped that the Age of Revolution would allow them to reorganize their commercial networks and free them from European markets and capital. The pursuit progressed in gradual stages, each facilitated by revolutionary fervor.

United States independence allowed North American merchants to pursue legal trade outside the confines of British mercantilism. With their independence, they sought open trade with Brazil. After the Portuguese court moved to Rio de Janeiro in 1808, many North Americans hoped to trade there with minimal restrictions. After 1816, they looked to Pernambuco and the Banda Oriental as regions that promised generous trade with fellow republicans. They viewed the turbulence in South America as an opportunity to gain the upper hand in new markets composed of merchants who shared common ideological commitments.

In Brazil, such promising trade remained elusive. Brazilians retained a monarchy more ideologically and commercially connected to Great Britain than to the United States. Brazil lacked an industrialized textile manufacturing sector, so it depended on importations of British textiles. British merchants maintained a strong advantage in terms of the value of goods exported to Brazil, and North Americans found their own Brazilian trade dependent on British capital and credit. United States banks could not offer the same amount of credit as British banking titans such as Baring Brothers & Co.[2]

Some North Americans blamed such disappointments on the innate inability of Brazilians to establish a republic, but Brazil exposed the fragility of North Americans' commitment to hemispheric republicanism and its tepid attachment to free trade. As they built a fledgling republic amid Atlantic geopolitical threats, U.S. authorities worried more about the government's international reputation than about republicanism in South America. They illustrated their governing priorities with the embargo of 1807, the removal of Joseph Ray and Thomas Halsey from their consular posts, the passage of neutrality laws, and the repression of Artigan privateers.

Sanguinary Revolts

By the 1820s, many white Southerners had grown wary of South American revolutions as a disorganized frenzy of blacks, Indians, "mixed breeds," and abolitionists. They drew a distinction between the supposedly restrained, orderly revolution in North America and the chaotic bouts for "universal emancipation" in South America. By 1826, many North Americans recoiled at the idea of U.S. participation in the Panama Congress, a pan-American conference organized by the firebrand South American revolutionary

Simón Bolívar. When the congress failed to map out a coherent vision for South America's future, even warm supporters worried that South Americans had proven incapable of republican government. Jared Sparks, editor of the *North American Review*, lamented, "Freedom will one day sit quietly down in South America and rule the land in peace, but I fear that day is more distant than I once thought."[3]

In 1839, the *United States Gazette* published a private letter from an unknown North American in Rio de Janeiro who promoted trade in Brazil. The writer provided a brief history of Brazilian commerce, beginning the sketch with the opening of Brazilian ports in 1808—the year that "light began to dawn upon this fertile and beautiful land." In 1817, as perceived by the author, Pernambucans "felt the advantages of free trade and liberal principles" and desired independence from Portugal. After Brazilians "had tasted . . . the sweets of liberal principles," they could accept no longer the rule of the Portuguese monarchy.[4]

By 1821, the author continued, Brazilians "became clamorous for new and extended privileges" and declared independence. Unfortunately, Dom Pedro "attempted to ape the 'great conqueror of Europe'" and dissolved the constituent assembly in 1823. After he returned calm by adopting a new constitution in 1824, he made the misstep of declaring an unpopular war on Buenos Aires over the Banda Oriental. The emperor "lost the confidence of the People" and abdicated the throne in 1831. He returned to Portugal and left his young son, Dom Pedro II, to reign under the tutelage of regents. As presented by the anonymous writer, Brazilian commerce had developed out of the fits and starts of liberal politics.[5]

Between 1835 and 1840, the Brazilian regency confronted revolutionary upheaval again in the northeastern and southern provinces. In 1835, residents in Rio Grande do Sul in southern Brazil had rebelled against Rio de Janeiro and adopted a republican government. The unknown writer had received word that other provinces would probably join the revolt, "which may result in a general revolution throughout the Empire." To that possibility, the author shrugged, "Nous verrons"—we'll see. Brazil had witnessed several republican uprisings that had come to naught. In the meantime, the author claimed, North Americans could still take advantage of high demand for flour in Rio de Janeiro.[6]

The letter revealed a continued belief that trade liberalization marched hand in hand with Brazilian independence and a liberal political order. At the same time, the writer observed the new republican uprisings with detached interest. Whether or not the revolutions succeeded, North Americans could engage in healthy commerce with Brazil so long as it retained an enlightened government committed to free trade. Another North American correspondent went even further, as reported in the *Commercial Advertiser* in 1840. Recounting revolts in Pará, Maranhão, and Rio Grande do Sul, the correspondent decried the "alarming frequency of disorder" in Brazil. The writer concluded a gloomy portrayal of Brazilian turmoil with the hope that "such may soon and forever cease to be the facts respecting Brazil." Another observer wondered, "What is the whole history of Portuguese and Spanish Colonies but a scene of revolution?" By the 1840s, North Americans had abandoned their hopes that revolution would spawn stable republics across South America.[7]

In late 1837, Bahian rebels declared a short-lived independence from Brazil before government forces suppressed the revolt in March 1838. The Sabinada, as it became known, began as a military mutiny and grew to encompass broad segments of the population—radical federalists, discontented (mainly black) soldiers, slaves, and others who felt marginalized by the government in Rio de Janeiro. The rebels convened a meeting of the city council and declared Bahia an independent republic. They had contradictory and nebulous goals regarding slavery and the future of the province, but the rebellion assumed the appearance of a race war and slave revolt. It attracted a wide variety of participants, including African-born slaves, creole slaves (born in Brazil), and free mulattos and blacks who acquired some of the principal leadership positions in the independent state. White elites feared for their safety and sought protection from the Brazilian government.[8]

North Americans feared slave revolts with continental reverberations, and they refused to equate the Sabinada with their own republican experiment. In 1837, a U.S. diplomatic report suggested that Bahian "separatists, nullifiers & revolutionists . . . refer to our history without understanding it" to agitate for reform, whereas loyalists improperly blamed the United States for the turmoil. The report disavowed Brazilian revolutionaries rather than cast them as a reflection of U.S. ideals. Accounts in the United States described the revolutionary armed forces as insurgents "composed chiefly of mulattoes and negroes" who attempted "to set the city on fire" and "blacks to whom the Rebels had . . . granted their freedom"—hardly subjects of pity in the United States.[9]

One South Carolina newspaper published an account of the Sabinada that turned earlier U.S. paradigms on their heads. According to the author,

"The state of this once flourishing country, under the old Portuguese Regime, is fast verging into its original state." The province had assumed "a most deplorable, desolated appearance" due to "a succession of sanguinary revolts and insurrections," the result of the "blind and reckless fury of the wild people" who rebelled. If monarchies were not ideal, at least they could control the enslaved and colored populations. In the future, slavery would unite U.S. and Brazilian interests.[10]

Divergence

Revolutionary tumult had altered core trade patterns of North American–Luso-Atlantic commerce between the 1760s and 1820s. During the Age of Revolution, traders displayed a remarkable capacity to cooperate and contravene state authority. Smugglers, revolutionaries, insurrectionists, rogue consuls, and privateers took advantage of commercial networks to achieve political objectives and used political turmoil to enhance their commercial prospects. Committed to the ideological syllogism of independence, republicanism, free trade, and prosperity, many North Americans had gambled on revolution. Most U.S. traders felt disposed to trade wherever they could earn a profit, but they operated in a political and commercial culture that took for granted the necessity of republicanism to liberate people and commerce. As the Age of Revolution advanced, however, they faced a disjunction between U.S. republican ideals and geopolitical realities.

Monarchists and republicans alike had imagined Brazil and the United States as "the two rising Americas," "the two Americas," "the two great powers of the western hemisphere," and "brethren of the same family." Their fates appeared intertwined—inseparable. At the same time, their relationship remained unsettled and fraught with tension. They had followed distinct paths to independence and commercial freedom, which resulted in conflicting national narratives about monarchy, republicanism, and the future of the Western Hemisphere.[11]

Many North Americans thought that Brazilians had betrayed the ideals they associated with the Americas. Worse still for U.S. free traders and revolutionary sympathizers, Brazil revealed that their ideologies could clash with their own republican government just as easily as they had with imperial states. It forced reconsideration of U.S. objectives in South America by inverting North American paradigms about independence, revolution, and political systems. Smugglers, pirates, and patriots had fractured empires, contested state power, and revolutionized Atlantic commerce. As the curtain fell on the Age of Revolution, however, North Americans abandoned faith that the United States would lead the Americas into a new era of republicanism and free trade.

Notes

Introduction

1. "Termo de Juramento e declaração que faz Jacob Leandro da Silva," July 23, 1818 (quotation), "Termo sobre a captura do Brigue *União de América*," July 17, 1818, "Instrumento Com Otheor de huns autos de Exame e averiguação do roubo Commetido no Bergantim união da America para Reclamações," July 3, 1818, "Termo de Juramento que faz Miguel Thadeo Montufas," July 3, 1818, all in box 116, MNE.

2. "Termo de Juramento e declaração que faz Jacob Leandro da Silva," July 23, 1818, "Termo sobre a captura do Brigue *União de América*," July 17, 1818, "Instrumento Com Otheor de huns autos de Exame e averiguação do roubo Commetido no Bergantim união da America para Reclamações," July 3, 1818, "Termo de Juramento que faz Miguel Thadeo Montufas," July 3, 1818, all in box 116, MNE. Around the Atlantic, observers used several terms such as "North Americans" and "English Americans" to distinguish U.S. nationals from Americans who lived in other parts of the Western Hemisphere. "English Americans" fails to capture the diversity of British-controlled colonies or the U.S. early republic. I use "North Americans" to refer broadly to those who lived in British dominions on the mainland during the colonial era and to U.S. nationals during the early republic. I also use "British Americans" when referring to people in the Americas subject to British political rule.

3. "Termo de Juramento e declaração que faz Jacob Leandro da Silva," July 23, 1818, "Termo sobre a captura do Brigue *União de América*," July 17, 1818, "Instrumento Com Otheor de huns autos de Exame e averiguação do roubo Commetido no Bergantim união da America para Reclamações," July 3, 1818 (quotation), "Termo de Juramento que faz Miguel Thadeo Montufas," July 3, 1818, "Termo de Juramento e Declaração que faz Manuel Francisco Cassilhas Contra Mestre do Bergantim União da América," July 3, 1818, all in box 116, MNE.

4. In recent years, historians have questioned Eurocentric notions of empire and the power of state institutions in shaping imperial commerce. Such scholarship focuses less on imperial political economy than on the agency of individual traders and consumers who shaped Atlantic commerce by private transactions. While not denying the limits of imperial power, other historians stress the state frameworks and high-level politics that gave shape to private networks. This book draws on both strands of scholarship. Fabrício Prado, *Edge of Empire: Atlantic Networks and Revolution in Bourbon Río de la Plata* (Oakland: University of California Press, 2015), 6–7; Pedro Cardim, Tamar Herzog, José Javier Ruiz Ibáñez, and Gaetano Sabatini, eds., *Polycentric Monarchies: How Did Early Modern Spain and Portugal*

Achieve and Maintain a Global Hegemony? (Portland, OR: Sussex Academic Press, 2012); João Fragoso and Manolo Florentino, *O arcaísmo como projeto: Mercado atlântico, sociedade agrária e elite mercantil em uma economia colonial tardia Rio de Janeiro, c. 1790–c. 1840*, 4th ed. (Rio de Janeiro: Civilização Brasileira, 2001); Thomas M. Doerflinger, *A Vigorous Spirit of Enterprise: Merchants and Economic Development in Revolutionary Philadelphia* (Chapel Hill: University of North Carolina Press, 1986); David Hancock, *Oceans of Wine: Madeira and the Emergence of American Trade and Taste* (New Haven, CT: Yale University Press, 2009); Sheryllynne Haggerty, *The British-Atlantic Trading Community, 1760–1810: Men, Women, and the Distribution of Goods* (Boston: Brill, 2006), 4; João Fragoso, Maria Fernanda Bicalho, and Maria de Fátima Silva Gouvêa, eds., *O antigo regime nos trópicos: A dinâmica imperial portuguesa (séculos XVI–XVIII)* (Rio de Janeiro: Civilização Brasileira, 2001); Manolo Florentino, *Em costas negras: Uma história do tráfico de escravos entre África e o Rio de Janeiro (séculos XVIII e XIX)* (Rio de Janeiro: Companhia das Letras, 1997); Ernst Pijning, "Controlling Contraband: Mentality, Economy, and Society in Eighteenth-Century Rio de Janeiro" (Ph.D. diss., Johns Hopkins University, 1997); Fabrício Prado, "Addicted to Smuggling: Contraband Trade in Eighteenth-Century Brazil and Rio de la Plata," in Christoph Rosenmüller, ed., *Corruption in the Iberian Empires: Greed, Custom, and Colonial Networks* (Albuquerque: University of New Mexico Press, 2017), 198; Zacarias Moutoukias, *Contrabando y control colonial en el siglo XVII: Buenos Aires, el Atlántico y el espacio peruano*, Biblioteca Universitarias (Buenos Aires: Centro Editor de América Latina, 1988), 151–66; Christian J. Koot, "Balancing Center and Periphery," *William and Mary Quarterly* 69 (January 2012), 41–46; John J. McCusker and Russell R. Menard, *The Economy of British America, 1607– 1789, with Supplementary Bibliography* (Chapel Hill: University of North Carolina Press, 1991); John Brewer, *The Sinews of Power: War, Money, and the English State* (New York: Alfred Knopf, 1989); Gabriel Paquette, *Imperial Portugal in the Age of Atlantic Revolutions* (New York: Cambridge University Press, 2013), 13–14.

5. Prado, *Edge of Empire*; Michael J. Jarvis, *In the Eye of All Trade: Bermuda, Bermudians, and the Maritime Atlantic World, 1680–1783* (Chapel Hill: University of North Carolina Press, 2010), 160–66; Gautham Rao, *National Duties: Custom Houses and the Making of the American State* (Chicago: The University of Chicago Press, 2016); Hancock, *Oceans of Wine*, xviii; Eric Hinderaker, *Elusive Empires: Constructing Colonialism in the Ohio Valley, 1673–1800* (New York: Cambridge University Press, 1997).

6. Prado, *Edge of Empire*, 6–8; Cardim et al., *Polycentric Monarchies*; Paquette, *Imperial Portugal*, 14; Nuala Zahedieh, *The Capital and the Colonies: London and the Atlantic Economy, 1660–1700* (New York: Cambridge University Press, 2010), 6–7; João Fragoso and Maria de Fátima Silva Gouvêa, "Nas rotas da governação portuguesa: Rio de Janeiro e Costa da Mina, séculos XVII e XVIII," in João Fragoso, Manolo Florentino, Antônio Carlos Jucá, and Adriana Campos, eds., *Nas rotas do império: Eixos mercantis, tráfico e relações sociais no mundo português* (Lisboa: ICCT, 2006)," 25–66; António Manuel Hespanha, "Antigo regime nos trópicos? Um debate sobre o modelo político do império colonial português," in João Fragoso and Maria de Fátima Gouvêa, eds., *Na trama das redes: Política e negócios no império português, séculos XVI–XVIII* (Rio de Janeiro: Civilização Brasileira, 2010), 51, 54.

7. For historiography of free trade and the Enlightenment, see Paul A. Gilje, *Free Trade and Sailors' Rights in the War of 1812* (New York: Cambridge University Press, 2013); Joyce Appleby, *Capitalism and a New Social Order: The Republican Vision of the 1790s* (New York:

New York University Press, 1984); Nicholas Onuf and Peter Onuf, *Nations, Markets, and War: Modern History and the American Civil War* (Charlottesville: University of Virginia Press, 2006); Fabrizio Simon, "Criminology and Economic Ideas in the Age of Enlightenment," *History of Economic Ideas* 17 (2009): 11–39; Michael Kwass, *Contraband* (Cambridge, MA: Harvard University Press, 2014), 288–98.

8. Valentim Alexandre, *Sentidos do império: Questão nacional e questão colonial na crise do antigo regime português* (Porto: Edições Afrontamento, 1993), 167–231; Prado, *Edge of Empire*, 154; Kirsten Schultz, *Tropical Versailles: Empire, Monarchy, and the Portuguese Royal Court in America, 1808–1821* (New York: Routledge, 2001), 83, 87, 189–90; José Luís Cardoso, "Nas malhas do império: A economia política e a política colonial de D. Rodrigo de Souza Coutinho," in José Luís Cardoso, ed., *A economia política e os dilemas do império luso-brasileiro (1790–1822)* (Lisbon: Comissão Nacional para as Comemorações dos Descobrimentos Portugueses, 2001), 79–94.

9. For North Americans' view of South American revolutions, see Caitlin Fitz, *Our Sister Republics: The United States in an Age of American Revolutions* (New York: W. W. Norton, 2016), 12–13.

10. Historians have encountered difficulty integrating the histories of the North and South Atlantics. Some successful studies have either taken comparative approaches to North and South America or have examined U.S.–Latin American relations in the early nineteenth century without placing them in broader Atlantic, interimperial contexts dating to the eighteenth century. Jorge Cañizares-Esguerra, *Puritan Conquistadors: Iberianizing the Atlantic, 1550–1700* (Stanford, CA: Stanford University Press, 2006), 218–20; Thomas Bender, foreword to Jorge Cañizares-Esguerra and Erik R. Seeman, *The Atlantic in Global History, 1500–2000* (Upper Saddle River, NJ: Pearson, 2007), xvii–xviii; David Armitage, "Three Concepts of Atlantic History," in David Armitage and Michael J. Braddick, eds., *The British Atlantic World, 1500–1800* (New York: Palgrave-MacMillan, 2002), 13–29; Alison Games, "Atlantic History: Definitions, Challenges, and Opportunities," *American Historical Review* 111 (June 2006), 747, 752; J. H. Elliott, *Empires of the Atlantic World: Britain and Spain in America, 1492–1830* (New Haven, CT: Yale University Press, 2006); Arthur P. Whitaker, *The United States and the Independence of Latin America, 1800–1830* (New York: W. W. Norton, 1964); Fitz, *Our Sister Republics*; David Head, *Privateers of the Americas: Spanish American Privateering from the United States in the Early Republic* (Athens: University of Georgia Press, 2015).

11. Tench Coxe to James Madison, January 1807, James Madison Papers, LOC.

12. Jeremy Adelman, *Sovereignty and Revolution in the Iberian Atlantic* (Princeton, NJ: Princeton University Press, 2006), 48; Ayşe Çelikkol, "Free Trade and Disloyal Smugglers in Scott's *Guy Manering* and *Redgauntlet*," *ELH* 4 (Winter 2007), 759; Gilje, *Free Trade*, 11; Steve Pincus, "Rethinking Mercantilism: Political Economy, the British Empire, and the Atlantic World in the Seventeenth and Eighteenth Centuries," *William and Mary Quarterly* 69 (January 2012), 4, 14.

13. Appleby, *Capitalism*; Drew McCoy, *The Elusive Republic: Political Economy in Jeffersonian America* (Chapel Hill: University of North Carolina Press, 1980).

14. For historiography linking free trade and republicanism, see Gilje, *Free Trade*; Appleby, *Capitalism*; McCoy, *Elusive Republic*; Onuf and Onuf, *Nations, Markets, and War*; Çelikkol, "Free Trade and Disloyal Smugglers," 759. For North American smuggling practices, see John W. Tyler, *Smugglers and Patriots: Boston Merchants and the Advent of the American*

Revolution (Boston: Northeastern University Press, 1986); Cathy Matson, *Merchants and Empire: Trading in Colonial New York* (Baltimore: Johns Hopkins University Press, 1998); Benjamin L. Carp, *Defiance of the Patriots: The Boston Tea Party and the Making of America* (New Haven, CT: Yale University Press, 2010); Thomas Truxes, *Defying Empire: Trading with the Enemy in Colonial New York* (New Haven, CT: Yale University Press, 2008); Joshua M. Smith, *Borderland Smuggling: Patriots, Loyalists, and Illicit Trade in the Northeast, 1783–1820* (Gainesville: University Press of Florida, 2006); Victor Enthoven, "'That Abominable Nest of Pirates': St. Eustatius and the North Americans, 1680–1780," *Early American Studies* 10 (Spring 2012), 239–301.

15. For North Americans' contrast of American republicanism with European monarchy, see Onuf and Onuf, *Nations, Markets, and War*, 234. For their perceptions of their South American neighbors, see James E. Lewis Jr., *The American Union and the Problem of Neighborhood: The United States and the Collapse of the Spanish Empire, 1783–1829* (Chapel Hill: University of North Carolina Press, 1998), 6.

16. Sociologists have theorized that networks develop according to growth and preferential attachment. They increase with the addition of new agents. Agents with more time and investment in a network tend to attract new agents, thereby exponentially reinforcing their own influence in the nexus. Albert-László Barabási and Réka Albert, "Emergence of Scaling in Random Networks," *Science* 286 (October 1999), 509–12. Early North Americans used the term "merchant" in a variety of ways, spanning from grocers to business princes engaged in global trade. For the purposes of this study, I apply the term to those engaged in overseas trade. Where necessary, I differentiate between merchants who conducted business on their own accounts and factors who acted as agents for others. Recently, scholars have greatly expanded our vision of Atlantic trade to encompass a wide variety of participants, including slaves, women, and composite farmers. I use "traders" to refer to the wider community of tradesmen and tradeswomen beyond merchants. See Tyler, *Smugglers and Patriots*, 7; Doerflinger, *Vigorous Spirit*, 17; Haggerty, *British-Atlantic Trading Community*; Ellen Hartigan-O'Connor, *The Ties That Buy: Women and Commerce in Revolutionary America* (Philadelphia: University of Pennsylvania Press, 2009); Richard Lyman Bushman, "Markets and Composite Farms in Early America," *William and Mary Quarterly* 55 (July 1998), 351–74.

17. Adrian Finucane, *The Temptations of Trade: Britain, Spain, and the Struggle for Empire* (Philadelphia: University of Pennsylvania Press, 2016), 12; Martin Robson, *Britain, Portugal, and South America in the Napoleonic Wars: Alliances and Diplomacy in Economic Maritime Conflict* (New York: I. B. Tauris, 2011), 10–20.

18. For useful scholarship on North American–Luso-Atlantic commercial networks, see James G. Lydon, "Fish and Flour for Gold, 1600–1800: Southern Europe in the Colonial Balance of Payments" (Philadelphia: Library Company of Philadelphia, 2008), http://library company.org/Economics/PDF%20Files/lydon_web.pdf (accessed October 8, 2014); Hancock, *Oceans of Wine*; Brooke Hunter, "Wheat, War, and the American Economy During the Age of Revolution," *William and Mary Quarterly* 62 (July 2005), 505–26; Jorge Manuel Martins Ribeiro, "Comércio e diplomacia nas relações luso-americanas (1776–1822)" (Ph.D. diss., University of Porto, 1997).

19. Eliga H. Gould, *Among the Powers of the Earth: The American Revolution and the Making of a New World Empire*, (Cambridge, MA: Harvard University Press, 2012), 3, 12–13; Like Gould, Nicholas and Peter Onuf note the early recognition in the United States of the

necessity of making the United States a traditional power. See Onuf and Onuf, *Nations, Markets, and War*, 234.

20. Prado, "Addicted to Smuggling," 197–212; Fragoso and Silva Gouvêa, "Nas rotas da governação," 38; Daniel B. Domingues da Silva, *The Atlantic Slave Trade from West Central Africa, 1780–1867* (New York: Cambridge University Press, 2017), 49; Roquinaldo Ferreira, *Cross-Cultural Exchange in the Atlantic World: Angola and Brazil During the Era of the Slave Trade* (New York: Cambridge University Press, 2012), 7–9; Moutoukias, *Contrabando y control*, 94, 100, 103; Luiz Felipe de Alencastro, "The African Slave Trade and the Construction of the Iberian Atlantic," in Kerry Bystrom and Joseph R. Slaughter, eds., *The Global South Atlantic* (New York: Fordham University Press, 2018), 38–39; João Luís Ribeiro Fragoso, *Homens de grossa aventura: Acumulação e heirarquia na praça mercantil do Rio de Janeiro (1790–1830)* (Rio de Janeiro: Arquivo Nacional Órgão do Ministério da Justiça, 1992), 19–27, 83–93.

21. For increased U.S. racialization of South American revolutions see Fitz, *Our Sister Republics*, 90, 201–13, 227.

22. Schulz, *Tropical Versailles*, 4, 7–8.

Part I

1. Celso Furtado, *Formação Econômica do Brasil* (1959; repr., São Paulo: Companhia Editora Nacional, 2005), 38–42; H. E. S. Fisher, *The Portugal Trade: A Study of Anglo-Portuguese Commerce, 1700–1770* (London: Methuen, 1971), 29; Hancock, *Oceans of Wine*, 117.

2. C. R. Boxer, "Brazilian Gold and British Traders in the First Half of the Eighteenth Century," *Hispanic American Historical Review* 49 (August 1969), 462; Moutoukias, *Contrabando y control*, 93–94; Fragoso and Silva Gouvêa, "Nas Rotas da Governação," 37; McCusker and Menard, *Economy of British America*, 199.

3. Gilje, *Free Trade*, 13–31, 32–45; Tyler, *Smugglers and Patriots*, 18, 22; Matson, *Merchants and Empire*, 8–9.

4. Adelman, *Sovereignty and Revolution*, 56–71, 121–22; Luis Felipe de Alencastro, *O trato dos viventes: Formação do Brasil no Atlântico Sul* (São Paulo: Companhia das Letras, 2000); Florentino, *Em costas negras*, 192–95; Fragoso, *Homens de grossa aventura*, 174–212; Walter Hawthorne, *From Africa to Brazil: Culture, Identity, and an Atlantic Slave Trade, 1600–1830* (New York: Cambridge University Press, 2010), 61.

Chapter 1

1. C. R. Boxer, *The Golden Age of Brazil, 1695–1750: Growing Pains of a Colonial Society* (Berkeley: University of California Press, 1962), 206; Furtado, *Formação Econômica*, 38–42; Lydon, "Fish and Flour," 9; Kenneth Maxwell, *Pombal: Paradox of the Enlightenment* (New York: Cambridge University Press, 1995), 46; *The Priviledges of an Englishman in the Kingdoms and Dominions of Portugal* (London, 1759).

2. Florentino, *Em Costas Negras*, 23, 121; Moutoukias, *Contrabando y control*, 18, 93–94, 100, 133; Fragoso and Silva Gouvêa, "Nas Rotas da Governação," 37–38; Prado, "Addicted to Smuggling," 204–5; Ernst Pijning, "Contrabando, ilegalidade e medidas políticas no Rio de Janeiro do século XVIII," *Revista Brasileira de História* 21 (2001), 399–402; Ferreira, *Cross-Cultural Exchange*, 7–9; José Roberto do Amaral Lapa, *O antigo sistema colonial* (São Paulo: Editora Brasiliense, 1982), 38–65.

3. Hancock, *Oceans of Wine*, 107–15, 125, esp. 107; T. Bentley Duncan, *Atlantic Islands: Madeira, the Azores and the Cape Verdes in Seventeenth-Century Commerce and Navigation* (Chicago: University of Chicago Press, 1972), 71; André L. Simon, ed., *The Bolton Letters: The Letters of an English Merchant in Madeira 1695–1714*, 2 vols. (London: T. Werner Laurie, 1928), 1:15–16; Lydon, "Fish and Flour," 137–47.

4. "Parecer (minuta) do conselho ultramarino sobre a carta do governador do Rio de Janeiro, António Pais de Sande, acerca do cumprimento das ordens para passar à vila de São Paulo, ao descobrimento das minas de prata e ouro," November 5, 1694, box 6, document 594, Administração Central, CU (quotation); Elizabeth W. Kiddy, *Blacks of the Rosary: Memory and History in Minas Gerais, Brazil* (University Park: Pennsylvania State University Press, 2005), 36; Boxer, *Golden Age of Brazil*, 35–36; Paul Chandler, *Bound to the Hearth by the Shortest Tether: Village Life in China, Brazil* (New York: University Press of America, 2006), 90–91; Adriana Romeiro, *Paulistas e emboabas no coração das Minas: Idéias, práticas e imaginário politico no século XVIII* (Belo Horizonte: Editora UFMG, 2008), 52.

5. Romeiro, *Paulistas e emboabas*, 50–53; "Parecer do conselho ultramarino sobre a incumbência do governador Artur de Sá e Meneses em averiguar a existência de minas de ouro e prata nas capitanias do Sul, com as mesmas ordens atribuídas ao ex-governador do Rio de Janeiro, António Pais de Sande, encarregando o governo desta capitania a Martim Gouveia Vasques," December 7, 1696, box 6, document 613, CU; Antônio Álvares da Cunha to Francisco Xavier de Mendonça Furtado, June 9, 1764, box 71, document 6544, CU (quotation).

6. Manoel S. Cardozo, "The Collection of the Fifths in Brazil, 1695–1709," *Hispanic American Historical Review* 20 (August 1940), 359–60; Boxer, "Brazilian Gold," 461; Sebastião de Castro e Caldas to Dom Pedro II, June 22, 1695, box 6, document 606, CU; "Parecer (minuta) do Conselho Ultramarino, sobre as denúncias feitas pelo governador do Rio de Janeiro [Luís Vahia Monteiro], quanto aos descaminhos do ouro, autorizando o dito governador para fazer buscas em qualquer casa cujo proprietário seja suspeito do crime de contrabando, inclusive em casas de eclesiásticos, devendo o produto ser confiscado e os culpados entregues aos respectivos prelados para serem sentenciados," March 7, 1731, box 22, document 2409, CU; Diogo de Mendonça to Gomes Freire de Andrade, March 21, 1751, box 44, document 4485, CU; Antônio Álvares da Cunha to Francisco Xavier de Mendonça Furtado, June 9, 1764, box 71, document 6544, CU.

7. "Parecer (minuta) do Conselho Ultramarino, sobre as denúncias feitas pelo governador do Rio de Janeiro [Luís Vahia Monteiro], quanto aos descaminhos do ouro," March 7, 1731, box 22, document 2409, CU; Diogo de Mendonça to Gomes Freire de Andrade, March 21, 1751, box 44, document 4485, CU (quotation).

8. Kathleen J. Higgins, *Licentious Liberty in a Brazilian Gold-Mining Region: Slavery, Gender, and Social Control in Eighteenth-Century Sabará, Minas Gerais* (University Park: Pennsylvania State University Press, 1999), 1–3; Boxer, "Brazilian Gold," 462–63; "Minutes of Committee of Privy Council for Plantation Affairs," June 25, 1735, item 608, vol. 41, Colonial State Papers, NAUK.

9. "A Brief View of the Weight and Consequence of the General Trade, and of some Considerable places In the Indies," 1701, film book 398, reel 9, materials on the history of Jamaica in the Edward Long Papers, BL (quotation); *Virginia Gazette*, September 9, 1737; Higgins, *Licentious Liberty*, 1–3; Governor Dudley to the Council of Trade and Plantations,

July 13, 1704, item 455, vol. 22, pp. 213–18, Colonial State Papers, NAUK; Governor Hart to the Council of Trade and Plantations, March 25, 1724, item 102, vol. 34, pp. 71–73, Colonial State Papers, NAUK; Boxer, "Brazilian Gold," 461; George Anson, *A Voyage Round the World in the Years MDCCXL, I, II, III, IV* (London, 1748), 42.

10. "Consulta sobre a expedição da Frota da Bahia," November 10, 1763, livro 109, roll 2110, Junta do Comércio, ANTT.

11. John Ayrey & Co. to Baynton & Wharton, February 21 and April 15, 1761, and Parr & Bulkeley to Baynton & Wharton, February 20 and April 18, 1762, all in MG 19, roll 2235, Baynton, Wharton, & Morgan Papers, PSA.

12. Parr & Bulkeley to Baynton & Wharton, November 7, December 5, and December 29, 1761, and February 29, 1762, all in MG 19, roll 2236, Baynton, Wharton, & Morgan Papers, PSA. A Portuguese quintal measured four arrobas (approximately 14.7 kg/arroba), equaling about 58.8 kg. See, John J. McCusker, *Essays in the Economic History of the Atlantic World* (New York: Routledge, 1997), 53, 60.

13. "Consulta sobre a expedição da Frota da Bahia," November 10, 1763, livro 109, roll 2110, Junta do Comércio, ANTT; Boxer, "Brazilian Gold," 463; *Virginia Gazette*, September 9, 1737.

14. Diogo de Mendonça to João Pacheco Pereira de Vasconcelos, June 1, 1753, box 46, document 4713, CU; Boxer, "Brazilian Gold," 461, 464; Thomas Riche to William Street, September 7, 1763, and Riche to William and Francis Street, September 28 and September 29, 1763, all in TRL, vol. 1a, HSP; Riche to William Street, February 4, 1769, TRL, vol. 4, HSP; *Pennsylvania Gazette* (Philadelphia), July 26, 1764; Bruce H. Mann, *Republic of Debtors: Bankruptcy in the Age of American Independence* (Cambridge, MA: Harvard University Press, 2002), 82; Duncan, *Atlantic Islands*, 127–30; Frédéric Mauro, "Political and Economic Structures of Empire, 1580–1750," in Leslie Bethell, ed., *Colonial Brazil*, 39–66 (New York: Cambridge University Press, 1987), 52–53; Gomes Freire de Andrade to Sebastião José de Carvalho e Melo, March 12, 1761, box 62, document 5943, CU.

15. Fábio Kühn, "Os Interesses do governador: Luiz Garcia de Bivar e os negociantes da Colônia do Sacramento (1749–1760)," *Topoi* 13 (January/June 2012), 35; Finucane, *Temptations of Trade*, 81, 86; Gomes Freire de Andrade to Francisco Xavier de Mendonça Furtado, February 6, 1761, box 61, document 5822, CU (quotations); *Public Register or The Daily Register of Commerce and Intelligence* (London), January 7, 1761; Luís de Almeida Portugal Soares de Alarcão Eça e Melo Silva e Mascarenhas to Martinho de Melo e Castro, September 23, 1770, box 91, document 7936, CU.

16. Joseph C. Miller, *Way of Death: Merchant Capitalism and the Angolan Slave Trade, 1730–1830* (Madison: University of Wisconsin Press, 1988), 463, 483–85; José de Lima Pinheiro e Aragão to Tomé Joaquim da Costa Corte Real, October 30, 1756, box 51, document 5110, CU; Corsino Medeiros dos Santos, *O Tráfico de Escravos do Brasil para o Rio da Prata* (Brasília: Senado Federal, 2010), 80–105.

17. Stephen Haber and Herbert S. Klein, "The Economic Consequences of Brazilian Independence," in Stephen Haber, ed., *How Latin America Fell Behind: Essays on the Economic Histories of Brazil and Mexico, 1800–1914* (Stanford, CA: Stanford University Press, 1997), 245–48; Boxer, "Brazilian Gold," 458–60; Jorge M. Pedreira, "From Growth to Collapse: Portugal, Brazil, and the Breakdown of the Old Colonial System (1760–1830)," *Hispanic American Historical Review* 80 (November 2000), 841; Lydon, "Fish and Flour," 35, 213; Alan

Taylor, *American Colonies: The Settling of North America* (New York: Penguin Group, 2001), 306; Riche to Parr & Bulkeley, November 5, 1764, TRL, vol. 2, HSP.

18. Florentino, *Em Costas Negras*, 23, 121; Fragoso and Silva Gouvêa, "Nas Rotas da Governação," 36–38; Herbert S. Klein, "The Portuguese Slave Trade from Angola in the Eighteenth Century," *Journal of Economic History* 32 (December 1972), 895; Miller, *Way of Death*, 570–71; Antonia Aparecida Quintão, *Lá vem o meu parente: As irmandades de pretos e pardos no Rio de Janeiro e em Pernambuco (século XVIII)* (São Paulo: Annablume editora, 2002), 174–75; Mariana Pinho Candido, *Fronteras de esclavización: Esclavitud, comercio e identidad en Benguela, 1780–1850* (Mexico City: El Colegio de México, 2011), 19–20, 25–42; Kenneth Maxwell, *Conflicts and Conspiracies: Brazil and Portugal, 1750–1808* (New York: Routledge, 2004), 3–5; Dauril Alden, *Royal Government in Colonial Brazil: With Special Reference to the Administration of the Marquis of Lavradio, 1769–1799* (Berkeley: University of California Press, 1968), 67–68.

19. Pinho Candido, *Fronteras de esclavización*, 19–20, 25–42; Maxwell, *Conflicts and Conspiracies*, 3–5; Alencastro, *O Trato dos viventes*.

20. Miller, *Way of Death*, 71–73, 94–100, 105–39, 179, 296–97, 463; "Carta dos oficiais da Câmara do Rio de Janeiro ao rei [D. José], solicitando, em nome dos lavradores e senhores de engenho de açúcar, providências para conter os abusos dos atravessadores de escravos negros naquela cidade e seu termo, que já vinham sendo penalizados, mas prosseguiam com aquele tráfico, o que os fez com que os mencionados lavradores insistissem em sua petição, já tendo recorrido, com a mesma queixa, até ao [vice-rei do Estado do Brasil], conde da Cunha, [D. Antônio Álvares da Cunha]," November 6, 1765, box 76, document 6877, CU; Romeiro, *Paulistas e emboabas*, 103.

21. Hancock, *Oceans of Wine*, 393.

22. Furtado, *Formação Econômica*, 38–42; Lydon, "Fish and Flour," 9; Maxwell, *Pombal*, 46; Boxer, "Brazilian Gold," 462.

23. Furtado, *Formação Econômica*, 38–42; Maxwell, *Conflicts and Conspiracies*, 7; Lydon, "Fish and Flour," 9–10; Fisher, *Portugal Trade*, 66–67; Maxwell, *Pombal*, 16, 41–42; John Rutherford, *The Importance of the Colonies to Great Britain* (London, 1761), edited by Jan-Michael Poff, 12, http://www.ncpublications.com/colonial/bookshelf/Tracts/Importance/Default.htm; H. E. S. Fisher, "Anglo-Portuguese Trade, 1700–1770," *Economic History Review* 16 (1963), 222; S. Sideri, *Trade and Power: Informal Colonialism in Anglo-Portuguese Relations* (Rotterdam: Rotterdam University Press, 1970), 49–53; Lucy S. Sutherland, *A London Merchant, 1695–1774* (London: Frank Cass, 1962), 17–19, 38.

24. Lydon, "Fish and Flour," 39; Henry Hill accounts, August, 17, 1763, John J. Smith Collection, LCP; Parr & Bulkeley to John Steinmetz, September 7, 1773, box 6, folder 1, Jasper Yeates Brinton Collection, HSP (quotation); Parr & Bulkeley to Clifford, December 8, 1761, Clifford Correspondence, vol. 3, Pemberton Papers, Clifford Family Papers, HSP; Samuel Galloway and Stephen Steward to James Russell, November 28, 1769, and December 7, 1769, Robert and John Pasley to Richard Bishoprick, December 7, 1769, and to James Russell, December 26, 1769, and n.d., all in box 75, Galloway-Maxcy-Markoe Papers, LOC; Parr & Bulkeley to Clifford, February 6, 1764, Clifford Correspondence, vol. 4, Pemberton Papers, Clifford Family Papers, HSP.

25. Boxer, "Brazilian Gold," 459; Max Savelle, *Empires to Nations: Expansion in America, 1713–1824* (St. Paul, MN: North Central, 1974), 132; *Pennsylvania Gazette*, July 31, 1735;

Virginia Gazette (Williamsburg), December 10, 1736; *South Carolina Gazette* (Charlestown), August 27, 1737.

26. Lydon, "Fish and Flour," 9–10; Boxer, "Brazilian Gold," 465 (quotation "freight, brokerage, commission"); Maxwell, *Pombal*, 46 (quotation "His Majesty's subjects").

27. John Delaforce, *The Factory House at Oporto* (London: Christie's Wine Publications, 1979), 1; A. H. Walford, *The British Factory in Lisbon* (Lisbon: Instituto britânico em Portugal, 1940); *Pennsylvania Gazette*, May 5, 1737; William Pardon, *A New and Compendious System of Practical Arithmetick* (London, 1737), 117; Lamar, Hill, Bisset, & Co. to Baynton, Wharton, & Morgan, May 21, 1767, box 2, Edward Wanton Smith Collection, HSP; Rose to Robert Davies, [July?] 27, 1779, to Anthony Van Dam, July [n.d.] 1779, to Charles Wetherell, July 30, 1779, and to Thomas and John Rowley, September 20, 1779, all in Cropley Rose Letterbook, HSP; Lydon, "Fish and Flour," 45.

28. Lydon, "Fish and Flour," 1–3, 8–9, 121.

29. Marien Lamar to Hill, July 27, 1771, and August 1, 1771, box 1, Sarah A. G. Smith Collection, HSP; Thomas Willing account book, ms. coll. no. 4, series III-B, Hare-Willing Family Papers, APS; Mifflin & Massey insurance accounts, November–December 1762, box 1, Mifflin & Massey Business Papers, HL; Parr & Bulkeley to Baynton & Wharton, February 29, 1762, MG 19, roll 2236, Baynton, Wharton, & Morgan Papers, PSA.

30. Lydon, "Fish and Flour," 121–22; Riche to Gurley & Stephens, June 28, 1764, and to Peter Gurley, June 28, 1764, July 16, 1764, and July 27, 1764; and Parr & Bulkeley to Clifford, April 22, 1765, and August 26, 1765, Clifford Correspondence, vol. 4, Pemberton Papers, Clifford Family Papers, HSP; Edward Burns & Sons to Galloway, August 9, 1765, and February 26, 1766, Galloway-Maxcy-Markoe Papers, vol. 8, LOC. Alqueires measured capacity of approximately thirteen liters. See, Boxer, *Golden Age of Brazil*, 356.

31. Manuel Nunes Dias, "Companhias versus companhias na competição colonial," *Revista de Historia de America* 84 (July–December 1977), 39; Frédéric Mauro, "Le Rôle économique de la fiscalité dans le Brésil Colonial (1500–1800)," *Caravelle* 5 (1965), 93–94; Conselho ultramarino to Dom João IV, December 19, 1650, box 2, document 205, CU; Tomé Correia de Alvarenga to Dom Alfonso VI, October 24, 1657, box 3, document 313, CU; Hancock, *Oceans of Wine*, 107–15, 125, esp. 107; Duncan, *Atlantic Islands*, 71; Simon, *Bolton Letters*, 15–16.

32. Hancock, *Oceans of Wine*, 14, 140; Duncan, *Atlantic Islands*, 54, 71.

33. William Bolton & Company to Robert Heysham, May 22, 1696, and September 4, 1698, both in Simon, *Bolton Letters*, 1:8, 40; Duncan, *Atlantic Islands*, 63–64; Lydon, "Fish and Flour," 114, 121. Moios measured approximately sixty alqueires. See, Boxer, *Golden Age of Brazil*, 356.

34. Simon, "Introduction," *Bolton Letters*, 8; Lydon, "Fish and Flour," 114, 121; Peter E. Pope, *Fish into Wine: The Newfoundland Plantation in the Seventeenth Century* (Chapel Hill: University of North Carolina Press, 2004), 93, 96, 375–82; Kearny & Gilbert to Newton & Gordon, March 30, 1767, and April 20, 1767, and Francis & Tilghman to Newton & Gordon, May 17, 1769, all in Newton & Gordon letters received, 1763–1775, Newton & Gordon Papers, ISM.

35. Joseph Jones to Thomas Clifford & Co., December 22, 1759; Lamar, Hill, Bisset, & Co. to Thomas Clifford & Co., December 22, 1759; and Hill, Lamar, & Hill to Clifford, Fox, & Morris, February 10, 1761 (quotation "impracticable to sell"), all three in Clifford

Correspondence, vols. 2–3, Pemberton Papers, Clifford Family Papers, HSP; Cropley Rose to Pat Larkan, October 31, 1779, Cropley Rose Letterbook, HSP (quotation "that brings Cash"); Robert Waln to Newton & Gordon, April 18, 1767, Newton & Gordon letters received, 1763–1775, Newton & Gordon Papers, ISM.

36. Hill accounts 1763–1775, October 31, 1763, John J. Smith Collection, LCP; Kearny & Gilbert to Newton & Gordon, March 26, 1764, Newton & Gordon letters received, 1763–1775, Newton & Gordon Papers, ISM; Searle to Galloway & Steward, February 16, 1765, Galloway-Maxcy-Markoe Papers, vol. 7, LOC; Riche to Shirley & Martin, August 1, 1764, TRL, vol. 1b, HSP.

37. Samuel Johnston to Newton & Gordon, February 2, 1764, and Kearny & Gilbert to Newton & Gordon, March 26, 1764, Newton & Gordon letters received, 1763–1775, Newton & Gordon Papers, ISM; Riche to William Street, June 22, 1764, and to Shirley & Martin, June 27, 1764, TRL, vol. 1b, HSP; Duncan, *Atlantic Islands*, 142.

38. Hancock, *Oceans of Wine*; Johnston to Newton & Gordon, February 2, 1764, Newton & Gordon letters received, 1763–1775, Newton & Gordon Papers, ISM.

39. Hancock, *Oceans of Wine*, 79–82, 98–99; Martins Ribeiro, "Comércio e diplomacia," 118; Rose to Robert Davies, [July?] 27, 1779, Cropley Rose Letterbook, HSP; Riche to Shirley & Martin, February 25, 1764, and October 17, 1764, TRL, vol. 1b, HSP; F. S. Hopkins, *An Historical Sketch of the Island of Madeira* (London, 1819), 51; Johnston to Newton & Gordon, February 2, 1764, Newton & Gordon letters received, 1763–1775, Newton & Gordon Papers, ISM.

40. Johnston to Newton & Gordon, February 2, 1764, Newton & Gordon letters received, 1763–1775, Newton & Gordon Papers, ISM.

41. Doerflinger, *Vigorous Spirit of Enterprise*, 87–88.

42. Holdsworth, Olive, & Newman to Baynton, Wharton, & Morgan, November 24, 1765, MG 19, roll 2237, Baynton, Wharton, & Morgan Papers, PSA; Kearny & Gilbert to Newton & Gordon, May 8, 1765, December 4, 1765, January 25, 1767, and March 30, 1767, Newton & Gordon letters received, 1763–1775, Newton & Gordon Papers, ISM; Silvanus Grove to Galloway, January 15, 1766, and Galloway & Steward to James Russell, October 29, 1769, and December 26, 1769, Galloway-Maxcy-Markoe Papers, vols. 8 and 9, LOC.

43. John Ayrey & Co. to Baynton & Wharton, January 21, 1761, MG 19, roll 2235, Baynton, Wharton, & Morgan Papers, PSA; Parr & Bulkeley to Keppelle & Steinmetz, September 2, 1773, box 6, folder 1, Jasper Yeates Brinton Collection, HSP.

44. Mayne & Co. to Galloway, January 18, 1766, Galloway-Maxcy-Markoe Papers, vol. 8, LOC; Robert Bisset to Henry Hill, January 31, 1775, box 1, Sarah A. G. Smith Collection, HSP.

45. Nicholas Shrady, *The Last Day: Wrath, Ruin, and Reason in the Great Lisbon Earthquake of 1755* (New York: Viking, 2008), 12, 18, 96; Malcom Jack, "Destruction and Regeneration: Lisbon, 1755," in Theodore E. D. Braun and John B. Radner, eds., *The Lisbon Earthquake of 1755: Representations and Reactions* (Oxford: Voltaire Foundation, 2005), 10 (quotation); Judite Nozes, *The Lisbon Earthquake of 1755: Some British Eye-Witness Accounts* (Lisbon: British Historical Society of Portugal, 1987), 72; Mark Molesky, *This Gulf of Fire: The Great Lisbon Earthquake, or Apocalypse in the Age of Science and Reason* (New York: Vintage Books, 2016), 293–94.

46. Molesky, *This Gulf of Fire*, 22; Maxwell, *Pombal*, 4, 23–24, 66.

47. Maxwell, *Pombal*, 2–7.

48. Susan Schneider, *O Marquês de Pombal e o Vinho do Porto: Dependência e subdesen-volvimento em Portugal no século XVIII* (Lisbon: A Regra do Jogo, 1980), 42–43; Oficiais da Câmara do Rio de Janeiro to Francisco Xavier de Mendonça Furtado, March 4, 1761, box 62, document 5919, CU; Gomes Freire de Andrade to Francisco Xavier de Mendonça Furtado, February 16,1761, box 61, document 5850, CU; Manuel Nunes Dias, "Os acionistas e o capital social da Companhia do Grão Pará e Maranhão (Os dois momentos: O da fundação (1755–1758) e o da véspera da extinção (1776))," *Cahiers du monde hispanique et luso-brésilien* 11 (1968), 29–52.

49. Maxwell, *Pombal*, 59–63, and *Conflicts and Conspiracies*, 42; also Kenneth Maxwell, *Naked Tropics: Essays on Empire and Other Rogues* (New York: Routledge, 2003), 99; Adriana Lopez, *De Cães a Lobos-de-Mar: Súditos Ingleses no Brasil* (São Paulo: Editora Senac São Paulo, 2007), 151–52 ; Adelman, *Sovereignty and Revolution*, 39; Alden, *Royal Government*, 395; Mesa da Inspeção to Tomé Joaquim da Costa Corte Real, July 18, 1759, box 57, document 5504, CU; Mesa da Inspeção to Francisco Xavier de Mendonça Furtado, February 12, 1761, box 61, document 5833, CU; João Tavares de Abreu to Francisco Xavier de Mendonça Furtado, February 28, 1761, box 61, document 5905, CU; Diogo Inácio de Pina Manique to Martinho de Melo e Castro, October 1, 1771, box 61, document 5905, CU; Paquette, *Imperial Portugal*, 52; Pijning, "Contrabando," 408.

50. Fisher, *Portugal Trade*, 41, 43; Maxwell, *Conflicts and Conspiracies*, 42, 49; Schneider, *Marquês de Pombal*, 14–16; *South Carolina and American General Gazette* (Charlestown), November 18, 1768; Sutherland, *London Merchant*, 36–40; Hancock, *Oceans of Wine*, 488n56.

51. Maxwell, *Conflicts and Conspiracies*, 49; Jacob M. Price, "New Time Series for Scotland's and Britain's Trade with the Thirteen Colonies and States, 1740–1791," *William and Mary Quarterly* 32 (April 1975), 324–25; Fisher, *Portugal Trade*, 41–49.

52. Lydon, "Fish and Flour," 133, 139–40; Parr & Bulkeley to Baynton & Wharton, May 22, May 30, August 4, and October 4, 1762, and July 12, 1763, and to Baynton, Wharton, & Morgan, January 16, 1766, all in MG 19, roll 2236, Baynton, Wharton, & Morgan Papers, PSA.

53. Parr & Bulkeley to Baynton & Wharton, May 22, May 30, August 4, and October 4, 1762, and July 12, 1763, and to Baynton, Wharton, & Morgan, January 16, 1766, all in MG 19, roll 2236, Baynton, Wharton, & Morgan Papers, PSA; Samuel Copland, *Wheat: Its History, Characteristics, Chemical Composition and Nutritive Properties* (London: Houlston & Wright, 1865), 67, 70.

54. Raymond & Dea to Baynton, Wharton, & Morgan, July 8, 1766, MG 19, roll 2236, Baynton, Wharton, & Morgan Papers, PSA.

55. Mayne & Co. to Galloway, March 9, 1765, and April 6, 1765, Galloway-Maxcy-Markoe Papers, vol. 7, LOC; Parr & Bulkeley to Baynton & Wharton, February 29, 1764, MG 19, roll 2238, Baynton, Wharton, & Morgan Papers, PSA.

56. R. B. Outhwaite, *Dearth, Public Policy and Social Disturbance in England, 1550–1800* (New York: Cambridge University Press, 1991), 31; Maxwell, *Conflicts and Conspiracies*, 59–60; Fisher, *Portugal Trade*, 41–43; Raymond & Dea to Baynton, Wharton, & Morgan, July 31, 1767, MG 19, roll 2236, Baynton, Wharton, & Morgan Papers, PSA; Edward Burns & Sons to Galloway, February 26, 1766, Galloway-Maxcy-Markoe Papers, vol. 8, LOC; McCusker, *Economic History*, 251; Lydon, "Fish and Flour," 40–41, 127; U.S. Bureau of the

Census, *Historical Statistics of the United States: Colonial Times to 1970*, bicentennial ed., part 2 (Washington, D.C., 1975), 1182.

Chapter 2

1. For contests over opposing visions of imperial political economies in the British and Portuguese Empires, see Pincus, "Rethinking Mercantilism," 3–34; Adelman, *Sovereignty and Revolution*, 121–22; Manuel Hespanha, "Antigo Regime nos trópicos," 51, 54; António Manuel Hespanha, *Poder e Instituições no Antigo Regime* (Lisbon: Edições Cosmos, 1992), 20–21; Paquette, *Imperial Portugal*, 39.

2. Gilje, *Free Trade*, 13; Adelman, *Sovereignty and Revolution*, 151–52; Luís de Almeida Portugal Soares de Alarcão Eça e Melo Silva e Mascarenhas to Martinho de Melo e Castro, September 11, 1770, box 91, document 7930, CU (quotation).

3. Wim Klooster, "Inter-imperial Smuggling in the Americas, 1600–1800," in Bernard Bailyn and Patricia L. Denault, eds., *Soundings in Atlantic History* (Cambridge, MA: Harvard University Press, 2009), 141.

4. Thomas Riche to William Street, September 7, 1763, to William and Francis Street, September 28, 1763, and September 29, 1763, TRL, vol. 1a, HSP; Riche to William Street, February 4, 1769, TRL, vol. 4, HSP; *Pennsylvania Gazette* (Philadelphia), July 26, 1764.

5. Riche to William Street, September 7, 1763, to William and Francis Street, September 28, 1763, and September 29, 1763, TRL, vol. 1a, HSP; Riche to William Street, February 4, 1769, TRL, vol. 4, HSP; Mann, *Republic of Debtors*, 82; Duncan, *Atlantic Islands*, 127–30; Mauro, "Political and Economic Structures," 52–53.

6. Riche to John and James Searle, April 18, 1761, to Francis Lewis, October 30, 1761, to Parr & Bulkeley, January 15, 1762, to Neate & Pigou, February 18, 1762, all in TRL, vol. 1a, HSP; Riche to John Riche, April 2, April 6, and June 14, 1764, to Samuel Cornell, June 9, 1764, to John Searle, June 16, 1764, and to John Manby, August 6, 1764, all in TRL, vol. 1b, HSP; James H. Soltow, "Thomas Riche's 'Adventure' in French Guiana, 1764–1766," *Pennsylvania Magazine of History and Biography* 83 (October 1959), 412.

7. Riche to William and Francis Street, September 28 and September 29, 1763, to Francis Street, November 11, 1763, and to George Ronnolds, September 28, 1763, all in TRL, vol. 1a, HSP; Andrew Jackson O'Shaughnessy, *An Empire Divided: The American Revolution and the British Caribbean* (Philadelphia: University of Pennsylvania Press, 2000), 60–63; Philip Coelho, "The Profitability of Imperialism," *Explorations in Economic History* 10 (Spring 1973), 260–65; Marc Egnal, "The Changing Structure of Philadelphia's Trade with the British West Indies, 1750–1775," *Pennsylvania Magazine of History and Biography* 99 (April 1975), 165; Riche to Peter Gurley, September [n.d.] 1764, TRL, vol. 1b, HSP; Stuart B. Schwartz, *Sugar Plantations in the Formation of Brazilian Society: Bahia, 1550–1835* (New York: Cambridge University Press, 1985), 498–501; Mayne & Co. to Samuel Galloway, July 5, 1762, Galloway-Maxcy-Markoe Papers vol. 7, LOC.

8. Riche to William and Francis Street, September 28 and September 29, 1763, to Francis Street, November 11, 1763, and to George Ronnolds, September 28, 1763, all in TRL, vol. 1a, HSP; Riche to William Street, March 31 April 4, April 24, and June 24, 1764, all in TRL, vol. 1b, HSP; Riche to Jacob Van Zandt, April 4, 1765, TRL, vol. 2, HSP.

9. Riche to Parr & Bulkeley, November 5, 1764, to John Searle, February 18, 1765, and to John Riche, October 25, 1764, all in TRL, vol. 2, HSP; Doerflinger, *Vigorous Spirit*, 86, 176, 181–82; Alvin Rabushka, *Taxation in Colonial America* (Princeton, NJ: Princeton University

Press, 2008), 797–98; Riche to John Riche, May 10, 1764, and June 14, 1764, to Jacob Van Zandt, May 19, 1764, to John Searle, June 16, 1764, and to William Street, June 24, 1764, all in TRL, vol. 1b, HSP.

10. Riche to William Street, March 31,1764, TRL, vol. 1b, HSP; Riche to William Street, March 28, 1765, TRL, vol. 2, HSP; S. Sombra, *História monetário do Brasil colonial* (Rio de Janeiro, 1938), 175; Duncan, *Atlantic Islands*, 127–30; Mauro, "Political and Economic Structures," 52–53; Boxer, "Brazilian Gold," 461, 464; Gomes Freire de Andrade to Francisco Xavier de Mendonça Furtado, February 6, 1761, box 61, document 5822, CU; Prado, "Addicted to Smuggling," 203; "Aviso do Secretário do Estado," February 4, 1764, livro 109, microfilm roll 2110, Junta do Comércio, ANTT; João Alves Simões to Diogo de Mendonça Corte Real, July 20, 1752, and Diogo de Mendonça Corte Real to João Alves Simões, December 1, 1752, box 45, documents 4599, 4621, CU; Gomes Freire de Andrade to Sebastião José de Carvalho e Melo, March 12, 1761, box 62, document 5943, CU; Parr & Bulkeley to Clifford, February 6, 1764, Clifford Correspondence, vol. 4, Pemberton Papers, Clifford Family Papers, HSP.

11. Riche to William Street, April 4, 1764, TRL, vol.1b, HSP; Riche to William Street, March 28, and April 1765, to Parr & Bulkeley, April 29, 1766, and to Richard and John Samuel, July 2 and October 24, 1766, all in TRL, vol. 2, HSP.

12. For smuggling as an unarticulated form of free trade, see Gilje, *Free Trade*, 20–21.

13. Pincus, "Rethinking Mercantilism," 3–34; Gilje, *Free Trade*, 13.

14. Peter Borschberg, *Hugo Grotius, the Portuguese, and Free Trade in the East Indies* (Singapore: NUS Press, 2011), 1, 3; Pincus, "Rethinking Mercantilism," 3–34; Kwass, *Contraband*, 288–98; Gilje, *Free Trade*, 15–17, 18; Pedro Doria, *1789: A História de Tiradentes e dos Contrabandistas, Assassinos, e Poetas que Lutaram pela Independência do Brasil* (Rio de Janeiro: Nova Fronteira, 2013), 124; John Berdell, *International Trade and Economic Growth in Open Economies: The Classical Dynamics of Hume, Smith, Ricardo, and Malthus* (Northampton, MA: Edward Elgar, 2002), 15–41.

15. Borschberg, *Hugo Grotius*, 78–80, 162–63.

16. Kwass, *Contraband*, 288–98.

17. Kwass, *Contraband*, 288–98.

18. Simon, "Criminology and Economic Ideas," 23–24.

19. Pincus, "Rethinking Mercantilism," 15–16.

20. David Ormrod, *The Rise of Commercial Empires: England and the Netherlands in the Age of Mercantilism, 1650–1770* (New York: Cambridge University Press, 2003), 36; Christopher Hill, *The Century of Revolution, 1603–1714*, 2nd ed. (New York: W. W. Norton, 1980), 16; Pauline Croft, "Free Trade and the House of Commons, 1605–6," *Economic History Review* 28 (February 1975), 18–19.

21. Pincus, "Rethinking Mercantilism," 22–23; Jonathan Eacott, *Selling Empire: India in the Making of Britain and America, 1600–1830* (Chapel Hill: University of North Carolina Press, 2016), 72, 75; Gilje, *Free Trade*, 18 (quotation); Jarvis, *Eye of All Trade*, 167–80.

22. Pincus, "Rethinking Mercantilism," 22–27, esp. 27 (quotation "if we cou'd obtain"); Finucane, *Temptations of Trade*, 32; Eacott, *Selling Empire*, 104; Gilje, *Free Trade*, 19 (quotation "conquered the Spaniards").

23. Pincus, *Rethinking Mercantilism*, 32–33; Benjamin Franklin to William Shirley, December 22, 1754, Founders Online, National Historical Publications and Records Commission, National Archives, http://founders.archives.gov/documents/Franklin/01-05-02-0127 (accessed September 20, 2016).

24. Matson, *Merchants and Empire*, 8–9; Tyler, *Smugglers and Patriots*, 18, 22, 168; O'Shaughnessy, *Empire Divided*, 59–65.

25. Pincus, *Rethinking Mercantilism*, 14–15, 28–29.

26. O'Shaughnessy, *Empire Divided*, 58–59; Tyler, *Smugglers and Patriots*, 17, 110, 260–62, 268–269; Matson, *Merchants and Empire*, 309, 311.

27. Truxes, *Defying Empire*, 39.

28. Carp, *Defiance of the Patriots*, 76; Tradesman of Philadelphia, "Address to the People of Pennsylvania," August 17, 1774, American Archives: Documents of the American Revolutionary Period, 1774–1776, Northern Illinois University, http://amarch.lib.niu.edu/islandora/object/niu-amarch%3A79275 (accessed September 20, 2016); Matson, *Merchants and Empire*, 299.

29. Ralph L. Ketcham, ed., *The Political Thought of Benjamin Franklin* (Indianapolis: Hackett Publishing, 1965), 171–75, esp. 173; "The Right of Taxing the Americans Considered," *Gentleman's and London Magazine*, January 1766, 43; John Vardill, "To the worthy inhabitants of the city of New-York" (New York, 1773).

30. *South Carolina and American General Gazette*, July 22, 1774 (quotations "carried on a trade" and "every political point"); *Scots Magazine* 36 (1774), 268 (quotation "As to the Americans").

31. *South Carolina Gazette*, June 8, 1773; Tradesman, "To the free-holders and free-men of the city; and province of New York" (New York, November 13, 1773); For an additional rebuttal to Vardill, see Mechanic, "To the Worthy Inhabitants of New-York" (New York, 1773), 3.

32. Tyler, *Smugglers and Patriots*, 17, 90, esp. 17 (quotation "for every penny"); "The Claims of the Americans Impartially Represented," *Gentleman's and London Magazine*, January 1766, 45 (quotation "their mother-country"); also see Ketcham, *Political Thought*, 171–75.

33. Thomas Jefferson, "A Summary View of the Rights of British America," The Avalon Project: Documents in Law, History, and Diplomacy, Yale School of Law, http://avalon.law.yale.edu/18th_century/jeffsumm.asp (accessed March 4, 2017); Philip Mazzei, "Observations of a Citizen of the World to an American," *Virginia Gazette*, August 24, 1776.

34. Guillaume Thomas Raynal, *The Sentiments of a Foreigner, on the Disputes of Great-Britain with North America* (Philadelphia, 1775), 8; also reprinted in *Virginia Gazette*, September 21 and 28, 1775; *Pennsylvania Gazette*, June 21, 1775.

35. Tyler, *Smugglers and Patriots*, 238; Ayşe Çelikkol, *Romances of Free Trade: British Literature, Laissez-Faire, and the Global Nineteenth Century* (New York: Oxford University Press, 2011), 24.

36. Adelman, *Sovereignty and Revolution*, 56–71, 121–22; Alencastro, *O Trato dos Viventes*; Fragoso, *Homens de grossa aventura*, 174–212.

37. Adelman, *Sovereignty and Revolution*, 56–71; Florentino, *Em Costas Negras*, 192–95; Fragoso, *Homens de grossa aventura*, 174–212; Hawthorne, *From Africa to Brazil*, 61.

38. Fragoso, *Homens de grossa aventura*, 22–23, 101–22; Adelman, *Sovereignty and Revolution*, 61–64.

39. Kenneth Maxwell, "The Spark: Pombal, the Amazon, and the Jesuits," *Portuguese Studies* 17 (2001), 175; Alden, *Royal Government*, 356; Maxwell, *Conflicts and Conspiracies*, 41–42; Hawthorne, *From Africa to Brazil*, 61; Eulália Maria Lahmeyer Lobo, "O comércio atlântico e a comunidade de mercadores no Rio de Janeiro e em Charleston no século XVIII,"

Revista de história 101 (1975), 72; Paquette, *Imperial Portugal*, 28–31; Florentino, *Em Costas Negras*, 30.

40. Fragoso and Florentino, *O Arcaísmo como projeto*, 169–219; Miller, *Way of Death*, 568; Kühn, "Interesses do governador," 35; Adelman, *Sovereignty and Revolution*, 28, 65–71; Paquette, *Imperial Portugal*, 30–32.

41. Paquette, *Imperial Portugal*, 31–34; Maxwell, *Conflicts and Conspiracies*, 77, 215, esp. 77 (quotation).

42. Adelman, *Sovereignty and Revolution*, 28, 119–21, esp. 28 (quotation); Miller, *Way of Death*, 278, 581; Maxwell, *Conflicts and Conspiracies*, 215; Paquette, *Imperial Portugal*, 33.

43. Maxwell, *Conflicts and Conspiracies*, 215 (quotation "a free trade"); Paquette, *Imperial Portugal*, 33 (quotation "become an entrepôt").

44. Maxwell, *Conflicts and Conspiracies*, 72–73, 215; Schwartz, *Sugar Plantations*, 417–18; Lahmeyer Lobo, "Comércio atlântico," 70–71; Carlos Guilherme Mota, *Nordeste 1817: Estruturas e Argumentos* (São Paulo: Editora da Universidade de São Paulo, 1972), 21.

45. Miller, *Way of Death*, 581n27; Maxwell, *Conflicts and Conspiracies*, 39 (quotation).

46. Maxwell, *Conflicts and Conspiracies*, 73 (quotation); Paquette, *Imperial Portugal*, 31.

47. *Virginia Gazette*, November 20, 1766, March 26, 1767, and October 13, 1768.

48. Maxwell, *Conflicts and Conspiracies*, 39, 78.

49. Paquette, *Imperial Portugal*, 35–36; Maxwell, *Conflicts and Conspiracies*, 73–74; Dias, "Os acionistas," 31–42, 50; Mota, *Nordeste 1817*, 21–22.

50. Maxwell, *Conflicts and Conspiracies*, 45; Diogo de Mendonça to Gomes Freire de Andrade, March 21, 1751, box 44, document 4485, CU; José Antonio da Silva Maia, *Memória da origem, progressos, e decadencia do quinto do ouro na provincia de Minas Geraes* (Rio de Janeiro, 1827), 13.

51. Silva Maia, *Memória*, 20–21; Maxwell, *Conflicts and Conspiracies*, 45.

52. Doria, *1789*, 45; Maxwell, *Conflicts and Conspiracies*, 108–9. A 1799 royal report claimed that Brazilians had only "scratched the surface" of Brazilian mines and that "the veins of the metals are for the most part intact in their center." See "Memória Sobre a Capitania das Minas Gerais," 1799, BNRJ. For an overview of smuggling practices in Brazil and the government's response, see Alden, *Royal Government*, 388–417.

53. Diogo de Mendonça to Gomes Freire Andrade, March 21, 1751, box 44, document 4485, CU.

54. José de Lima Pinheiro e Aragão to Tomé Joaquim da Costa Corte Real, October 30, 1756, box 51, document 5110, CU; João Marques Bacalhau to Tomé Joaquim da Costa Corte Real, November 11, 1756, box 51, document 5114, CU; Francisco Xavier Mendonça Furtado to Antônio Álvares da Cunha, January 25, 1764, box 71, document 6493, CU; Antônio Álvares da Cunha to Francisco Xavier Mendonça Furtado, June 9, 1764, box 71, document 6544, CU. For the role of inspectors in Luso-Atlantic commerce, see Manuel Hespanha, *Poder e Instituições*, 48–49.

55. Kühn, "Interesses do governador," 30, 32–35, 37; Prado, *Edge of Empire*, 24–25, 69–81; Maxwell, *Conflicts and Conspiracies*, 100–102; João Pacheco Pereira de Vasconcelos to Dom José I, October 15, 1753, box 46, document 4725, CU.

56. Ronald Raminelli, *Nobrezas do Novo Mundo: Brasil e ultramar hispânico, séculos XVII e XVIII* (Rio de Janeiro: Editora FGV, 2015), 17; Kühn, "Interesses do governador," 32–35, 37 (quotation); Prado, *Edge of Empire*, 69–81; Prado, "Addicted to Smuggling," 201–2, 208–11; Pijning, "Controlling Contraband," 148–82.

57. Prado, "Addicted to Smuggling," 204–8; Pijning, "Contrabando," 399–402; Maxwell, *Conflicts and Conspiracies*, 99–103.

58. Luís de Almeida Portugal Soares de Alarcão Eça e Melo Silva e Mascarenhas to Martinho de Melo e Castro, September 11, 1770, box 91, document 7930, CU (quotations "grave consequences," "plague of states," and "mount against me"); Adelman, *Sovereignty and Revolution*, 21 (quotation "multiplied damages").

59. Prado, *Edge of Empire*, 13–33; Pijning, "Contrabando," 398–400; Adelman, *Sovereignty and Revolution*, 121; Kühn, "Intereses do governador," 36.

60. Adelman, *Sovereignty and Revolution*, 121–22.

61. Maxwell, *Conflicts and Conspiracies*, 79.

62. Adelman, *Sovereignty and Revolution*, 56–101; Florentino, *Em Costas Negras*, 23, 121; Fragoso, *Homens de grossa aventura*, 19–27, 83–93.

Part II

1. Matson, *Merchants and Empire*, 283–311.
2. Hancock, *Oceans of Wine*, 107–8.

Chapter 3

1. Alan Taylor, *American Revolutions: A Continental History, 1750–1804* (New York: W. W. Norton, 2016), 51.

2. Gordon S. Wood, *The American Revolution: A History* (Toronto: Modern Library, 2002), 23–24; Hancock, *Oceans of Wine*, 119; *Virginia Gazette*, September 5, 1751 (quotation "only remedy") and February 9, 1775 (quotation "a great grievance"); Riche to Parr & Bulkeley, April 30, 1764, and to William Street, June 22, 1764, TRL, vol. 1b, HSP.

3. Hancock, *Oceans of Wine*, 119; "An Account of the Duties Inwards on the undermentioned Goods imported from Portugal and Spain into Great-Britain," March 1, 1765, sent from Joseph Banfield to Keppelle & Steinmetz, n.d., box 12, folder 6, Jasper Yeates Brinton Collection, HSP. The full text copy of the Sugar Act is at "Great Britain: Parliament—The Sugar Act, 1764," The Avalon Project: Documents in Law, History, and Diplomacy, Yale Law School, http://avalon.law.yale.edu/18th_century/sugar_act_1764.asp (accessed January 14, 2017).

4. Riche to Francis Street, November 11, 1763, and to Parr & Bulkeley, November 12, 1763, TRL, vol. 1a, HSP; Riche to Parr & Bulkeley, June 11, 1764, and to John Davidson, June 22, 1764, TRL, vol. 1b, HSP; "Great Britain: Parliament—The Sugar Act, 1764," Avalon Project.

5. Riche to William Street, June 22, 1764, to Searle, June 16, 1764, and June [n.d.], 1764, to John Davidson, June 22, 1764, and to John Kenny, June 23, 1764, TRL, vol. 1b, HSP; Hancock, *Oceans of Wine*, 118, 212–13; CO 5/1227–28, Naval Office Shipping Lists for New York, 1739–1765, NAUK; Searle to Galloway, June 20, 1764, Galloway-Maxcy-Markoe Papers, vol. 7, LOC; Kearny & Gilbert to Newton & Gordon, March 30, 1767, and November 30, 1767, Newton & Gordon letters received, 1763–1775, Newton & Gordon Papers, ISM; Riche to William Street, June 23, 1768, TRL, vol. 4, HSP.

6. Tyler, *Smugglers and Patriots*, 84–86, esp. 84. While the "Proposals" lucidly represent the complaints of British-American traders, the committee never sent them to England since, in Tyler's words, "they were outmoded by the addition of new grievances," including the

Currency Act and Stamp Act; "Great Britain: Parliament—The Sugar Act, 1764," Avalon Project.

7. Hancock, *Oceans of Wine*, 119; Samuel Johnston to Newton & Gordon, February 2, 1764, Newton & Gordon letters received, 1763–1775, Newton & Gordon Papers, ISM; Riche to Searle, June 16, 1764, June [n.d.], 1764, and September 23, 1764, TRL, vol. 1b, HSP; U.S. Bureau of the Census, *Historical Statistics*, 1198; Charles Wharton to Alvário Antônio Texeira Lona, December 3, 1767, Charles Wharton letterbook, 1766–1769, Sarah A. G. Smith Collection, HSP; Mayne & Co. to Baynton, Wharton, & Morgan, February 12, 1765, MG 19, roll 2237, Baynton, Wharton, & Morgan Papers, PSA; Searle to Galloway & Steward, February 16, 1765, Galloway-Maxcy-Markoe Papers, vol. 7, LOC; Kearny & Gilbert to Newton & Gordon, March 30, November 30, 1767, Newton & Gordon letters received, 1763–1775, Newton & Gordon Papers, ISM; Riche to Parr & Bulkeley, April 26, 1766, to Searle, April 21, 1765, TRL, vol. 2, HSP; Riche to William Street, June 23, 1768, TRL, vol. 4, HSP; Lydon, "Fish and Flour," 227; Riche to Searle, April 13, 1766, to Thomas Gilbraith, December 2, 1767, to John Riche, December 3, 1767, and to Samuel Devonshire, December 3, 1767, TRL, vol. 3, HSP.

8. O'Shaughnessy, *Empire Divided*, 67–68; Charles Francis Adams, et. al., "Annual Meeting, April 1910," *Proceedings of the Massachusetts Historical Society* 43 (October 1909–June 1910), 478–479; Riche to William Street, June 23, 1768, TRL, vol. 4, HSP; Arthur M. Schlesinger, *The Colonial Merchants and the American Revolution, 1763–1776* (New York: Columbia University, 1918), 98n3 (quotation); Tyler, *Smugglers and Patriots*, 20; Virginia D. Harrington, *The New York Merchant on the Eve of the Revolution* (New York: Columbia University Press, 1935; reprint, Gloucester, MA: P. Smith, 1964), 269–70.

9. Tyler, *Smugglers and Patriots*, 16, 17, 70, 115, 247, 258–77; While Sewall succeeded in confiscating Hancock's sloop in mid-August, he dropped the additional suit four months after initiating the action. See John Ferling, *John Adams: A Life* (New York: Oxford University Press, 1992), 58–59.

10. Hancock, *Oceans of Wine*, 500n15; Harrington, *New York Merchant*, 245–46; Francis & Tilghman to Newton & Gordon, December 4, 1770, Newton & Gordon letters received, 1763–1775, Newton & Gordon Papers, ISM; Riche to George Ronnolds, September 28, 1763, to Francis Street, November 11, 1763, and to Parr & Bulkeley, November 12, 1763, TRL, vol. 1a, HSP; Riche to Parr & Bulkeley, June 11, 1764, and to John Davidson, June 22, 1764, TRL, vol. 1b, HSP.

11. Schlesinger, *Colonial Merchants*, 101; Ferling, *John Adams*, 58.

12. T. H. Breen, *The Marketplace of Revolution: How Consumer Politics Shaped American Independence* (New York: Oxford University Press, 2004), 10–26.

13. Taylor, *American Revolutions*, 96–103.

14. Taylor, *American Revolutions*, 101–2; Parr & Bulkeley to Baynton, Wharton, & Morgan, January 16, 1766, MG 19, roll 2236, Baynton, Wharton, & Morgan Papers, PSA; John Chew to Galloway, November 7, 1765, Galloway-Maxcy-Markoe Papers, vol. 8, LOC; Tyler, *Smugglers and Patriots*, 91; *Pennsylvania Gazette*, November 7, 1765; Joseph T. Tiedemann, *Reluctant Revolutionaries: New York City and the Road to Independence, 1763–1776* (Ithaca, NY: Cornell University Press, 1997), 71, 74.

15. Michelle L. Craig, "Grounds for Debate? The Place of the Caribbean Provisions trade in Philadelphia's Prerevolutionary Economy," *Pennsylvania Magazine of History and Biography*, 128 (April 2004), 150–51.

16. Parr & Bulkeley to Baynton, Wharton, & Morgan, January 16, 1766, MG 19, roll 2236, Baynton, Wharton, & Morgan Papers, PSA.

17. Holdsworth, Olive, & Newman to Baynton, Wharton, & Morgan, April 21, 1766, MG 19, roll 2237, Baynton, Wharton, & Morgan Papers, PSA; O'Shaughnessy, *Empire Divided*, 67–68; Adams, et. al., "Annual Meeting," 478–79.

18. Robert J. Chaffin, "The Townshend Acts of 1767," *William and Mary Quarterly* 27 (January 1970), 95, 115–16; Lydon, "Fish and Flour," 226–27; Hancock, *Oceans of Wine*, 119.

19. Lydon, "Fish and Flour," 226–27; "A Portugal Merchant" to the printer of the *London Chronicle*, March 10, 1768, Benjamin Franklin Papers, APS; Hancock, *Oceans of Wine*, 119; Chaffin, "Townshend Acts of 1767," 115–16.

20. Chaffin, "Townshend Acts of 1767," 116, 119; Lydon, "Fish and Flour," 227.

21. David Morgan, *The Devious Dr. Franklin, Colonial Agent: Benjamin Franklin's Years in London* (Macon, GA: Mercer University Press, 1996), xiii, 1; Benjamin Franklin to the printer of the *London Chronicle*, [n.d.] 1768, Benjamin Franklin Papers, APS; "A Portugal Merchant" to the printer of the *London Chronicle*, March 10, 1768, Benjamin Franklin Papers, APS.

22. Keppelle & Steinmetz to Parr, Bulkeley, & Co., June 21, 1773, see also loose account records, April 7, 1773, both in box 9, folder 11, Jasper Yeates Brinton Collection, HSP; Joseph Banfield to Keppelle & Steinmetz, April 7, 1773, box 9, folder 18, Jasper Yeates Brinton Collection, HSP; Charles Wharton to Parr & Bulkeley, July 7, 1768, Charles Wharton letterbook 1766–1799, Sarah A. G. Smith Collection, HSP; Susan E. Gay, *Old Falmouth: The Story of the Town from the Days of the Killigrews to the Earliest Part of the 19th Century* (London: Headley Brothers, 1903), 74–75; Benjamin Franklin to the printer of the *London Chronicle*, [n.d.] 1768, Benjamin Franklin Papers, APS (quotation).

23. Doerflinger, *Vigorous Spirit*, 173–77; Lydon, "Fish and Flour," 87, 225, 230; Riche to Parr & Bulkeley, April 30, 1765, and to William Street, May 7, 1765, TRL, vol. 2, HSP; Charles Wharton to Parr & Bulkeley, August 24, 1768, Charles Wharton letterbook 1766–1799, Sarah A. G. Smith Collection, HSP.

24. Carl Ubbelohde, *The Vice-Admiralty Courts and the American Revolution* (Chapel Hill: University of North Carolina Press, 1960), 90–91.

25. Riche to Parr & Bulkeley, April 30, 1765, and to William Street, May 7, 1765, TRL, vol. 2, HSP.

26. Riche to Parr & Bulkeley, April 30, 1765 (quotation "good deal oneasy"), and to William Street, May 7, 1765, TRL, vol. 2, HSP; Lydon, "Fish and Flour," 87 (quotation "great Quantitys").

27. Hancock, *Oceans of Wine*, 118; Doerflinger, *Vigorous Spirit*, 173–77; Lamar, Hill, & Bisset to Galloway & Steward, March 7, 1770, Galloway-Maxcy-Markoe Papers, vol. 10, LOC (quotation).

28. Benjamin Franklin to the printer of the *London Chronicle*, [n.d.] 1768, Benjamin Franklin Papers, ASP.

29. Tiedemann, *Reluctant Revolutionaries*, 128–29; Tyler, *Smugglers and Patriots*, 112–116; Doerflinger, *Vigorous Spirit*, 189–191; Robert Middlekauff, *The Glorious Cause: The American Revolution, 1763–1789* (New York: Oxford University Press, 1982), 183.

30. Doerflinger, *Vigorous Spirit*, 189–190; Thomas Lamar to Henry Hill, June 12, 1770, Sarah A.G. Smith collection, box 1, HSP (quotation).

31. Middlekauff, *Glorious Cause*, 208–9; Lydon, "Fish and Flour," 229 (quotation).

32. John Smith & Sons to Parr, Bulkeley, & Co., December 20, 1774 (quotation "immediate dispatch"), January 2, 1775, and April 20, 1775 (quotation "too narrowly watch'd"), John Smith & Sons Letterbook, vol. 1, MHS; Lydon, "Fish and Flour," 191–92, 229.

33. Keppelle & Steinmetz to Samuel Davison, June 24, 1773, box 9, folder 11, Jasper Yeates Brinton Collection, HSP; "Account of Duty and Charges on the Cargo of the Ship Charming Peggy," Joseph Banfield to Keppelle & Steinmetz, September 23, 1773, and "Port Charges and Disbursements," Joseph Banfield to Keppelle & Steinmetz, September 25, 1773, both in box 10, folder 2, Jasper Yeates Brinton Collection, HSP; Parr, Bulkeley, & Co. to Keppelle & Steinmetz, August 3, 1774, box 6, folder 4, Jasper Yeates Brinton Collection, HSP; McCusker, *Essays*, 14–25.

34. Clifford Correspondence, vols. 4–6, Pemberton Papers, Clifford Family Papers, HSP; Lydon, "Fish and Flour," 145, 229. The historian James G. Lydon has insisted that the "Lisbon/Philadelphia trade enjoyed phenomenal growth 1769–1774" (145), although his data show a significant decline after the peak years of 1769–1770. His numbers also indicate an increase in ships returning in ballast from Lisbon to British America, with cargoes of heavy but non-merchantable material solely to increase sailing stability.

35. Parr, Bulkeley, & Co. to Keppelle & Steinmetz, October 11, 1772, February 22, 1773, May 2, 1773 (imports from Porto and Vienna), box 6, folder 3, Jasper Yeates Brinton Collection, HSP; Parr, Bulkeley, & Co. to Keppelle & Steinmetz, December 9, 1773 (Parliament to allow English grain exports), box 6, folder 1, Jasper Yeates Brinton Collection, HSP; Parr, Bulkeley, & Co. to Keppelle & Steinmetz, March 1, 1774, box 6, folder 2, Jasper Yeates Brinton Collection, HSP; Parr, Bulkeley, & Co. to Keppelle & Steinmetz, August 9, 1774 (quotation "a fairer prospect"), September 6, 1774, and December 20, 1774 (quotation, April, May, and June as season of "briskest Consumption") box 6, folder 4, Jasper Yeates Brinton Collection, HSP.

36. Parr, Bulkeley, & Co. to Keppelle & Steinmetz, September 6, 1774, box 6, folder 4, Jasper Yeates Brinton Collection, HSP.

37. Breen, *Marketplace of Revolution*, 10–13, 19–20; Gilje, *Free Trade*, 23.

38. Worthington Chauncey Ford, Gaillard Hunt, et al., eds., *Journals of the Continental Congress, 1774–1789*, vol. 1 (Washington, D.C.: Government Printing Office, 1904), 76–77.

39. Keppelle & Steinmetz to Thomas Dowman, December 12, 1774 and to Parr, Bulkeley, & Co., December 12, 1774 (quotation "not at liberty"), box 9, folder 11, Jasper Yeates Brinton Collection, HSP; Robert Bisset to Henry Hill, January 31, 1775 (quotation "filling our stores"), box 1, Sarah A. G. Smith Collection, HSP; *Pennsylvania Gazette*, February 15, 1775 (quotation "declared his intention").

40. John Smith & Sons to Parr, Bulkeley, & Co., December 20, 1774, John Smith & Sons Letterbook, vol. 1, MHS; Pasley's & Co. to Keppelle & Steinmetz, April 27, 1775 (quotations "disputes between" and "escuse us") and Parr, Bulkeley, & Co. to Keppelle & Steinmetz, January 31, 1775 (rumors of port closures), and April 18, 1775 (quotation "America produce"), all in box 6, folder 5, Jasper Yeates Brinton Collection, HSP.

41. Keppelle & Steinmetz to Parr, Bulkeley, & Co., December 12, 1774, box 9, folder 11, Jasper Yeates Brinton Collection, HSP (quotation "We are not bound"); Parr, Bulkeley, & Co. to Keppelle & Steinmetz, May 12, 1775, box 6, folder 5, Jasper Yeates Brinton Collection, HSP (quotation "distressing").

42. Harry M. Ward, *The War for Independence and the Transformation of American Society* (New York: Routledge, 1999), 12; Parr, Bulkeley, & Co. to Keppelle & Steinmetz, April 14, 1775, and June 13, 1775 (quotation), box 6, folder 5, Jasper Yeates Brinton Collection, HSP.

43. Parr, Bulkeley, & Co. to Keppelle & Steinmetz, April 14, 1775 (quotations "We are puzzled" and "need of divining"), and Pasley's & Co. to Keppelle & Steinmetz, April 28, 1775 (quotation "may operate"), box 6, folder 5, Jasper Yeates Brinton Collection, HSP; John Smith & Sons to Parr, Bulkeley, & Co., April 20, 1775, John Smith & Sons Letterbook, vol. 1, MHS.

44. John Smith & Sons to Parr, Bulkeley, & Co., May 14, 1775, John Smith & Sons Letterbook, vol. 1, MHS.

45. Keppelle & Steinmetz to Thomas Dowman, July 16, 1775, to John Whitmore, Senior & Junior, December 9, 1775, and to Thomas Gage, December 9, 1775, and petition of Henry Keppelle to Continental Congress, October 7, 1776, and to Victualling Office, October 5, 1775, and affidavit of Thomas Dowman, December 26, 1775, all in box 9, folder 18, Jasper Yeates Brinton Collection, HSP; Ford, Hunt, et. al., *Journals*, 2:200; Memorial of Keppelle & Steinmetz to Continental Congress, December 27, 1775, box 10, folder 1, Jasper Yeates Brinton Collection, HSP.

46. Keppelle & Steinmetz to John Whitmore, Senior & Junior, December 9, 1775 (quotation "just & legal trade"), and February 24, 1776, and petition of Henry Keppelle to Continental Congress, October 7, 1776, all in box 9, folder 18, Jasper Yeates Brinton collection, HSP; Stephen Collins to John Steinmetz, August 8, 1776, box 10, folder 1, Jasper Yeates Brinton Collection, HSP; Schlesinger, *Colonial Merchants*, 68; Keppelle & Steinmetz to Thomas Dowman, July 16, 1775, box 9, folder 18, Jasper Yeates Brinton Collection, HSP (quotation "present Disputes"); Robert Pasley & Co. to Keppelle & Steinmetz, February 15, 1777 (quotation "present calamities") and Parr, Bulkeley, & Co. to Keppelle & Steinmetz, December 17, 1777 (quotation "unhappy contest"), both in box 6, folder 7, Jasper Yeates Brinton Collection, HSP. In July 1781, a British admiralty court finally awarded them the value of the ship and cargo. See "Copy of Decree of Admiralty Court London on Ship Charming Peggy & Cargo," n.d., box 9, folder 10, Jasper Yeates Brinton Collection, HSP.

47. John Smith & Sons to Parr, Bulkeley, & Co., September 8, 1775, John Smith & Sons Letterbook, vol. 1, MHS.

48. Martins Ribeiro, "Comércio e diplomacia," 290 (quotation "make common cause"), 298; *Virginia Gazette*, June 22, 1776 (quotation "bad consequences"); H. T. Dickinson, *Britain and the American Revolution* (New York: Routledge, 1998), 199–200; H. M. Scott, *British Foreign Policy in the Age of the American Revolution* (New York: Oxford University Press, 1990), 222; Timothy Walker, "Atlantic Dimensions of the American Revolution: Imperial Priorities and the Portuguese Reaction to the North American Bid for Independence (1775–1783)," *Journal of Early American History* 2 (2012)," 263.

49. Dauril Alden, "The Marquis of Pombal and the American Revolution," *Americas*, 17 (April 1961), 370–71, 374–75; Maxwell, *Pombal*, 127, 140–41; Júlio Rodrigues da Silva, "A guerra da independência dos E.U.A. e os diplomatas portugueses. Luís Pinto de Sousa Coutinho e os primórdios do conflito (1774–1776)," in vol. 2 of *Actas do XV colóquio de história militar—Portugal militar nos séculos XVII e XVIII até às vésperas das invasões francesas* (Lisbon, Comissão Portuguesa de História Militar, 2006), http://www.fcsh.unl.pt/chc/pdfs/guerrainde pendencia.pdf (accessed November 29, 2014); Alden, "Marquis of Pombal," 374–75.

50. Marquis of Pombal to George III, November 28, 1775, appended to Alden, "Marquis of Pombal," 377–82.

51. Marquis of Pombal to George III, November 28, 1775, appended to Alden, "Marquis of Pombal," 377–82, esp. 381 (quotation); Weldon A. Brown, *Empire or Independence: A Study in the Failure of Reconciliation, 1774–1783*, 2nd ed. (Port Washington, NY: Kennikat Press, 1966), 1–8.

52. Dickinson, *Britain and the American Revolution*, 199–200; Scott, *British Foreign Policy*, 222; Maxwell, *Conflicts and Conspiracies*, 49; Walker, "Atlantic Dimensions," 263.

53. Benjamin Franklin to Arthur Lee, March 21, 1777, Founders Online, http://founders.archives.gov/documents/Franklin/01-23-02-0328 (accessed December 3, 2014); Francis Wharton, comp., *The Revolutionary Diplomatic Correspondence of the United States* (Washington, D.C.: Government Printing Office, 1889), 2:307 (quotations).

54. Gilje, *Free Trade*, 36–37, esp. 36.

55. Walker, "Atlantic Dimensions," 274–75; Samuel Morris, Jr., to Robert Murray, February 5, 1781, reel 1, Morris Family Papers, HL; Charles Wharton to John Bulkeley & Co., August 18, 1779, Charles Wharton letterbook 1779–1785, Sarah A. G. Smith Collection, HSP.

56. Larry G. Bowman, "The Scarcity of Salt in Virginia During the American Revolution," *Virginia Magazine of History and Biography* 77 (October 1969), 464–66; Joseph Wharton to the American commissioners, September 26, 1778, Benjamin Franklin Papers, APS (quotation).

57. Walker, "Atlantic Dimension," 269–71; Martins Ribeiro, "Comércio e diplomacia," 306–10; Robert Pasley & Co. to Keppelle & Steinmetz, February 15, 1777, and Parr, Bulkeley, & Co. to Keppelle & Steinmetz, December 17, 1777, both in box 6, folder 7, Jasper Yeates Brinton Collection, HSP.

58. "Memorial and Petition of Arnold Henry Dohrman," July 19, 1786 (quotation), and John Adams to Arnold Henry Dohrman, May 16, 1780, both in *ASP:Cl*, 1:510–11, esp. 510; Martins Ribeiro, "Comércio e diplomacia," 333–34; George Anderson to the American commissioners, February 16, 1779, and Arnold Henry Dohrman to Benjamin Franklin, May 5, 1778, Benjamin Franklin Papers, ASP.

59. George Anderson to the American commissioners, February 16, 1779, Benjamin Franklin Papers, ASP; "Memorial and Petition of Arnold Henry Dohrman," July 19, 1786, *ASP:Cl*, 1:510 (quotation).

60. Thomas Jefferson to Arnold Henry Dohrman, May 24, 1780, *ASP:Cl*, 1:511; Levi Hollingsworth to Arnold Henry Dohrman, December 1, 1781, outgoing correspondence, vol. 1, Hollingsworth Family Papers, HSP; "Memorial and Petition of Arnold Henry Dohrman," July 19, 1786, and "By the United States in Congress Assembled," October 1, 1787, and petition of Rachael Dohrman, January 6, 1817, all in *ASP:Cl*, 1:508–10, 512.

61. Dohrman to Adams, February 19, 1783, *Papers of John Adams*, vol. 14, http://www.masshist.org/publications/apde2/view?mode=p&vol=PJA14&page=280 (accessed December 4, 2014) (quotation "own interest lies"); "Memorial and Petition of Arnold Henry Dohrman," July 19, 1786, "By the United States in Congress Assembled," October 1, 1787, Petition of Rachael Dohrman, January 6, 1817, James Ross to Rufus King, January 13, 1817, all in *ASP:Cl*, 1:508–10, 512–14; Deposition of Arnold Henry Dohrman, August 3, 1791, Alexander Nelson to John Wilcocks, June 29, 1783 (quotation "merchantile abilities"), Josh Wentworth to Arnold Henry Dohrman, August 23, 1783, and invoice from Jacob Dohrman & Co. to

Arnold Henry Dohrman, April 27, 1804, all in box 3, McAllister Collection, LCP; Doerflinger, *Vigorous Spirit*, 289–90. While Dohrman claimed over $25,000 in expenses incurred during the Revolutionary War, the U.S. Treasury reimbursed him for just under $6,000, claiming that many of his receipts were too general to meet the standard for reimbursement. Recognizing, however, that Dohrman had incurred many expenses that could not be catalogued by receipts (such as housing North Americans during the war), they recommended an annual back salary of $1,600 from the time he first received appointment as a U.S. consul in Lisbon, as well as land in the West. See Martins Ribeiro, "Comércio e diplomacia," 344–45.

62. Martins Ribeiro, "Comércio e diplomacia," 336–37, 341, 347. Unfortunate circumstances later left Dohrman in great want. After fires twice destroyed their home in New York, the Dohrmans moved to Ohio. In 1813, Arnold died deeply in debt, leaving Rachael and their eleven children dependent on a meager income, help from neighbors, and ultimately the U.S. government for support. See Petition of Rachael Dohrman, January 6, 1817, James Ross to Rufus King, January 13, 1817, *ASP:Cl*, 1:508–9, 513–14.

63. Hancock, *Oceans of Wine*, 120–21, 154–55; Lydon, "Fish and Flour," 246 (quotation).

64. Walker, "Atlantic Dimensions," 275–76; John Adams to John Jay, May 15, 1780, in Wharton, *Revolutionary Diplomatic Correspondence*, 3:678; George Anderson to the American Commissioners, February 16, 1779, Benjamin Franklin Papers, APS; Caetano Beirão, *Dona Maria I, 1777–1792: Subsídios para a Revisão da História do seu Reinado*, 4th ed. (Lisbon: Empresa Nacional de Publicidade, 1944), 220; Homer Bast, "Tench Tilghman—Maryland Patriot," *Maryland Historical Magazine* 42 (June 1947), 90. Although they did not make the reason explicit, the Baltimore firm John Smith & Sons severed their ties with Parr, Bulkeley, & Co., despite close relations before the war. After the war ended, they turned to the Lisbon firm of Daniel Bowden & Son upon receiving an introduction from Gregory Turnbull of London. See John Smith & Sons to Daniel Bowden & Son, April 24, 1784, John Smith & Sons Letterbook, vol. 1, MHS.

65. John Adams to John Jay, May 15, 1780, in Wharton, *Revolutionary Diplomatic Correspondence*, 3:678 (quotation); John Bondfield to Adams, May 14, 1782, AP; Jonathan Williams, Jr., to William Temple Franklin, May 16, 1782, William Temple Franklin Papers, APS; Coppens fils to Benjamin Franklin, May 21, 1782, Benjamin Franklin Papers, APS; João Gomes de Araujo to Martinho de Melo e Castro, December 3, 1777, box 105, document 8839, CU; Luís de Vasconcelos e Sousa to Martinho de Melo e Castro, April 23, 1779, box 109, document 9116, CU; James J. Piecuch, "A War Averted: Luso-American Relations in the Revolutionary Era, 1775–1786," *Portuguese Studies Review* 5 (Fall–Winter), 31.

66. Charles Wharton to John Bulkeley & Co., August 18, 1779, Charles Wharton letterbook 1779–1785, Sarah A. G. Smith Collection, HSP; John Ehrman, *The British Government and Commercial Negotiations with Europe, 1783–1793* (New York: Cambridge University Press, 1962), 8; William Tonkin to John Steinmetz, March 12, 1783, box 6, folder 10, Jasper Yeates Brinton Collection, HSP; Lydon, "Fish and Flour," 245.

67. Mayne & Co. to Galloway, April 6, 1765, Galloway-Maxcy-Markoe Papers, vol. 7, LOC.

68. Hancock, *Oceans of Wine*, 107–8.

Chapter 4

1. Thomas Jefferson to John Adams, November 27, 1785, TJP.

2. Lydon, "Fish and Flour," 141, 248; *ASP:CN*, 1:34, 138, 248, 294, 312, 342, 362, 384, 417, 431, 453, 489, 507, 543, 590–91, 671, 696, 721.

3. William Jarvis to James Madison, November 19, 1806, CD, Lisbon, NARA–CP; Irving Brant, "Two Neglected Letters," *William and Mary Quarterly* 3 (October 1946), 569, 587.

4. David Humphreys to George Washington, July 23, 1792, GWP.

5. Martins Ribeiro, "Comércio e diplomacia," 318, n. 95 (quotation), 319–20; Adams to Jefferson, November 5, 1785, TJP; Geoffrey Gilbert, "The Role of Breadstuffs in American Trade, 1770–1790," *Explorations in Economic History* 14 (1977), 379.

6. John Bulkeley & Son. to John Wilcocks, March 22, 1786, "Account of Insurance on the Hull & Apparel of the American ship St Anne, Miscellaneous MS Collection, APS; Lydon, "Fish and Flour," 40–42; Willing, Morris, & Swanwick to Tench Tilghman & Co., November 10, 1784, box 1, folder F4, Willing, Morris, & Swanwick Papers, PSA (quotation).

7. Lydon, "Fish and Flour," 40–41; John Smith & Sons to Daniel Bowden & Son, November 12, 1784, John Smith & Sons Letterbook, vol. 1, MHS.

8. Joseph Wharton to Charles Thomson, October 26, 1784, as an enclosure in Thomson to Jefferson, October 26, 1784, TJP; Lydon, "Fish and Flour," 42.

9. Joseph Wharton to Charles Thomson, October 26, 1784, as an enclosure in Thomson to Jefferson, October 26, 1784, TJP.

10. Gould, *Among the Powers*, 119; Thomson to Jefferson, October 26, 1784, and Adams to Jefferson, November 5, 1785 (quotation), TJP; Martins Ribeiro, "Comércio e diplomacia," 134.

11. Martins Ribeiro, "Comércio e diplomacia," 320, 324; Adams to Jefferson, January 25, 1787, TJP.

12. Lydon, "Fish and Flour," 141, 248; John Smith & Sons to Daniel Bowden & Son, November 12, 1781, John Smith & Sons Letterbook, vol. 1, MHS; Scott, Pringle, & Co. to Willing, Morris, & Swanwick, September 23, 1784, box 1, folder F4, Willing, Morris, & Swanwick Papers, PSA; Gilbert, "Role of Breadstuffs," 379; Hunter, "Wheat, War," 513; Brooke Hunter, "The Prospect of Independent Americans: The Grain Trade and Economic Development during the 1780s," *Explorations in Early American Culture* 5 (2001), 266–67.

13. Robert J. Allison, *The Crescent Obscured: The United States and the Muslim World, 1776–1815* (Chicago: University of Chicago Press, 1995), xv, 7–8.

14. John Smith & Sons to William Rathbone, May 16, 1785 (quotation "jobbing rise"), and to Daniel Bowden & Son, October 27, 1785, December 1, 1785, and December 31, 1785 (quotation "risk of the Algerines"), all in John Smith & Sons Letterbook, vol. 1, MHS; Daniel Bowden & Son to Tench Tilghman & Co., March 11, 1786, box 1, Tench Tilghman Papers, MHS; Allison, *Crescent Obscured*, 13.

15. Hunter, "Prospect of Independent Americans," 269.

16. Doerflinger, *Vigorous Spirit*, 109; Gilbert, "Role of Breadstuffs," 381; John Bulkeley & Son to John Clifford, January 5, 1790, Clifford Correspondence, vol. 9, Pemberton Papers, Clifford Family Papers, HSP; Jean B. Lee, *The Price of Nationhood: The American Revolution in Charles County* (New York: W. W. Norton, 1994), 248; *ASP:CN*, 1:150, 152, 158, 160.

17. Hunter, "Prospect of Independent Americans," 261 (quotation); John Bulkeley & Son to John Clifford, January 5, 1790, Clifford Correspondence, vol. 9, Pemberton Papers, Clifford Family Papers, HSP; *ASP:CN*, 1:122, 30–31.

18. *ASP:CN*, 1:26– 27, 113.

19. *ASP:CN*, 1:26–27, 30–31; U.S. Department of Agriculture, *Agricultural Statistics* (Washington: Government Printing Office, 2005), ix, n25; Peter Tracy Dondlinger, *The Book*

of Wheat: An Economic History and Practical Manual of the Wheat Industry (London: O. Judd, 1908), 277; *Parliamentary Papers, House of Commons and Command*, vol. 49, part 2 (1846), 1059.

20. *ASP:CN*, 1:26–27, 30–31, 114, 122, 226, 235.

21. *ASP:CN*, 1:26–27, 30–31, 114, 122, 226, 235.

22. John Bulkeley & Son to Thomas Clifford, January 26, 1790 (quotation "extravagant pri[c]es"), and Manoel Martins Neiva to John Clifford, April 10, 1790 (quotation "exorbitant prices"), both in Clifford Correspondence, vol. 9, Pemberton Papers, Clifford Family Papers, HSP; Martins Ribeiro, "Comércio e diplomacia," 108.

23. Per capita, Portugal surpassed other European countries in the importation of U.S. breadstuff. In 1790, with an estimated combined population of Great Britain and the British West Indies at 10,268,700, the regions imported an approximate value of $0.23 per capita of grains and flour combined. That same year, with an estimated combined population of 3,342,600, Portugal, Madeira, and the Azores imported a per capita value of $0.33. The approximately 11,027,000 inhabitants of Spain, Florida, and the Spanish West Indies imported far less than either the British or Portuguese Empires, with a per capita value of just $0.14. The figures include only the regions where U.S. merchants could legally trade with those empires. R. D. Lee and R. S. Schofield, "British Population in the Eighteenth Century," in Roderick Floud and Donald McCloskey, eds., *The Economic History of Britain Since 1700*, vol. 1 (New York: Cambridge University Press, 1981), 21–23; McCusker, *Essays*, 206–207; *Annals of the General Assembly of the Church of Scotland* (Edinburgh: John Johnstone, 1840), v; David Allan, *Scotland in the Eighteenth Century: Union and Enlightenment* (New York: Routledge, 2002), 82; Nuno Valério, ed., *Estatísticas históricas portuguesas*, vol. 1 (n.p.: Instituto Nacional de Estatística Portugal, 2001), 33; Hancock, *Oceans of Wine*, 8–9; Duncan, *Atlantic Islands*, 80, 117, 255–56; Conde de Floridablanca, *Censo Español Executado de Órden del Rey Comunicada por el Excelentísimo Señor Conde de Floridablanca* (n.p., n.d.); William R. Lux, "French Colonization in Cuba, 1791–1809," *Americas* 29 (July 1972), 57; Luis A. Figueroa, *Sugar, Slavery, and Freedom in Nineteenth-Century Puerto Rico* (Chapel Hill: University of North Carolina Press, 2005), 26; Jane Landers, *Black Society in Spanish Florida* (Chicago: University of Illinois Press, 1999), 82; Marcus Rainsford, *An Historical Account of the Black Empire of Hayti*, Paul Youngquist and Grégory Pierrot, eds., (Durham, NC: Duke University Press, 2013), 300n136; *ASP:CN*, 1:26–27, 30–31.

24. Gilbert, "Role of Breadstuffs," 384.

25. Fisher, *Portugal Trade*, 42; *ASP:CN*, 1:30, 122, 235; *Report from the Select Committee on the Sale of Corn* (London, 1834), 28.

26. Jefferson to Adams, November 27, 1785, TJP; Martins Ribeiro, "Comércio e diplomacia," 102, 135; Edward Church to Jefferson, October 8, 1793, CD, Lisbon, NARA–CP; John Bulkeley to Thomas Clifford, January 26, 1790, Clifford Correspondence, vol. 9, Pemberton Papers, Clifford Family Papers, HSP (quotation).

27. Hunter, "Wheat, War," 518; *ASP:CN*, 1:34, 138, 248, 294, 312, 342, 362, 384, 417, 431, 453, 489, 507, 543, 590–91, 671, 696, 721.

28. Bouillon & Co. to Dutilh & Wachsmuth, September 7, 1792, box 1, Dutilh & Wachsmuth Papers (accession 1003), HL (quotation); Luke Morris receipt book, April 4, 1791, Morris Family Papers, vol. 6, HSP; Greg H. Williams, *The French Assault on American Shipping, 1793–1813: A History and Comprehensive Record of Merchant Marine Losses* (Jefferson,

NC: McFarland, 2009), 86; Christopher Kingston, "Marine Insurance in Philadelphia During the Quasi-War with France, 1795–1801," *Journal of Economic History* 71 (March 2011), 162; Louise Rau, "Dutilh Papers," *Bulletin of the Business Historical Society* 13 (November 1939), 73; Doerflinger, *Vigorous Spirit*, 244; Willing, Morris, & Swanwick to Tench Tilghman & Co., August 31, 1785, box 1, folder F5, Willing, Morris, & Swanwick Papers, PSA; "Invoice of sundry Merchandises shipped on board the Abigail," July 18, 1793, and Invoice from John Dutilh, August 13, 1795, both in Dutilh & Wachsmuth Papers (accession 1097), HL; Jacques Buillon to E. Dutilh & Co., March 4, 1787, box 1, Dutilh & Wachsmuth Papers (accession 1003), HL; Rufus King to Nicholas Low, February 16, 1794, Nicholas Low Papers, NYHS.

29. Sheryllynne Haggerty, *'Merely for Money'? Business Culture in the British Atlantic, 1750–1815* (Liverpool: Liverpool University Press, 2012), 194; H. McAusland to Andrew Clow & Co., November 9, 1790, Andrew Clow material (accession 1063), HL; "Copy of the entry made at the custom house of the goods by the ship Mercedes," n.d., Andrew Clow material, HL; Douat, Labate, & Planté to Andrew Clow & Co., February 12, 1790, Miscellaneous Philadelphia items, HL; De Arabet, Gautier, Manning, & Co. to Andrew Clow & Co., March 7, 1796, Miscellaneous Philadelphia concerns, HL (quotation); Valentín Riera & Co. to Tench Tilghman & Co., October 19, 1785, box 1, Tench Tilghman Papers, MHS.

30. Jacob and Thomas Walden to Grivignée & Co., July 11, 1805, and to Gould Brothers & Co., July 11, 1805, both in Jacob and Thomas Walden Letterbook, NYHS.

31. John Bulkeley & Son to John Clifford, July 6, 1785, Clifford Correspondence, vol. 7, Pemberton Papers, Clifford Family Papers, HSP; Hancock, *Oceans of Wine*, 7–8; Theodore Richter to John Clifford, January 11, 1790, Clifford Correspondence, vol. 9, Pemberton Papers, Clifford Family Papers, HSP (quotation).

32. Adams to Robert Livingston, August 1, 1783, in Wharton, *Revolutionary Diplomatic Correspondence* 6:628 (quotation); *ASP:CN*, 1:323. For the years 1789–1794, the *ASP* combined importations of Faial and Tenerife wines which belonged to the Portuguese and Spanish Empires respectively. For the purposes of approximating Portuguese Empire imports, I divided the imports from Tenerife and Faial in half. Any difference would produce only a minimal change to the overall percentage.

33. Hancock, *Oceans of Wine*, 117; *ASP:CN*, 1:323.

34. Scott, Pringle, & Co. to Willing, Morris, & Swanwick, September 23, 1784, and Willing, Morris, & Co. to Tench Tilghman & Co., November 16, 22, 1784, both in box 1, folder F4, Willing, Morris, & Swanwick Papers, PSA; Graham & Dent to Tench Tilghman & Co., August 26, 1785, and Tench Tilghman & Co. sale of merchandize, 1786–1791, both in box 2, Tench Tilghman Papers, MHS; John Street to Madison, November 16, 1803, CD, Faial, NARA–CP.

35. Willing, Morris, & Swanwick to Tench Tilghman, August 8, 1785, box 1, folder F5, Willing, Morris, & Swanwick Papers, PSA (quotation "must lie long"); List of entrances and clearances, Lamar, Hill, Bisset, & Co. business papers, 1763–1796, box 2, Edward Wanton Smith Collection, HSP; Manoel Martins Neiva to John Clifford, January 31, 1789 (quotation "immense"), and William Seton & Co. to John Clifford, April 19, 1790, both in Clifford Correspondence, vol. 9, Pemberton Papers, Clifford Family Papers, HSP; Prices current at Philadelphia, December 13, 1794, Jones & Clarke Papers, HSP.

36. Willing, Morris, & Swanwick to Tench Tilghman, August 2, 1785, box 1, folder F5, Willing, Morris, & Swanwick Papers, PSA.

37. Domingos d'Oliveira to John Clifford, October 24, 1785, Clifford Correspondence, vol. 7, Pemberton Papers, Clifford Family Papers, HSP; Domingos d'Oliveira to John Clifford, July 26, 1786, Clifford Correspondence, vol. 8, Pemberton Papers, Clifford Family Papers, HSP.

38. Hancock, *Oceans of Wine*, 152–53; Hill to Mary Lamar, June 5, 1785, box 1, Sarah A. G. Smith Collection, HSP; Charles Wharton to Lamar, Hill, Bisset, & Co., September 17, 1785, Charles Wharton Letterbook, 1779–1785, box 2, Sarah A. G. Smith Collection, HSP.

39. Robert Bisset to Thomas Lamar, January 25, 1789, box 1, Sarah A. G. Smith Collection, HSP; Hancock, *Oceans of Wine*, 152–53.

40. Hancock, *Oceans of Wine*, 123, 152–53.

41. Reed & Forde to Andrew Arnold, August 5, 1797, and to John Inlay, Jr., August 5, 1797, both in Reed & Forde Papers, vol. 4, HSP; *ASP:CN*, 1:34, 138, 248, 294, 312, 342, 362, 384, 417, 431; Tench Coxe, "Notes of the Commercial and Navigating Regulations of the Kingdom of Portugal and Its Dominions," n.d., enclosed in Tench Coxe to Thomas Jefferson, June 30, 1791, Thomas Jefferson Papers, LOC.

42. Hancock, *Oceans of Wine*, 178–79, 479n7; Martins Ribeiro, "Comércio e diplomacia," 354–56; Lewis Pintard to John Marsden Pintard, December 1, 1795, and January 7, January 16, February 1, February 5, April 1 (quotation "where you know"), April 11, April 20, and June 25, 1796, and August 7, November 26, 1797 (quotation "dissolute life"), and January 26, 1799 (quotation "met with misfortunes"), and to Campbell Wilson, May 19, 1796, all in Lewis Pintard Letterbook, November 1795–January 1799, NYHS.

43. Hancock, *Oceans of Wine*, 138, 479n7.

44. Martins Ribeiro, "Comércio e diplomacia," 105, 557.

45. William Ashhurst receipt from Henry Sheaff, April 22, 1806, box 6, Ashhurst Family Papers, HSP; Henry Sheaff to Jefferson, March 18, 1801, http://rotunda.upress.virginia.edu/founders/default.xqy?keys = FOEA-print-04–01–02–0778, (accessed March 9, 2015); Richard Ashhurst receipt from Charles L. Smith, March 3, 1810, box 6, Ashhurst Family Papers, HSP; Entrances, 1784–1785, reel 1, Baltimore Customs Records, MHS; Entrances, 1782–1784, 1786–1788, reel 2, Baltimore customs records, MHS; Port of Philadelphia Captain's Reports, 1797–1802, HSP.

46. T. C. W. Blanning, *The Pursuit of Glory: Europe, 1648–1815* (New York: Viking, 2007), 611–25.

47. Noah Feldman, *The Three Lives of James Madison: Genius, Partisan, President* (New York: Random House, 2017), 372–73.

48. Silvia Marzagalli, "Establishing Transatlantic Trade Networks in Time of War: Bordeaux and the United States, 1793–1815," *Business History Review* 79 (Winter 2005), 811–13; *ASP:CN*, 1:34, 138, 248, 294, 312, 342, 362, 384, 417, 431, 453, 489, 507, 543, 591, 671, 696, 721.

49. Marzagalli, "Establishing Transatlantic Trade Networks," 811–13, 819; Martins Ribeiro, "Comércio e diplomacia," 102, 135; Mark Pringle to Edmund Morris, February 16, 1797, Mark Pringle Letterbook, vol. 1, MHS; *ASP:CN*, 1:34, 138, 248, 294, 312, 342, 362, 384, 417, 431, 453, 489, 507, 543, 591, 671, 696, 721.

50. *ASP:CN*, 1:284, 425, 430; Port of Philadelphia Captain's Reports, 1797–1802, HSP.

51. Francisco Lopez Rodrigues, "Discursos sobre varios artigos interessantes ao Reyno de Portugal e suas colonias," 1798, BNRJ (quotation); Port of Philadelphia Captain's Reports,

1797–1802, HSP; Adrien Balbi, *Essai Statistique sur le Royaume de Portugal et D'Algarve, Comparé aux autres États de L'Europe* (Paris: Rey et Gravier, 1822), 1:439–40; Lydon, "Fish and Flour," 33, 127, 172.

52. Church to Jefferson, July 31, 1793, CD, Lisbon, NARA–CP (quotation "immensely rich"); Lydon, "Fish and Flour," 152, 154; John Bulkeley & Son to John Clifford, January 5, 1790, Clifford correspondence, vol. 9, Pemberton Papers, Clifford Family Papers, HSP (quotation "we are old friends").

53. Lydon, "Fish and Flour," 137–47; John W. Jordon, ed., *Colonial and Revolutionary Families of Pennsylvania: Genealogical and Personal Memoirs* (Baltimore: Clearfield, 1978), 1:219–20; Waln correspondence, 1799–1819, box 1, folder 4, Robert Waln Papers, HSP; Port of Philadelphia Captain's Reports, 1797–1802, HSP.

54. The average number of vessels entering Philadelphia is based on Lydon's tonnage figures divided by the average tonnage of vessels trading between Philadelphia and Lisbon during that period. Port of Philadelphia Captain's Reports, 1797–1802, HSP; Lydon, "Fish and Flour," 145–47; Thomas Sergeant and William Rawle, Jr., *Reports of Cases Adjudged in the Supreme Court of Pennsylvania*, 3rd ed., vol. 1 (Philadelphia: Kay & Brother, 1872), 242.

55. William Jarvis to James Madison, May 3, 1806, CD, Lisbon, NARA–CP.

Part III

1. M. N. S. Sellers, *American Republicanism: Roman Ideology in the United States Constitution* (New York: New York University Press, 1994), 86, 123, 208; Tyler, *Smugglers and Patriots*, 17; John T. Agresto, "Liberty, Virtue, and Republicanism," *Review of Politics* 39 (1977), 473–504; J. G. A. Pocock, *The Machiavellian Moment: Florentine Political Thought and the Atlantic Republican Tradition* (Princeton, NJ: Princeton University Press, 1975), 506–52; Appleby, *Capitalism*, 97; Raúl Coronado, *A World Not to Come: A History of Latino Writing and Print Culture* (Cambridge, MA: Harvard University Press, 2013), 114.

2. Adelman, *Sovereignty and Revolution*, 13–55; Schultz, *Tropical Versailles*; José Jobson de Andrade Arruda, *Uma colônia entre dois impérios: A abertura dos portos brasileiros, 1800–1808* (Bauru: EDUSC, 2008); Jurandir Malberba, *A Corte no Exílio: Civilização e poder no Brasil às vésperas da Independência (1808 a 1821)* (São Paulo: Companhia das Letras, 2000); Patrick Wilcken, *Empire Adrift: The Portuguese Court in Rio de Janeiro, 1808–1821* (New York: Bloomsbury, 2005).

Chapter 5

1. Sellers, *American Republicanism*, 86, 123, 208; James L. Huston, "Virtue Besieged: Virtue, Equality, and the General Welfare in the Tariff Debates of the 1820s," *Journal of the Early Republic* 14 (Winter 1994), 527; Agresto, "Liberty, Virtue, and Republicanism," 489–92, 495–96, 503–4; Appleby, *Capitalism*, 97–100.

2. Appleby, *Capitalism*, 103; Coronado, *World Not to Come*, 116; Gilje, *Free Trade*, 11; Donald Campbell to Meneses e Souto Maior, April 1, 1801, box 191, document 13757, and Donald Campbell to Rodrigo de Souza Coutinho, September 8, 1801, box 194, document 13889, both in CU.

3. Brian Loveman, *No Higher Law: American Foreign Policy and the Western Hemisphere Since 1776* (Chapel Hill: University of North Carolina Press, 2010), 21–22; Rufus King to Robert R. Livingston, July 12, 1802, Robert R. Livingston Papers, LOC (quotation).

4. Alexandre, *Sentidos do império*, 78–80.

5. Fragoso and Florentino, *Arcaísmo como projeto*, 97–103; Fragoso, *Homens de grossa aventura*, 19–27, 83–93; Florentino, *Em Costas Negras*, 23, 121; *National Intelligencer and Washington Advertiser*, February 6, 1805 (quotation "may be considered"); Maxwell, *Conflicts and Conspiracies*, 78 (quotation "Portugal without Brazil").

6. Maxwell, *Conflicts and Conspiracies*, 181–83; Sven Beckert, *Empire of Cotton: A Global History* (New York: Alfred A. Knopf, 2015), 93–94; Adelman, *Sovereignty and Revolution*, 115–20; Alexandre, *Sentidos do império*, 37–44; 62–69; Joze da Gama Lobo Coelho, Alyxo Maria Caetano, and Joze Pereira da Cunha to Rodrigo de Souza Coutinho, February 3, 1800, códice 107, vol. 1, ANRJ; Pijning, "Controlling Contraband," 85; William Jarvis to James Madison, September 27, 1806, CD, Lisbon, NARA–CP.

7. John Adams to Robert R. Livingston, July 12, 1783, AP; Martins Ribeiro, "Comércio e diplomacia," 317–19.

8. Maxwell, *Conflicts and Conspiracies*, 63, 67, 78, 79, 84–114, 126, esp. 79 (quotation); Martinho de Melo e Castro to Luís de Vasconcelos e Sousa, January 5, 1785, box 125, document 10009, CU.

9. "Auto de Perguntas feitas ao Alferes Joaquim José de Silva Xavier," May 22, 1789, códice 5, vol. 5, p. 4, ANRJ (quotation "the English Americans"); José Joaquim Maia e Barbalho to Thomas Jefferson, October 2, November 21, 1786, TJP (quotation "resolved to follow").

10. Francis D. Cogliano, *Emperor of Liberty: Thomas Jefferson's Foreign Policy* (New Haven, CT: Yale University Press, 2014), 5, 175, esp. 5 (quotation "empire of liberty"); Jefferson to James Monroe, August 28, 1785, TJP (quotation "our commerce").

11. Eacott, *Selling Empire*, 3–4. For limited Spanish and French West Indies trade, see Jefferson to Monroe, June 17, 1785, in Brett F. Woods, ed., *Thomas Jefferson: Diplomatic Correspondence* (New York: Algora Publishing, 2016), 40n1; Doron S. Ben-Atar, *The Origins of Jeffersonian Commercial Policy and Diplomacy* (New York: Palgrave-MacMillan, 1993), 77–78; Linda K. Salvucci, "Atlantic Intersections: Early American Commerce and the Rise of the Spanish West Indies (Cuba)," *Business History Review* 79 (2005), 795; Jefferson to Adams, November 27, 1785, TJP (quotation).

12. Jefferson to Adams, November 27, 1785, and to John Jay, May 4, 1787 (quotation), and Maia e Barbalho to Jefferson, January 5, 1787, all in TJP; Maxwell, *Conflicts and Conspiracies*, 67, 79, 81, 84–114; Doria, *1789*, 41, 128, 146–50; Júnia Ferreira Furtado, "José Joaquim da Rocha and the Proto-Independence Movement in Colonial Brazil," in Martin Brückner, ed., *Early American Cartographies* (Chapel Hill: University of North Carolina Press, 2001), 129–32.

13. Jefferson to Jay, May 4, 1787, TJP.

14. Jefferson to Jay, May 4, 1787, TJP.

15. Jefferson to Jay, May 4, 1787, TJP; Maxwell, *Conflicts and Conspiracies*, 81–82.

16. George Washington to the United States Senate, February 18, 1791, n. 3, GWP; Jefferson to David Humphreys, April 11, 1791, TJP.

17. Tench Coxe, "Notes of the commercial and navigating regulations of the Kingdom of Portugal and its dominions, which affect the exports, imports, and vessels of the United States," enclosed in Coxe to Jefferson, June 30, 1791, Thomas Jefferson Papers, LOC; Huston, "Virtue Besieged," 527.

18. "Memorandum on Meeting with Senate Committee," January 4, 1792, and Humphreys to Jefferson, December 23, 1791, both in TJP.

19. Thomas Mann Randolph to Jefferson, May 23, 1801, TJP.

20. Humphreys to Jefferson, December 23, 1791, TJP.

21. Maxwell, *Conflicts and Conspiracies*, 13, 65, 84–114.

22. Maxwell, *Conflicts and Conspiracies*, 67, 79; "Auto de Perguntas feitas ao Alferes Joaquim José de Silva Xavier," May 22, 1789, códice 5, vol. 5, p. 4, ANRJ (quotations); Doria, *1789*, 77–78; Alden, *Royal Government*, 303–4.

23. Maxwell, *Conflicts and Conspiracies*, 44, 101, 119–20; "Auto de Perguntas feitas ao Alferes Joaquim José de Silva Xavier," May 22, 1789, códice 5, vol. 5, p. 2, ANRJ.

24. Doria, *1789*, 120–26; Alexandre, *Sentidos do império*, 78–80.

25. Maxwell, *Conflicts and Conspiracies*, 115–17, 126, 135–37.

26. Maxwell, *Conflicts and Conspiracies*, 127–28, 135–37, 141–44, 171, 198–99; "Auto de Continuação de Perguntas feitas ao Alferes Joaquim José de Silva Xavier," May 27, 1789, códice 5, vol. 5, p. 6, ANRJ; Luís de Vasconcelos e Sousa to Martinho de Melo e Castro, June 16, 1789, box 134, document 10640, CU; Inconfidência Mineira collection, boxes 1004 and 1004A, ANRJ.

27. "Auto de continuação de perguntas feitas ao Conego Luís Vieira da Silva," July 21, 1790, códice 5, vol. 5, p. 132, ANRJ (quotation "spoke with much pleasure"); Gerald Horne, *The Deepest South: The United States, Brazil, and the African Slave Trade* (New York: New York University Press, 2007), 18; Doria, *1789*, 18; Maxwell, *Conflicts and Conspiracies*, 117, 135–39, 182, esp. 136 (quotations "freedom of commerce" and "an English America"); "Auto de Cotinuação de Perguntas feitas ao Alferes Joaquim José de Silva Xavier," May 27, 1789, códice 5, vol. 5, p. 6, ANRJ.

28. "Auto de continuação de perguntas feitas ao Coronel Ignácio José de Alvarenga," January 14, 1790, códice 5, vol. 5, p. 57, ANRJ (quotations "english Americas," "dominant passion," and "richness and happiness"); Sebastião Xavier de Vasconcelos Coutinho to Martinho de Melo e Castro, Frebruary 20, 1791, box 140, document 10988, CU (quotation "cause of the uprising"); Maxwell, *Conflicts and Conspiracies*, 117, 135–39, 182; "Auto de continuação de perguntas feitas ao Conego Luís Vieira da Silva," July 21, 1790, códice 5, vol. 5, p. 132, ANRJ.

29. Jorge de Abreu Castelo Branco to Martinho de Melo e Castro, January 8, 1791, box 139, document 10950, CU; Adelman, *Sovereignty and Revolution*, 119–20.

30. Adelman, *Sovereignty and Revolution*, 119–20.

31. Cardoso, "Nas malhas do império," 79, 92–93.

32. Paquette, *Imperial Portugal*, 17–83; Cardoso, "Nas Malhas do Império," 92–93; António Manuel Hespanha, "A constituição do Império português: Revisão de alguns enviesamentos correntes," in João Fragoso, Maria Fernanda Bicalho, and Maria de Fátima Gouvêa, eds., *Antigo regime nos trópicos: A dinâmica imperial portuguesa (séculos XVI–XVIII)* (Rio de Janeiro: Civilização Brasileira, 2001), 163–88; Maria Fernanda Bicalho, "As câmaras ultramarinas e o governo do Império," in Fragoso, Bicalho, and Gouvêa, *Antigo regime*, 189–222; Maria de Fátima Gouvêa, "Poder politico e administração na formação do complexo atlântico português (1645–1808)," in Fragoso, Bicalho, and Gouvêa, *Antigo regime*, 285–316; Adelman, *Sovereignty and Revolution*, 14–15, 127; António Penalves Rocha, "A economia política na desagregação do império português," in Cardoso, *A economia política*, 154.

33. Guilherme Pereira das Neves, "Guardar mais silêncio do que falar: Azeredo Coutinho, Ribeiro dos Santos e a escravidão," in Cardoso, *A economia política*, 18–19; Cardoso, "Nas malhas do império," 69–72; Adelman, *Sovereignty and Revolution*, 71, 125–26, 150–51.

34. Schultz, *Tropical Versailles*, 27 (quotation); Bruno Aidar, "Uma substituição luminosa: Tributação e reforma do Antigo Regime português em D. Rodrigo de Souza Coutinho ao final do século XVIII," *Nova Economia* 21 (January–April 2011), 138–54; Cardoso, "Nas malhas do império," 65–66, 72–79, 83–85; Adelman, *Sovereignty and Revolution*, 127–31.

35. Adelman, *Sovereignty and Revolution*, 121–22, 131; Miller, *Way of Death*, 531.

36. Moutoukias, *Contrabando y control*, 92, 94, 100, 117, 133; Prado, *Edge of Empire*, 67–69, 131–152; Adelman, *Sovereignty and Revolution*, 121–22, 131.

37. Miller, *Way of Death*, 531; Alex Borucki, *From Shipmates to Soldiers: Emerging Black Identities in the Río de la Plata* (Albuquerque: University of New Mexico Press, 2015), 5, 29.

38. Cardoso, "Nas malhas do império," 84–85.

39. Adelman, *Sovereignty and Revolution*, 125–31, 142–46, 150–52.

40. Adelman, *Sovereignty and Revolution*, 125.

41. Fragoso, *Homens de grossa aventura*, 179–81; Lahmeyer Lobo, "Comércio atlântico," 72–75, 84–85; Miller, *Way of Death*, 364–65, 456–57, 463; Domingues da Silva, *Atlantic Slave Trade*, 46–48.

42. Scholars have generally connected North American contraband and ideology by focusing on colonial smugglers who imported illegal goods to protest British mercantilism. But North Americans extended ideological justifications of smuggling chronologically into the early republic and geographically beyond the British Atlantic. Tyler, *Smugglers and Patriots*; Carp, *Defiance of the Patriots*; Smith, *Borderland Smuggling*; Enthoven, "That Abominable Nest"; Klooster, "Inter-imperial Smuggling," 141.

43. Gilje, *Free Trade*, 19–28, 32–68; Tyler, *Smugglers and Patriots*, 238, 250; Carp, *Defiance of the Patriots*, 76; Enthoven, "That Abominable Nest," 239–41.

44. C. R. Ritcheson, "The Earl of Shelburne and Peace with America, 1782–1783: Vision and Reality," *International History Review* 5 (August 1983), 322–45; Hunter, "Prospect of Independent Americans," 268–69; Ernesto Bassi, *An Aqueous Territory: Sailor Geographies and New Granada's Transimperial Greater Caribbean World* (Durham, NC: Duke University Press, 2016), 121–27; *American Recorder* (Boston, MA), April 11, 1786 (quotation).

45. "State of Connecticut in Convention," *Pennsylvania Gazette*, January 30, 1788 (quotation "too favourable"); *Annals of Congress*, 1 Cong., 1 Sess., May 9, 1789, p. 311 (quotation "unjust or unpopular"); Samuel Allardice, Alexander Lawson, and John James Barralet, *The History of the British Empire, from the year 1765, to the end of 1783*, 2 vols. (Boston, 1798), 1:99. For histories of merchants agreeing to import only smuggled tea, see William Gordon, *The History of the Rise, Progress, and Establishment, of the Independence of the United States of America*, 3 vols. (New York, 1789), 1:199.

46. Gilje, *Free Trade*, 11; Thomas Jefferson, "First Inaugural Address," March 4, 1801, The Avalon Project: Documents in Law, History, and Diplomacy (Yale Law School), avalon.law.yale.edu/19th_century/jefinau1.asp (accessed August 23, 2016); Appleby, *Capitalism*; Çelikkol, *Romances of Free Trade*, 22.

47. *Annals of Congress*, 1 Cong., 1 Sess., May 9, 1789, p. 311; Gilje, *Free Trade*, 20.

48. Baltazar da Silva Lisboa to Martinho de Melo e Castro, July 2, 1792, box 145, document 11257, CU; José Luís de Castro to Martinho de Melo e Castro, November 21, 1793, box 149, document 11470, CU; Martinho de Melo e Castro to José Luís de Castro, March 6, 1790, box 136, document 10760, CU.

49. José Luís de Castro to Luís Pinto de Sousa Coutinho, July 17, 1795, box 155, document 11714, CU; José Luís de Castro to Rodrigo de Souza Coutinho, November 7, 1798, box

167, document 12445, CU; José Antônio Ribeiro Freire to João Rodrigues de Sá e Melo Meneses e Souto Maior, June 20, 1803, box 211, document 14697, CU. For procedures of treating foreign vessels, see Alden, *Royal Government*, 403–8.

50. Bassi, *Aqueous Territory*, 5; Jorge de Abreu Castelo Branco to Martinho de Melo e Castro, January 8, 1791, box 139, document 10950, CU; Adelman, *Sovereignty and Revolution*, 119–20.

51. David Humphreys to Thomas Jefferson, August 22, 1791, TJP (quotation "too freely"); *Pennsylvania Gazette*, October 31, 1792 (quotation "very frequent"); *Diary or Wood-fall's Register* (London, England), July 1, 1793 (quotation "where they intended"). The newspaper reproduced a report from May that stated the arrests had occurred several months earlier; Schultz, *Tropical Versailles*, 50–57.

52. Maxwell, *Naked Tropics*, 122; Schultz, *Tropical Versailles*, 57; Evaldo Cabral de Mello, *A outra independência: O federalismo pernambucano de 1817 a 1824* (São Paulo: Editora 34, 2004), 25–26; Fabiana Schondorfer Braz and Paulo Fillipy de Souza Conti, "D. José da Cunha de Azeredo Coutinho: Um bispo ilustrado em Pernambuco," *Revista Tempo Histórico* 5 (2013), 9; Manuel Correia de Andrade, *A Guerra dos Cabanos*. 2nd ed. (Recife: Editora Universitaria, 2005), 27–28; Manuel Correia de Andrade, *As raízes do separatismo no Brasil* (São Paulo: Editora UNESP Fundação, 1998), 61–62.

53. Schondorfer Braz and Souza Conti, "D. José da Cunha de Azeredo Coutinho," 5–6, 9; Pereira das Neves, "Guardar mais silêncio," 18–19; E. Bradford Burns, "The Role of Azeredo Coutinho in the Enlightenment of Brazil," *Hispanic American Historical Review* 44 (May 1964), 145–56, 158; Antonio Jorge Siqueira, "Bispo Coutinho e o clero ilustrado de Pernambuco na Revolução de 1817," *Revista Brasileira de História das Religiões* 14 (September 2012), 159–64; James E. Wadsworth, *In Defence of the Faith: Joaquim Marquês de Araújo, A Comissário in the Age of Inquisitional Decline* (Montreal: McGill-Queen's University Press, 2013), 78–80, 84, 126, 135–37; Cabral de Mello, *A outra independência*, 25–26. Historians have varied in their interpretations of Azeredo Coutinho's recall. While some have viewed it as a pretext for removing his liberal ideologies from Pernambuco, others have assumed that the court wanted to employ his abilities in Portugal. Regardless, he undoubtedly drew the ire of more conservative clerics during his time in Pernambuco, and those clashes contributed to his recall.

54. Adelman, *Sovereignty and Revolution*, 115–23; Klooster, "Inter-imperial Smuggling," 148; Martinho de Melo e Castro to Luís de Vasconcelos e Sousa, January 5, 1785, box 125, document 10009, CU.

55. Martins Ribeiro, "Comércio e diplomacia," 89, 358, 385.

56. *Reports of cases argued and determined in the Supreme Judicial Court of the commonwealth of Massachusetts*, vol. 6 (Newburyport, 1811), 234; *Gazette of the United States*, August 10, 1802.

57. Boxer, "Brazilian Gold," 461, 464; Alexandre, *Sentidos do império*, 85; Joze da Gama Lobo Coelho, Alyxo Maria Caetano, and Joze Pereira da Cunha to Rodrigo de Souza Coutinho, February 3, 1800, códice 107, vol. 1, ANRJ; Charles Lyon Chandler, "List of United States Vessels in Brazil, 1792–1805, Inclusive," *Hispanic American Historical Review* 4 (November 1946), 611. The number of U.S. ships that entered Brazilian ports may have been higher for both periods, but clerics and scribes in Brazil frequently referred to North American vessels as "English" without using the distinguishing description of "English American."

58. Donald Campbell to João Rodrigues de Sá e Melo Meneses e Souto Maior, March 9, 1802, box 199, document 14086, CU; D. Fernando José de Portugal e Castro to João Rodrigues de Sá e Melo Meneses e Souto Maior, February 21, 1804, box 216, document 14921, CU; "Auto de exame realizado no Rio de Janeiro ao navio americano, Elizabeth, por ordem do vice-rei do Estado do Brasil," November 12, 1806, box 241, document 16443, CU; Donald Campbell to Rodrigo de Souza Coutinho, February 10, 1801, box 189, document 13660, CU (quotations "innumerable vessels" and "difficulty of discovering"); Thomas Lindley, *Authentic Narrative of a Voyage from the Cape of Good Hope to Brasil* (London, 1808), 81; Luís Beltrão de Gouveia de Almeida to Rodrigo de Souza Coutinho, May 1, 1801, box 192, document 13793, CU (quotation "greatest excess").

59. Donald Campbell to João Rodrigues de Sá e Melo Meneses e Souto Maior, April 1, 1801, box 191, document 13757, CU; Donald Campbell to Rodrigo de Souza Coutinho, September 8, 1801, box 194, document 13889, CU.

60. José Pires de Carvalho e Albuquerque to the customs house provider, "Registro de Portarias do provedor da Alfândega da Bahia," April 24, 1806, p. 47–48, Códice 212—Alfândega da Bahia, ANRJ; Royal Provision, February 27, 1807, assorted documents of Bahia, BNRJ (quotation).

61. Schultz, *Tropical Versailles*, 3–8.

Chapter 6

1. Madison made the argument in favor of a provision in the 1795 naturalization law that would require applicants for citizenship to renounce former titles of nobility. He assumed that republicanism might become so widespread that old elites would "be thrown out of that part of the world." If they came to the United States, they would have to lose their titles in conformity with the Constitution. Madison was cited in the *Philadelphia Gazette*, January 2, 1795; Pierre Samuel du Pont de Nemours to James Madison, July 25, 1815, James Madison Papers, LOC.

2. Schultz, *Tropical Versailles*, 3–5.

3. *ASP:CN*, 1:869.

4. Rufus King to Nicholas Low, August 16, 1796, Nicholas Low Papers, NYHS (quotations "much concern" and "feeble resistance"); Schultz, *Tropical Versailles*, 15 (quotations "no longer the best" and "its Sovereign").

5. Schultz, *Tropical Versailles*, 2–3, 15, 7–8, 77, esp. 15.

6. Katherine B. Aaslestad and Johan Joor, eds., *Revisiting Napoleon's Continental System: Local, Regional and European Experiences* (New York: Palgrave, 2014), 2; Wilcken, *Empire Adrift*, 12–13.

7. Robson, *Britain, Portugal*, xiv; Wilcken, *Empire Adrift*, 12.

8. Adelman, *Sovereignty and Revolution*, 224–25, 227, 232; Laurentino Gomes, *1808: Como uma rainha louca, um príncipe medroso e uma corte corrupta enganaram Napoleão e mudaram a História de Portugal e do Brazil* (São Paulo: Planeta, 2007), 67–68; Wilcken, *Empire Adrift*, 21–29; Schultz, *Tropical Versailles*, 29.

9. Wilcken, *Empire Adrift*, 74–79, esp. 78; Cardoso, "Nas malhas do império," 94–95.

10. Caetano Pinto de Miranda Montenegro to João Rodrigues de Sá e Melo, January 4, 1808, Junta do Comércio, Mesas de Inspeção de Pernambuco, ANRJ.

11. Adelman, *Sovereignty and Revolution*, 228.

12. "Nota de alguns artigos duvidozos," January 4, 1808, Junta do Comércio, Mesas de Inspeção de Pernambuco, ANRJ.

13. "Carta Régia de D. João, Principe Regente, declarando abertos os portos do Brasil ao comércio com as nações amigas," January 28, 1808, BNRJ.

14. Rodrigo Ricupero, "O Estabelecimento do Exclusivo Comercial Metropolitano e a Conformação do Antigo Sistema Colonial no Brasil," *História* 35 (December 19, 2016), 2–3, https://dx.doi.org/10.1590/1980–436920160000000100 (accessed August 10, 2018), esp. 2; Adelman, *Sovereignty and Revolution*, 235–36; Schultz, *Tropical Versailles*, 189–90, 202–5.

15. "Rellação das Embarcações que tem chegado a este Porto vindas do Estrangeiros com negócio, e arribadas na forma declarada, desde 26 de Março athé hoje 17 de Junho 1808," Junta do Comércio, Mesas de Inspeção de Pernambuco, ANRJ.

16. Genealogical notes, box 1, folder 3, Henry Hill Papers, TJDC; Henry Hill to James Madison, February 17, 1808, CD, St. Salvador, NARA–CP (quotations).

17. Hill to Madison, February 17, 1808, CD, St. Salvador, NARA–CP.

18. Hill to Madison, February 17, 1808, CD, St. Salvador, NARA–CP.

19. Hill to Madison, February 17, 1808, CD, St. Salvador, NARA–CP.

20. Hill to Madison, February 17, 1808, CD, St. Salvador, NARA–CP.

21. Hill to Madison, February 17, 1808, CD, St. Salvador, NARA–CP.

22. "Mapa das fazendas e generos importados na Alfandega da Cidade do Rio de Janeiro em anno de 1803," and "Mapa das fazendas e generos importados na Alfandega da Cidade do Rio de Janeiro em Anno de 1804," both in BNRJ; Gregory G. Brown, "The Impact of American Flour Imports on Brazilian Wheat Production: 1808–1822," *Americas*, 47 (January 1991), 319–21; Hill, "A View of the Commerce of Brazil," November 17, 1808, CD, St. Salvador, NARA–CP.

23. John M. Owen, *Liberal Peace, Liberal War: American Politics and International Security* (Ithaca, NY: Cornell University Press, 1997), 76; Mlada Bukovansky, "American Identity and Neutral Rights from Independence to the War of 1812," *International Organization* 51 (Spring 1997), 227–28; Peter Andreas, *Smuggler Nation: How Illicit Trade Made America* (New York: Oxford University Press, 2013), 67–68.

24. Andreas, *Smuggler Nation*, 67–71; James Monroe and William Pinckney to James Madison, January 3, 1807, U.S. House of Representatives Records, roll 1, NARA–CP.

25. Andreas, *Smuggler Nation*, 74–80.

26. Andreas, *Smuggler Nation*, 74–78, esp. 74 (quotation "greater public object"); Jefferson to Albert Gallatin, August 11, 1808, Papers of Albert Gallatin, NYHS (quotation "growth of fraud"); Smith, *Borderland Smuggling*, 51; "An Act laying an Embargo on all ships and vessels in the ports and harbors of the United States," 1 Stat. 451–53, esp. 453 (1807); Rao, *National Duties*, 141, 143, 154; Jeffrey A. Frankel, "The 1807–1809 Embargo Against Great Britain," *Journal of Economic History* 42 (June 1982), 294; James W. Stevens to Madison, March 2, 1809, JMP (quotation "the facility").

27. *Gazette of the United States*, August 10, 1802.

28. To collect duties on U.S. imports, the British government had an incentive to record accurately U.S. imports whether smuggled or not, making British records a fairly reliable indicator of the effectiveness of the embargo. Frankel, "1807–1809 Embargo," 295, 297.

29. Gautham Rao points out that courts frequently acquitted embargo violators, but the seizures and court cases impeded the violators from smuggling in the meantime. Rao,

National Duties, 141–42, 144–45; Andreas, *Smuggler Nation*, 78–79; George C. Herring, *From Colony to Superpower: U.S. Foreign Relations Since 1776* (New York: Oxford University Press, 2008), 120–21; Lewis, *American Union*, 42–48.

30. Hill to Madison, November 10, 1808 (quotation "wished for a monopoly"), and Hill, "A View of the Commerce of Brazil," November 17, 1808, both in CD, St. Salvador, NARA–CP; "Mappa dos Navios que Entrarão e sahirão do Porto da Capitania da Bahia em 1808," and "Mapas de importação e exportação—nordeste," box 448, pacote 1, ANRJ; Schultz, *Tropical Versailles*, 190, 210, esp. 190 (quotation "an emporium"); "Rellação das Embarcações que tem chegado a este Porto vindas do Estrangeiros com negócio, e arribadas na forma declarada, desde 26 de Março athé hoje 17 de Junho 1808," Junta do Comércio, Mesas de Inspeção de Pernambuco, ANRJ. Crews that entered immediately after the opening of the ports may likely have been surprised to learn that they could legally trade in Brazil.

31. Livermore's speech reprinted in the *National Intelligencer and Washington Advertiser* (Washington, DC), March 25, 1808; *Pittsburgh Gazette* (Pittsburgh, PA), April 5, 1808 (quotation "an equal footing"); "Mr. Lloyd's speeches in the Senate of the United States, on Mr. Hillhouse's resolution to repeal the embargo laws" (n.p., 1808), 12–13; "Mr. White's speech in the Senate of the United States on Mr. Hillhouse's resolution to repeal the Embargo laws" (n.p. 1808), 8.

32. "Mr. Livermore's speech in the House of Representatives" (n.p. [Washington?], n.d. [1809]), 22–23; *National Intelligencer and Washington Advertiser*, January 25 (quotation "Brazils will assist") and April 7, 1809; *Supporter* (Chillicothe, OH), January 19, 1809 (quotation "make the Americans").

33. *Evening Post*, January 10, 1809.

34. Hill to Madison, November 17, 1808 and April 10, 1809, CD, St. Salvador, NARA–CP.

35. James Madison to Henry Hill, May 8, 1808, Consular Instructions of the Department of State, RG 59, NARA–CP; "Copy of a memorandum delivered to His Excellency D. Rodrigo de Souza Coutinho," September 24, 1808, and Henry Hill to Rodrigo de Souza Coutinho, September 2, 1808, CD, St. Salvador, NARA–CP.

36. Andreas, *Smuggler Nation*, 80; Gilje, *Free Trade*, 195.

37. "Speech of Mr. Newton delivered in the House of Representatives of the United States," (n.p. [Washington?], 1810), 7.

38. Hill to Lucy Hill, April 29, 1809, Henry Hill Papers, box 1, folder 18, TJDC; *ASP:CN*, 1:815, 869.

39. Robson, *Britain, Portugal*, 220–25; Alexandre, *Sentidos do império*, 184–85; Collective letter from Pernambuco ministers to Dom João, August 27, 1808, Junta do Comércio, Mesas de Inspecção de Pernambuco, ANRJ; Henry Didier to John D'Arcy, June 4, 1809, and to Ronanez, June 5, 1809, Henry Didier letterbook, Charles Didier Collection, MHS; H. B. Stewart to William Waln, February 13, February 18, 1810, H. B. Stewart Letterbook, HSP.

40. Fat. O'Connor to Robert Waln, August 22, 1808, box 1, folder 4, Robert Waln Papers, HSP; Levi Hollingsworth to Daniel Smith, August 30, 1809, outgoing correspondence, vol. 5, Hollingsworth Family Papers, HSP (quotation); Baring Brothers & Co. to Robert Oliver, April 4, 1809, box 1, incoming correspondence, Robert Oliver Papers, MHS; Robert Oliver to Baring Brothers & Co., October 25, 1809, to John A. Morton, March 9, 1810, and to George and Robert Blackburn, June 30, 1810, all in letterbook 20, Robert Oliver Papers, MHS; H. B. Stewart to William Waln, December 15, December 25, 1809, H. B. Stewart Letterbook, HSP.

41. W. Freeman Galpin, "The American Grain Trade to the Spanish Peninsula, 1810–1814," *American Historical Review* 28 (October 1922), 25–26, 28–29; Robert and John Oliver to Baring Brothers & Co., April 11, 1811, and to George and Robert Blackburn & Co., April 11, 1811, both in letterbook 20, Robert Oliver Papers, MHS.

42. John Bulkeley & Son to Robert Waln, May 30 and November 24, 1810, box 1, folder 4, Robert Waln Papers, HSP.

43. Martins Ribeiro, "Comércio e diplomacia," 473; William Jarvis to Madison, January 17, 1806, January 22, 1807, CD, Lisbon, NARA–CP.

44. Robert and John Oliver to George and Robert Blackburn, & Co., October 24, 1810, letterbook 20, Robert Oliver Papers, MHS; Holford, Gonne, & Lucas to John Johnston and John McKean, March 20, 1811, box 454, folder 17, Chew Family Papers, HSP; Mark Pringle to James Ullman, May 2, 1811, and to Joseph de Cruz da Acenção, June 20, 1811, both in Mark Pringle Letterbooks, vol. 2, MHS.

45. Mark Pringle to Paca Smith, January 15 and February 4, 1812, to G. Galway, April 15, 1812, and to Lyttleton Gale, April 19, 1811, all in Mark Pringle Letterbooks, vol. 2, MHS; John Bulkeley & Son to Robert Waln, C. Ross, and John Smith, October 22, 1812, box 1, folder 4, Robert Waln Papers, HSP.

46. Alfred Thayer Mahan, *Sea Power in Its Relations to the War of 1812* (Boston, 1905), 1:410; *ASP:CN*, 1:696, 815; Remarks on July 22 and September 16, 17, 1812, *Comet* log book, John L. Thomas Ship Logs and Papers, MHS; Galpin, "American Grain Trade," 28–29.

47. Desmond Gregory, *The Beneficent Usurpers: A History of the British in Madeira* (Cranbury, NJ: Associated University Presses, 1988), 57–64; Oliver to John A. Morton, March 9, 1810, and to George and Robert Blackburn, June 30, 1810, both in letterbook 20, Robert Oliver Papers, MHS; Port of Philadelphia Captain's Reports, 1797–1802, HSP; Outward Foreign Manifests for the Port of Philadelphia, RG 36, NARA–MA.

48. Port of Philadelphia Captain's Reports, 1797–1802, HSP; Outward Foreign Manifests, RG 36, NARA–MA.

49. Victor S. Clark, *History of Manufactures in the United States, 1607–1860* (Washington, DC: Carnegie Institution of Washington, 1916), 321–22; John Bach McMaster, *A History of the People of the United States* (1883; repr., New York: Cosimo, 2006), 3:502–4; Mary Pepperell Sparhawk Jarvis Cutts, *The Life and Times of Hon. William Jarvis* (New York: Hurd and Houghton, 1869), 274–75.

50. Jarvis Cutts, *Life and Times*, 276–77, 282; Livros de receitas de lãs merinas, 1809–1812, Alfândegas de Lisboa, ANTT; *National Intelligencer* (Washington, DC), April 2, 1811 (quotation); Mark Pringle to Joseph de Cruz da Acenção, June 20, 1811, Mark Pringle Letterbooks, vol. 2, MHS; Receipt from Gillman to Daniel Rea, April 10, 1811, Daniel Rea Papers, ISM; *Daily National Intelligencer* (Washington, DC), April 21, 1815.

51. *Liverpool Mercury*, reprinted in *National Intelligencer*, December 7, 1811; *National Intelligencer*, March 23, 1809 (quotation). Madison's patriotic apparel was also reported by the *Enquirer* (Richmond, VA), March 10, 1809, the *New York Commercial Advertiser* (New York, NY), March 13, 1809, and the *New-Jersey Telescope* (Newark), March 13, 1809.

52. Holford, Gonne, and Lucas to John Johnston and John McKean, March 8, 1811 and George and Robert Blackburn to John Johnston and John McKean, August 16, 1811, both in box 454, folder 17, Chew Family Papers, HSP; John Bulkeley & Son to Robert Waln, C. Ross, and John C. Smith, October 22, 1812, box 1, folder 4, Robert Waln Papers, HSP; Baring

Brothers & Co. to Robert and John Oliver, November 3, 1808, box 1, Robert Oliver Papers, MHS; Robert and John Oliver to Baring Brothers & Co., February 11 and April 11, 1811, and to Henry F. Sampayo, April 10, 1811, all in letterbook 20, Robert Oliver Papers, MHS.

53. Petition of merchants of Philadelphia, December 24, 1810, *ASP:CN*, 1:822; David O. Stewart, *Madison's Gift: Five Partnerships that Built America* (New York: Simon & Schuster, 2015), 235.

54. *Niles' Weekly Register*, vol. 2 (Baltimore, MD), 119; Mahan, *Sea Power*, 381. In May 1810, the Macon Bill no. 2 had restored trade with Britain and France so long as they respected U.S. neutrality. In November, Madison had declared a renewal of nonintercourse with Britain unless they repealed orders in council blockading U.S. ships from Europe.

55. John Bulkeley & Son to Robert Waln, C. Ross, and John Smith, October 22, 1812, box 1, folder 4, Robert Waln Papers, HSP; Robert and John Oliver to George and Robert Blackburn, February 8, 1813, letterbook 20, Robert Oliver Papers, MHS; Outward Foreign Manifests, RG 36, NARA–MA.

56. "Parecer sobre a questão da paz da América Inglesa [S.I.]," January 12, 1815, Coleção Linhares 1803–1817, MS 554, reel 2, document 46, BNRJ (quotation "interests of the kingdom"); Robert and John Oliver to Brown, Reid, & Co., April 23, 1815, letterbook 20, Robert Oliver Papers, MHS (quotation "our respective markets").

57. Hancock, *Oceans of Wine*, 122; Robert and John Oliver to George and Robert Blackburn, & Co., October 24, 1810, November 15, 1811, letterbook 20, Robert Oliver Papers, MHS.

58. Robert and John Oliver to George and Robert Blackburn, & Co., January 1, January 8, and February 8, 1813, April 20, 1815, March 23, 1816 (quotation), July 1 and August 28, 1817, and to Scott & Co., April 11, 1811, all in letterbook 20, Robert Oliver Papers, MHS; Outward Foreign Manifests, RG 36, NARA–MA.

59. "Tratado de Commercio, e Navegação Entre os Muito Altos, e Muito Poderosos Senhores O Principe Regente de Portugal, e ElRey do Reino Unido da Grande Bretanha e Irlanda," February 19, 1810, CD, St. Salvador, NARA–CP; Fragoso, *Homens de grossa aventura*, 182–183; Cardoso, "Nas Malhas do Império," 98–99, 102; Domingues, *Atlantic Slave Trade*, 49, 132.

60. *ASP:CN*, 1:815, 869, 892, 965, 994

61. Henry Hill vs. Thomas Reely, Henry Hill Papers, box 2, folder 57, TJDC; Outward Foreign Manifests, RG 36, NARA–MA.

Part IV

1. Conde de Barça to José Corrêa da Serra, February 21, 1807, box 114, MNE. Recognizing Brazil's importance to the Portuguese Empire, Dom João elevated Brazil's status to a kingdom to resist calls from Portugal and Great Britain to return the seat of empire to its traditional place in Lisbon. See Adelman, *Sovereignty and Revolution*, 312–13.

Chapter 7

1. Henry Hill to Mariano Moreno, November 3, 1810, and to Thomas Sumpter, September 20, 1809, both in CD, St. Salvador, NARA–CP; Nicolas Shumway, *The Invention of Argentina* (Berkeley: University of California Press, 1991), 24–46.

2. Hill to Mariano Moreno, November 3, 1810, and to Thomas Sumpter, September 20, 1809, both in CD, St. Salvador, NARA–CP.

3. Hill to Sumpter, September 20, 1809, CD, St. Salvador, NARA–CP.

4. Hill to Sumpter, September 20, 1809, CD, St. Salvador, NARA–CP; Schultz, *Tropical Versailles*, 198.

5. Adelman, *Sovereignty and Revolution*, 314; Schultz, *Tropical Versailles*, 101–4; Caitlin Fitz, "A Stalwart Motor of Revolutions: An American Merchant in Pernambuco, 1817–1825," *Americas*, 65 (July 2008), 38–39; Henry Koster, *Travels in Brazil* (London, 1816), 32 (quotation); Ana Rosa Cloclet da Silva, *Inventando a Nação: Intelectuais Ilustrados e Estadistas Luso-Brasileiros na Crise do Antigo Regime Português (1750–1822)* (São Paulo: Editora Hucitec, 2006), 270–73; Mota, *Nordeste 1817*, 21–23.

6. Fitz, "Stalwart Motor," 38–39; Maxwell, *Conflicts and Conspiracies*, 74; Cloclet da Silva, *Inventando a Nação*, 270–73; Mota, *Nordeste 1817*, 14–17, 21–28.

7. Cloclet da Silva, *Inventando a nação*, 270–73; Adelman, *Sovereignty and Revolution*, 315; *Caledonian Mercury* (Edinburgh, Scotland), May 31, 1817; Marcus J. M. de Carvalho, "O outro lado da independência: Quilombolas, negros e pardos em Pernambuco (Brazil), 1817–23," *Luso-Brazilian Review* 43 (2006), 1–30.

8. Adelman, *Sovereignty and Revolution*, 315; Wadsworth, *In Defence of the Faith*, 79–80; *National Advocate*, May 2, 1817 (quotations).

9. Adelman, *Sovereignty and Revolution*, 314–16; Mota, *Nordeste 1817*, 31, 34–36, esp. 35 (quotation "its Franklin") and 36 (quotation "two Americas"); Flávio José Gomes Cabral, *Conversas reservadas: "Vozes públicas," conflitos políticos e rebeliões em Pernambuco no tempo da Independência do Brasil* (Rio de Janeiro: Arquivo Nacional, 2013), 83; Fitz, *Our Sister Republics*, 54; *Daily National Intelligencer*, May 5, 1817 (quotations "like the revolutions" and "partial to the Americans"); Corrêa da Serra to Conde de Barça, May 31, 1817, box 552, MNE.

10. Fitz, *Our Sister Republics*, 54 (quotation "Imitators of English America); Mota, *Nordeste 1817*, 31, 34–35, esp. 31 (quotation "given many proofs").

11. *National Advocate* (New York), April 30, 1817 (quotation "for their model"); May 1, 1817 (quotation "hailed as brothers") and May 20, 1817 (quotation "must fail").

12. *Aeolian Harp* (New York, 1817), 1:42–43.

13. Moses Ray to James Monroe, March 23, 1820, Miscellaneous Letters of the Department of State, RG 59, NARA–CP.

14. "Demonstração do valor total da Mercadorias Importadas no Reino de Portugal, que formão o Debito da Balança Geral do Commercio com o Reino do Brazil, e Dominios, no Anno de 1816," códice 731, vol. 1, p. 13, ANRJ; *Morning Chronicle*, March 31, 1817; Outward Foreign Manifests, RG 36, NARA–MA.

15. Outward Foreign Manifests, RG 36, NARA–MA; Jerônimo Martiniano Figueira de Mello, *Ensaio sobre a Estatística Civil e Política da Província de Pernambuco*, draft, Chapter 7, BNRJ; Whitaker, *United States*, 13–14, 132–33; Fitz, "Stalwart Motor," 45.

16. *Daily National Intelligencer*, May 5, 1817 (quotation "most valuable part"); *National Advocate*, April 30, 1817; *Providence Patriot, Columbian Phenix* (RI), May 3, 1817 (quotation flourishing and populous") and May 10, 1817 (quotation "highly interesting"); *Boston Patriot*, reprinted in *Daily National Intelligencer*, May 27, 1817 (quotation "friendship of the patriots").

17. *Daily National Intelligencer*, June 3, 1817.

18. *Savannah Republican*, May 3, 1817.

19. Corrêa da Serra to Conde de Barça, July 25, 1817, box 552, MNE; Theodorick Bland to John Quincy Adams, "Report on South America," November 2, 1818, box 5, Theodorick

Bland Papers, MHS; Joseph Eugene Agan, "Corrêa da Serra," *Pennsylvania Magazine of History and Biography* 49 (1925), 26–27; Henry Brackenridge, *South America: A Letter on the Present State of that Country to James Monroe, President of the United States* (Washington, 1817), 35–36. In April 1817, Jean-Guillaume Hyde de Neuville, the French minister plenipotentiary in Washington, made the same argument as Brackenridge. He claimed, "The inhabitants of the province of Pernambuco do not even have the pretext of fighting for local Institutions, for their Sovereign is in their midst" (Jean-Guillaume Hyde de Neuville to Richard Rush, April 28, 1817, box 552, MNE).

20. Brackenridge, *South America*, 35–36.

21. [Antônio Gonçalves da Cruz], "Reply to the Author of the Letter on South America and Mexico" (Philadelphia, 1817), 13–14, 18.

22. Gilje, *Free Trade*, 23–24; Eacott, *Selling Empire*, 422.

23. Eacott, *Selling Empire*, 421–23, esp. 423 (quotation "calmly look on"); *Annals of Congress*, 14 Cong., 2 Sess., January 4–5, 1816, pp. 454–58, and February 4, 1816, pp. 877 (quotation "restrictive system"), 881 (quotation "inviting a change").

24. Eacott, *Selling Empire*, 421–23; Randolph B. Campbell, "The Spanish American Aspect of Henry Clay's American System," *Americas* 24 (July 1967), 6; Onuf and Onuf, *Nations, Markets, and War*, 176.

25. Corrêa da Serra to Conde de Barça, May 31, 1817, box 552, MNE; Flávio José Gomes Cabral, " 'Highly Important! Revolution in Brazil': A divulgação da república de Pernambuco de 1817 nos Estados Unidos," *Clio* 33, no. 1 (2015), 11; *Examiner* (London, England), June 1, 1817; *Daily National Intelligencer* (Washington, DC), May 1, 1817; "Note laying forth the insurrections and following acquisition of power by a revolutionary faction in the captaincy of Pernambuco," May 19, 1817, MS-554, reel 2, Coleção Linhares, 1803–1817, BNRJ; *National Advocate*, April 30, 1817; Bill of Lading, April 10, 1822, box 195, Inward Foreign Manifests, Port of Philadelphia, NARA–MA.

26. Corrêa da Serra to Conde de Barça, May 31, 1817, box 552, MNE; Cabral, " 'Highly Important!,' " 11–12; Fitz, "Stalwart Motor," 39, 45; Fitz, *Our Sister Republics*, 54 (quotation). The quotation is also in Mota, *Nordeste 1817*, 35.

27. Fitz, "Stalwart Motor," 39 (quotation "friendly disposition"), 45 (quotation "absolute liberty"); Mota, *Nordeste 1817*, 31, 34–35; Adelman, *Sovereignty and Revolution*, 314–16; *Morning Chronicle* (London), May 27, 1817 (quotation "like the North American"); Mota, *Nordeste 1817*, 34–35; *National Advocate*, April 30, 1817 (quotation "intercourse with them").

28. Corrêa da Serra to Conde de Barça, May 31 and August 30, 1817, and to João Paulo Bezerra, February 5, 1818, all in box 552, MNE. Newspapers across the United States reprinted the greeting of the *Boston Patriot* to the Pernambucans and the newspaper's comparison to Adams and Hancock. See, for example, *Providence Patriot, Columbian Phenix*, May 24, 1817; *Savannah Republican*, May 31, 1817; *Supporter* (Chillicothe, OH), June 3, 1817.

29. Mota, *Nordeste 1817*, 32–33, 33n68, 35; Fitz, "Stalwart Motor," 39–40; Corrêa da Serra, Correspondência com o governo—N. 2, n.d., box 552, MNE; Cloclet da Silva, *Inventando a Nação*, 272; Corrêa da Serra to Conde de Barça, May 31 and August 30, 1817, and to João Paulo Bezerra, February 5, 1818 (quotation), all in box 552, MNE; Ruiz do Rego Barretto to Tomás Antônio Vilanova Portugal, February 24, 1819, Série Interior, IJJ9–243, ANRJ.

30. Alexandre, *Sentidos do império*, 347; Bathazar de Sousa Botelho de Vasconcelos to Simplicio Dias da Silva, May 11, 1817, Ministério dos Estrangeiros e da Guerra, 4H-152,

ANRJ; Cloclet da Silva, *Inventando a Nação*, 272; "Relação dos principais cúmplices na revolução de Pernambuco, conduzidos prezos no Navio Carrasco chegado a Bahia a 8 de Junho de 1817," BNRJ; Corrêa da Serra to Richard Rush, May 13, 1817, box 552, MNE (quotation); Denis Antônio de Mendonça Bernardes, *O patriotismo constitucional: Pernambuco, 1820–1822* (São Paulo: Editora Universitária UFPE, 2006), 194.

31. Fitz, "Stalwart Motor," 41–42.

32. Joseph Ray to Richard Rush, July 20, 1817, CD, Pernambuco, NARA–CP; Fitz, "Stalwart Motor," 41–45; Report of the government of Ceará to Tomás Antônio Vilanova Portugal, November 13, 1818, Série Interior, IJJ9–169, ANRJ; Corrêa da Serra to João Paulo Bezerra, March 5, 1818, and to Vilanova Portugal, June 1, 1818, both in box 552, MNE.

33. Fitz, "Stalwart Motor," 45–46; Mota, *Nordeste 1817*, 43 (quotation); *Savannah Republican*, July 1, 1817; *National Advocate*, June 20, 1817; Schultz, *Tropical Versailles*, 214, 217–19; Mota, *Nordeste 1817*, 43.

34. Schultz, *Tropical Versailles*, 214, 217–19, esp. 219; Fitz, "Stalwart Motor," 45–46.

35. Fitz, "Stalwart Motor," 45–46, esp. 45; Corrêa da Serra to John Quincy Adams, October 15, 1818, Corrêa da Serra Papers, APS.

36. Fitz, "Stalwart Motor," 46; Moses Ray to James Monroe, March 23, 1820, Miscellaneous Letters of the Department of State, NARA-CP; Moses Ray to Mary Ray, June 28, 1822, Mary Ray Papers, ISM (quotations).

37. *Gazeta do Rio de Janeiro* (Brazil), April 19, 1817; Figueira de Mello, *Ensaio sobre a Estatística Civil e Política*, draft, Chapter 7, BNRJ.

38. *Daily National Intelligencer*, May 5, 1817, and June 18, 1817; *Providence Patriot, Columbian Phenix*, May 17, 1817, and May 10, 1817; *National Advocate*, May 7, 1817 (quotation "the glorious cause"); *Caledonian Mercury*, June 2, 1817; Mota, *Nordeste 1817*, 36; *Documentos Históricos da Biblioteca Nacional*, Divisão de Obras Raras e Publicações, vol. 101 (112 vols., 1953), 35, 154.

39. *Daily National Intelligencer*, May 5, 1817 (quotations) and June 18, 1817; *Providence Patriot, Columbian Phenix*, May 17, 1817; *National Advocate*, May 7, 1817; Holford, Gonne, & Lucas to John Johnston and John McKean, March 20, 1811, box 454, folder 17, Chew Family Papers, HSP; *Caledonian Mercury*, June 2, 1817.

40. Corrêa da Serra, "Correspondência com o governo—N. 2," n.d., box 552, MNE; *Daily National Intelligencer*, May 12 and May 27, 1817; *Savannah Republican*, June 10, 1817 (quotation) and 25, 1817. Revolutionaries in Ceará heard rumors that the provisional government in Pernambuco was constructing a fortress to clear the way for U.S. vessels, though it is unclear if such rumors reached the United States (Mota, *Nordeste 1817*, 36).

41. Bill of lading, May 16, 1817, Outward Foreign Manifests, RG 36, NARA–MA; *Savannah Republican*, October 22, 1817.

42. Figueira de Mello, *Ensaio sobre a Estatística Civil e Política*, draft, Chapter 7, BNRJ; "Demonstração do Valor total das Mercadorias Exportadas de Portugal, que formão o Credito da Balança Geral do Commercio com o Reino do Brazil e Dominios no Anno de 1817," códice 731, vol. 1, p. 14, ANRJ; "Demonstração do Valor total das Mercadorias Exportadas do Reino de Portugal, que formão o Credito da Balança Geral do Commercio com o Reino do Brazil e Dominios no Anno de 1817," códice 731, vol. 2, p. 63, ANRJ.

43. *Daily National Intelligencer*, October 23, 1817; *National Advocate*, November 24, 1817.

44. *Savannah Republican*, August 16, 1817 (quotation "hang together"); Corrêa da Serra to Conde de Barça, August 30, 1817, box 552, MNE (quotation "absolutely defeat"); Joseph Ray to John Quincy Adams, February 18, 1818, CD, Pernambuco, NARA–CP (quotation "fire which burst").

45. Corrêa da Serra to Conde de Barça, August 30, 1817, box 552, MNE; *Daily National Intelligencer*, August 29, 1817 (quotations).

46. *Savannah Republican*, October 22, 1817.

47. Report of the government of Ceará to Tomás Antônio Vilanova Portugal, November 13, 1818, Série Interior, IJJ9–169, ANRJ (quotation "fugitives of Pernambuco"); Corrêa da Serra to Conde de Barça, August 30, 1817, to João Paulo Bezerra, March 5, 1818 (quotations "infernal intrigue" and "fragments of rebellions") and to Vilanova Portugal, June 1 and July 13, 1818 (quotations "demons" and "mysterious personages"), all in box 552, MNE.

48. Figueira de Mello, *Ensaio sobre a Estatística Civil e Política*, draft, Chapter 7, BNRJ.

49. Mota, *Nordeste 1817*, 35–36; *Daily National Intelligencer*, September 18, 1818; Moses Ray to James Monroe, March 23, 1820, Miscellaneous Letters of the Department of State, NARA–CP; *National Advocate* quotation, reprinted in *Providence Patriot, Columbian Phenix*, October 27, 1821.

50. Mendonça Bernardes, *O patriotismo constitucional*, 194.

51. Corrêa da Serra to Vilanova Portugal, December 9, 1819, box 552, MNE (quotation); Fitz, "Stalwart Motor," 47. As Fitz notes of Ray's involvement with the corsairs, "The evidence . . . is entirely circumstantial, which suggests either that he was not involved or else that he, like many privateering agents, covered his tracks like a tried professional."

Chapter 8

1. *Savannah Republican*, November 25, 1817.

2. Thomas U. P. Charlton to James Madison, June 5, 1815, James Madison Papers, LOC.

3. Janice E. Thomson, *Mercenaries, Pirates, and Sovereigns: State-Building and Extraterritorial Violence in Early Modern Europe* (Princeton, NJ: Princeton University Press, 1994), 3–4.

4. Gould, *Among the Powers*, 3, 12–13, esp. 3; Lauren Benton, *A Search for Sovereignty: Law and Geography in European Empires, 1400–1900* (New York: Cambridge University Press, 2010), 2; Adelman, *Sovereignty and Revolution*, 318–19.

5. Prado, *Edge of Empire*, 99, 134; Mario Rodríguez, "Dom Pedro of Braganza and Colônia do Sacramento, 1680–1705," *Hispanic American Historical Review* 38 (May 1958), 195; Maxwell, "Portuguese America," 542; Mark D. Szuchman, "From Imperial Hinterland to Growth Pole: Revolution, Change, and Restoration in the Río de la Plata," in Mark D. Szuchman and Jonathan C. Brown eds., *Revolution and Restoration: The Rearrangement of Power in Argentina, 1776–1860* (Lincoln: University of Nebraska Press, 1994), 1–26; Lyman L. Johnson, *Workshop of Revolution: Plebeian Buenos Aires and the Atlantic World, 1776–1810* (Durham, NC: Duke University Press, 2011), 275–76; Shumway, *Invention of Argentina*, 18–21; José Carlos Chiaramonte, *Ciudades, Provincias, Estados: Orígenes de la Nación Argentina, 1800–1846* (Buenos Aires, 2007); John Chasteen, *Americanos: Latin America's Struggle for Independence* (New York: Oxford University Press, 2008); Charles Lyon Chandler, "United States Shipping in the La Plata Region, 1809–1810," *Hispanic American Historical Review* 3 (May 1920), 172; *Geneva Gazette* (NY), August 28, 1811.

6. Prado, *Edge of Empire*, 154, 157–58; Rafe Blaufarb, "The Western Question: The Geopolitics of Latin American Independence," *American Historical Review* 112 (June 2007), 758–59; Shumway, *Invention of Argentina*, 47–80.

7. Sujay Rao, "Arbiters of Change: Provincial Elites and the Origins of Federalism in Argentina's Littoral, 1814–1820," *Americas*, 64 (April 2008), 514–15; Adelman, *Sovereignty and Revolution*, 282; Theodorick Bland to Adams, November 2, 1818, box 5, Theodorick Bland Papers, MHS; Agustín Beraza, *Los corsarios de Artigas, 1816–1821* (Montevideo: Revista Histórica, 1949), 13–19; Ana Frega, "La virtud y el poder: La soberania particular de los pueblos en el proyecto artiguista," in Noemí Goldman and Ricardo Salvatore, eds., *Caudillismos rioplatenses: Nuevas miradas a un viejo problema* (Buenos Aires: Eudeba, 1998), 106–114.

8. John Street, *Artigas and the Emancipation of Uruguay* (New York: Cambridge University Press, 1959), 295, 300; Adelman, *Sovereignty and Revolution*, 317 (quotations); Shumway, *Invention of Argentina*, 64; Blaufarb, "Western Question," 758–59; Agan, "Corrêa da Serra," 17–18; Charles C. Griffin, "Privateering from Baltimore During the Spanish American Wars of Independence," *Maryland Historical Magazine* 35 (March 1940), 1–25; Fred Hopkins, "For Freedom and Profit: Baltimore Privateers in the Wars of South American Independence," *Northern Mariner / Le marin du nord*, 18 (July–October 2008), 93–104.

9. David Head, "Sailing for Spanish America: The Atlantic Geopolitics of Privateering from the United States in the Early Republic," (Ph.D. diss., University at Buffalo, State University of New York, 2009), 4, 27, 86, 198; "Sketch of Instructions for Agents for South America," March 24, 1819, in Stanislaus Murray Hamilton, ed., *The Writings of James Monroe, including a collection of his public and private papers and correspondence now for the first time printed*, 7 vols. (New York, 1902), 6:99; Rodrigo José Ferreira Lobo to Nova Portugal, February 28, 1818, in Comisión Nacional, *Archivo Artigas*, 35:60–61; Juan Martín de Pueyrredón to Barón de la Laguna, July 2, 1818, in Comisión Nacional, *Archivo Artigas*, 35:66–67 (quotation). For sources on the number of Artigan vessels, see sources for Figure 11.

10. Laura Bornholdt, "Baltimore as a Port for Spanish-American Propaganda, 1810–1823" (Ph.D. diss., Yale University, 1945), 14–15; Jerome R. Garitee, *The Republic's Private Navy: The American Privateering Business as Practiced by Baltimore During the War of 1812* (Middletown, CT: Wesleyan University Press, 1977); Hopkins, "For Freedom and Profit," 94.

11. Conde de Barça to Corrêa da Serra, April 4, 1817, box 114, MNE (quotation); Corrêa da Serra to James Monroe, December 20, 1816, box 552, MNE; "General Table of the value claimed by subjects of Portugal, in consequence of captures made by American Privateers, under insurgent Flags, specially Artigas," n.d., box 116, MNE; Léon Bourdon, ed., *José Corrêa da Serra: Ambassadeur du royaume-uni de Portugal et Brésil a Washington, 1816–1820* (Paris: Fundação Calouste Gulbenkian, 1975), 98.

12. Thomas Lloyd Halsey to James Monroe, May 5, 1815, in William Ray Manning, *Diplomatic Correspondence of the United States Concerning the Independence of the Latin-American Nations* (New York, 1925), 1:337.

13. Prado, *Edge of Empire*, 155–56; Johnson, *Workshop of Revolution*, 250–60; Francis and Charles Bradbury to James Madison, December 19, 1806, British Spoliations, 1794–1824, RG 76, NARA–CP; *Gazeta Extraordinária de Madrid*, December 24, 1806; Whitaker, *United States*, 9; Henry L. DeKoven to Low & Wallace, March 4, 1807, Nicholas Low Papers, NYHS (quotation).

14. Chandler, "United States Shipping," 160–61, 172; Whitaker, *United States*, 9; *Geneva Gazette* (NY), August 28, 1811; Alexander Thomas to John Johnston and Joseph Y. Singleton, July 2, 6 1811, Marcus Whyte to John Johnston and John McKean, July 22, 1811, and Thomas Bedwell to Joseph Y. Singleton and John Johnston, July 6, 1811, all in box 454, folder 17, Chew Family Papers, HSP.

15. Beraza, *Corsarios de Artigas*, 22, 30–31; Corrêa da Serra to Tomás Antônio Vilanova Portugal, January 2, 1819, box 552, MNE; Barão da Laguna to Conde dos Arcos, July 18, 1818, in Comisión Nacional, *Archivo Artigas*, 55:86; Contract between Thomas Lloyd Halsey and George W. Hockley, June 21, 1820, box 15, Papers of Jonathan Meredith, LOC; Head, "Sailing for Spanish America," 81, 81n12, 198; Head, *Privateers of the Americas*, 74.

16. David Head, "New Nations, New Connections: Spanish American Privateering from the United States and the Development of Atlantic Relations," *Early American Studies* 11 (Winter 2013), 164–66; Head, *Privateers of the Americas*, 66–74; Joaquim José Vasques, "Lista das acçoens que intentei como Consul Geral da Nação Portugueza ad interim, as quaes se acham ainda por decidir," July 10, 1820, box 116, MNE.

17. *Alexandria Gazette*, November 4, 1817 (quotations "deserving patriots" and "ripe for independence"); *Baltimore Patriot*, August 4, 1817 (quotations "scandalous" and "king John"); *Daily National Intelligencer*, November 4, 1817 and September 22, 1818; *Maryland Censor* quoted in *Daily National Intelligencer*, September 22 (quotations "most unprovoked" and "we care not") and September 25, 1818 (*Maryland Censor*'s citation of "we care not"); Portuguese translation of newspaper clip enclosed in correspondence of Corrêa da Serra to Vilanova Portugal, September 16, 1818, box 552, MNE, retranslated into English (quotation "before long").

18. Corrêa da Serra to Adams, March 17, 1819, in Bourdon, *José Corrêa da Serra*, 468–69; Corrêa da Serra to Marquês de Aguiar, December 28, 1816, March 8, 1817, box 552, MNE; Head, *Privateers of the Americas*, 128; Charles Francis Adams, ed., *Memoirs of John Quincy Adams* (Philadelphia: J.B. Lippincott & Co., 1875), 4:134 (quotations).

19. Corrêa da Serra to Monroe, December 20, 1816, in Bourdon, *José Corrêa da Serra*, 240–42, esp. 241–42.

20. *Annals of Congress*, 14 Cong., 2 Sess., January 24, 1817, pp. 719–20, esp. 719.

21. *Annals of Congress*, 14 Cong., 2 Sess., January 24, 1817, pp. 720, 727, 733, 742.

22. *Annals of Congress*, 14 Cong., 2 Sess., January 24, 1817, p. 735 (quotation); Tyson Reeder, "Liberty with the Sword: Jamaican Maroons, Haitian Revolutionaries, and American Liberty," *Journal of the Early Republic* 37 (Spring 2017), 100–101.

23. *Annals of Congress*, 14 Cong., 2 Sess., January 24, 1817, p. 742.

24. "An Act more effectually to preserve the neutral relations of the United States," 3 Stat. 370, 371 (1817); Ben Herzog, *Revoking Citizenship: Expatriation in America from the Colonial Era to the War on Terror* (New York: New York University Press, 2015), 29–31. Critics of the Neutrality Act cited Spain as the beneficiary of the legislation. Since 1815, Luis de Onís, Spain's minister in Washington, had pressured the U.S. government to prohibit vessels flying the flags of South American revolutionary governments from entering U.S. ports. President Monroe, however, credited passage of the act to Corrêa da Serra, averring in 1820 that "nothing could then [in 1817] have been done at the instance of Mr. Onis" (*Annals of Congress*, 14 Cong., 2 Sess., January 24, 1817, pp. 719–20, 722, 727, 733, 742; "An Act more effectually to preserve the neutral relations of the United States," 3 Stat. 370–71, esp. 370 [1817]; Agan, "Corrêa da Serra," 18, 20; *Gazeta de Lisboa* [Lisbon, Portugal], July 7, 1817).

25. W. G. D. Worthington to John Quincy Adams, January 10, 1818, in Manning, *Diplomatic Correspondence*, 368, 379, esp. 368; Adams, *Memoirs of John Quincy Adams*, 4:70.

26. For sources on the number of captures, see sources for Figure 11. The numbers for captured vessels are based on captures for which a definite year is known: Garitee, *Republic's*

Private Navy, 129, 193; "Autos Civeis de Requerimento, Justificação e Protesto," box 117, MNE; Head, *Privateers of the Americas*, 77–78.

27. Corrêa da Serra to Count of Palmela, September 17, 1818, box 183, MNE; Beraza, *Corsarios de Artigas*, 57; Bourdon, *José Correa da Serra*, 103–5; J. L. Anderson, "Piracy and World History: An Economic Perspective on Maritime Predation," *Journal of World History* 6 (Fall 1995), 199; Ernst Ekman, "A Swedish Career in the Tropics: Johan Norderling (1760–1828)," *Swedish Pioneer* 15 (January 1964), 21; Han Jordaan and Victor Wilson, "The Eighteenth-Century Danish, Dutch, and Swedish Free Ports in the Northeastern Caribbean: Continuity and Change," in Gert Oostindie and Jessica V. Roitman, eds., *Dutch Atlantic Connections, 1680–1800: Linking Empires, Bridging Borders* (Boston, 2014), 34, 276–80; Enthoven, "That Abominable Nest," 246, 253–55; Vasques to João Gomes de Oliveira e Silva, September 9, 1818, box 117, MNE (quotation).

28. "Conta de Ricardo Alsop," [1819 or 1820], box 273, MNE (quotation); "General Table of the value claimed by subjects of Portugal, in consequence of captures made by American Privateers, under insurgent Flags, specially Artigas," n.d., box 116, MNE; Bassi, *Aqueous Territory*, 24.

29. Vasques to Forjaz, August 18, 1819, box 273, MNE; "Lista das Embarcações que tem sido armadas, e esquipadas nos Portos dos Estados Unidos, e dentro da sua Jurisdicção," n.d., box 552, MNE; Head, "Sailing for Spanish America," 240; "Conta de Ricardo Alsop," [1819 or 1820], box 273, MNE (quotation).

30. "Conta de Ricardo Alsop," [1819 or 1820], box 273, MNE; Corrêa da Serra to Vilanova Portugal, September 16, 1818, box 552, MNE; Robert Monroe Harrison to Corrêa da Serra, June 21, 1822, in Bourdon, *José Correa da Serra*, 626 (quotation "enormous sum"); Ekman, "Swedish Career in the Tropics," 19, 22 (quotation "Since I began"); [José Amado Grehon], "Resumo dos passos dados pelo Ministro de S. M. nos Estados-Unidos, à cerca dos Corsarios," ca. 1822, box 117, MNE.

31. Benton, *Search for Sovereignty*, 2; Bassi, *Aqueous Territory*, 4.

32. "Depoimento de José Antonio Moreira, Capitão da Galera Maria de Lisboa," September 7, 1819, 64–82, Claim documents, box 117, MNE; "Termo de Juramento que faz Miguel Thadeo Montufas," July 3, 1818, box 116, MNE; "Remonstração da Tripulação da Maria de Lisboa," [1819?], box 117, MNE.

33. John Torpey, *The Invention of the Passport: Surveillance, Citizenship, and the State* (Cambridge: Cambridge University Press, 2000), 4. Torpey builds on Max Weber's theory that states hold monopolies on the legitimate means of violence.

34. "Termo sobre a captura do Brigue *União de América*," July 17, 1818, box 116, MNE; "Termo de Juramento que faz Miguel Thadeo Montufas," July 3, 1818, Testimony of Gabriel Lacayo y Coronado, July 20, 1818, "Termo de Juramento e declaração que faz Jacob Leandro da Silva," July 23, 1818, "Termo de Juramento e declaração que faz João Borges Tristão," July 3, 1818, "Termo de Juramento e declaração que faz Manuel Francisco Cassilhas," July 3, 1818, all in box 116, MNE.

35. Testimony of Gabriel Lacayo y Coronado, July 20, 1818, "Termo de Juramento e declaração que faz Jacob Leandro da Silva," July 23, 1818, both in box 116, MNE.

36. Testimony of Gabriel Lacayo y Coronado, July 20, 1818, box 116, MNE.

37. Douglas L. Stein, *American Maritime Documents, 1776–1860* (Mystic, CT: Mystic Seaport Museum, 1992), http://library.mysticseaport.org/initiative/ImText.cfm?BibID=

6405&ChapterID = 17 (accessed August 13, 2018); Torpey, *Invention of the Passport*, 94–96; Martin Lloyd, *The Passport: The History of Man's Most Travelled Document* (Stroud, UK: Sutton, 2003), 71–73.

38. "Termo de Juramento que faz Miguel Thadeo Montufas," July 3, 1818, box 116, MNE.

39. "Declaração que faz João Luiz Victor," August 12, 1818, Série Interior, IJJ9–243, ANRJ.

40. Testimony of Gabriel Lacayo y Coronado, July 20, 1818 (quotation "from the prizes") and "Termo de Juramento e declaração que faz Manuel Francisco Cassilhas," July 3, 1818 (quotation "appeared to him"), both in box 116, MNE.

41. "Depoimento de Agostinho Luis Pinto de Carvalho," February 19, 1822, part of "Registo de Reclamações 94," box 117, MNE (quotation); Comisión Nacional, *Archivo Artigas*, 35:86.

42. "Registo de Reclamações 94," October 17, 1822, box 117, MNE.

43. United States v. Henry Ford, Criminal Case Files of the U.S. Circuit Court for the District of Maryland, 1795–1860 (microfilm: reel 1), Records of District Courts of the United States, RG 21, NARA–DC.

44. United States v. Henry Ford, Criminal Case Files of the U.S. Circuit Court for the District of Maryland, 1795–1860 (microfilm: reel 1), Records of District Courts of the United States, RG 21, NARA–DC.

45. "General Table of the value claimed by subjects of Portugal, in consequence of captures made by American Privateers, under insurgent Flags, specially Artigas," n.d., box 116, MNE.

46. "Processo verbal e Sumario sobre roubo feito no Brigue Correio 'Infante D. Sebastião,'" enclosed in Vilanova Portugal to Corrêa da Serra, April 24, 1820, box 114, MNE.

47. "Processo verbal e Sumario sobre roubo feito no Brigue Correio 'Infante D. Sebastião,'" enclosed in Vilanova Portugal to Corrêa da Serra, April 24, 1820, box 114, MNE; W. Jeffrey Bolster, *Black Jacks: African American Seamen in the Age of Sail* (Cambridge, MA: Harvard University Press, 1997), 44–67; Carlos Lopes, ed., *Mansas, escravos, grumetes e gentio: Cacheu na encruzilhada de civilizaçoes* (Lisbon: Instituto Nacional de Estudos e Pesquisa, Imprensa Nacional—Casa da Moeda, 1993), 14; Ray Costello, *Black Salt: Seafarers of African Descent on British Ships* (Liverpool: Liverpool University Press, 2012), 15; Hawthorne, *From Africa to Brazil*, 82, 101–7; George E. Brooks, "The Observance of All Souls' Day in the Guinea-Bissau Region: A Christian Holy Day, an African Harvest Festival, an African New Year's Celebration, or All of the Above(?)," *History in Africa* 11 (January 1984), 16–17, 24–25; John Ladhams, "In Search of West African Pidgin Portuguese," *Revista Internacional de Lingüística Iberoamericana* 4 (January 2006), 90–91.

48. "Processo verbal e Sumario sobre roubo feito no Brigue Correio 'Infante D. Sebastião,'" enclosed in Vilanova Portugal to Corrêa da Serra, April 24, 1820, box 114, MNE; Bolster, *Black Jacks*, 4–5, 131–57.

49. Torpey, *Invention of the Passport*, 4.

50. Head, "Sailing for Spanish America," 3n5, 190, 193.

51. Head, "Sailing for Spanish America," 180, 184, 190, 193, 195, 198, 200–203; Carlos Vidales, "Corsarios y piratas de la Revolución Francesa en las aguas de la emancipación hispanoamericana," *Caravelle* 54 (1990), 256–57.

52. Corrêa da Serra to Madison, July 10, 1816, in Bourdon, *José Corrêa da Serra*, 219 (quotation); Agan, "Corrêa da Serra," 1–17; E. Corrêa da Serra to John Vaughan, July 1, 1823, John Vaughan Papers, APS.

53. Richard Beale Davis, "The Abbe Corrêa da Serra in America: The Contributions of the Diplomat and Natural Philosopher to the Foundations of Our National Life," *Transactions of the American Philosophical Society* 45 (1955), 90–121; Corrêa da Serra to Vilanova Portugal, June 25, 1819, box 552, MNE (quotation "fear of the people"); Corrêa da Serra to Adams, August 26, 1820, box 118, MNE (quotation "disgraced the commission"); Corrêa da Serra to Barça, May 31 and July 25, 1817 (quotation "revolutionary tendencies"), to Vilanova Portugal, September 16, 1818 (quotation "has no power"), and to Adams, May 13, 1817 (quotation "the lukewarm acts"), all in box 552, MNE.

54. Corrêa da Serra to Vilanova Portugal, January 2, 1819, box 552, MNE.

55. José Corrêa da Serra, *An Appeal to the Government and Congress of the United States Against the Depredations Committed by American Privateers on the Commerce of Nations at Peace with Us* (New York, 1819), 56, 61; Corrêa da Serra to Vilanova Portugal, June 25, 1819, box 552, MNE; Bourdon, *José Corrêa da Serra*, 147.

56. Corrêa da Serra to Vilanova Portugal, January 30, 1819, in Bourdon, *José Corrêa da Serra*, 455; Hill to Adams, January 1, 1819, CD, Rio de Janeiro, NARA–CP; Benjamin Etting journal, ISM (quotation).

57. Corrêa da Serra to Vilanova Portugal, January 30, 1819, in Bourdon, *José Corrêa da Serra*, 455.

58. Corrêa da Serra to Adams, March 17, 1819, in Bourdon, *José Corrêa da Serra*, 468 (quotation); "An Act in addition to the 'Act for the punishment of certain crimes against the United States,' and to repeal the acts therein mentioned," 3 Stat. 447–450 (1818); Adams to Corrêa da Serra, February 9, 1819, reel 446, Adams Family Papers, MAHS.

59. Graham to Vilanova Portugal, September 18, 1819, in Bourdon, *José Corrêa da Serra*, 510; Vilanova Portugal to Graham, September 25, 1819, in Bourdon, *José Corrêa da Serra*, 515.

60. Corrêa da Serra to Vilanova Portugal, March 23, 1819, in Bourdon, *José Corrêa da Serra*, 473 (quotation "hook and bait"); Corrêa da Serra to Vilanova Portugal, March 29, 1819, in Bourdon, *José Corrêa da Serra*, 474 (quotation "our objectives"); Corrêa da Serra to Vilanova Portugal, April 8, 1819, in Bourdon, *José Corrêa da Serra*, 478–79 (quotation "I believe").

61. James F. Vivian, "The Paloma Claim in United States and Venezuelan-Colombian Relations, 1818–1826," *Caribbean Studies* 14 (January 1975), 60–61; Ruiz do Rego Barretto to Tomás Antônio Vilanova Portugal, February 24, 1819, Série Interior, IJJ9–243, ANRJ; "An act to protect the commerce of the United States, and punish the crime of piracy," 2 Stat. 510–514 (1819). "Sketch of Instructions for Agents for South America," March 24, 1819, in Hamilton, *Writings of James Monroe*, 6:93 (quotation "operate principally"); Monroe to Adams, September 4, 1820, in Bourdon, *José Corrêa da Serra*, 583 (quotation "whole maritime force").

62. Adams, *Memoirs of John Quincy Adams*, 4:316–17 (quotations "most energetic manner," "displeasure," and "amicable"); Ekman, "Swedish Career," 18–19; Palmela, "Note du Comte de Palmela aux plénipotentiaires des puissances alliées réunies à Aix-la-Chapelle," November 15, 1818, in Bourdon, *José Corrêa da Serra*, 435–36 (quotations "crews gathered" and "found means").

63. Matthew McCarthy, *Privateering, Piracy and British Policy in Spanish America, 1810–1830* (Rochester: University of Rochester Press–Boydell and Brewer, 2013), 17; Corrêa da Serra to Vilanova Portugal, September 6, 1820, box 552, MNE (quotation); Gould, *Among the Powers*, 3, 12–13, esp. 3.

64. Agan, "Corrêa da Serra," 30; Adams, *Memoirs of John Quincy Adams*, 4:317 (quotations).

65. Adams to Elias Glenn, April 12, 1819, in Bourdon, *José Corrêa da Serra*, 480; Adams, *Memoirs of John Quincy Adams*, 4:316–18, 339.

66. Head, "Sailing for Spanish America," 235–39; Corrêa da Serra to Vilanova Portugal, January 2, 1819, box 552, MNE (quotation); "Commodore Taylor—A Law Case," *Niles' Weekly Register*, December 19, 1818, 15:290.

67. Glenn to Adams, April 19, 1819, Miscellaneous Letters of the Department of State, NARA–CP; Corrêa da Serra to Vilanova Portugal, January 2, 1819, box 552, MNE; Head, "Sailing for Spanish America," 235–39; Graham to Vilanova Portugal, September 18, 1819, in Bourdon, *José Corrêa da Serra*, 512–13.

68. Vivian, "Paloma Claim," 61–62.

69. Vasques to Pereira Forjaz, June 19, 1819, box 273, MNE. On his selection of Richard Alsop, see Vasques to Vilanova Portugal, January 6, 1819, box 273, MNE.

70. On Alsop's residence in New York, see Richard Alsop to Frances M. Alsop, March 2, 1814, folder 78, box 5, Series I: Correspondence, 1776–1912, ms 34, Alsop Family Papers, MA–YUL. On José Joaquim Vasques's establishment in New York, see "Certificate of Public Instrument," October 21, 1816, box 273, MNE. On Alsop's prospects in Lisbon, see Richard Alsop to Mary Wyllys Pomeroy Alsop, June 25 and October 20, 1815, folder 88, box 5, Series I: Correspondence, Alsop Family Papers, MA–YUL. For Alsop's departure date, see Corrêa da Serra to Forjaz, June 4, 1819, in Bourdon, *José Correa da Serra*, 493–94. On Alsop's cooperation with M. C. Von Hausewolff and information on his mission, see "Conta de Ricardo Alsop," [1819 or 1820], box 273, MNE.

71. "Conta de Ricardo Alsop," [1819 or 1820], box 273, MNE.

72. Corrêa da Serra to Vilanova Portugal, June 9, 1820, box 552, MNE.

73. James Monroe, "Third Annual Message," December 7, 1819, The American Presidency Project, John T. Woolley and Gerhard Peters, eds., http://www.presidency.ucsb.edu/ws/?pid=29461 (accessed August 13, 2018); "An Act designating the ports within which only foreign armed vessels shall be permitted to enter," 3 Stat. 597–98 (1820); Head, *Privateers of the Americas*, 85.

74. Guy Chet, *The Ocean Is a Wilderness: Atlantic Piracy and the Limits of State Authority, 1688–1856* (Amherst: University of Massachusetts, 2014), 3–4.

75. "An Act to continue in force 'An act to protect the commerce of the United States, and punish the crime of piracy,' and also to make further provisions for punishing the crime of piracy," 3 Stat. 600–601, esp. 601 (1820); *Annals of Congress*, 16 Cong., 1 Sess., May 8, 1820, pp. 2207–11, esp. 2210; Head, *Privateers of the Americas*, 78; *National Advocate*, December 22, 1818; *Daily National Intelligencer*, January 19, 1819; Testimony of Gabriel Lacayo y Coronado, July 20, 1818, box 116, MNE; "Termo de Juramento e Declaração que faz Manuel Francisco Cassilhas," July 3, 1818, box 116, MNE; "Processo verbal e Sumario sobre roubo feito no Brigue Correio 'Infante D. Sebastião,'" enclosed in Vilanova Portugal to Corrêa da Serra, April 24, 1820, box 114, MNE; Beraza, *Corsarios*, 124–26, 257–58; Horacio Rodríguez and

Pablo E. Arguindeguy, *El corso ríoplatense* (Buenos Aires: Instituto Browniano, 1996), 324; U.S. vs. Henry Ford, Criminal Case Files of the U.S. Circuit Court for the District of Maryland, 1795–1860 (reel 1), Records of District Courts of the United States, RG 21, NARA–DC.

76. *Annals of Congress*, 16 Cong., 1 Sess., May 10, 1820, pp. 2222–29, esp. 2226; Monroe to Adams, July 24, 1820, in Hamilton, *Writings of James Monroe*, 6:142 (quotation "increased vigilance"), 145; Adams to Corrêa da Serra, July 20, 1820, in *Annals of Congress*, 18 Cong., 1 Sess., May 10, 1824, pp. 3042–44, esp. 3043 (quotation "the determination"); "Resumo dos passos," n.d., box 117, MNE (quotation "very desirous").

77. Corrêa da Serra to Vilanova Portugal, September 6, 1820, box 552, MNE (quotation "numerous death sentences"); "Resumo dos passos," n.d., box 117, MNE (quotations "oratory harangues" and "the punishment"); Head, *Privateers of the Americas*, 86; Adams, *Memoirs of John Quincy Adams*, 5:150.

78. See sources for Figure 11; Henning Hillman and Christina Gathmann, "Overseas Trade and the Decline of Privateering," *Journal of Economic History* 71 (September 2011), 731; Alejandro Colás and Bryan Mabee, "The Flow and Ebb of Private Seaborne Violence in Global Politics: Lessons from the Atlantic World, 1689–1815," in Alejandro Colás and Bryan Mabee, eds., *Mercenaries, Bandits, Pirates and Empires: Private Violence in Historical Perspective* (New York: Columbia University Press, 2010), 84; Chet, *Ocean is a Wilderness*, 3–4; Head, *Privateers of the Americas*, 90–91.

79. Street, *Artigas and the Emancipation of Uruguay*, 309, 320–28; "General Table of the value claimed by subjects of Portugal, in consequence of captures made by American Privateers, under insurgent Flags, specially Artigas," n.d., box 116, MNE; Head, "Sailing for Spanish America," 8, 119–20, 208–15, 224–32; Head, *Privateers of the Americas*, 89.

Chapter 9

1. Worthington C. Ford, ed., *Writings of John Quincy Adams* (New York, 1917), 7:68–70, esp. 70; Agan, "Corrêa da Serra," 47, 39–40.

2. Adelman, *Sovereignty and Revolution*, 308–43. For export percentages, see sources to Figure 13.

3. Jay Sexton, *The Monroe Doctrine: Empire and Nation in Nineteenth-Century America* (New York: Hill and Wang, 2011), 47–48.

4. Sexton, *Monroe Doctrine*, 47–48.

5. Campbell, "Spanish American Aspect," 14–15; Gilje, *Free Trade*, 313–20.

6. Gould, *Among the Powers*, 170–71, 179, 213, 218, esp. 218; Nicholas Dungan, *Gallatin: America's Swiss Founding Father* (New York: New York University Press, 2010), 129; Peter J. Kastor, *The Nation's Crucible: The Louisiana Purchase and the Creation of America* (New Haven, CT: Yale University Press, 2004), 4; Trans-Atlantic Slave Trade Database, http://slavevoyages.org/voyages/F3OxRNZ3 (accessed September 18, 2018); Matthew Mason, "Keeping Up Appearances: The International Politics of Slave Trade Abolition in the Nineteenth-Century Atlantic World," *William and Mary Quarterly* 66 (October 2009), 821–22; David F. Long, *Gold Braid and Foreign Relations: Diplomatic Activities of U.S. Naval Officers, 1798–1883* (Annapolis: Naval Institute Press, 1988), 60–64.

7. Brian R. Hamnett, "Process and Pattern: A Re-examination of the Ibero-American Independence Movements, 1808–1826," *Journal of Latin American Studies* 29 (May 1997), 309; Schultz, *Tropical Versailles*, 67; Alexandre, *Sentidos do império*, 338, 341–56, 411–20; Ana Frega, "Alianzas y proyectos independistas en los inicios del 'Estado Cisplatino," in Ana Frega,

ed., *Historia regional e independencia del Uruguay: Proceso histórico y revisión crítica de sus relatos* (Montevideo: Ediciones de la Banda Oriental, 2009), 19–23.

8. Alexandre, *Sentidos do império*, 355–56, 367–69, esp. 355.

9. Maxwell, "Portuguese America," 532; Schultz, *Tropical Versailles*, 236–37.

10. [Francisco Cailhé de Geine?], "Le Roy et la famille Royale de Bragance doivent-ils, dans les circonstances présents, retourner en Portugal, ou bien rester au Brésil?" caixas topográficas, 740.1, ANRJ (quotation "revolutionary tempest"); Francisco Adolfo Varnhagen, *Historia Geral do Brasil*, ed. Antonio Paim, (Salvador: Centro de Documentação do Pensamento Brasileiro, 2011), 337, www.cdpb.org.br/varnhagen_historia_geral.pdf (accessed August 10, 2015); Schultz, *Tropical Versailles*, 242 (quotations "most interesting part," "suffocate the giant," and "Brazil so abandoned"); Lúcia Maria Bastos Pereira das Neves, *Corcundas e constitucionais: A cultura política da independência, 1820–1822* (Rio de Janeiro: Revan, FAPERJ, 2003), 242–47.

11. Adelman, *Sovereignty and Revolution*, 321–26; Alexandre, *Sentidos do império*, 346.

12. Rocha, "Economia política," 172–73, 176, 192, esp. 173.

13. Cabral de Mello, *A outra independência*, 65–76; *Daily National Intelligencer*, October 20, 1821; *Providence Patriot, Columbian Phenix*, October 27, 1821.

14. Adelman, *Sovereignty and Revolution*, 330–34, 380.

15. Rocha, "Economia política," 152–56; Chasteen, *Americanos*, 145–47.

16. Peter Sartoris to Adams, October 7, 1821, in Manning, *Diplomatic Correspondence*, 2:725 (quotation); Rocha, "Economia política," 152–56; Chasteen, *Americanos*, 146–47, 151.

17. Adams, *Memoirs of John Quincy Adams*, 5:171, 176, esp. 176; Paul H. Silverstone, *The Sailing Navy, 1775–1854* (New York: Routledge, 2006), 24.

18. Brown, "Impact of American Flour Imports," 320, 330; George Wells to Jesse Tyson & Son, April 13, 1822, box 1, Jesse Tyson Records, MHS; *ASP:CN*, 2:694; Hill to Madison, February 17, 1808, CD, St. Salvador, NARA–CP.

19. G. Terry Sharrer, "The Merchant-Millers: Baltimore's Flour Milling Industry, 1783–1860," *Agricultural History* 56 (January 1982), 138–50; *Register of Pennsylvania* (Philadelphia), October 11, 1828; *ASP:CN*, 2:694; George Wells to Jesse Tyson, February 7, 1823, box 2, Jesse Tyson Records, MHS (quotation); Hill to Madison, February 17, 1808, CD, St. Salvador, NARA–CP.

20. Outward Foreign Manifests, NARA–MA; Letter from Richard Willing, March 25, 1829, box 1, Willing Family Papers, HSP; Last will and testament of Paul Beck, Jr., 1, HSP.

21. Outward Foreign Manifests, NARA–MA; Richard Alsop to Frances M. Alsop, March 2, 1814, MS 34, folder 78, box 5, Alsop Family Papers, MA–YUL; Richard Alsop to Mary Wyllys Pomeroy Alsop, June 25, 1815, and October 20, 1815, folder 79, box 5, Alsop Family Papers, MA–YUL; Richard Alsop to Samuel W. Dana, March 5, 1820, folder 80, box 5, Alsop Family Papers, MA–YUL.

22. *Maryland Gazette and Political Intelligencer* (Annapolis), March 7, 1822; Richard F. Fox, "Condition of Brazil," *Daily National Intelligencer*, October 20, 1821; *Daily National Intelligencer*, February 22 and October 17, 1822.

23. *Daily National Intelligencer*, February 22 and October 17, 1822 (quotation).

24. Sartoris to Adams, June 13, 1822, in Manning, *Diplomatic Correspondence*, 2:737.

25. José Amado Grehon to Adams, April 1, 1822, *Annals of Congress*, 18 Cong., 1 Sess., Appendix, 348; Adams to Grehon, April 30, 1822, box 116, MNE; Adams to Henry Dearborn, June 25, 1822, *Annals of Congress*, 18 Cong., 1 Sess., Appendix, 3037–40, esp. 3040.

26. Adams to Henry Dearborn, June 25, 1822, *Annals of Congress*, 18 Cong., 1 Sess., Appendix, 3037–40, esp. 3040; Dearborn to Adams, October 10, 1822, *Annals of Congress*, 18 Cong., 1 Sess., Appendix, 3051–52; Stanley K. Hornbeck, "The Most-Favored-Nation Clause," *American Journal of International Law* 3 (July 1909), 620.

27. Dearborn to Adams, October 10, 1822, March 3, June 4, and November 27, 1823, *Annals of Congress*, 18 Cong., 1 Sess., Appendix, 3051–52, 3056–57, 3063, esp. 3063.

28. Dearborn to the Marquis of Palmela, November 7, 1823, *Annals of Congress*, 18 Cong., 1 Sess., Appendix, 3062 (quotations "subject of a treaty" and "disposition to urge"); Dearborn to Silvestre Pinheiro Ferreira, April 18, 1823, *Annals of Congress*, 18 Cong., 1 Sess., Appendix, 3059–60, esp. 3060 (quotation "readily acquiesce"); Dearborn to Adams, January 26, March 4, 1824, *Annals of Congress*, 18 Cong., 1 Sess., Appendix, 3064 (quotation "existing circumstances"), 3065 (quotation "quite at leisure").

29. Theodorick Bland to Adams, November 2, 1818, box 5, Theodorick Bland Papers, MHS; Frabrício P. Prado, "In the Shadows of Empires: Trans-Imperial Networks and Colonial Identity in Bourbon Rio de la Plata" (Ph.D. diss., Emory University, 2009), 197–99; Prado, *Edge of Empire*, 81; Robert Hamilton to Jesse Tyson & Son, June 12, 1822, box 1, Jesse Tyson Records, MHS; Paul Beck, Jr., to Samuel Woodhouse, October 17, 1820, vol. 24, P.1845, Staufer Collection, HSP; Nixon & Walker to Thomas Hockley, June 13, 1821, "Account sales of Sundries received from on board the Ship Cherub," September 27, 1821, and "Amount sales of flour, &c. received from on board the Ship Little Cherub," November 24, 1821, box 2, Thomas Hockley letterbook, Hockley Family Papers, HSP.

30. William Gilchrist Miller to Adams, April 17, June 8, and September 14, 1821, CD, Montevideo, NARA–GA; Street, *Artigas and the Emancipation of Uruguay*, 329–36.

31. Street, *Artigas and the Emancipation of Uruguay*, 335–36.

32. Street, *Artigas and the Emancipation of Uruguay*, 335–36; Frega, "Alianzas y proyectos independistas," 19–63.

33. William Gilchrist Miller to Adams, September 14, 1821, CD, Montevideo, NARA–GA; Outward Foreign Manifests, NARA–MA.

34. Robert Hamilton to Jesse Tyson & Son, June 12, 1822, and Calvin Beck to Jesse Tyson & Son, June 20, 1822, both in box 1, Jesse Tyson Records, MHS; Prado, *Edge of Empire*, 178–80; Street, *Artigas and the Emancipation of Uruguay*, 337; William P. Ford to Thomas Tyson, August 5, 1823, box 2, Jesse Tyson Records, MHS; Outward Foreign Manifests, NARA–MA.

35. Prado, *Edge of Empire*, 1–11, 158.

36. Prado, *Edge of Empire*, 163–64, 166–67, 170; Ana Frega, "Cidadania e representação em tempos revolucionários: A banda/província oriental, 1810–1820," in José Murilo de Carvalho and Adriana Campos, eds., *Perspectivas da cidadania no Brasil império* (Rio de Janeiro: Civilização Brasileira, 2011), 59–86.

37. *Porstmouth Journal of Literature and Politics* (New Hampshire), March 23, 1822; *Independent Chronicle and Boston Patriot*, August 3, 1825.

38. Condy Raguet to Adams, September 11 (quotations) and September 12, 1824, Condy Raguet Official Letters, vol. 1, HSP; Sanford W. Higginbotham, "Philadelphia Commerce with Latin America, 1820–1830," *Pennsylvania History* 9 (October 1942), 262n28; Copy of Circular of Luis José de Carvalho e Melo, August 27, 1824, Condy Raguet Official Letters, vol. 1, HSP; Stephen Meardon, "Negotiating Free Trade in Fact and Theory: The Diplomacy and Doctrine of Condy Raguet," *European Journal of the History of Economic Thought* 21 (2014), 41–77.

39. Raguet to Adams, September 12, 1824, Condy Raguet Official Letters, vol. 1, HSP.

40. Hill to Adams, December 21, 1818, CD, St. Salvador, NARA–CP.

41. Hill to Adams, December 21, 1818, CD, St. Salvador, NARA–CP.

42. Raguet to John Vaughan, April 8, 1823, American Philosophical Society archives, APS; Raguet to Adams, October 5, 1824, Condy Raguet Official Letters, vol. 1, HSP.

43. Raguet to Adams, October 5, 1824, Condy Raguet Official Letters, vol. 1, HSP.

44. Hill to Sumpter, September 20, 1809, CD, St. Salvador, NARA–CP; Raguet to Adams, September 12, 1824, Condy Raguet Official Letters, vol. 1, HSP.

45. Raguet to Adams, October 5 and December 18, 1824, Condy Raguet Official Letters, vol. 1, HSP.

46. Paquette, *Imperial Portugal*, 147, 155–64; Kildare Gonçalves Carvalho, *Direito Constitucional: Teoria do Estado e da Constituição Direito Constitucional Positivo*, 14th ed. (São Paulo: Del Rey Editoria, 2008), 581–84; Roderick J. Barman, *Brazil: The Forging of a Nation, 1798–1852* (Stanford, CA: Stanford University Press, 1988), 66.

47. Cabral de Mello, *A outra independência*, 11–12; Adelman, *Sovereignty and Revolution*, 389 (quotation); Fitz, "Stalwart Motor," 48–49.

48. Cabral de Mello, *A outra independência*, 163–64, esp. 163 (quotation "American in ideas"); *Daily National Intelligencer*, September 23, 1824 (quotation "firm republican principles"); Fitz, "Stalwart Motor," 49.

49. Cabral de Mello, *A outra independência*, 163–64; Jeffrey C. Mosher, *Political Struggle, Ideology, and State Building: Pernambuco and the Construction of Brazil, 1817–1850* (Lincoln: University of Nebraska Press, 2008), 64–73.

50. Cabral de Mello, *A outra independência*, 164 (quotation "appease the court"); Fitz, "Stalwart Motor," 49 (quotation "showcasing their own"); *National Advocate*, November 25, 1823 (quotation "change of system"), and June 19, 1824.

51. Fitz, "Stalwart Motor," 49; *National Advocate*, June 19, 1824 (quotation).

52. Fitz, "Stalwart Motor," 46, 49–50, esp. 50.

53. Fitz, "Stalwart Motor," 51–52; Raguet to Adams, February 17, 1825, Condy Raguet Official Letters, vol. 1, HSP (quotation); Petition to James H. Bennett, September 21, 1824, CD, Pernambuco, NARA–CP.

54. Fitz, "Stalwart Motor," 53; J. P. B. Storer to John Vaughan, April 22, [n.d.], John Vaughan Papers, APS (quotation).

55. *Newport Mercury*, February 26, 1825; Figueira de Mello, *Ensaio sobre a Estatística Civil e Política*, draft, Chapter 7, BNRJ.

56. Figueira de Mello, *Ensaio sobre a Estatística Civil e Política*, draft, Chapter 7, BNRJ; Raguet to Adams, January 31, 1825, Condy Raguet Official Letters, vol. 1, HSP (recognition).

57. Higginbotham, "Philadelphia Commerce," 262–63; Raguet to Clay, January 9, 1827, Condy Raguet Official Letters, vol. 2, HSP. Girard does not appear as a shipper in any of the Outward Foreign Manifests destined to Brazil.

58. Meardon, "Negotiating Free Trade," 46–47.

59. Meardon, "Negotiating Free Trade," 47–48; Prado, *Edge of Empire*, 179–80.

60. Meardon, "Negotiating Free Trade," 47–49; Raguet to Clay, September 1, 1826, Condy Raguet Official Letters, vol. 2, HSP (quotation).

61. Raguet to Clay, September 23 and October 2, 1826, Condy Raguet Official Letters, vol. 2, HSP; José Silvestre Rebello to Henry Clay, November 14, 1827, in Manning, *Diplomatic Correspondence*, 2:862.

62. *National Advocate*, February 14, 1824; *Independent Chronicle and Boston Patriot*, August 3, 1825.

63. Outward Foreign Manifests, NARA–MA; "From Pernambuco," *Daily National Intelligencer*, November 29, 1824.

64. William Tudor to Henry Clay, September 11, 1828, in Manning, *Diplomatic Correspondence*, 2:865–66; Street, *Artigas and the Emancipation of Uruguay*, 368; Ana Frega, "La mediación británica en la guerra entre las Provincias Unidas y el Imperio del Brasil (1826–1828): Una mirada desde Montevideo," in Frega, *Historia regional*, 101–30; James C. Knarr, *Uruguay and the United States, 1903–1929: Diplomacy in the Progressive Era* (Kent, OH: Kent State University Press, 2012), 6; Peter Winn, "British Informal Empire in Uruguay in the Nineteenth Century," *Past and Present* 73 (November 1976), 100–108; "Treaty of Amity, Commerce, and Navigation," December 12, 1828, The Avalon Project: Documents in Law, History, and Diplomacy, Yale Law School, http://avalon.law.yale.edu/19th_century/brazil01.asp (accessed August 29, 2015); "Tratado de comércio e navegação, em catorze artigos, entre Portugal e os Estados Unidos da América," August 26, 1840, Direção-Geral do Livro, dos Arquivos e das Bibliotecas, https://digitarq.arquivos.pt/details?id = 4613547 (accessed September 18, 2018).

65. Bill of lading, October 22, 1823, box 210, Inward Foreign Manifests for the Port of Philadelphia, NARA–MA; B. H. Devereux to John Devereux, July 3, 1839, and to Baring Brothers & Co., August 8, 1840, and September 30, 1821, all in B. H. Devereux Letterbook, HSP.

66. Horne, *Deepest South*, 28 (quotation); Bruna Iglezias Mota Dourado, "Comércio de grosso trato e interesses mercantis no Recife, Pernambuco (c. 1837–c. 1871): A trajetória do negociante João Pinto de Lemos" (Ph.D. diss., Universidade Federal Fluminense, 2015), 34; Figueira de Mello, *Ensaio sobre a Estatística Civil e Política*, draft, Chapter 7, BNRJ; Haber and Klein, "Economic Consequences," 251.

67. Fitz, "Stalwart Motor," 48; *Pennsylvania Register*, October 11, 1828; Mota Dourado, "Comércio de grosso trato," 63–64; Haber and Klein, "Economic Consequences," 251.

68. Leonardo Marques, *The United States and the Transatlantic Slave Trade to the Americas, 1776–1867* (New Haven, CT: Yale University Press, 2016), 118–21; Horne, *Deepest South*, 8–10.

69. Marques, *United States*, 143, 223; Dale W. Tomich, "Civilizing America's Shore: British World-Economic Hegemony and the Abolition of the International Slave Trade (1814–1867)," in Dale W. Tomich, *The Politics of the Second Slavery* (New York: State University of New York Press, 2016), 15; Domingues da Silva, *Atlantic Slave Trade*, 28.

70. Horne, *Deepest South*, 8, 56, 58, esp. 56.

71. Horne, *Deepest South*, 113–14.

72. Horne, *Deepest South*, 107–27; Fitz, *Our Sister Republics*, 240–48.

73. Matthew Karp, *This Vast Southern Empire: Slaveholders at the Helm of American Foreign Policy* (Cambridge, MA: Harvard University Press, 2016), 58, 70–71, esp. 58.

74. Karp, *This Vast Southern Empire*, 58, 70–71, esp. 58. The *Liberator* quoted the *Southern Standard* at length and decried the plan "to reinstate slavery in St. Domingo and other places where it has been abolished, and plant it on all the interesting countries between Brazil and the United States (*Liberator* [Boston], April 28, 1854).

75. Horne, *Deepest South*, 103–4, 124, 127, 128–49.

Epilogue

1. Jefferson to William Short, August 4, 1820, in H. A. Washington, ed., *The Writings of Thomas Jefferson* (New York: Cambridge University Press, 2011), 7:168. First published 1854.

2. Haber and Klein, "Economic Consequences," 252–53.

3. Fitz, *Our Sister Republics*, 201–13, 227, esp. 205 (quotation "universal emancipation"), 208 (quotation "mixed breeds"), 227 (quotation "freedom will"); Karp, *This Vast Southern Empire*, 57–58.

4. "Sketch of Brazil," *Daily National Intelligencer*, November 20, 1839.

5. "Sketch of Brazil," *Daily National Intelligencer*, November 20, 1839; Paquette, *Imperial Portugal*, 382.

6. "Sketch of Brazil," *Daily National Intelligencer*, November 20, 1839; Mark Harris, *Rebellion on the Amazon: The Cabanagem, Race, and Popular Culture in the North of Brazil, 1798–1840* (New York: Cambridge University Press, 2010); Barman, *Brazil*, 182–88.

7. *Commercial Advertiser*, February 1, 1840; *Daily Picayune* (New Orleans), February 3, 1838.

8. Juliana Serzedello Crespim Lopes, "Liberdade, Liberdades: Dilemas da escravidão na Sabinada (Bahia, 1837–1838)," *Sankofa* 3 (December 2010), 25–42; Hendrik Kraay, "Daniel Gomes de Freitas: Liberal Conspiracy in the Early National Period," in Peter M. Beattie, ed., *The Human Tradition in Modern Brazil* (Wilmington, DE: SR Books, 2004), 16–19. The rebels moderated their declaration of independence days later, declaring their independence until Pedro II assumed majority age.

9. Horne, *Deepest South*, 28–29 (quotation "separatists, nullifiers & revolutionists"); *New Hampshire Gazette* (Portsmouth), April 3, 1838 (quotation "composed chiefly"); *Sun* (Baltimore), May 1, 1838 (quotations "city on fire" and "granted their freedom"); *Sun* quotations also in *Southern Patriot* (Charleston, SC), May 4, 1838.

10. *Southern Patriot*, February 23, 1838.

11. Extract of William Bainbridge to Henry Hill, December 12, 1812, CD, St. Salvador, NARA–CP; Mota, *Nordeste 1817*, 36; Adams, *Memoirs of John Quincy Adams*, 5:176; Jefferson to William Short, August 4, 1820, in Washington, *Writings of Thomas Jefferson*, 7:168.

Bibliography

MANUSCRIPT COLLECTIONS

Brazil

ARQUIVO NACIONAL, RIO DE JANEIRO

Códice 5—Inconfidência Mineira
Códice 107—Correspondência de Santa Catarina sobre Assuntos Diversos
Códice 212—Alfândega da Bahia
Códice 731—Balança do Comércio
Inconfidência Mineira—3A
Junta do Comércio, Mesas de Inspeção
Mapas de Importação e Exportação—Nordeste
Ministério dos Estrangeiros e da Guerra—4H-152
SDH—Miscellaneous boxes
Série Interior

BIBLIOTECA NACIONAL, RIO DE JANEIRO

Carta Régia, January 28, 1808
Coleção Linhares, 1803–1817
Discursos sobre vários artigos interessantes ao Reyno de Portugal e suas colônias
Documentos Diversos sobre a Bahia
Ensaio sobre Estatística Civil e Política da Província de Pernambuco, draft, Chapter 7
Mapa das fazendas e generos importados na Alfandega da Cidade do Rio de Janeiro em anno
  de 1803
Mapa das fazendas e generos importados na Alfandega da Cidade do Rio de Janeiro em anno
  de 1804
Mappa dos Trigos, Estrangeiros que se venderão no Terreiro Publico de Lisboa desde o anno
  de 1797 até 1812
Memória Sobre a Capitania das Minas Gerais
Relação dos principais cúmplices na revolução de Pernambuco, conduzidos prezos no Navio
  Carrasco chegado a Bahia a 8 de Junho de 1817

Portugal

ARQUIVO HISTÓRICO ULTRAMARINO, LISBON

Conselho Ultramarino

ARQUIVO NACIONAL—TORRE DO TOMBO, LISBON

Alfândegas de Lisboa
Junta do Comércio
Ministério dos Negócios Estrangeiros

United Kingdom

BRITISH LIBRARY, LONDON

Edward Long Papers

NATIONAL ARCHIVES, LONDON

Colonial State Papers
Naval Office Shipping Lists for New York

United States

CONNECTICUT

Thomas J. Dodd Center, Storrs

Henry Hill Papers

Yale University Library, New Haven

Alsop Family Papers

DELAWARE

Hagley Library, Wilmington

Andrew Clow Material
Dutilh & Wachsmuth Material
Dutilh & Wachsmuth Papers
Mifflin & Massey Business Papers
Miscellaneous Philadelphia Concerns
Miscellaneous Philadelphia Items
Morris Family Papers

DISTRICT OF COLUMBIA

Library of Congress, Washington

Galloway-Maxcy-Markoe Papers
James Madison Papers
Papers of Jonathan Meredith
Robert R. Livingston Papers
Thomas Jefferson Papers

National Archives and Records Administration, Washington
Records of District Courts of the United States

GEORGIA

National Archives and Records Administration, Atlanta
Despatches from U.S. Consuls in Montevideo

MARYLAND

Maryland Historical Society, Baltimore
Baltimore Customs Records
Charles Didier Collection
Jesse Tyson Records
John L. Thomas Ship Logs and Papers
John Smith & Sons Letterbooks
Mark Pringle Letterbooks
Robert Oliver Papers
Tench Tilghman Papers
Theodorick Bland Papers

National Archives and Records Administration, College Park
British Spoliations
Consular Instructions of the Department of State
Despatches from U.S. Consuls in Faial
Despatches from U.S. Consuls in Lisbon
Despatches from U.S. Consuls in Pernambuco
Despatches from U.S. Consuls in Rio de Janeiro
Despatches from U.S. Consuls in St. Salvador
Maryland Criminal Case Files
Miscellaneous Letters of the Department of State
U.S. House of Representatives Records

MASSACHUSETTS

Massachusetts Historical Society, Boston
Adams Family Papers

NEW YORK

New York Historical Society, New York
Jacob and Thomas Walden Letterbook
Lewis Pintard Letterbook
Nicholas Low Papers
Papers of Albert Gallatin

PENNSYLVANIA

American Philosophical Society, Philadelphia

American Philosophical Society Archives
Benjamin Franklin Papers
Corrêa da Serra Papers
Hare-Willing Family Papers
John Vaughan Papers
Miscellaneous Manuscripts Collection
William Temple Franklin Papers

Historical Society of Pennsylvania, Philadelphia

Ashhurst Family Papers
B. H. Devereux Letterbook
Chew Family Papers
Clifford Family Papers
Condy Raguet Official Letters
Cropley Rose Letterbook
Edward Wanton Smith Collection
H. B. Stewart Letterbook
Hockley Family Papers
Hollingsworth Family Papers
Jasper Yeates Brinton Collection
Jones & Clarke Papers
Morris Family Papers
Paul Beck, Last Will and Testament
Port of Philadelphia Captain's Reports
Reed & Forde Papers
Robert Waln Papers
Sarah A. G. Smith Collection
Staufer Collection
Thomas Riche Records
Willing Family Papers

Independence Seaport Museum, Philadelphia

Benjamin Etting Journal
Daniel Rea Papers
Mary Ray Papers
Newton & Gordon Papers

Library Company of Philadelphia, Philadelphia

John J. Smith Collection
McAllister Collection

National Archives and Records Administration, Mid-Atlantic, Philadelphia

Inward Foreign Manifests, Port of Philadelphia
Outward Foreign Manifests, Port of Philadelphia

Pennsylvania State Archives, Harrisburg
Baynton, Wharton, & Morgan Papers
Willing, Morris, & Swanwick Papers

NEWSPAPERS AND PERIODICALS

Alexandria Gazette
American Recorder
Baltimore Patriot
Caledonian Mercury
Commercial Advertiser
Daily National Intelligencer
Daily Picayune
Diary or Woodfall's Register
Enquirer
Evening Post
Examiner
Gazeta de Lisboa
Gazeta de Madrid
Gazeta do Rio de Janeiro
Gazette of the United States
Geneva Gazette
Gentleman's and London Magazine
Independent Chronicle and Boston Patriot
Liberator
Maryland Gazette and Political Intelligencer
Morning Chronicle
National Advocate
National Intelligencer
National Intelligencer and Washington Advertiser
New Hampshire Gazette
New-Jersey Telescope
Newport Mercury
New York Commercial Advertiser
Niles' Weekly Register
North American Review
Pennsylvania Gazette
Pennsylvania Journal and the Weekly Advertiser
Pittsburgh Gazette
Portsmouth Journal of Literature and Politics
Providence Patriot, Columbian Phenix
Public Register or the Daily Register of Commerce and Intelligence
Register of Pennsylvania
Savannah Republican

Scots Magazine
South Carolina and American General Gazette
South Carolina Gazette
Southern Patriot
Southern Standard
Sun
Supporter
United States Gazette
Virginia Gazette

PUBLISHED/EDITED PRIMARY SOURCES

Adams, Charles Francis, ed. *Memoirs of John Quincy Adams*. 5 vols. Philadelphia: J. B. Lippincott, 1875.

Aeolian Harp. 2 vols. New York, 1817.

Allardice, Samuel, Alexander Lawson, and John James Barralet. *The History of the British Empire, from the year 1765, to the end of 1783*. 2 vols. Boston, 1798.

"American Archives: Documents of the American Revolutionary Period, 1774–1776." DeKalb, IL: Northern Illinois University, 2015. http://amarch.lib.niu.edu/islandora/object/niu-amarch%3A79275.

American State Papers: Claims. Washington, DC: Gales and Seaton, 1834.

American State Papers: Commerce and Navigation. 2 vols. Washington, DC: Gales and Seaton, 1832–1834.

Annals of Congress. Debates and Proceedings, 1789–1824. 42 vols. Washington, DC: Gales and Seaton, 1834–1856.

Annals of the General Assembly of the Church of Scotland. Edinburgh: John Johnstone, 1840.

Anson, George. *A Voyage Round the World in the Years MDCCXL, I, II, III, IV*. London, 1748.

Balbi, Adrien. *Essai Statistique sur le Royaume de Portugal et D'Algarve, Comparé aux autres États de L'Europe*. 2 vols. Paris: Rey et Gravier, 1822.

Bourdon, Léon, ed. *José Corrêa da Serra: Ambassadeur du royaume-uni de Portugal et Brésil a Washington, 1816–1820*. Paris: Fundação Calouste Gulbenkian, 1975.

Brackenridge, Henry. *South America: A Letter on the Present State of that Country to James Monroe, President of the United States*. Washington, 1817.

Comisión Nacional. *Archivo Artigas*. 36 vols. Montevideo: Fanelcor, 2005.

Conde de Floridablanca. *Censo Español Executado de Órden del Rey Comunicada por el Excelentísimo Señor Conde de Floridablanca*. n.p., n.d.

Corrêa da Serra, José. *An Appeal to the Government and Congress of the United States Against the Depredations Committed by American Privateers on the Commerce of Nations at Peace with Us*. New York, 1819.

Crackel, Theodore J., ed. The Papers of George Washington Digital Edition. University of Virginia Press, 2008.

Documentos Históricos. Biblioteca Nacional, Divisão de Obras Raras e Publicações. 112 vols. 1928–1958.

Ford, Worthington C., ed. *Writings of John Quincy Adams*. 7 vols. New York, 1917.

Ford, Worthington C., Gaillard Hunt, et. al., eds. *Journals of the Continental Congress, 1774–1789.* 34 vols. Washington, DC: Government Printing Office, 1904.

Founders Online. National Historical Publications and Records Commission, National Archives. http://founders.archives.gov/.

[Gonçalves da Cruz, Antônio]. "Reply to the Author of the Letter on South America and Mexico." Philadelphia, 1817.

Gordon, William. *The History of the Rise, Progress, and Establishment, of the Independence of the United States of America.* 3 vols. New York, 1789.

Hamilton, Stanislaus Murray, ed. *The Writings of James Monroe, including a collection of his public and private papers and correspondence now for the first time printed.* 7 vols. New York, 1902.

Hopkins, F. S. *An Historical Sketch of the Island of Madeira.* London, 1819.

Jefferson, Thomas. "First Inaugural Address, March 4, 1801." The Avalon Project: Documents in Law, History, and Diplomacy. Yale Law School. avalon.law.yale.edu/19th_century/jefinaul.asp.

———. "A Summary View of the Rights of British America." 1774. The Avalon Project: Documents in Law, History, and Diplomacy. Yale Law School. avalon.law.yale.edu/18th_century/jeffsumm.asp.

Ketcham, Ralph L., ed. *The Political Thought of Benjamin Franklin.* Indianapolis: Hackett Publishing, 1965.

Koster, Henry. *Travels in Brazil.* London, 1816.

Lindley, Thomas. *Authentic Narrative of a Voyage from the Cape of Good Hope to Brasil.* London, 1808.

Livermore, Edward St. Loe. "Mr. Livermore's Speech in the House of Representatives." n.p. [Washington?], n.d. [1809?].

Lloyd, James. "Mr. Lloyd's Speeches in the Senate of the United States, on Mr. Hillhouse's Resolution to Repeal the Embargo Laws." n.p. 1808.

Manning, William Ray. *Diplomatic Correspondence of the United States Concerning the Independence of the Latin-American Nations.* 3 vols. New York, 1925.

Monroe, James, "Third Annual Message." December 7, 1819. The American Presidency Project, John Wooley and Gerhard Peters, eds. http://www.presidency.ucsb.edu/ws/?pid=29461.

Newton, Thomas. "Speech of Mr. Newton delivered in the House of Representatives of the United States." n.p. [Washington, DC?], 1810.

Oberg, Barbara B., and J. Jefferson Looney, eds. The Papers of Thomas Jefferson Digital Edition. University of Virginia Press, Rotunda, 2008–2015.

Pardon, William. *A New and Compendious System of Practical Arithmetick.* London, 1737.

Parliamentary Papers, House of Commons and Command. Vol. 49, pt. 2. London, 1846.

The Priviledges of an Englishman in the Kingdoms and Dominions of Portugal. London, 1759.

Rainsford, Marcus. *An Historical Account of the Black Empire of Hayti.* Edited by Paul Youngquist and Grégory Pierrot. Durham, NC: Duke University Press, 2013.

Raynal, Guillaume Thomas. *The Sentiments of a Foreigner, on the Disputes of Great-Britain with North America.* Philadelphia, 1775.

Report from Select Committee on the Sale of Corn. London, 1834.

Reports of Cases Argued and Determined in the Supreme Judicial Court of the Commonwealth of Massachusetts. Newburyport, 1811.

Reports of Cases Determined in the Circuit Court of the United States, for the Third Circuit. 2nd ed. Philadelphia: T. & J. W. Johnson, 1852.

Rutherford, John. *The Importance of the Colonies to Great Britain*. London, 1761. Edited by Jan-Michael Poff. The Colonial Records Project. http://www.ncpublications.com/colo nial/bookshelf/Tracts/Impo rtance/Defaul t.htm.

Sergeant, Thomas, and William Rawle, Jr. *Reports of Cases Adjudged in the Supreme Court of Pennsylvania*. 3rd ed. Vol. 1. Philadelphia: Kay & Brother, 1872.

Silva Maia, José Antonio da. *Memória da origem, progressos, e decadencia do duinto do ouro na provincia de Minas Geraes*. Rio de Janeiro, 1827.

Stagg, J. C. A., ed. The Papers of James Madison, Digital Edition. University of Virginia Press, 2010.

Taylor, C. James, ed. The Adams Papers, Digital Edition. University of Virginia Press, Rotunda, 2008–2015.

"Tratado de comércio e navegação, em catorze artigos, entre Portugal e os Estados Unidos da América." August 26, 1840. Direção-Geral do Livro, dos Arquivos e das Bibliotecas. https://digitarq.arquivos.pt/details?id=4613547.

"Treaty of Amity, Commerce, and Navigation." December 12, 1828. The Avalon Project: Documents in Law, History, and Diplomacy. Yale Law School. http://avalon.law.yale.edu/ 19th_century/brazil01.asp.

Tyng, Dudley Atkins. *Reports of Cases Argued and Determined in the Supreme Judicial Court of the Commonwealth of Massachusetts*. 16 vols. Newburyport, MA, 1811.

Vardill, John. "To the Worthy Inhabitants of the City of New-York." New York, 1773.

Washington, H. A., ed. *The Writings of Thomas Jefferson*. 9 vols. New York: Cambridge University Press, 2011. First published 1854.

Wharton, Francis, comp. *The Revolutionary Diplomatic Correspondence of the United States*. 6 vols. Washington, DC: Government Printing Office, 1889.

White, Samuel. "Mr. White's Speech in the Senate of the United States on Mr. Hillhouse's Resolution to Repeal the Embargo Laws." n.p. 1808.

Woods, Brett F., ed. *Thomas Jefferson: Diplomatic Correspondence*. New York: Algora Publishing, 2016.

PUBLISHED MONOGRAPHS/ARTICLES/COMPILATIONS

Aaslestad, Katherine B., and Johan Joor, eds. *Revisiting Napoleon's Continental System: Local, Regional and European Experiences*. New York: Palgrave, 2014.

Adams, Charles Francis, et. al. "Annual Meeting, April, 1910." *Proceedings of the Massachusetts Historical Society* 43 (October 1909–June 1910): 460–543.

Adelman, Jeremy. *Sovereignty and Revolution in the Iberian Atlantic*. Princeton, NJ: Princeton University Press, 2006.

Agan, Joseph Eugene. "Corrêa da Serra." *Pennsylvania Magazine of History and Biography* 49 (1925): 1–43.

Agresto, John T. "Liberty, Virtue, and Republicanism." *Review of Politics* 39 (1977): 473–504.

Aidar, Bruno. "Uma substituição luminosa: Tributação e reforma do antigo regime português em D. Rodrigo de Souza Coutinho ao final do século XVIII." *Nova Economia* 21 (January/April 2011): 138–56.

Alden, Dauril. "The Marquis of Pombal and the American Revolution." *Americas* 17 (April 1961): 369–76.

———. *Royal Government in Colonial Brazil: With Special Reference to the Administration of the Marquis of Lavradio, 1769–1799.* Berkeley: University of California Press, 1968.

Alexandre, Valentim. *Os sentidos do império: Questão nacional e questão colnial na crise do antigo regime português.* Porto: Edições Afrontamento, 1993.

Allan, David. *Scotland in the Eighteenth Century: Union and Enlightenment.* New York: Routledge, 2002.

Allison, Robert J. *The Crescent Obscured: The United States and the Muslim World, 1776–1815.* Chicago: University of Chicago Press, 1995.

Anderson, J. L. "Piracy and World History: An Economic Perspective on Maritime Predation." *Journal of World History* 6 (Fall 1995): 175–99.

Andreas, Peter. *Smuggler Nation: How Illicit Trade Made America.* New York: Oxford University Press, 2013.

Appleby, Joyce. *Capitalism and a New Social Order: The Republican Vision of the 1790s.* New York: New York University Press, 1984.

Armitage, David. "Three Concepts of Atlantic History." In David Armitage and Michael J. Braddick, eds. *The British Atlantic World, 1500–1800*, 13–29. New York: Palgrave-MacMillan, 2002.

Arruda, José Jobson de Andrade. *Uma colônia entre dois impérios: A abertura dos portos brasileiros, 1800–1808.* Bauru: EDUSC, 2008.

Barabási, Albert-László, and Réka Albert. "Emergence of Scaling in Random Networks." *Science* 286 (October 1999): 509–12.

Barman, Roderick J. *Brazil: The Forging of a Nation, 1798–1852.* Stanford, CA: Stanford University Press, 1988.

Bassi, Ernesto. *An Aqueous Territory: Sailor Geographies and New Granada's Transimperial Greater Caribbean World.* Durham, NC: Duke University Press, 2016.

Bast, Homer. "Tench Tilghman—Maryland Patriot." *Maryland Historical Magazine* 42 (June 1947): 71–94.

Beckert, Sven. *Empire of Cotton: A Global History.* New York: Alfred A. Knopf, 2015.

Beirão, Caetano. *Dona Maria I, 1777–1792: Subsídios para a Revisão da História do seu Reinado.* 4th ed. Lisbon: Empresa Nacional de Publicidade, 1944.

Ben-Atar, Doron S. *The Origins of Jeffersonian Commercial Policy and Diplomacy.* New York: Palgrave-MacMillan, 1993.

Benton, Lauren. *A Search for Sovereignty: Law and Geography in European Empires, 1400–1900.* New York: Cambridge University Press, 2010.

Beraza, Agustín. *Los corsarios de Artigas, 1816–1821.* Montevideo: Revista Histórica, 1949.

Berdell, John. *International Trade and Economic Growth in Open Economies: The Classical Dynamics of Hume, Smith, Ricardo, and Malthus.* Northampton, MA: Edward Elgar, 2002.

Blanning, T. C. W. *The Pursuit of Glory: Europe, 1648–1815.* New York: Viking, 2007.

Blaufarb, Rafe. "The Western Question: The Geopolitics of Latin American Independence." *American Historical Review* 112 (June 2007): 742–63.

Bolster, W. Jeffrey. *Black Jacks: African American Seamen in the Age of Sail.* Cambridge, MA: Harvard University Press, 1997.

Bornholdt, Laura. "Baltimore as a Port for Spanish-American Propaganda, 1810–1823." Ph.D. diss., Yale University, 1945.

Borschberg, Peter. *Hugo Grotius, the Portuguese, and Free Trade in the East Indies.* Singapore: NUS Press, 2011.

Borucki, Alex. *From Shipmates to Soldiers: Emerging Black Identities in the Río de la Plata.* Albuquerque: University of New Mexico Press, 2015.

Bowman, Larry G. "The Scarcity of Salt in Virginia During the American Revolution." *Virginia Magazine of History and Biography* 77 (October 1969): 464–72.

Boxer, C. R. "Brazilian Gold and British Traders in the First Half of the Eighteenth Century." *Hispanic American Historical Review* 49 (August 1969): 454–72.

———. *The Golden Age of Brazil, 1695–1750: Growing Pains of a Colonial Society.* Berkeley: University of California Press, 1962.

Brant, Irving. "Two Neglected Letters." *William and Mary Quarterly* 3 (October 1946): 569–87.

Breen, T. H. *The Marketplace of Revolution: How Consumer Politics Shaped American Independence.* New York: Oxford University Press, 2004.

Brewer, John. *The Sinews of Power: War, Money, and the English State.* New York: Alfred Knopf, 1989.

Brooks, George E. "The Observance of All Souls' Day in the Guinea-Bissau Region: A Christian Holy Day, an African Harvest Festival, an African New Year's Celebration, or All of the Above(?)" *History in Africa* 11 (January 1984): 1–34.

Brown, Gregory G. "The Impact of American Flour Imports on Brazilian Wheat Production: 1808–1822." *Americas* 47 (January 1991): 315–36.

Brown, Weldon A. *Empire or Independence: A Study in the Failure of Reconciliation, 1774–1783.* 2nd ed. Port Washington, NY: Kennikat Press, 1966.

Bukovansky, Mlada. "American Identity and Neutral Rights from Independence to the War of 1812." *International Organization* 51 (Spring 1997): 209–43.

Burns, E. Bradford, "The Role of Azeredo Coutinho in the Enlightenment of Brazil." *Hispanic American Historical Review* 44 (May 1964): 145–60.

Bushman, Richard Lyman. "Markets and Composite Farms in Early America." *William and Mary Quarterly* 55 (July 1998): 351–74.

Cabral, Flávio José Gomes. *Conversas reservadas: "Vozes públicas," conflitos políticos e rebeliões em Pernambuco no tempo da independência do Brasil.* Rio de Janeiro: Arquivo Nacional, 2013.

———. " 'Highly Important! Revolution in Brazil': A divulgação da república de Pernambuco de 1817 nos Estados Unidos." *Clio* 33, no. 1 (2015): 5–22.

Cabral de Mello, Evaldo. *A outra independência: O federalismo pernambucano de 1817 a 1824.* São Paulo: Editora 34, 2004.

Campbell, Randolph B. "The Spanish American Aspect of Henry Clay's American System." *Americas* 24 (July 1967): 3–17.

Cañizares-Esguerra, Jorge. *Puritan Conquistadors: Iberianizing the Atlantic, 1550–1700.* Stanford, CA: Stanford University Press, 2006.

Cañizares-Esguerra, Jorge, and Erik R. Seeman. *The Atlantic in Global History, 1500–2000.* Upper Saddle River, NJ: Pearson, 2007.

Cardim, Pedro, Tamar Herzog, José Javier Ruiz Ibáñez, and Gaetano Sabatini, eds. *Polycentric Monarchies: How Did Early Modern Spain and Portugal Achieve and Maintain a Global Hegemony?* Portland, OR: Sussex Academic Press, 2012.

Cardoso, José Luís. "Nas malhas do império: A economia política e a política colonial de D. Rodrigo de Souza Coutinho." In José Luís Cardoso, ed. *A economia política e os dilemas do império luso-brasileiro (1790–1822)*, 63–109. Lisbon: Comissão Nacional para as Comemorações dos Descobrimentos Portugueses, 2001.

Cardozo, Manoel S. "The Collection of the Fifths in Brazil, 1695–1709." *Hispanic American Historical Review* 20 (August 1940): 359–79.

Carp, Benjamin L. *Defiance of the Patriots: The Boston Tea Party and the Making of America*. New Haven, CT: Yale University Press, 2010.

Carvalho, Kildare Gonçalves. *Direito constitucional: Teoria do estado e da constituição direito constitucional positivo*. 14th ed. São Paulo: Del Rey Editora, 2008.

Carvalho, Marcus J. M. de. "O outro lado da independência: Quilombolas, negros e pardos em Pernambuco (Brazil), 1817–23." *Luso-Brazilian Review* 43 (2006): 1–30.

Çelikkol, Ayşe. "Free Trade and Disloyal Smugglers in Scott's *Guy Manering* and *Redgauntlet*." *ELH* 4 (Winter 2007): 759–82.

———. *Romances of Free Trade: British Literature, Laissez-Faire, and the Global Nineteenth Century*. New York: Oxford University Press, 2011.

Chaffin, Robert J. "The Townshend Acts of 1767." *William and Mary Quarterly* 27 (January 1970): 90–121.

Chandler, Charles Lyon. "List of United States Vessels in Brazil, 1792–1805, Inclusive." *Hispanic American Historical Review* 4 (November 1946): 599–602.

———. "United States Shipping in the La Plata Region, 1809–1810." *Hispanic American Historical Review* 3 (May 1920): 159–76.

Chandler, Paul. *Bound to the Hearth by the Shortest Tether: Village Life in China, Brazil*. New York: University Press of America, 2006.

Chasteen, John. *Americanos: Latin America's Struggle for Independence*. New York: Oxford University Press, 2008.

Chet, Guy. *The Ocean Is a Wilderness: Atlantic Piracy and the Limits of State Authority, 1688–1856*. Amherst: University of Massachusetts Press, 2014.

Chiaramonte, José Carlos. *Ciudades, Provincias, Estados: Orígenes de la Nación Argentina, 1800–1846*. Buenos Aires: Ariel Historia, 2007.

Clark, Victor S. *History of Manufactures in the United States, 1607–1860*. Washington, DC: Carnegie Institution of Washington, 1916.

Cloclet da Silva, Ana Rosa. *Inventando a nação: Intelectuais ilustrados e estadistas luso-brasileiros na crise do antigo regime português (1750–1822)*. São Paulo: Editora Hucitec, 2006.

Coelho, Philip. "The Profitability of Imperialism." *Explorations in Economic History* 10 (Spring 1973): 253–80.

Cogliano, Francis D. *Emperor of Liberty: Thomas Jefferson's Foreign Policy*. New Haven, CT: Yale University Press, 2014.

Colás, Alejandro, and Bryan Mabee. "The Flow and Ebb of Private Seaborne Violence in Global Politics: Lessons from the Atlantic World, 1689–1815." In Alejandro Colás and Bryan Mabee, eds. *Mercenaries, Bandits, Pirates and Empires: Private Violence in Historical Perspective*, 83–106. New York: Columbia University Press, 2010.

Copland, Samuel. *Wheat: Its History, Characteristics, Chemical Composition and Nutritive Properties*. London: Houlston and Wright, 1865.

Coronado, Raul. *A World Not to Come: A History of Latino Writing and Print Culture.* Cambridge, MA: Harvard University Press, 2013.

Correia de Andrade, Manuel. *A guerra dos Cabanos.* 2nd ed. Recife: Editora Universitaria, 2005.

———. *As raízes do separatismo no Brasil.* São Paulo: Editora UNESP Fundação, 1998.

Costello, Ray. *Black Salt: Seafarers of African Descent on British Ships.* Liverpool: Liverpool University Press, 2012.

Craig, Michelle L. "Grounds for Debate? The Place of the Caribbean Provisions Trade in Philadelphia's Prerevolutionary Economy." *Pennsylvania Magazine of History and Biography* 128 (April 2004): 149–77.

Crespim Lopes, Juliana Serzedello. "Liberdade, Liberdades: Dilemas da escravidão na Sabinada (Bahia, 1837–1838)." *Sankofa* 3 (December 2010): 25–44.

Croft, Pauline. "Free Trade and the House of Commons, 1605–6." *Economic History Review* 28 (February 1975): 17–27.

Davis, Richard Beale. "The Abbe Corrêa da Serra in America: The Contributions of the Diplomat and Natural Philosopher to the Foundations of Our National Life." *Transactions of the American Philosophical Society* 45 (1955): 90–121.

Delaforce, John. *The Factory House at Oporto.* London: Christie's Wine Publications, 1979.

Dias, Manuel Nunes. "Companhias versus companhias na competição colonial." *Revista de Historia de America* 84 (July–December 1977): 83–104.

———. "Os acionistas e o capital social da Companhia do Grão Pará e Maranhão (Os dois momentos: O da fundação (1755–1758) e o da véspera da extinção (1776))." *Cahiers du monde hispanique et luso-brésilien* 11 (1968): 29–52.

Dickinson, H. T. *Britain and the American Revolution.* New York: Routledge, 1998.

Doerflinger, Thomas M. *A Vigorous Spirit of Enterprise: Merchants and Economic Development in Revolutionary Philadelphia.* Chapel Hill: University of North Carolina Press, 1986.

Domingues da Silva, Daniel B. *The Atlantic Slave Trade from West Central Africa, 1780–1867.* New York: Cambridge University Press, 2017.

Dondlinger, Peter Tracy. *The Book of Wheat: An Economic History and Practical Manual of the Wheat Industry.* London: O. Judd, 1908.

Doria, Pedro. *1789: A história de Tiradentes e dos contrabandistas, assassinos, e poetas que lutaram pela independência do Brasil.* Rio de Janeiro: Nova Fronteira, 2013.

Duncan, T. Bentley. *Atlantic Islands: Madeira, the Azores and the Cape Verdes in Seventeenth-Century Commerce and Navigation.* Chicago: University of Chicago Press, 1972.

Dungan, Nicholas. *Gallatin: America's Swiss Founding Father.* New York: New York University Press, 2010.

Eacott, Jonathan. *Selling Empire: India in the Making of Britain and America, 1600–1830.* Chapel Hill: University of North Carolina Press, 2016.

Egnal, Marc. "The Changing Structure of Philadelphia's Trade with the British West Indies, 1750–1775." *Pennsylvania Magazine of History and Biography* 99 (April 1975): 156–79.

Ehrman, John. *The British Government and Commercial Negotiations with Europe, 1783–1793.* New York: Cambridge University Press, 1962.

Ekman, Ernst. "A Swedish Career in the Tropics: Johan Norderling (1760–1828)." *Swedish Pioneer* 15 (January 1964): 3–32.

Elliott, J. H. *Empires of the Atlantic World: Britain and Spain in America, 1492–1830.* New Haven, CT: Yale University Press, 2006.

Enthoven, Victor. "'That Abominable Nest of Pirates': St. Eustatius and the North Americans, 1680–1780." *Early American Studies* 10 (2012): 239–301.

Feldman, Noah. *The Three Lives of James Madison: Genius, Partisan, President.* New York: Random House, 2017.

Felipe de Alencastro, Luiz. *O trato dos viventes: Formação do Brasil no Atlântico Sul.* São Paulo: Companhia das Letras, 2000.

———. "The African Slave Trade and the Construction of the Iberian Atlantic." In Kerry Bystrom and Joseph R. Slaughter, eds. *Global South Atlantic,* 33–45. New York: Fordham University Press, 2018.

Ferling, John. *John Adams: A Life.* New York: Oxford University Press, 1992.

Ferreira, Roquinaldo. *Cross-Cultural Exchange in the Atlantic World: Angola and Brazil During the Era of the Slave Trade.* New York: Cambridge University Press, 2012.

Figueroa, Luis A. *Sugar, Slavery, and Freedom in Nineteenth-Century Puerto Rico.* Chapel Hill: University of North Carolina Press, 2005.

Finucane, Adrian. *The Temptations of Trade: Britain, Spain, and the Struggle for Empire.* Philadelphia: University of Pennsylvania Press, 2016.

Fisher, H. E. S. "Anglo-Portuguese Trade, 1700–1770." *Economic History Review* 16 (1963): 219–33.

———. *The Portugal Trade: A Study of Anglo-Portuguese Commerce, 1700–1770.* London: Methuen, 1971.

Fitz, Caitlin. *Our Sister Republics: The United States in an Age of American Revolutions.* New York: W. W. Norton, 2016.

———. "A Stalwart Motor of Revolutions: An American Merchant in Pernambuco, 1817–1825." *Americas* 65 (July 2008): 35–62.

Florentino, Manolo. *Em costas negras: Uma história do tráfico de escravos entre África e o Rio de Janeiro (séculos XVIII e XIX).* Rio de Janeiro: Companhia das Letras, 1997.

Fragoso, João Luís Ribeiro. *Homens de grossa aventura: Acumulação e heirarquia na praça mercantil do Rio de Janeiro (1790–1830).* Rio de Janeiro: Arquivo Nacional Órgão do Ministério da Justiça, 1992.

Fragoso, João and Manolo Florentino. *O Arcaísmo como projeto: Mercado atlântico, sociedade agrária e elite mercantile emu ma economia colonial tardia Rio de Janeiro, c. 1790–c. 1840.* 4th ed. Rio de Janeiro: Civilização Brasileira, 2001.

Fragoso, João and Maria de Fátima Silva Gouvêa. "Nas rotas da governação portuguesa: Rio de Janeiro e Costa da Mina, séculos XVII e XVIII." In João Fragoso, Manolo Florentino, Antônio Carlos Jucá, and Adriana Campos, eds. *Nas rotas do império: Eixos mercantis, tráfico e relações sociais no mundo português,* 25–72. Lisboa: ICCT, 2006.

Fragoso, João, Maria Fernanda Bicalho, and Maria de Fátima Silva Gouvêa, eds. *O antigo regime nos trópicos: A dinâmica imperial portuguesa (séculos XVI–XVIII).* Rio de Janeiro: Civilização Brasileira, 2001.

Frankel, Jeffrey A. "The 1807–1809 Embargo Against Great Britain." *Journal of Economic History* 42 (June 1982): 291–308.

Frega, Ana. "Alianzas y proyectos independistas en los inicios del 'Estado Cisplatino." In Ana Frega, ed. *Historia regional e independencia del Uruguay: Proceso histórico y revisión crítica de sus relatos,* 19–64. Montevideo: Ediciones de la Banda Oriental, 2009.

———. "Cidadania e representação em tempos revolucionários: A banda/província oriental, 1810–1820." In José Murilo de Carvalho and Adriana Campos, eds. *Perspectivas da cidadania no Brasil império,* 59–86. Rio de Janeiro: Civilização Brasileira, 2011.

———. "La mediación británica en la guerra entre las Provincias Unidas y el Imperio del Brasil (1826–1828): Una mirada desde Montevideo." In Ana Frega, ed. *Historia regional e independencia del Uruguay: Proceso histórico y revisión crítica de sus relatos*, 101–30. Montevideo: Ediciones de la Banda Oriental, 2009.

———. "La virtud y el poder: La soberania particular de los pueblos en el proyecto artiguista." In Noemí Goldman and Ricardo Salvatore, eds. *Caudillismos rioplatenses: Nuevas miradas a un viejo problema*, 101–34. Buenos Aires: Eudeba, 1998.

———. ed. *Historia regional e independencia del Uruguay: Proceso histórico y revisión crítica de sus relatos*. Montevideo: Ediciones de la Banda Oriental, 2009.

Furtado, Celso. *Formação econômica do Brasil*. 1959. Reprint, São Paulo: Companhia Editora Nacional, 2005.

Furtado, Júnia Ferreira. "José Joaquim da Rocha and the Proto-Independence Movement in Colonial Brazil." In Martin Brückner, ed. *Early American Cartographies*, 116–41. Chapel Hill: University of North Carolina Press, 2001.

Galpin, W. Freeman. "The American Grain Trade to the Spanish Peninsula, 1810–1814." *American Historical Review* 28 (October 1922): 24–44.

Games, Alison. "Atlantic History: Definitions, Challenges, and Opportunities." *American Historical Review* 111 (June 2006): 741–57.

Garitee, Jerome R. *The Republic's Private Navy: The American Privateering Business as Practiced by Baltimore During the War of 1812*. Middletown, CT: Wesleyan University Press, 1977.

Gay, Susan E. *Old Falmouth: The Story of the Town from the Days of the Killigrews to the Earliest Part of the 19th Century*. London: Headley Brothers, 1903.

Gilbert, Geoffrey. "The Role of Breadstuffs in American Trade, 1770–1790." *Explorations in Economic History* 14 (1977): 378–87.

Gilje, Paul A. *Free Trade and Sailors' Rights in the War of 1812*. New York: Cambridge University Press, 2013.

Gomes, Laurentino. *1808: Como uma rainha louca, um príncipe medroso e uma corte corrupta enganaram Napoleão e mudaram a História de Portugal e do Brasil*. São Paulo: Planeta, 2007.

Gould, Eliga H. *Among the Powers of the Earth: The American Revolution and the Making of a New World Empire*. Cambridge, MA: Harvard University Press, 2012.

Gregory, Desmond. *The Beneficent Usurpers: A History of the British in Madeira*. Cranbury, NJ: Associated University Presses, 1988.

Griffin, Charles C. "Privateering from Baltimore During the Spanish American Wars of Independence." *Maryland Historical Magazine* 35 (March 1940): 1–25.

Haber, Stephen, and Herbert S. Klein. "The Economic Consequences of Brazilian Independence." In Stephen Haber, ed. *How Latin America Fell Behind: Essays on the Economic Histories of Brazil and Mexico, 1800–1914*, 243–66. Stanford, CA: Stanford University Press, 1997.

Haggerty, Sheryllynne. *The British-Atlantic Trading Community, 1760–1810: Men, Women, and the Distribution of Goods*. Boston: Brill, 2006.

———. *'Merely for Money'? Business Culture in the British Atlantic, 1750–1815*. Liverpool: Liverpool University Press, 2012.

Hamnett, Brian R. "Process and Pattern: A Re-examination of the Ibero-American Independence Movements, 1808–1826." *Journal of Latin American Studies* 29 (May 1997): 279–328.

Hancock, David. *Oceans of Wine: Madeira and the Emergence of American Trade and Taste.* New Haven, CT: Yale University Press, 2009.

Harrington, Virginia D. *The New York Merchant on the Eve of the Revolution.* New York: Columbia University Press, 1935. Reprint, Gloucester, MA: P. Smith, 1964.

Harris, Mark. *Rebellion on the Amazon: The Cabanagem, Race, and Popular Culture in the North of Brazil, 1798–1840.* New York: Cambridge University Press, 2010.

Hartigan-O'Connor, Ellen. *The Ties That Buy: Women and Commerce in Revolutionary America.* Philadelphia: University of Pennsylvania Press, 2009.

Hawthorne, Walter. *From Africa to Brazil: Culture, Identity, and an Atlantic Slave Trade, 1600–1830.* New York: Cambridge University Press, 2010.

Head, David. "New Nations, New Connections: Spanish American Privateering from the United States and the Development of Atlantic Relations." *Early American Studies* 11 (Winter 2013): 161–75.

———. *Privateers of the Americas: Spanish American Privateering from the United States in the Early Republic.* Athens: University of Georgia Press, 2015.

———. "Sailing for Spanish America: The Atlantic Geopolitics of Privateering from the United States in the Early Republic." Ph.D. diss., University at Buffalo, State University of New York, 2009.

Herring, George C. *From Colony to Superpower: U.S. Foreign Relations Since 1776.* New York: Oxford University Press, 2008.

Herzog, Ben. *Revoking Citizenship: Expatriation in America from the Colonial Era to the War on Terror.* New York: New York University Press, 2015.

Hespanha, António Manuel. "A constituição do império português: Revisão de alguns enviesamentos correntes." In João Fragoso, Maria Fernanda Bicalho, and Maria de Fátima Silva Gouvêa, eds. *Antigo regime nos trópicos: A dinâmica imperial portuguesa (séculos XVI–XVIII),* 163–88. Rio de Janeiro: Civilização Brasileira, 2001.

———. "Antigo regime nos trópicos? Um debate sobre o modelo político do império colonial português." In João Fragoso and Maria de Fátima Gouvêa, eds. *Na trama das redes: Política e negócios no império português, séculos XVI–XVIII,* 43–93. Rio de Janeiro: Civilização Brasileira, 2010.

———. *Poder e instituições no antigo regime.* Lisbon: Edições Cosmos, 1992.

Higginbotham, Sanford W. "Philadelphia Commerce with Latin America, 1820–1830." *Pennsylvania History* 9 (October 1942): 252–66.

Higgins, Kathleen J. *Licentious Liberty in a Brazilian Gold-Mining Region: Slavery, Gender, and Social Control in Eighteenth-Century Sabará, Minas Gerais.* University Park: Pennsylvania State University Press, 1999.

Hill, Christopher. *The Century of Revolution, 1603–1714.* 2nd ed. New York: W. W. Norton, 1980.

Hillman, Henning, and Christina Gathmann. "Overseas Trade and the Decline of Privateering." *Journal of Economic History* 71 (September 2011): 730–61.

Hinderaker, Eric. *Elusive Empires: Constructing Colonialism in the Ohio Valley, 1673–1800.* New York: Cambridge University Press, 1997.

Hopkins, Fred. "For Freedom and Profit: Baltimore Privateers in the Wars of South American Independence." *Northern Mariner / Le marin du nord* 18 (July–October 2008): 93–104.

Hornbeck, Stanley K. "The Most-Favored-Nation Clause." *American Journal of International Law* 3 (July 1909): 619–47.

310   Bibliography

Horne, Gerald. *The Deepest South: The United States, Brazil, and the African Slave Trade.* New York: New York University Press, 2007.

Hunter, Brooke. "The Prospect of Independent Americans: The Grain Trade and Economic Development during the 1780s." *Explorations in Early American Culture* 5 (2001): 260–87.

———. "Wheat, War, and the American Economy During the Age of Revolution." *William and Mary Quarterly* 62 (July 2005): 505–26.

Huston, James L. "Virtue Besieged: Virtue, Equality, and the General Welfare in the Tariff Debates of the 1820s." *Journal of the Early Republic* 14 (Winter 1994): 523–47.

Jack, Malcom. "Destruction and Regeneration: Lisbon, 1755." In Theodore E. D. Braun and John B. Radner, eds. *The Lisbon Earthquake of 1755: Representations and Reactions,* 7–20. Oxford: Voltaire Foundation, 2005.

Jarvis, Michael J. *In the Eye of All Trade: Bermuda, Bermudians, and the Maritime Atlantic World, 1680–1783.* Chapel Hill: University of North Carolina Press, 2010.

Jarvis Cutts, Mary Pepperell Sparhawk. *The Life and Times of Hon. William Jarvis.* New York: Hurd and Houghton, 1869.

Johnson, Lyman L. *Workshop of Revolution: Plebeian Buenos Aires and the Atlantic World, 1776–1810.* Durham, NC: Duke University Press, 2011.

Jordaan, Han, and Victor Wilson. "The Eighteenth-Century Danish, Dutch and Swedish Free Ports in the Northeastern Caribbean: Continuity and Change." In Gert Oostindie and Jessica V. Roitman, eds. *Dutch Atlantic Connections, 1680–1800: Linking Empires, Bridging Borders,* 275–308. Boston: Brill, 2014.

Jordon, John W., ed. *Colonial and Revolutionary Families of Pennsylvania: Genealogical and Personal Memoirs.* 3 vols. Baltimore: Clearfield, 1978.

Karp, Matthew. *This Vast Southern Empire: Slaveholders at the Helm of American Foreign Policy.* Cambridge, MA: Harvard University Press, 2016.

Kastor, Peter J. *The Nation's Crucible: The Louisiana Purchase and the Creation of America.* New Haven, CT: Yale University Press, 2004.

Kent, Neil. *The Soul of the North: A Social, Architectural and Cultural History of the Nordic Countries, 1700–1940.* London: Reaktion, 2000.

Kiddy, Elizabeth W. *Blacks of the Rosary: Memory and History in Minas Gerais, Brazil.* University Park: University of Pennsylvania Press, 2005.

Kingston, Christopher. "Marine Insurance in Philadelphia During the Quasi-War with France, 1795–1801." *Journal of Economic History* 71 (March 2011): 162–84.

Klein, Herbert S. "The Portuguese Slave Trade from Angola in the Eighteenth Century." *Journal of Economic History* 32 (December 1972): 894–918.

Klooster, Wim. "Inter-imperial Smuggling in the Americas, 1600–1800." In Bernard Bailyn and Patricia L. Denault, eds. *Soundings in Atlantic History,* 141–80. Cambridge, MA: Harvard University Press, 2009.

Knarr, James C. *Uruguay and the United States, 1903–1929: Diplomacy in the Progressive Era.* Kent, OH: Kent State University Press, 2012.

Koot, Christian J. "Balancing Center and Periphery." *William and Mary Quarterly* 69 (January 2012): 41–46.

Kraay, Hendrik. "Daniel Gomes de Freitas: Liberal Conspiracy in the Early National Period." In Peter M. Beattie, ed. *The Human Tradition in Modern Brazil,* 5–22. Wilmington, DE: SR Books, 2004.

Kühn, Fábio. "Os interesses do governador: Luiz Garcia de Bivar e os negociantes da Colônia do Sacramento (1749–1760)." *Topoi* 13 (January/June 2012): 29–42.

Kwass, Michael. *Contraband.* Cambridge, MA: Harvard University Press, 2014.

Ladhams, John. "In Search of West African Pidgin Portuguese." *Revista Internacional de Lingüística Iberoamericana* 4 (January 2006): 87–105.

Lahmeyer Lobo, Eulália Maria. "O comércio atlântico e a comunidade de mercadores no Rio de Janeiro e em Charleston no século XVIII." *Revista de história* 101 (1975): 49–106.

Landers, Jane. *Black Society in Spanish Florida.* Chicago: University of Illinois Press, 1999.

Lapa, José Roberto do Amaral. *O antigo sistema colonial.* São Paulo: Editora Brasiliense, 1982.

Lee, Jean B. *The Price of Nationhood: The American Revolution in Charles County.* New York: W. W. Norton, 1994.

Lee, R. D., and R. S. Schofield. "British Population in the Eighteenth Century." In Roderick Floud, and Donald McCloskey, eds. *The Economic History of Britain Since 1700.* vol. 1, 17–35. New York: Cambridge University Press, 1981.

Lewis, James E., Jr. *The American Union and the Problem of Neighborhood: The United States and the Collapse of the Spanish Empire, 1783–1829.* Chapel Hill: University of North Carolina Press, 1998.

Lloyd, Martin. *The Passport: The History of Man's Most Travelled Document.* Stroud, UK: Sutton, 2003.

Long, David F. *Gold Braid and Foreign Relations: Diplomatic Activities of U.S. Naval Officers, 1798–1883.* Annapolis: Naval Institute Press, 1988.

Lopes, Carlos, ed. *Mansas, escravos, grumetes e gentio: Cacheu na encruzlihada de civilizaçoes.* Lisbon: Instituto Nacional de Estudos e Pesquisa, Imprensa Nacional—Casa da Moeda, 1993.

Lopez, Adriana. *De cães a lobos-de-mar: Súditos ingleses no Brasil.* São Paulo: Editora Senac São Paulo, 2007.

Loveman, Brian. *No Higher Law: American Foreign Policy and the Western Hemisphere Since 1776.* Chapel Hill: University of North Carolina Press, 2010.

Lux, William R. "French Colonization in Cuba, 1791–1809." *Americas* 29 (July 1972): 57–61.

Lydon, James G. "Fish and Flour for Gold, 1600–1800: Southern Europe in the Colonial Balance of Payments." Philadelphia: Library Company of Philadelphia, 2008. www.library company.org/economics/PDF%20Files/lydon_we b.pdf.

Mahan, Alfred Thayer. *Sea Power in Its Relations to the War of 1812.* 2 vols. Boston: Little, Brown, 1905.

Malberba, Jurandir. *A corte no exílio: Civilização e poder no Brasil às vésperas da independência (1808 a 1821).* São Paulo: Companhia das Letras, 2000.

Mann, Bruce H. *Republic of Debtors: Bankruptcy in the Age of American Independence.* Cambridge, MA: Harvard University Press, 2002.

Marques, Leonardo. *The United States and the Transatlantic Slave Trade to the Americas, 1776–1867.* New Haven, CT: Yale University Press, 2016.

Martins Ribeiro, Jorge Manuel. "Comércio e diplomacia nas relações luso-americanas (1776–1822)." Ph.D. diss., University of Porto, 1997.

Marzagalli, Silvia. "Establishing Transatlantic Trade Networks in Time of War: Bordeaux and the United States, 1793–1815." *Business History Review* 79 (Winter 2005): 811–44.

Mason, Matthew. "Keeping Up Appearances: The International Politics of Slave Trade Abolition in the Nineteenth-Century Atlantic World." *William and Mary Quarterly* 66 (October 2009): 809–32.

Matson, Cathy. *Merchants and Empire: Trading in Colonial New York*. Baltimore: Johns Hopkins University Press, 1998.

Mauro, Frédéric. "Le Rôle économique de la fiscalité dans le Brésil Colonial (1500–1800)." *Caravelle* 5 (1965): 93–102.

———. "Political and Economic Structures of Empire, 1580–1750." In Leslie Bethell, ed. *Colonial Brazil*, 39–66. New York: Cambridge University Press, 1987.

Maxwell, Kenneth. *Conflicts and Conspiracies: Brazil and Portugal, 1750–1808*. New York: Routledge, 2004.

———. *Naked Tropics: Essays on Empire and Other Rogues*. New York: Routledge, 2003.

———. *Pombal: Paradox of the Enlightenment*. New York: Cambridge University Press, 1995.

———. "Portuguese America." *International History Review* 6 (November 1984): 529–50.

———. "The Spark: Pombal, the Amazon, and the Jesuits." *Portuguese Studies* 17 (2001): 168–83.

McCarthy, Matthew. *Privateering, Piracy and British Policy in Spanish America, 1810–1830*. Rochester: University of Rochester Press–Boydell and Brewer, 2013.

McCoy, Drew. *The Elusive Republic: Political Economy in Jeffersonian America*. Chapel Hill: University of North Carolina Press, 1980.

McCusker, John J. *Essays in the Economic History of the Atlantic World*. New York: Routledge, 1997.

McCusker, John J., and Russell R. Menard. *The Economy of British America, 1607– 1789, with Supplementary Bibliography*. Chapel Hill: University of North Carolina Press, 1991.

McMaster, John Bach. *A History of the People of the United States*. 1883. 8 vols. Reprint, New York: Cosimo, 2006.

Meardon, Stephen. "Negotiating Free Trade in Fact and Theory: The Diplomacy and Doctrine of Condy Raguet." *European Journal of the History of Economic Thought* 21 (2014): 41–77.

Medeiros dos Santos, Corsino. *O tráfico de escravos do Brasil para o Rio da Prata*. Brasília: Senado Federal, 2010.

Mendonça Bernardes, Denis Antônio de. *O patriotismo constitucional: Pernambuco, 1820–1822*. São Paulo: Editora Universitária UFPE, 2006.

Middlekauff, Robert. *The Glorious Cause: The American Revolution, 1763–1789*. New York: Oxford University Press, 1982.

Miller, Joseph C. *Way of Death: Merchant Capitalism and the Angolan Slave Trade, 1730–1830*. Madison: University of Wisconsin Press, 1988.

Molesky, Mark. *This Gulf of Fire: The Great Lisbon Earthquake, or Apocalypse in the Age of Science and Reason*. New York: Vintage Books, 2016.

Morgan, David. *The Devious Dr. Franklin, Colonial Agent: Benjamin Franklin's Years in London*. Macon, GA: Mercer University Press, 1996.

Morrison, A. J. "Arnold Henry Dohrman." *Ohio Archaeological and Historical Publications* 23 (1914): 227–31.

Mosher, Jeffrey C. *Political Struggle, Ideology, and State Building: Pernambuco and the Construction of Brazil, 1817–1850*. Lincoln: University of Nebraska Press, 2008.

Mota, Carlos Guilherme. *Nordeste 1817: Estruturas e argumentos*. São Paulo: Editora da Universidade de São Paulo, 1972.

Mota Dourado, Bruna Iglezias. "Comércio de grosso trato e interesses mercantis no Recife, Pernambuco (c. 1837–c.1871): A trajetória do negociante João Pinto de Lemos." Ph.D. diss., Universidade Federal Fluminense, 2015.

Moutoukias, Zacarías. *Contrabando y control colonial en el siglo XVII: Buenos Aires, el Atlántico y el espacio peruano.* Biblioteca Universitarias, Buenos Aires: Centro Editor de América Latina, 1988.

Nozes, Judite. *The Lisbon Earthquake of 1755: Some British Eye-Witness Accounts.* Lisbon: British Historical Society of Portugal, 1987.

Onuf, Nicholas, and Peter Onuf. *Nations, Markets, and War: Modern History and the American Civil War.* Charlottesville: University of Virginia Press, 2006.

Ormrod, David. *The Rise of Commercial Empires: England and the Netherlands in the Age of Mercantilism, 1650–1770.* New York: Cambridge University Press, 2003.

O'Shaughnessy, Andrew Jackson. *An Empire Divided: The American Revolution and the British Caribbean.* Philadelphia: University of Pennsylvania Press, 2000.

Outhwaite, R. B. *Dearth, Public Policy and Social Disturbance in England, 1550–1800.* New York: Cambridge University Press, 1991.

Owen, John M. *Liberal Peace, Liberal War: American Politics and International Security.* Ithaca, NY: Cornell University Press, 1997.

Paquette, Gabriel. *Imperial Portugal in the Age of Atlantic Revolutions.* New York: Cambridge University Press, 2013.

Pedreira, Jorge M. "From Growth to Collapse: Portugal, Brazil, and the Breakdown of the Old Colonial System (1760–1830)." *Hispanic American Historical Review* 80 (November 2000): 839–64.

Pereira das Neves, Guilherme. "Guardar mais silêncio do que falar: Azeredo Coutinho, Ribeiro dos Santos e a escravidão." In José Luís Cardoso, ed. *A economia política e os dilemas do império luso-brasileiro (1790–1822),* 13–62. Lisbon: Comissão Nacional para as Comemorações dos Descobrimentos Portugueses, 2001.

Pereira das Neves, Lúcia Maria Bastos. *Corcundas e constitucionais: A cultura política da independência, 1820–1822.* Rio de Janeiro: Revan, FAPERJ, 2003.

Piecuch, James J. "A War Averted: Luso-American Relations in the Revolutionary Era, 1775–1786." *Portuguese Studies Review* 5 (Fall–Winter): 22–36.

Pijning, Ernst. "Contrabando, ilegalidade e medidas políticas no Rio de Janeiro do século XVIII." *Revista Brasileira de História* 21 (2001): 397–414.

———. "Controlling Contraband: Mentality, Economy, and Society in Eighteenth-Century Rio de Janeiro." Ph.D. diss., Johns Hopkins University, 1997.

Pincus, Steve. "Rethinking Mercantilism: Political Economy, the British Empire, and the Atlantic World in the Seventeenth and Eighteenth Centuries." *William and Mary Quarterly* 69 (January 2012): 3–34.

Pinho Candido, Mariana. *Fronteras de esclavización: Esclavitud, comercio e identidad en Benguela, 1780–1850.* Mexico City: El Colegio de México, 2011.

Pocock, J. G. A. *The Machiavellian Moment: Florentine Political Thought and the Atlantic Republican Tradition.* Princeton, NJ: Princeton University Press, 1975.

Pope, Peter E., *Fish into Wine: The Newfoundland Plantation in the Seventeenth Century.* Chapel Hill: University of North Carolina Press, 2004.

Prado, Fabrício. "Addicted to Smuggling: Contraband Trade in Eighteenth-Century Brazil and Rio de la Plata." In Christoph, Rosenmüller, ed. *Corruption in the Iberian Empires: Greed, Custom, and Colonial Networks,* 197–214. Albuquerque: University of New Mexico Press, 2017.

———. *Edge of Empire: Atlantic Networks and Revolution in Bourbon Río de la Plata*. Oakland: University of California Press, 2015.

———. "In the Shadows of Empires: Trans-Imperial Networks and Colonial Identity in Bourbon Rio de la Plata." Ph.D. diss., Emory University, 2009.

Price, Jacob M. "New Time Series for Scotland's and Britain's Trade with the Thirteen Colonies and States, 1740–1791." *William and Mary Quarterly* 32 (April 1975): 307–25.

Quintão, Antonia Aparecida. *Lá vem o meu parente: As irmandades de pretos e pardos no Rio de Janeiro e em Pernambuco (século XVIII)*. São Paulo: Annablume editora, 2002.

Rabushka, Avlin. *Taxation in Colonial America*. Princeton, NJ: Princeton University Press, 2008.

Raminelli, Ronald. *Nobrezas do Novo Mundo: Brasil e ultramar hispânico, séculos XVII e XVIII*. Rio de Janeiro: Editora FGV, 2015.

Rao, Gautham. *National Duties: Custom Houses and the Making of the American State*. Chicago: University of Chicago Press, 2016.

Rao, Sujay. "Arbiters of Change: Provincial Elites and the Origins of Federalism in Argentina's Littoral, 1814–1820." *Americas* 64 (April 2008): 511–46.

Rau, Louise. "Dutilh Papers." *Bulletin of the Business Historical Society* 13 (November 1939): 73–74.

Reeder, Tyson. "Liberty with the Sword: Jamaican Maroons, Haitian Revolutionaries, and American Liberty." *Journal of the Early Republic* 37 (Spring 2017): 81–115.

Ricupero, Rodrigo. "O estabelecimento do exclusivo comercial metropolitano e a conformação do antigo sistema colonial no Brasil." *História* 35 (December 19, 2016). https://dx.doi.org/10.1590/1980–436920160000000100.

Ritcheson, C. R. "The Earl of Shelburne and Peace with America, 1782–1783: Vision and Reality." *International History Review* 5 (August 1983): 322–45.

Robson, Martin. *Britain, Portugal, and South America in the Napoleonic Wars: Alliances and Diplomacy in Economic Maritime Conflict*. New York: I. B. Tauris, 2011.

Rocha, António Penalves. "A economia política na desagregação do império português." In José Luís Cardoso, ed. *A economia política e os dilemas do império luso-brasileiro (1790–1822)*, 149–97. Lisbon: Comissão Nacional para as Comemorações dos Descobrimentos Portugueses, 2001.

Rodrigues da Silva, Júlio. "A guerra da independência dos E.U.A. e os diplomatas portugueses. Luís Pinto de Sousa Coutinho e os primórdios do conflito (1774–1776)." In vol. 2 of *Actas do XV colóquio de história militar—Portugal militar nos séculos XVII e XVIII até às vésperas das invasões francesas*. Lisbon: Comissão Portuguesa de História Militar, 2006. http://www.fcsh.unl.pt/chc/pdfs/guerraindependencia.pdf.

Rodríguez, Horacio, and Pablo E. Arguindeguy. *El corso rioplatense*. Buenos Aires: Instituto Browniano, 1996.

Rodríguez, Mario. "Dom Pedro of Braganza and Colônia do Sacramento, 1680–1705." *Hispanic American Historical Review* 38 (May 1958): 179–208.

Romeiro, Adriana. *Paulistas e emboabas no coração da Minas: Idéias, práticas, e imaginário político no século XVIII*. Belo Horizonte: Editora UFMG, 2008.

Salvucci, Linda K. "Atlantic Intersections: Early American Commerce and the Rise of the Spanish West Indies (Cuba)." *Business History Review* 79 (2005): 781–809.

Savelle, Max. *Empires to Nations: Expansion in America, 1713–1824*. St. Paul, MN: North Central, 1974.

Schlesinger, Arthur M. *The Colonial Merchants and the American Revolution, 1763–1776.* New York: Columbia University, 1918.

Schneider, Susan. *O Marquês de Pombal e o vinho do Porto: Dependência e subdesenvolvimento em Portugal no século XVIII.* Lisbon: A Regra do Jogo, 1980.

Schondorfer Braz, Fabiana, and Paulo Fillipy de Souza Conti. "D. José da Cunha de Azeredo Coutinho: Um bispo ilustrado em Pernambuco." *Revista Temmpo Histórico* 5 (2013): 1–18.

Schultz, Kirsten. *Tropical Versailles: Empire, Monarchy, and the Portuguese Royal Court in America, 1808–1821.* New York: Routledge, 2001.

Schwartz, Stuart B. *Sugar Plantations in the Formation of Brazilian Society: Bahia, 1550–1835.* New York: Cambridge University Press, 1985.

Scott, H. M. *British Foreign Policy in the Age of the American Revolution.* New York: Oxford University Press, 1990.

Sellers, M. N. S. *American Republicanism: Roman Ideology in the United States Constitution.* New York: New York University Press, 1994.

Sexton, Jay. *The Monroe Doctrine: Empire and Nation in Nineteenth-Century America.* New York: Hill and Wang, 2011.

Sharrer, G. Terry. "The Merchant-Millers: Baltimore's Flour Milling Industry, 1783–1860." *Agricultural History* 56 (January 1982): 138–50.

Shrady, Nicholas. *The Last Day: Wrath, Ruin, and Reason in the Great Lisbon Earthquake of 1755.* New York: Viking, 2008.

Shumway, Nicolas. *The Invention of Argentina.* (Berkeley: University of California Press, 1991).

Sideri, S. *Trade and Power: Informal Colonialism in Anglo-Portuguese Relations.* Rotterdam: Rotterdam University Press, 1970.

Silverstone, Paul H. *The Sailing Navy, 1775–1854.* New York: Routledge, 2006.

Simon, André L., ed. *The Bolton Letters: The Letters of an English Merchant in Madeira 1695–1714.* 2 vols. London: T. Werner Laurie, 1928.

Simon, Fabrizio. "Criminology and Economic Ideas in the Age of Enlightenment." *History of Economic Ideas* 17 (2009): 11–39.

Siqueira, Antonio Jorge. "Bispo Coutinho e o clero ilustrado de Pernambuco na Revolução de 1817." *Revista Brasileira de História das Religiões* 14 (September 2012): 153–65.

Smith, Joshua M. *Borderland Smuggling: Patriots, Loyalists, and Illicit Trade in the Northeast, 1783–1820.* Gainesville: University Press of Florida, 2006.

Soltow, James H. "Thomas Riche's 'Adventure' in French Guiana, 1764–1766." *Pennsylvania Magazine of History and Biography* 83 (October 1959): 409–19.

Sombra, S. *História monetário do Brasil colonial.* Rio de Janeiro, 1938.

Stein, Douglas L. *American Maritime Documents, 1776–1860.* Mystic, CT: Mystic Seaport Museum, 1992.

Stewart, David O. *Madison's Gift: Five Partnerships that Built America.* New York: Simon & Schuster, 2015.

Street, John. *Artigas and the Emancipation of Uruguay.* New York: Cambridge University Press, 1959.

Sutherland, Lucy S. *A London Merchant, 1695–1774.* London: Frank Cass, 1962.

Szuchman, Mark D. "From Imperial Hinterland to Growth Pole: Revolution, Change, and Restoration in the Río de la Plata." In Mark D. Szuchman, and Jonathan C. Brown, eds.

Revolution and Restoration: The Rearrangement of Power in Argentina, 1776–1860, 1–26. Lincoln: University of Nebraska Press, 1994.

Taylor, Alan. *American Colonies: The Settling of North America*. New York: Penguin Group, 2001.

———. *American Revolutions: A Continental History, 1750–1804*. New York: W. W. Norton, 2016.

Thomson, Janice E. *Mercenaries, Pirates, and Sovereigns: State-Building and Extraterritorial Violence in Early Modern Europe*. Princeton, NJ: Princeton University Press, 1994.

Tiedemann, Joseph T. *Reluctant Revolutionaries: New York City and the Road to Independence, 1763–1776*. Ithaca, NY: Cornell University Press, 1997.

Tomich, Dale W. "Civilizing America's Shore: British World-Economic Hegemony and the Abolition of the International Slave Trade (1814–1867)." In Dale W. Tomich. *The Politics of the Second Slavery*, 1–24. New York: State University of New York Press, 2016.

Torpey, John. *The Invention of the Passport: Surveillance, Citizenship, and the State*. Cambridge: Cambridge University Press, 2000.

Trans-Atlantic Slave Trade Database. http://slavevoyages.org/voyages/F3OxRNZ3.

Truxes, Thomas M. *Defying Empire: Trading with the Enemy in Colonial New York*. New Haven, CT: Yale University Press, 2008.

Tyler, John W. *Smugglers and Patriots: Boston Merchants and the Advent of the American Revolution*. Boston: Northeastern University Press, 1986.

Ubbelohde, Carl. *The Vice-Admiralty Courts and the American Revolution*. Chapel Hill: University of North Carolina Press, 1960.

U.S. Bureau of the Census, *Historical Statistics of the United States: Colonial Times to 1970*. Bicentennial ed. Part 2. Washington, DC, 1975.

U.S. Department of Agriculture. *Agricultural Statistics*. Washington, DC: Government Printing Office, 2005.

Valério, Nuno, ed. *Estatísticas históricas portuguesas*. 2 vols. Lisbon: Instituto Nacional de Estatística Portugal, 2001.

Varnhagen, Francisco Adolfo. *Historia geral do Brasil*. Edited by António Paim. Salvador: Centro de Documentação do Pensamento Brasileiro, 2011. www.cdpb.org.br/varnhagen_historia_geral.pdf.

Vidales, Carlos. "Corsarios y piratas de la Revolución Francesa en las aguas de la emancipación hispanoamericana." *Caravelle* 54 (1990): 247–62.

Vivian, James F. "The Paloma Claim in United States and Venezuelan-Colombian Relations, 1818–1826." *Caribbean Studies* 14 (January 1975): 57–72.

Wadsworth, James E. *In Defence of the Faith: Joaquim Marquês de Araújo, A Comissário in the Age of Inquisitional Decline*. Montreal: McGill-Queen's University Press, 2013.

Walford, A. H. *The British Factory in Lisbon*. Lisbon: Instituto britânico em Portugal, 1940.

Walker, Timothy. "Atlantic Dimensions of the American Revolution: Imperial Priorities and the Portuguese Reaction to the North American Bid for Independence (1775–1783)." *Journal of Early American History* 2 (2012): 247–85.

Ward, Harry M. *The War for Independence and the Transformation of American Society*. New York: Routledge, 1999.

Whitaker, Arthur P. *The United States and the Independence of Latin America*. New York: W. W. Norton, 1964.

Wilcken, Patrick. *Empire Adrift: The Portuguese Court in Rio de Janeiro, 1808–1821*. New York: Bloomsbury, 2005.

Williams, Greg H. *The French Assault on American Shipping, 1793–1813: A History and Comprehensive Record of Merchant Marine Losses*. Jefferson, NC: McFarland, 2009.

Winn, Peter. "British Informal Empire in Uruguay in the Nineteenth Century." *Past and Present* 73 (November 1976): 100–26.

Wood, Gordon S. *The American Revolution: A History*. Toronto: Modern Library, 2002.

Zahedieh, Nuala. *The Capital and the Colonies: London and the Atlantic Economy, 1660–1700*. New York: Cambridge University Press, 2010.

Index

126–32, 138–39, 142, 231–33; of
brazilwood, 126; in British America, 8, 16,
35, 38, 45–49, 47, 63–64, 67–68, 71–75,
79, 80, 272n42; in Buenos Aires, 8; in
Cabinda, 51; in Canada, 142; in Cayenne,
71; by claiming distress at sea, 19, 20, 92,
126, 129–31, 141–42, 273n57; claims of
benefits to British Empire, 48; complicity
of officials in, 8, 15, 16, 17–18, 20, 55–56,
57, 123, 128, 232; of corks, 71; defined, 38;
of diamonds, 56, 127; and economic
development, 55, 56–57; during embargo
of 1807, 141–43, 145, 194–96, 205, 208,
231; in England, 35; as free trade, 37–38,
41–43, 46–49, 54–55, 57, 106, 109, 112,
113, 124–26, 131, 143; in Genesee County,
142; of gold, 13, 15, 17, 18, 19, 20, 21, 35,
39, 41, 49, 55, 126; of Lisbon wine, 65,
71–72, 73–74, 75; in Luanda, 51, 52; in
Madeira, 100; of Madeira wine, 66–68, 67,
69, 83, 84; of manufactures, 15, 114; in
Mina Coast, 21, 49, 51; networks, 35,
38–39, 41, 56, 65, 67, 71, 85–86, 129; in
New York, 66, 142; in Nova Colônia do
Sacramento, 55–56; in Philadelphia, 40,
67, 71–72, 142–43; of pieces of eight, 100;
in Portugal/Portuguese Empire, 8, 13, 15,
20, 35, 51; in Portuguese Atlantic islands,
19–20; prosecuted in vice-admiralty
courts, 71; as resistance, 3, 5, 42, 43, 46,
47, 56, 61, 66–68, 111–12, 124–26, 129,
143; in Rio de Janeiro, 56; in Río de la
Plata region, 20, 122; of silver, 21, 122–23;
of slaves, 8, 10, 15, 21, 49, 122–23, 126,
194–96, 197–98, 211, 231–33, 234; of
snuff, 100; of soap, 100; in Spanish
America; 15, 20, 49, 56; of sugar, 19,
39–40, 41, 47; of tea, 47; of Tenerife wine,
66; in United States, 83; in Vermont, 142;
in West Indies, 45, 97, 125, 142, 204, 205
Sousa Coutinho, Vincente de, 90, 113
South Sea Company: and asiento, 6; established, 44

southern Europe, 13, 25, 29, 33, 35, 46,
66–67, 68–69, 92, 96–97
Souza Coutinho, Domingos Antônio de, 136
Souza Coutinho, Rodrigo de, 121, 126, 127;
advocates court's relocation to Brazil,
134–36; reforms of, 122–23
Spain/Spanish Empire: political economy of,
90, 112, 139, 185, 222; population of,
266n23; Portuguese union with, 13; and
Seven Years' War, 33; as threat to Portuguese sovereignty, 23, 122, 136
Spanish Company, 44
Spanish-Portuguese War (1735–1737), 24
Stamp Act, 63, 68, 69, 73
staves: Hamburg, 28; trade of, 98, 100
Storer, J. P. B., 227
Street, Francis, 39, 40, 41
Street, William, 27–28, 39, 40, 41; smuggles
wine, 65, 71–72
Suassuna Conspiracy, 127–28
sugar: cultivation of, 16, 140, 190; duties on,
165; price of, 39–40, 48; produced by
slaves, 22, 50; production of, 31, 52, 165;
trade of, 19, 22, 25, 39, 48, 51, 66, 113,
114, 116, 144. See also smuggling, of sugar
Sugar Act (American Duties Act), 63–69,
71, 75

tariffs: of 1816, 170; of 1824, 210
Taylor, Thomas, 184, 185, 186
Tea, 98. See also smuggling, of tea
Tea Act (1773), 47
Tenerife, 100, 267n32
Tenerife wine: price of, 27; trade of, 66, 99,
102, 267n32. See also smuggling, of
Tenerife wine
terreiro, 93; complaints about, 35, 89
textiles, 124; manufacture of, 22, 237;
production of, 152; trade of, 21–22, 32,
237
Tiradentes. See Silva Xavier, Joaquim José da
(Tiradentes)
tobacco: cultivation of, 16, 92; trade of, 39,
51, 98, 143, 144

Acknowledgments

I owe many debts to individuals and organizations that have assisted me in producing this book. The list includes those who have offered material, intellectual, and emotional support. Such support has not only made this book possible, but it has made writing it a fulfilling, exhilarating, and enjoyable experience. During those times of research and writing that did not seem so fulfilling, exhilarating, or enjoyable, that support and encouragement was all the sweeter.

Close colleagues have added much to this book. I am grateful to Alan Taylor, whom I am happy to consider both a colleague and a mentor at the University of Virginia. His unparalleled insight and constructive criticism has pushed me to reach higher levels of analysis, argue more effectively, and write more clearly. Ellen Hartigan-O'Connor and Chuck Walker have provided invaluable advice that has strengthened this book significantly. Ellen's incisive questions led me to reconsider my assertions, strengthen my evidentiary basis, and improve my analysis. Chuck's seamless blending of constructive criticism and encouraging input kept me grounded and motivated simultaneously. By pointing me toward Philadelphia customs records at the Mid-Atlantic National Archives and Records Administration, Cathy Matson helped me get my research started on the right foot. Her feedback during the early stages of my work helped me clarify my analytical framework. Sally McKee, David Biale, John Smolenski, and Ari Kelman provided wonderful help, particularly relating to Chapter 8. Jefferson Moak at the Mid-Atlantic National Archives provided very helpful information about the customs collections there. I thank Fabrício Prado for pointing me in very rewarding directions in my archival research and for a fruitful exchange of ideas and research information.

I have enjoyed a supportive intellectual community at the University of Virginia. John Stagg, Angela Kreider, David Mattern, Mary-Parke Johnson,

Anne Colony, Armin Mattes, Katharine Harbury, Stacy Diggs-Allen, and Sarah Marshall of the James Madison Papers have provided support as trusted and expert colleagues. Alan Taylor, Max Edelson, Andrew O'Shaughnessy, John Ragosta, and the community at the Early American Seminar sponsored by the Corcoran Department of History and the Robert H. Smith International Center for Jefferson Studies at Monticello have provided a stimulating intellectual environment for studying early America.

I presented chapter drafts of this book at conferences sponsored by the American Historical Association, the Rocky Mountain Council for Latin American Studies, a research fellows colloquium at the Library Company of Philadelphia, and a research symposium at the University of California, Davis. This book benefited greatly from collegial feedback at those conferences. Jeremy Baskes, Jane Landers, and Lyman Johnson provided very useful advice on chapter drafts. Paul Gilje and Fabrício Prado reviewed the book in its manuscript form, and their feedback strengthened its narrative and analytical frameworks. Also, colleagues such as Edward Pompeian, Olga González-Silen, Laura Jarnagin Pang, Joshua Smith, Alex Borucki, and Jesse Cromwell have provided important insights into the commercial cultures of the early U.S. republic and South America. Caitlin Fitz's scholarship and collegiality provided helpful observations about the commercial relationships between Brazil and the United States. Eliga Gould helped significantly strengthen the analytical framework of the book, especially as it relates to U.S. state building through foreign relations. The working group organized among colleagues at the Joseph Smith Papers reviewed drafts of chapters and helped me crystallize my research. Christopher Blythe, Mason Allred, Jordan Watkins, David Grua, and Jeffrey Mahas all provided valuable comments. Bob Lockhart offered his expertise and support to bring this book to fruition.

Portions of this book were published previously in the *Journal of American History* as "'Sovereign Lords' and 'Dependent Administrators': Artigan Privateers, Atlantic Borderwaters, and State Building in the Early Nineteenth Century." Financial support for this project came from the Hemispheric Institute on the Americas, Reed-Smith Travel Grants, the Program in Early American Economy and Society at the Historical Society of Pennsylvania and Library Company of Philadelphia, the Henry Belin du Pont Research Grant at the Hagley Library, the Hagley Library Exploratory Grant, the Lord Baltimore Fellowship at the Maryland Historical Society, the Emile G. Scholz Prize, the Roland Marchand Research Grant, and grants from the Institute for Social Sciences and the Institute of Governmental Affairs. Such generous support made this book possible. I am also grateful to the helpful and knowledgeable staffs and archivists at the many archives and libraries I consulted, especially the Historical Society of Pennsylvania, the Hagley Library, the Maryland Historical Society, the Arquivo Nacional–Torre do Tombo, the Library Company of Philadelphia, and the National Archives and Records Administration at College Park and Mid-Atlantic. During my research, I benefited from the hospitality of Spencer Mac-Donald, Paddy Kean, Rosangela Ribeiro, the Ramirez family, the Pavón family, Shawn Merrill, Eric Hitimana, Ricky Wyman, and Dan Kowalski.

I am very fortunate to have a wonderful network of family support. The endless supply of encouragement from my mother, Laura Reeder, gave me the confidence to start and the fortitude to finish this book. My father, Douglas Reeder, instilled in me a love for learning and intellectual curiosity. My parents-in-law, Lynn and Jeanne Taylor, provided encouragement and support throughout the process of writing. Having many siblings means receiving much encouragement, and I thank Ryan, Burke, Cody, Steffanie, Kammi, and B. J. for theirs. Steffanie, Kammi, B. J., and Meg Reeder all made useful design suggestions. My children—Matthew, TC, and Cody—have added much-needed color to my life as I have written this book, keeping me focused on the things that matter most. Finally, I give special gratitude to my wife, Karen. She has provided unfailing support and encouragement. She has willingly moved across the United States three times to support my career and research. She has frequently shouldered additional responsibilities when my archival research has compelled me to travel for extended periods of time. I thank her for reading drafts, providing feedback, and in many other ways making this book possible.